Advances in Teacher Education Volume 3

Editors:

Martin Haberman
University of Wisconsin—Milwaukee

Julie M. Backus
School District of Kewaskum, Wisconsin

Ablex Publishing Corporation
Norwood, New Jersey 07648

ADVANCES IN TEACHER EDUCATION
series editors
LILIAN G. KATZ
JAMES D. RATHS

University of Illinois, Urbana-Champaign

ISBN: 0-89391-396-0
ISSN: 0748-0067

Ablex Publishing Corporation
355 Chestnut Street
Norwood, New Jersey 07648

Contents

The Need for Research-Based Decisions in Teacher Education

Martin Haberman

University of Wisconsin, Milwaukee

There is likely to be more change in teacher education between now and the year 2000 than there has been in the entire history of teacher education. The reason is clear: The demand for more competent teachers in the public schools is being expanded into demands that universities also improve their teacher education programs. The call for excellence in elementary and secondary schools, the continuing commitment to equal educational access for minorities, women, and the handicapped, and the expectation that secondary schools should prepare teenagers for entry into the world of work will continue to increase pressures on public education. In the past these pressures were largely limited to elementary and secondary schools. Advocates of Headstart, the "right to read," bilingual education, multicultural programs, and other equity programs rarely focused their criticisms on schools of education or on the state departments of teacher certification. As taxpayers, readers of national reports, and consumers of educational services, however, the public has become increasingly sophisticated: they now see a clearer relationship between teacher preparation and school effectiveness.

In the recent past, financial support for the entire university and for their schools of education has stabilized or decreased. Spiraling health, welfare, and other costs no longer protect the university from major state cutbacks. As a result, teacher education is being forced to scale down budgetarily from within, at the same time that it is being required to be more responsive to the demands of external constituencies. "Do more with less" will be the mandate for public schools, for the university, and for schools of education.

To their credit, many schools of education are seeking not only to change but to base their program revisions on some rational basis. The usual pattern of having a faculty simply vote on new courses or program requirements is giving way to systematic self-study, studies of comparable institutions, and, we would hope, to reviews of the research.

What is known about how children learn in school settings is an expanding and useful literature. It is more frequently being referred to, as institutions seek to upgrade the quality of their programs and graduates. This effectiveness literature has become generally known as the knowledge base in teacher education. While effective public school teaching/learning should comprise the *content* of our teacher education programs, we cannot overlook the *processes* by which adult students of varying ages and with different needs actually learn this content in the course of becoming teachers. There is another whole field of inquiry undergirding these processes of teacher education which has its own theoretic, experiential, and research underpinnings.

But to expect that universities, as they hear more about how pupils learn and how teachers teach, will automatically and inevitably improve their programs of teacher education is one of those logical expectations that is simple, neat, and wrong. The description Conant made of American teacher education in 1963 would still pertain to many current programs. Indeed, the programs offered in 1950 would still describe most secondary teacher education programs and a good many elementary ones.

In sum, the pressures on teacher education to change are greater now than in the past because they represent demands which emanate from within the university as well as from external groups. These program changes will, in part, be based on the growing research literature related to effective teaching and administration in the K–12 schools. What is needed for all of this to occur, however, is a set of clear guidelines by which teacher education programs can be specifically changed. These guidelines must be both usable and research-based. Our group of authors has accepted the challenge to provide such a set of research-based guidelines.

Our volume focuses on the research basis which supports or refutes specific ways to prepare better teachers. What is known about recruitment and selection of teacher candidates? What is known about direct experiences which lead to greatest student change? Which people-factors influence the greatest student changes? In what ways? What knowledge is most likely to be implemented? How can candidates be evaluated for certification? We do not focus on specialized forms of preparation — for example, teachers of reading, math, science, and so on. We feel that it is vital to update the research regarding the generic processes of preservice teacher education. Our contention is that the knowledge base related to effective teaching will never be translated into teacher education without a simultaneous concern for using the research base related to the processes for actually preparing teachers.

Chapter 1

Teacher Selection Reconsidered

Kenneth R. Howey and Sharon M. Strom

University of Minnesota–Minneapolis

This chapter first reviews policies and practices concerned with the admission of students to teacher preparation programs. It examines as well data which speak to the general intellectual ability and prior academic achievement of prospective teachers. Primarily, however, this chapter suggests a more intellectually and morally defensible response to the extremely important questions:

1. What type of person do we value as a teacher?
2. What does the answer to question 1 suggest about preservice selection (and retention) policy and practice?

We maintain that little serious consideration has in fact been given to these questions, especially as they relate one to the other. Programs of teacher preparation tend not to be guided by explicit conceptions of a teacher or teaching. When such conceptualization does occur, it tends to focus on the technical dimension of teaching and not upon the multidimensional aspects of the teaching role or the personal qualities which it requires for success. Beyond this it is rare for those conceptions of the teacher and teaching which do exist to be explicitly linked to key elements of the teacher preparation program.

Policy-making, relative to the selection of teachers, is largely limited to identifying level of prior academic success desired as reflected in a minimum grade point average (GPA). Increasingly, some assessment of minimal competence in reading, writing, and mathematical computation is a matter of

1

concern as well. There are, also, some programs which require minimal scores on a standardized test of intellectual aptitude.

We maintain that there should be more attention given to the matter of admission and selection policies and practices than what normative practice suggests. These are moral and political exercises that call for serious consideration of complex issues. They are moral in the sense that policy choices regarding selection criteria have human, and therefore, social consequences. Because control is exercised through the limits set over who has access to programs, these decisions are, also, highly political. There are several complexities involved: the determination of values and standards to use as criteria in selecting prospective teachers involves conceptualization of teaching (and learning) and, also, a consideration of the personal qualities considered desirable in teachers. Additionally, the needs and wants of all parties with a vested interest in teacher education and the quality of teachers should be considered including prospective teachers, teacher educators, those who certify teachers, future employers, and the general public.

Context feeds into a consideration of which criteria to use in selection: the present and historical set of circumstances in teacher education; interpretations of competing professional values; the expectations of the public; the needs of prospective students; and resources such as time, money, faculty knowledge, and skill available to promote personal qualities considered desirable in teachers are but a few of the relevant considerations in determining selection criteria.

We are especially concerned that the formulation of criteria include consideration of relevant and accurate factual information about (a) the specific personal qualities which appear to be related to effective, humane teaching, and (b) the modifiability of these qualities in teacher education programs. Further, the critique of selection criteria involves weighing the probable consequences of upholding particular values and the acceptability of these values to various stakeholders. When the process of resolving policy problems like this one is deliberate and rational, both value and factual reasons given to support policy choices are clearly interpreted and examined for their legitimacy (Gauthier, 1963; Raz, 1978).

We assert that selection criteria and procedures employed early in programs of teacher preparation are not simply policy questions. They can have far-reaching ramifications. The search for ways to resolve selection (and retention) problems should become a matter for more critical reflection and dialogue than is currently exhibited in the profession. Following an examination of some of the limitations in current selection policies and practices, an illustrative framework is provided for explicating and applying more expanded and explicit selection criteria. Through this procedure we hope to open more critical examination of some of the central issues concerned with the selection (and retention) of prospective teachers.

NORMATIVE ADMISSONS POLICIES AND PRACTICES

Carpenter (1972) examined admissions procedures in 180 randomly selected institutions and reported that GPAs and letters of recommendation were the primary criteria employed in the selection of students to preservice teacher education programs. At that time less than one in five respondents (17%) indicated that they employed any form of standardized testing in admissions decisions; the most common measure reported was the Minnesota Teacher Attitude Inventory.

In a survey of admission procedures at 240 institutions preparing teachers in a sample stratified by type, size, and geography, Joyce, Yarger, Howey, Harbeck, and Kluwin (1977) reported that about one fifth of the institutions admitted students to programs as freshman (22%). Approximately the same number (21%) had students entering as sophomores. In contrast, the majority of institutions and teacher education programs, especially those which prepare general elementary or secondary teachers, admit students as juniors. This, also, indicates that education majors in most instances will have demonstrated at least satisfactory academic achievement for 2 years in a postsecondary context prior to admission to a teacher preparation program. Just as Carpenter, however, these investigators report that GPA and letters of recommendation were commonly the two factors considered in admitting students to programs. Another one fifth of the respondents in the present study reported that they examined autobiographical statements. Approximately one third engaged prospective students in some form of personal interview. The actual persons involved in the admission process were invariably limited to faculty in the programs to which the students were seeking admission. Little involvement by faculty in the arts and sciences, counselors, practicing teachers, or administrators was noted. This lack of involvement by others is understandable given the limited data reviewed and the minimal first-hand involvement with the perspective teacher candidate in the selection process in most instances.

In a study of 121 institutions, Laman and Reeves (1980) reported that the medium overall GPA required for admission to programs was 2.20 on a 4.0 scale with a 2.50 GPA required in the major. More recently, Ishler (1984) reported that GPAs required for admission ranged from 2.0 to 3.0 on a 4-point scale. Almost half of the responding institutions required a GPA of 2.0 for admissions with about another one fourth requiring a GPA between 2.0 and 2.25. Another one fourth required GPAs between 2.5 and 3.0. Ishler also found that 68% of the programs surveyed required basic skills testing for admission to teacher education. This appears to represent a major change in practice in a relatively short time given Carpenter's findings a decade previously. The tests identified as used during admissions included the Pre-Professional Skills Test, the California Achievement Test, the American

College Testing Program test, the Scholastic Aptitude Test, and a variety of tests developed locally or at the state level.

These data are consistent with another survey by the American Association of Colleges for Teacher Education (1984) which revealed that 64% of all the reporting institutions (N = 356) employ some standardized test in the admission process, almost always focused upon measuring level of competence in reading, writing, or mathematics. For example, 74% of those institutions employed tests which assessed skills in reading, 69% in mathematics, and 89% in writing ability.

Further, Sandefur's (1984) analysis of admission and selection procedures revealed that 23 states either have implemented or are planning to implement revised standards for admission to teacher preparation programs. Thus, admission standards are increasingly becoming a policy matter at the state level. Six of these states examined American College Test (ACT) or Scholastic Aptitude Test (SAT) scores. The range of minimal ACT scores that were reported as acceptable for admission is from 16 to 18. The range of SAT scores reported as allowable for admission is from 745 to 835.

In addition to the 23 states which now have uniform standards for admission to programs, another 21 states require explicit admission standards relative to demonstrated competency in the basic skills and a minimal GPA, but allow the individual institutions of higher education to identify the tests they employ, the cut-off scores they will require, and the GPAs which are acceptable for admission. The state does maintain ultimate control in the majority of these latter instances through the program approval process. In 1984 only 9 states reported no state board of education policies relative to admission to teacher education programs.

This recent nation-wide movement to employ tests of basic skills and general aptitude has been stimulated to a large extent by the recent trendline data from general measures of aptitude and achievement which show that prospective teachers' scores generally have declined on measures of aptitude and achievement and at a more rapid rate than for students pursuing other majors. For example, the College Entrance Examination Board (1983) reported that students seeking admission to teacher preparation programs in 1983 in the aggregate presented a mean SAT verbal score of 394, 29 points below the average for other majors. This mean score, also, reflects a decline of 24 points from the mean scores of prospective teachers a decade earlier. Likewise, average SAT mathematics scores fell 48 points below the national average (M = 418) and represented a diminishment of 31 points from those recorded by prospective teachers in 1972–73.

Concerns about the quality of prospective teachers also have been noted relative to those states which recently initiated forms of basic skills testing upon entry to teacher preparation programs. Minority students especially appear to have problems with these tests as reported by G. P. Smith in this volume.

Bethune (1984) drew upon data from the National Longitudinal Study (NLS) of the High School Class of 1972 to examine teacher preparation selection patterns. These NLS data include information obtained from approximately 20,000 high school seniors in more than 1,300 high schools. A base survey was conducted in 1972 and four follow-up surveys were implemented in 1973, 1974, 1976, and 1979. The sample for Bethune's study included NLS respondents who entered college during the fall of 1972 following their senior year in high school and who remained continuously enrolled in college through 1975. Due to small numbers, nonwhites and males were excluded and the final sample consisted of 848 white females, 270 of whom remained in teacher education programs as college seniors.

Bethune's descriptive analyses indicated that relative to females in other fields, freshman in education tended to be enrolled in colleges with less selective standards and tended to have lower ability, come from lower socioeconomic status families (SES), and have lower scores on a measure of self-esteem. He further reported that almost 25% of the original education majors left education for other fields. Generally those who left were in more selective colleges and had higher scores of general aptitude and self-esteem than those who remained in education programs.

On the other hand, recruits to education comprised almost two fifths (38%) of the education seniors in Bethune's (1984) sample. These students chose education after initially pursuing another major. These students were most frequently enrolled in less selective colleges. He reported that they generally were of lower ability than students in other fields but nonetheless generally of higher ability than the original persistors in teacher preparation programs. Bethune hypothesizes that these students, having experienced difficulty in other fields, turn to education because of relatively easy access.

There is mounting evidence that there are regional and institutional differences in the quality of students who are admitted to teacher preparation programs. For example, in a 1984 study in the state of Minnesota, 4 of the 8 teacher preparation institutions who examined scores from the preliminary SAT test reported that means for their education students were higher than the state and national means for all college bound juniors. Likewise 11 of the 14 institutions reported mean cumulative GPAs of 2.9 or more for their students entering in 1983–84 and 9 out of 11 institutions reported mean high school ranks of the 70th percentile or higher. Thus, it would appear that although there is considerable evidence for concern relative to the general academic ability of entering students, more study and analysis of differences across regions and institutions are needed.

Whatever differences in the quality of students exist from one program to the next, there is no doubt that those within and outside teacher education should be concerned about the academic ability and general intellectual aptitude of prospective teachers. Standardized measures of achievement and aptitude should be employed as indices of the quality of students entering programs of teacher preparation. Care does need to be taken so that tests do not reflect cultural bias and are understood in terms of what they measure and predict. There is little empirical data, for example, which would support general aptitude as measured by the SAT or the ACT tests as predictive of various aspects of teaching performance. In fact, some studies found that principals' or supervisors' ratings of teacher performance were not positively related to scores on these measures (Baker, 1970; Ducharme, 1970). Also, studies of the relationship between on-the-job performance as measured by principals' ratings and college GPAs are also mixed. Some studies revealed a small positive relationship (Ducharme, 1970; Druva & Anderson, 1983), but others such as Baker (1970) found no relationship. Similarly, Denton and Smith (1984) found no relationship between the grades of education majors and specific measures of cognitive achievement of students which they taught. Further, Eash and Rasher (1977) found that principals evaluated student teachers with higher grades on only 2 of the 27 performance items upon which they were assessed.

Studies such as those just mentioned are few in number and generally represent small sample sizes. Caution is needed in both interpretation and generalization. Yet it should be no great surprise that aptitude in and of itself hardly assures success in teaching. There have been studies of success in a number of professions which have revealed little correlation with academic intelligence. Sprinthall and Thies-Sprinthall (1983) in reviewing studies of predictors of later adult success refer to the following:

> Most recently, Heath's longitudinal studies with college-age samples reached similar conclusions. Carefully identified constructs such as ego maturity and competence were significantly related to a broad and multiple definition of life success, while academic achievement was not (Heath, 1977). The ability to symbolize one's experience, to act allocentrically with compassion, to act autonomously with self-control and a disciplined commitment to humane values — these formed part of the core of psychological maturity. (p. 79)

In his cross-cultural study, Heath (1977) found that adolescent males' (from the U.S.) scholastic aptitude as well as other measures of their intelligence did not predict several hundred measures of adaptation and competence observed during their early 30s. In fact, scholastic aptitude was inversely related to many measures of adult psychological maturity and judged interpersonal competence. Although it is ultimately sensible to seek academically talented and intelligent teachers, it appears that the aforementioned references indicate that other human qualities may be equally important.

ESTABLISHING SELECTION CRITERIA

We maintain that the establishment of selection criteria requires a relatively complete and coherent conceptualization of teacher and teaching. In this section we provide a rationale for the basic goal of teacher education and a model for evaluation research in teacher education to illustrate one way of providing for a fuller explication of the personal qualities considered desirable in teachers.

The Basic Goal of Teacher Education

We are indebted to the pioneering work of Marjorie Brown who introduced a developmentally focused teacher preparation program at the University of Minnesota in the early 1970s and have drawn heavily from her thinking on this topic. Professional action, viewed from an interactionist perspective (Lewin, 1935; Hunt, 1975; Hunt & Sullivan, 1974), is a product of (a) the mental system of concepts, motives, memories, and reasoning skills with which the teacher perceives the world, (b) elements of the actual situation, and (c) an interaction of these dispositional and situational factors.

The outstanding characteristic of the world in which teachers are prepared to teach is complexity (Schroder, 1977). The world in which they begin teaching will be in many ways different from that in which they were prepared. These changes will be reflected in schools, in community expectations, in pupil needs, in subject matter, in curriculum, in instructional equipment and materials, and in school organization among other things. Similarly, the immediate teaching situation will be in constant flux. There will be a need to make moment-to-moment decisions to accomplish tasks, tasks for which a consideration of different and conflicting perspectives is often warranted.

Such change and complexity come about in ways that can't be predicted. Therefore, teacher preparation can't proceed as if we know what the future holds. Instead teachers can be helped to gain the mental tools needed to meet professional tasks in ways that are adaptive, questioning, critical, inventive, creative, and self-renewing (Harvey, Hunt, & Schroder, 1961). That is, we can assist with the development of mental systems which will interact with elements of (now) unknown future environments in those ways.

The concept mental system is derived from a synthesis of theory and research on conceptual, moral, and ego development (e.g., Habermas, 1979, 1984; Harvey et al., 1961; Kegan, 1982; Kohlberg, 1976; Loevinger, 1976; Piaget, 1972; Rest, 1979). According to these theorists, a mental system involves what the person knows, believes, values, and so forth, as the substance of perceiving and thinking, the objects of feeling, and the basis for action. The structure of the mental system involves the patterns of interrelationship among concepts, motives, reasoning skills, and perceptions. The structure determines how the person will use what is known, perceived, and felt.

A *simple, concrete structure* is defined by poorly differentiated concepts, self-centered motives, distorted perceptions, underdeveloped reasoning skills, greater anxiety in coping with life situations, and lack of integration of concepts and motives resulting in contradictions and inconsistencies. A *complex, abstract structure* has clearly differentiated concepts, a rational–moral principle orientation to motives, realistic perceptions, well-developed reasoning skills, minimal anxiety in coping with life situations, and integration of concepts and motives resulting in adaptive qualities in coping. Each person's mental system is somewhere on a continuum between these extremes in terms of how knowledge, perceptions, and values are used.

The mental system a person has is a product of interaction with the particular environment and is subject to change. Change in the mental system is a result of interaction of the existing mental system with an appropriate (i.e., change-inducing) environment. Change in *content* occurs by addition, replacement, or reorganization. Change in *structure* occurs through a long-range process by which reorganization of the system of concepts, motives, and so on takes the place of the previous system structure. Change in content (even considerable change) does not necessarily result in change in structure of the mental system.

The work of teaching is such that teachers commonly affect the lives of those whom they teach in purposeful ways. They also affect their students out of mindlessness which does not question purpose or the consequences of teaching, or out of inadequacy of knowledge and skill to reach purpose. Therefore, there are moral consequences to teaching.

Professional responsibleness in teaching requires that knowledge and moral values combine in reflective decision-making and action. Without knowledge, derived from and open to rational inquiry, teaching (no matter how "good" the intention) becomes whimsical, nonrational, and irresponsible. Such behavior can be destructive both to learners and to society through failure to promote learner growth as well as through more specific harmful practices. Similarly, without an orientation to moral principle, teachers may not use knowledge for the welfare of learners and society.

Given the complex, interactive and moral nature of teaching and the rapid changes and diversity in schools (and in society), we maintain that the professional preparation of teachers should have as its basic goal the development of teachers as persons who have conceptual systems characterized by qualities of being adaptable, questioning, critical, inventive, creative, self-renewing, and oriented to moral principles. In teaching such persons would:

- Form and use multiple concepts; consider different and conflicting perspectives in thinking and decision-making.
- Organize and use ideas in a creative manner in problem-solving.
- Understand and use others' perspectives in communication.

- Seek beliefs–practice congruity
- Perceive and use conceptions regarding the needs of diverse groups.
- Evaluate the impact of their actions on other people.
- Develop a personally meaningful work identity.

Our rationale for a fuller consideration of these qualities in initial selection activities is based upon the following propositions:

1. When qualities such as those just mentioned, or those exemplified in persons reflecting a high level of psychological maturity are made explicit, they provide a clearer and loftier vision of the type of teacher we consider desirable. These particular qualities suggest a noble and select vocation as opposed to the pedestrian, technist conception of teaching that is so prevalent in much of the literature and discussions about teachers today.
2. The vision we have of a teacher is critical for a number of reasons. Our conception of a teacher tends to be a self-fulfilling prophecy in terms of: (a) the goals toward which our teacher preparation activities are oriented, (b) the roles assumed and behaviors modeled by teachers, and (c) the images of teaching which the public accepts and is willing to support.
3. We are largely unclear about the extent to which persons who enter teacher preparation programs possess these qualities. We believe that they are important, definable, and to an extent measurable.
4. The assessment of selected qualities, especially across institutions over time, would allow systematic study of their relationship to measures of teaching effectiveness. In instances where they are demonstrated as predictive of effectiveness, or valued for some other reason, the question of whether these qualities can/should be used in selection or can/should be developed within the context of teacher preparation can then be addressed. Our assumption is that it would be more efficacious for institutions to attend to certain qualities in early screening or selection procedures as well as to assist education students with career decision-making.

We do not wish to detract from the issues of the quality of prospective teachers and how this can be determined. Various measures of academic aptitude and achievement should be employed to ensure that intellectually able persons enter teaching. Although these are important criteria for selection, we maintain that they represent but part of the picture. It is important that we specify as clearly as possible other qualities which both common sense and logic, and, in certain instances, empirical data suggest are also related to teaching effectiveness. We have identified examples of these. We hope to illustrate more clearly what these are and how we might address them in the next section of this chapter.

Model for Evaluation Research in Teacher Education

Based on this view of teaching, a framework was developed to explore ways the research base in teacher education might be expanded. Although we have recommended that certain personal qualities and general abilities conceptualized as desirable in teaching should be addressed as part of an expanded admissions process, we recognize that the interactive relationship between these characteristics and various aspects of the preparation program is not fully known. We have much to learn about which qualities might be induced and how this might be done given the resources available in teacher education. It was hoped that the framework which follows would stimulate questions about possible interactions among personal, contextual–environmental, and behavioral outcome variables. No attempt was made to be exhaustive; in fact, parts of the model presented in Figure 1 are developed more fully than others.

Our approach was multivariate and interactive because of a growing uneasiness over the adequacy with which current research paradigms in education handle individual differences and interpretation of context (Cronbach & Snow, 1978; Shulman, 1970; Snow, 1974). There was an interest in determining how preservice students experience the educational environment and evaluating the impact of educational programs on characteristics and behaviors conceptualized as desirable in teachers. Provision was made for both *contemporaneous* analyses to investigate the differential effects of the program/classroom variables on preservice students and *developmental* analyses to explore relatively stable changes in preservice students characteristics that take place over time and what might be done to induce student development.

The model includes criterion factors, environmental factors, and contingency factors. First, *criterion factors* (defined in achievement and process terms) refer to teacher characteristics and behaviors considered desirable to ensure effectiveness in promoting pupil growth (the educational objectives in teacher education). In program evaluation attention would be given to both intended and unintended consequences. Next, *environmental factors* refer to selected dimensions of the educational environment which appear associated with preservice growth in cognitive functioning, change in attitudes, affective involvement, and teaching skill. Finally, *contingency factors* refer to variables believed to moderate the effects of educational process on the development of valued teacher characteristics and behaviors (outcomes). Included are preservice student characteristics (personality, attitudes, abilities, aptitude, and achievement) and faculty and institutional variables.

In this chapter we are concerned with how student characteristics (contingency factors) might be assessed early in the preservice program for use in selection. Some student characteristics in the model have educational implications and are considered modifiable in adults, while others are not given the

FIGURE 1. Model For Evaluation Research In Teacher Education[a]

Contingency Factors	Environmental Factors	Criterion Factors (Outcomes)

Contingency Factors

I. Student Variables

A. Personality
1. Style of working with information (cognitive orientation)
   a. Field independence-dependence
   b. Scanning
   c. Breadth of categorizing
   d. Conceptualizing styles
   e. Cognitive complexity-simplicity
   f. Reflectiveness-impulsivity
   g. Leveling-sharpening
   h. Constricted-Flexible control
   i. Tolerance of ambiguity and uncertainty
   j. Creative problem-solving
2. Style of working with people (motivational orientation)
   a. Moral responsibleness
      1) awareness of consequences
      2) ascription of responsibility
      3) moral sensitivity and judgment
   b. Needs and values
   c. Social perspective-taking
   d. Interactive competence
3. Attitudes
   a. General attitude toward people
   b. Internal-external locus of control
   c. Self-esteem
   d. Learning-style
   e. Attitude toward work and career
      1) attitudes toward specific aspects of teaching, e.g., control, roles
      2) general attitude toward career
      3) beliefs about teaching
      4) overall satisfaction with career choice
      5) career salience
      6) central life interest
B. Abilities
1. Logical
2. Critical thinking
3. Communicative competence
   a. Oral expression
   b. Written expression
4. Reading competence
   a. Basic skills
   b. Attitude toward reading

Environmental Factors

I. Program Variables

II. Classroom Variables
A. Content of intervention
   1. Elements of content taught
   2. Mental processes fostered (e.g., reasoning skills)
   3. Skill-content emphasized
B. Form of intervention
   1. Structure of presentation
      a. Amount of teacher control
      b. Complexity (number and difficulty) of concepts and materials dealt with
      c. Degree of concept differentiation-integration in classroom discourse
   2. Form of feedback and evaluation
      a. Values upheld in feedback
      b. Degree of attention to individual differences
   3. Approach to value issues
   4. Qualities of atmosphere
   5. Principles of teacher-student interaction
      a. Social
      b. Intellectual

III. Educational Environment Variables
A. Student perceptions of department or unit
B. Faculty perceptions of department or unit

Criterion Factors (Outcomes)

I. Conception of Teaching and Research
A. Degree of concept differentiation-integration (complexity)
B. Value of orientation to teaching
C. Perception of purpose
D. Content of beliefs about teaching/research

II. Performance in Teaching
A. Teacher strength (capacity to structure or organize classroom)
   1. Diagnosing
   2. Planning
      a. Objectives selected, justified, and taught
      b. Choice of strategies for purpose
      c. Selection and organization of curriculum content
   3. Instructing
      a. Skilled use of strategies
      b. Flexibility in approaches used
      c. Quality of reasoning used
   4. Evaluating
      a. Form of feedback and reward
      b. Evaluation skills
B. Teacher adaptability
   1. Sensitivity or the ability to sense and use another perspective in communication
   2. Flexibility or the capacity to react appropriately to learner frame-of-reference
      a. Skill in discrimination
      b. Skill in radiating environments
      c. Skill in flexible modulation from one environment to another
C. Interpersonal qualities displayed
   1. Accepts others as worthwhile and capable of development
   2. Actively listens to each person
   3. Creates a warm and open climate
      a. Exhibits genuineness
      b. Empathizes with others' needs and feelings
   4. Engages in open examination of ideas with students

III. Personality Development

(Continued)

11

FIGURE 1. *(Continued)*

Contingency Factors	Environmental Factors	Criterion Factors (Outcomes)

C. Entering student characteristics
  1. Aptitude
  2. Achievement
  3. Work experience
 	
II. Faculty Variables
A. Faculty personality
B. Orientation toward teaching and schooling
 	
III. Institutional Variables
A. University climate
B. College of Education climate
		IV. Attitudes Toward Self, Others, and Work
		A. Conceptualization of self as creative person and potentially creative teacher
		  1. Feels worthwhile, accepted, trustworthy
		  2. Feels capable of succeeding in teaching
		  3. Perceives experience accurately
		  4. Shows willingness to take risks
		  5. Acts independently
		  6. Accepts responsibility for own actions
		B. Perception of student behavior
		C. Commitment to examining beliefs, feelings, behavior (e.g., ethical consequences)
		D. Experimental attitude toward identifying and providing appropriate learning conditions
		V. Leadership Qualitites

[a]Developed by Sharon Strom to use with the Subcouncil on Teacher Education, University of Minnesota, October, 1984.

present state of our knowledge. Still others would be difficult to induce with limited resources. For example, because the basis for teaching (learning) is communicative interaction, educators would probably agree that teacher sensitivity (the ability to sense and use another's perspective in communication) is desirable. Are attempts to induce sensitivity warranted if we find, for example, that (a) it is a relatively stable personality characteristic despite short-term educational efforts to change it (Schroder & Talbot, 1966), and/or (b) there is not enough time, money, and staff support available to bring about the needed changes? In this situation screening to assess for some minimum level of this characteristic may be appropriate. Also, some student characteristics may be of interest in diagnosis and planning for individual differences rather than for use in selection—for example, moral sensitivity and judgment.

USING SELECTION CRITERIA

To this point, the argument has been made that certain personal qualities and general cognitive abilities which contribute to effective, humane teaching can be determined using sound rationale. Only in rare instances, however, are these personal qualities and general abilities made explicit, related to the goals and activities in the teacher preparation program, and considered at the time of admissions. Again, the general personal qualities and abilities which we have identified to receive systematic attention early in a preservice teacher education program include: cognitive orientation, creative problem-solving, interpersonal competence (with an emphasis on adaptability in interactive situations), beliefs–practice congruence, sensitivity to the needs of diverse groups (e.g., ethnic or cultural groups, gender, socioeconomic class or disabled students), awareness of ethical consequences, and integration of self and role. We turn now to how these might be examined.

Cognitive Orientation

Information about preservice students' level of cognitive functioning would provide insight about how they organize and interpret experience (including those experiences which involve both learning and teaching roles). Conceptual and methodological revisions of an initial provisional statement about cognitive development (Harvey et al., 1961) have led to three derivative theories (Harvey, 1967; Hunt, 1971; Schroder, Driver & Streufert, 1967). The major difference among these conceptual system derivatives is relative emphasis on motivation (or content) and conceptual complexity (or structure).

In Hunt's Conceptual Level Theory (CL), for example, there is an assumed interrelation between the integrative complexity with which information is cognitively processed and degree of interpersonal maturity. Points along a continuous dimension represent changes in the way a person interprets, combines, and acts upon information in the environment as well as differences in self-understanding, awareness of others, and self-responsibility. Simple and highly concrete structures show little differentiation of concepts; there is categorical thinking and a dependence on others for rules and norms to guide thinking, feeling, and action. The more abstract and complex structures contain highly differentiated concepts; there are interpretive categories for relating and synthesizing large amounts of information and explaining alternative interpretations as well as an interdependence in relationships with others.

The Paragraph Completion Method (PCM) (Hunt, Butler, Noy, & Rosser, 1978) was designed to measure CL. Because observational data on CL need to represent a person's cognitive and motivational orientations when responding in a concrete situation, the PCM was developed to meet two conditions: (1) participants are required to generate their own responses to a cognitive task, and (2) participants are required to respond to tasks demanding cognitive work in the interpersonal domain. Respondents construct answers to sentence stems in the areas of personal uncertainty, interpersonal conflict, and authority. Completed responses are analyzed structurally and "clinical judgments" are used to assign a CL score. The scoring manual for the PCM gives generic referents for each score on the CL dimension and specific protocals and examples of responses to each stem.

In contrast, Harvey (1967) has focused upon the motivation or system-specific content characteristics and has developed measures for assigning persons to one of four belief-system categories. System one individuals are characterized by high absolutism, a positive attitude toward tradition and authority, and an inability to change set or think creatively under conditions of high involvement or stress. At the fourth or highest level, a more open-minded attitude toward seeking information, a predisposition toward problem-solving, and a greater ability to change set and withstand stress are manifested.

Two instruments were designed to measure belief systems. The This I Believe (TIB) test is a projective device consisting of nine completion tasks. Respondents are asked to give a two-sentence response to stimulus words such as "religion," "marriage," and "the American way of life," words presumed to be highly ego-involving. Like most projective tests, this one is fairly difficult to score and interpret. As a result, an objective device, the Conceptual Systems Test (CST), was derived from actual responses to the TIB and has gone through a number of revisions. Respondents rate 48 statements on a Likert scale indicating degree of acceptance or rejection of theoretically relevant statements. Responses to the CST are cluster analyzed using six clusters — Divine Fate Control, Need for Structure–Order, Need to Help People, Need for People, Interpersonal Aggression, and General Pessimism. Persons are assigned a system description based on their scores on the six CST clusters (Harvey & Hoffmeister, 1975).

In both of these approaches there have been numerous investigations of teacher cognitive orientation and its relationship to various patterns of teaching behavior (see Miller's 1981 review of literature). For example, concrete teachers tend to be dictatorial and rule oriented, use questioning approaches in teaching which emphasize the "right" answer, teach isolated facts, discourage divergent thinking, and reward conformity and rote learning. In contrast, abstract teachers regard knowledge as tentative rather than absolute; consider situations from multiple viewpoints, in fact, seek alternative explanations; show more empathetic awareness of others; and tend to encourage problem-solving calling for information searches. Students of abstract teachers in contrast to students of concrete teachers also behaved differently — they were described as more cooperative, more involved in classroom activities, more active, more helpful, less nuturance seeking, and less concrete in their responses (Harvey, Prather, White, & Hoffmeister, 1968). Furthermore, they perceived teachers differently. Abstract teachers were rated higher by their students on fostering exploration, cooperation, and esprit de corps, whereas concrete teachers were rated higher on fostering hostility (Coates & Neva, 1970).

Assessments of cognitive orientation could serve multiple purposes. First, it could assist in designing learning environments that are more accommodative to basic differences in preservice students. Several studies have demonstrated forms of structure that appear requisites for students of less conceptual complexity to succeed (see Miller's 1981 review of conceptual matching models). Others have identified program elements and activities which appear to promote cognitive complexity (Brown & Strom, 1975-1976; Sprinthall & Thies-Sprinthall, 1983).

Finally, although teaching is not unique in the type of personal qualities it demands, a continuing interaction with relatively large numbers of students over relatively long periods of time in relatively confined spaces places a premium on the ability to withstand stress, change set, remain open to new ideas, and use information creatively. A variety of observational and laboratory experiences could be provided which vividly portray the dynamic, changing nature of teaching and the need for multidimensional thinking in teachers. The intent here would be to induce self-screening early in the program. Those with rigid belief systems and a need for relatively stable, nonstressful settings would be more likely to experience increasing discrepancy. Opportunities for such self-selection exist in most preservice programs that provide entering preservice teachers with multiple perspectives of the teaching experience. Rarely, however, have these experiences been systematically examined in the light of preservice teachers' cognitive orientation and predisposition for behaving. Results of formal assessments are one means of sharing data in this regard.

Early counseling could help facilitate this evaluation process. Attempts have been made to involve counseling or developmental psychologists in preservice programs either directly, in the provision of clinical feedback to students or indirectly, by assisting faculty in making such analyses. The involvement of counselors was, for example, one of the primary features of the Personalized Teacher Preparation Program (PTPP) piloted by the Research and Development Center for Teacher Educators at the University of Texas in the early 1970s. Here student self-confrontation was encouraged through early focused microteaching and systematic examination of personal motives and perceptions.

Creative Problem-Solving

In many respects this general ability is embedded in the conceptions of cognitive complexity reviewed earlier. There are, however, other means of examining one's attitude toward and ability to engage in problem-solving. The predisposition for engaging in and resolving problems has been viewed as the essence of creativity. In efforts to foster the creative process in teachers, G. I. Brown (1972) elaborated upon Barron's definition of the creative person:

> Barron (1963) describes the creative person as one who seeks out complexity and chaos. The creative person is willing to experience the tension or frustration or pain of a temporarily unresolved chaotic condition in that part of the uni-

verse in which he intentionally places himself. According to Barron, he does this in anticipation of what satisfaction he will experience when through the creative process he creates order out of chaos, simplicity out of complexity, or meaning out of confusion. Barron's description is intriguing and there are dimensions of Perls' work that add much to it. The creative person is first aware that chaos exists. He is then willing to confront this chaos and to "stay with" it. The person who is busily engaged in maintaining his status quo is unwilling to move into new experience, chaotic or otherwise, for he never knows whether it will be chaotic or not. He is not only unwilling to move into new experience, but he cannot perceive the reality of new possibilities even when directly confronted with them. (p. 95–96)

As can be inferred from this definition, an orientation toward resolving problems may well hinge on personal characteristics as well as abilities. The Barron-Welch Art Scale and the Barron Complexity Score were both developed to measure preference for complexity as well as other aspects of creativity and have been validated against operational criteria of originality and creativity (Barron, 1963).

In contrast to tests of creativity that emphasize factorial purity (e.g., Guilford, 1967), the Torrance Tests of Creative Thinking (Torrance, 1962) are structured as word and picture games and are considered useful in classrooms from kindergarten through graduate school. Student work on these activities is scored for the number of relevant responses, variety in response classes, and originality. An additional criterion, elaboration, is used with figural tests.

In addition to tests of creativity, Torrance is known for efforts over the years to engage students in Grades K–12 in creative problem-solving. He has designed numerous exercises to facilitate problem-solving ability. Most recently the Future Problem Solving Bowl, a year-long program involving four-person teams in Grades 4–12, was developed to creatively address future-oriented problems (Torrance, Torrance, & Crabbe, 1980–81). Several hundred schools and thousands of students have been involved in this creative problem-solving approach which incorporates the following phases:

1. Identifying and listing subproblems
2. Identifying and stating the underlying problems
3. Producing alternative solutions
4. Developing criteria for juding alternative solutions
5. Evaluating alternative solutions
6. Planning implementation of solution
7. Selling the solution (p. 7)

Schemes such as this could be adapted to focus on teaching-related problems and used to develop problem-solving tactics in preservice teachers.

Also, they could be employed as diagnostic measures to acquire base-line data on preservice students' orientation toward and ability to resolve problems. For example, preservice students could be presented with any number of problems and asked within prescribed time frames to respond to the problems in a three-step process. First, they would be asked to identify as many alternative solutions as possible to resolve the problem situation. After they completed this process, the students would then generate criteria for judging the solutions. Torrance et al. (1980–81) provide examples of criteria which might be employed in making judgments about suggested solutions:

> Which solution will be the most acceptable?
> Which solution will be the easiest to understand?
> Which solution will cost the least?
> Which solution will be the most workable?
> Which solution will be the most long-lasting?
> Which solution will be the quickest to implement?
> Which solution will cause the least disruption?
> Which solution will be the most ethically sound?
> Which solution will have the fewest adverse side effects?
> Which solution will have the most potential for sustained success? (p. 19)

Finally, as a third step, students would be asked to apply their criteria to these solutions which they proposed in step one and then to rank their solutions.

The problem or problems posed to the students would be of a general nature in order that specific previous knowledge would not be a differentiating factor among them. An example of a non–teaching-related problem of a general nature is: What could be done to enhance the quality of life for senior citizens generally? A teaching-related problem that would not be embedded in specific prior knowledge is: How can new curriculum, reflective of changes in today's society, be incorporated into schools when they already are characterized as having an overcrowded curriculum? Exercises such as these could be incorporated easily in any number of activities early in a students' preservice program. Simulations of real classroom settings can be conducted using paper and pencil in-basket tests of performance or through interaction with the microcomputer.

Whether employing simple paper and pencil assessment, more sophisticated interactive simulations, or validated instrumentation it would seem that indicators of creative problem-solving ability and preference for such activity can be assessed in relatively facile ways. Our perception is that much of a teacher's daily activity can or should be characterized as problem-solving in nature. We believe that attention to student willingness and ability to resolve problems early in a preservice program should be given. Again diagnostic data could be employed in planning educational experiences for the student and the information could be employed to note the lack of congruence between the student's present orientation and those abilities and qualities deemed necessary to be effective in the classroom.

Interpersonal Competence/Adaptability

In teaching, interpersonal competence consists of two related social tasks: the ability to understand and use another's perspective in communication and the capacity to react appropriately to that person's frame of reference. Of the diverse theoretical orientations and techniques employed to investigate differences in interpersonal understanding and interaction, three approaches of relevance to teaching are presented here for consideration.

First, studies of helping relationships provide empirical support that specific communication conditions are necessary for effective interpersonal functioning. These facilitative conditions include empathy, respect, genuineness, and concreteness among others (Carkhuff, 1969; Rogers, 1983). It is worth noting, in turn, that these conditions are related to the degree of self-understanding helpers possess. Carkhuff developed 5-point rating scales to assess the quality of interpersonal functioning displayed in the helping process (Carkhuff, 1969, 1971). Using the scales, research has demonstrated a relationship between these conditions and human development. For example, teachers who communicate high levels of empathetic understanding, respect, and genuineness are more likely to facilitate cognitive and affective growth in students than those who rank low (Aspy, 1965).

On all scales, level 3 is defined as the minimally effective level of functioning. High-level functioning consists of:

1. Empathetic understanding, which is the ability to merge with another's experience, to reflect on that experience while suspending judgment and tolerating one's own anxiety, and to communicate this understanding.
2. Respect, which refers to communication of deep appreciation of another's worth and his or her potential for growth.
3. Facilitative genuineness, which involves congruence between the helper's words and action and personal feelings and attitudes.
4. Concreteness, which is reflected in the degree of specificity achieved in communication about one's own and others ideas, feelings, and experiences.

Although Carkhuff believes these skills can be learned, low-level functioning is considered reflective of an unhealthy personality. Faculty and/or peer ratings of verbal material from teaching simulations could be used to encourage self-screening early in the preservice program. Students with low ratings, who set interpersonal development goals, could be referred for group counseling.

From another theoretical vantage point, investigations of social cognition have been used to explain the development of mature understanding of social relationships, that is, patterns of thinking about persons and relationships between persons (Selman, 1980). Selman analyzed solutions given to hypothetical dilemmas and open-ended questions focused on social problems to determine the complexity of thinking used in the social reasoning process. At the most abstract level there is (a) differentiation between experiences and one's own core beliefs, attitudes, and values, (b) reliance on a differentiated view of self and the similarities and differences between self and others, and (c) perception of alternative forms of relatedness between self and others — dependence, independence, interdependence.

This means that interpersonally mature teachers would use complex inferences about students' concepts, feelings, attitudes, and actions in their interactions with students. In addition to structural analysis of written material produced by preservice students in response to dilemmas focused on teacher–student relationship problems, several other approaches could be used to assess level of interpersonal understanding. For example, situational tests such as (a) a panel interview administered at the time of admission, (b) interactional analysis of verbal interaction in teaching simulations or roleplays, and (c) analysis of student observation reports (anecdotal records of atypical behavior or case studies) all could provide information about level of interpersonal functioning.

Finally, we are indebted to David Hunt for his continuing reminder that the interaction between teachers and students is hardly unidirectional (notwithstanding the contributions of active or direct teaching in various institutional contexts) and cannot be fully understood in those terms. The interactive pull of students, let alone their motivation for and responsibility to learning, has simply not received adequate attention. A teacher's adaptation to students is often at the heart of the teaching/learning process. Here adaptation refers to the moment-to-moment shifts by a teacher in response to an individual student, a group of students, or an entire class as well as shifts over longer periods of time. Hunt (1976) suggests that teacher adaptation is occurring constantly and indicates that a conservative estimate would be 100 occurrences an hour. Based on intensive observation and study, Hunt indicates that teacher adaptation varies enormously.

The two key communication skills in adaptation are a sensitization to student "pull" and an ability to "flex" or modulate teaching behavior appropriately. Hunt (1970) studied preservice teachers adaptation in a micro-teaching situation. In this particular experiment the task consisted of one-to-one microteaching in which the trainee was given a short time to communicate a particular idea or concept to a roleplaying listener. The trainee was given information about the concept to be taught, the specific objective, and (in some cases) information about the student (listener). During the trainee's attempt to communicate, the listener interjected specific obstacles at prespecified intervals. Interest then centered on the trainee's approach and how it was modulated in response to the obstacles. Hunt (1976) described the intervention as follows:

> The trainee was first given material describing the checks and balances system; next, he was told that he was to meet a Venezuelan emigrant, "George Lopez," who wanted to learn about the balance of power in order to pass a citizenship examination. Before meeting George, he was given a one-page description about him. Finally, the trainee met with the role player for 12 to 15 minutes and presented the concept in any way he or she wished. The role player systematically introduced five obstacles as appropriate, e.g., "The judges are like priests . . . they tell us what's right and wrong," or "The president is in charge . . . he tells everybody what to do." (p. 271)

The variation between teacher trainees was considerable ranging from those who were completely unresponsive to the role-player and were unremitting to their mini-lecture to those who spent the majority of time getting to know George Lopez and his frame of reference. In order to calibrate differences, Hunt (1976) developed the following adaptability index based upon the prospective teachers reaction to each of the five obstacles inserted by Lopez:

RATING	BEHAVIORAL REFERENT
1	Completely insensitive.
3	Aware of obstacle, but does not modulate.
5	Aware of obstacles and makes some attempt to modulate.
7	Shifts and modulates presentation in flexible fashion.
9	Modulates and explores for more information from listener's frame of reference. (p. 271)

Although there is an increasing emphasis on assessing written and oral competence as part of the selection procedure in many teacher preparation programs, it is rare for attention to be given to the skills needed in the type of interactive discourse teachers use repeatedly. Our impression is that the simple exercise which Hunt devised could be replicated or similar assessments designed. Such an assessment could be incorporated in a structured interview at the time of admission, for example. The type of adaptive behavior displayed may well reflect both a reasonable respect for another person's frame of reference as well as interpersonal flexibility.

Critical analyses of actual interpersonal discourse are also possible employing a number of systems designed to describe verbal behavior. Such analyses could reveal in behavioral terms much about one's sensitivity to and empathy towards others. We applaud the increasing concern about preservice teachers' ability to communicate but emphasize that communicative action is interpersonal and multidirectional in nature. As such it involves the ability to observe, listen, and interpret others' motives, meanings, and actions (Habermas, 1979) as well as speak with skill. Unfortunately the conception of teaching as largely telling is still prevalent. The sooner a prospective teacher contrasts this faulty perception of teaching with a more differenti- ated conception of effective interpersonal interaction the better in terms of an enlightened career choice.

Beliefs–Practice Congruency

Although recent research provides evidence that some novice teachers are able to maintain and even further strengthen beliefs and conceptions about teaching they regard as important (Tabachnick & Zeichner, 1984), other evi- dence shows that many beginning teachers alter teaching practices to con- form to norms and conventions counter to their beliefs. Weinberg, McHugh, and Lamb (1970) suggested that even experienced teachers over time rational- ized such concessions and as a result did not feel especially alienated. In sum- marizing their study Weinberg (1972) reported:

> The researchers inferred that these teachers generally had abandoned their real self to achieve security in a system which was not, and is not, significant in their lives. Such teachers either identify with the new reference group whose commit- ment is primarily to stability, or they are simply role playing in the sense of doing what is expected. Their jobs are secured, and mobility, if they wish it, is not endangered. Another possible interpretation of the findings is that self-role conflicts are obviated by the disappearance of the self. As long as the person's ex- pectations for his own behavior is incongruent with the expectations of others within the system, and as long as these expectations of others prevail (which they invariably do in schools), there will be alienating effects. The fact that the teacher alienation study was unable to discover many of these effects suggests that the study component was so rationalized, or that the dissonance was so re- duced, that the incongruence did not confront these persons. (p. 77)

Furthermore, Weinberg notes that rationalization occurs in a variety of ways. Some female teachers defer the teaching role to a primary family role. Others perceive considerable limitations in terms of what one person can do in their difficult role in any event. Still others submerge themselves to system interests in maintaining a sense of order and stability in the school, character- istics which are largely reinforced as desirable.

There is also evidence that beginning teachers may well lack a theoretical framework or well-thought-out belief system to guide their teaching. In fact, they may be seriously deficient in such a core skill as planning for instruction. Griffin (1983) summarized recent research on beginning teacher planning:

However, if one ignores the sharp differences in researchers' methods and intentions (always a risky undertaking), a picture emerges of teachers beginning the school year concentrating planning activities on students but spending the most energy on decisions about classroom activity. Even decisions about classroom activity are made from a relatively narrow range of options. When the teacher does consider students in planning and proactive decision making, the information used is associated more with observed achievement than actual ability. This condition is more than likely a consequence of the lack of a systematic and reasoned strategy for gathering information on decision making. Once initial planning decisions are made, our profile teacher seldom deviates from the mental script that emerged from the planning. (p. 20)

We believe that beginning teachers should possess more than a set of technical skills that have been demonstrated at an acceptable level of performance at the completion of their programs. Articulate conceptions of the nature of knowledge in a classroom, ways of knowing or learning, the nature of motivation, and the art and science of teaching are also essential. In fact, this is what it means to be professional. Although some would argue that these are unrealistic goals, Dobson and Dobson (1983) have demonstrated that continuing dialogue with and among the preservice teacher and focused upon assumptions and their evidential bases for these assumptions relative to the core activities of a teacher can run like threads throughout programs of preparation.

Further, we maintain that early in the preservice program, in what we conceive as largely a selection phase, much could be done to assess both candidate ability to articulate and justify important beliefs and values and candidate willingness to defend and to stay with that position. Several devices and procedures provide information about teacher beliefs and values. In addition to use of the Minnesota Teacher Attitude Inventory (MTAI) (Cook, Leeds, & Callis, 1951) to determine the extent to which teachers view the educational process as one in which a state of harmonious relations (mutual affection and sympathetic understanding) with pupils is maintained, Wheling and Charters (1969) developed a questionnaire to assess the complex organization of teachers beliefs about classroom teaching and learning. Students respond to 76 items about teaching in terms of their agreement or disagreement with the statements. Statements are not considered true or false in a factual sense but in terms of what is believed. Scores are obtained on eight dimensions: subject matter emphasis, personal adjustment ideology, student autonomy versus teacher direction, consideration of student viewpoint, classroom order, integrative learning, emotional disengagement, and student challenge. The relationship between these belief dimensions and level of teacher concreteness–abstractness has been examined in several studies (Rathbone, 1970; Victor, 1970).

It is worth noting also that the instruments described previously, namely, the TIB test (Harvey, 1966) and the CST (Harvey & Hoffmeister, 1975), could provide information about the content of teacher belief systems. Recall that teacher beliefs are defined in terms of primary motivational concern in working with people, for example, rigid, authority oriented; affiliation oriented; and flexible, independence oriented.

Other devices which may be helpful include (a) assessment of Internal–External Locus of Control (Rotter, 1966), (b) deCharms's pawn-origin approach to examining personal causation (deCharms, 1968; deCharms & Shea, 1976), and (c) identification of teachers' implicit psychological theory using an adaptation of the Role Construct Repertory Test (Hunt, 1976). Similarly Argyris and Schon (1977) offered a case-study–group-discussion approach to the assessment of teacher belief systems. Here prospective teachers would write case studies describing both difficult and easy teaching episodes that they have already experienced or expect to experience in the near future. The case study consists of (a) description of purpose and context, (b) comment regarding strategy — objectives, approach, and rationale, (c) sample dialogue with personal thoughts which occurred during the exchange, and (d) assumptions about effective teaching shown in the episode. In this approach group interaction is crucial to eliciting teachers' theories-in-use. The process unfolds one case at a time with each participant working to help make the theory-in-use explicit. There is joint assessment of self and other perceptions operant in the case situation and an assessment of teacher effectiveness. In addition to teacher effectiveness, two other criteria, internal consistency and congruence, are used to evaluate the relationship between espoused theory (beliefs and expectancies) and actual practice.

Weinberg (1972) designed what is referred to as the integrated-self game or the reference-group game which involves defense of a personal position against a peer or reference group. The reference group must maintain a consistent, normative stance other than that subscribed to by the individual defending their position. The structure of the "game" is not to present individual hostilities as much as contrasting norms. It seems conceivable that similar exercises could be designed early in a preparation program to assess a person's ability to articulate and defend important beliefs. Again, the subject matter need not be specific to educational process at the outset where one could not expect a rich knowledge base. However, there is virtually no end to the traditional or contemporary issues which could be addressed. Although the clear expression of an important belief or position and its defense can doubtlessly be improved with practice over time, we suggest that severe limitations in articulating a position of some consequence and in defending it raises a very real cautionary red flag relative to that particular teacher candidate.

Critical Consciousness of Diversity and Special Needs

Martin Haberman (1984) recently noted the following demographic projection:

> In 1982, almost one of every six students enrolled in the public schools was from a poor family and almost one of every ten was handicapped. More than one of every four students enrolled was a member of a minority. All these data were up from the previous decade.
>
> If present trends continue — and there is every reason to believe they will accelerate — the public schools in 2000 will have substantial numbers of minority, low-income, and handicapped students. An increasing number of cities (and states) will have schools where the majority of students will be characterized by one or more of these attributes (that is, minority, poverty, handicapped).
>
> In some states, where the minority population will constitute the majority of students, Spanish speakers will dominate (for example, Texas and New Mexico). In other states, the new majority will be composed primarily of Spanish speakers and Blacks but will also include several minorities, such as Asiatics and Haitans (for example, California, New York, and Florida).
>
> In almost every major city of over 500,000 in population, the majority of students will be those now defined as minority, poverty, handicapped. The shift in the general population from the older industrial areas to the Sunbelt will not mitigate this trend. Although the Sunbelt has almost all the fastest-growing urban areas, it is also characterized by large and rapidly increasing minority populations and increasing number of poor people. (pp. 498–499)

The increase in ethnic diversity and the number of persons in impoverished situations is hardly limited to this country; in fact, there are even more dramatic demographic trends internationally. Contrast these projected statistics with descriptive data about our prospective teachers (recall that the percentage of minorities entering teaching at this time in our country has declined). Yarger, Howey, and Joyce (1977) developed the following profile of a typical prospective teacher:

> A discussion with this average teacher candidate about her background creates several impressions. One is of provincialism. She still tends to come from a small city or from a rural area. She and her colleagues are clearly monolingual, with only three percent stating that they could use either Spanish or French as a medium for instruction (fewer than one percent specified any other language). Five out of six of the students attended College in their home state, with an amazing two-thirds attending college within 100 miles of their home. She and most of her colleagues selected their teacher training institution because of the programs that were available, the cost factor, convenience to home, and what was perceived as adequate job prospects upon graduation. (p. 34)

Obviously there are major differences among individuals and across institutions which prepare teachers but the largely white, monolingual, and somewhat parochial perspective of these teachers appears generalizable. For example, in this same study of preservice programs when teacher education students were asked about their preferences of a context for teaching, only one in three suggested they would prefer to teach in a multiracial setting. The majority wanted to teach in either a suburban or small town setting; only 12% expressed a preference for an urban setting.

Devices used to determine (a) conceptual maturity, (b) close-mindedness, and (c) general attitude toward people (Wrightsman, 1974) could provide information about the way prospective teachers adhere to beliefs about differences associated with cultural and ethnic group membership, SES, gender, and disability. First, studies examining the relationship between conceptual maturity, human relations, and the potential for prejudice indicate that ability to handle diversity is associated with creativity and adaptability in interactive situations (Schroder, Karlins, & Phares, 1973). When individuals use fewer and less well-integrated conceptions of other people, they are more likely to evaluate others as either very good or very bad. If other people are perceived as "different" or are seen as a threat to one's well-being, the effect for the conceptually immature is to increase the psychological distance between self and others; the chances for hostile action are enhanced. Thus, the indices of conceptual maturity mentioned previously can provide an estimate of interpersonal and intergroup functioning.

Another possible assessment involves the Dogmatism Scale (Rokeach, 1960). This scale was designed to measure individual differences in openness or closedness of belief systems. According to Rokeach, openness refers to "the extent to which the person can receive, evaluate and act on relevant information received from the outside on its own intrinsic merits, unencumbered by irrelevant factors in the situation arising from within the person or from the outside" (p. 57). As such the scale was constructed to measure adherence to beliefs rather than specific content of beliefs. Because we are concerned in teacher education with an understanding of the needs of diverse groups, this device could provide an indication of the prospective teacher's openness to change in perspective.

In addition to these formal devices, other procedures may be useful in determining a prospective teacher's approach to understanding diversity and special needs. Friere's (1981) problem-posing model for dialogue could be adapted for use in teacher education. In this approach, investigative teams examine generative themes to expose and critique unnecessary social constraints and personal blindness or ignorance. In teacher education small group experiences could be designed to explore issues surrounding existing school practices (e.g., ability grouping) and to encourage self-reflection about personal beliefs/practices which may have a distorting affect upon students from diverse backgrounds. The goal would be to develop critical awareness of personal theories-in-use as well as the probable consequences of upholding these views (Argyris & Schon, 1977; Goldenberg, 1978). Group interaction could be examined for the openness with which students examine school practices and their own beliefs/practices.

The prospective teacher should be confronted in multiple ways with a global perspective and a multicultural reality early in their programs, and concerns about cultural pluralism should be addressed more systematically (Varga, 1984). Teaching in the public schools calls for an understanding and a valuing of diversity. An insular posture, a parochial perspective cannot be tolerated among our teachers even though some teach in the midst of cultural homogeneity. In this situation teachers need a commitment to and an understanding and appreciation of differences among people so that this can be communicated to their students.

There are numerous ways in which prospective teachers at the outset of their training both in situ and vicariously can be exposed to the multicultural nature of teaching. Hopefully bias and prejudice on whatever grounds will eventually be eliminated through knowledge and experience. However, observations and assessment of potential teachers specific prejudices should be confronted early in the preparation program. A deep concern for social injustice inherent in a democratic society and in public school teaching particularly and its translation into teaching practice must be made eminently clear to our future teachers early on.

Awareness of Ethical Consequences

Choices in teaching often involve complex moral judgments (Tom, 1984). For this reason teachers must act with responsibleness, that is, action should be based on careful, reflective thought about which response is professionally right in a particular situation. This type of evaluation requires application of personal standards derived from an examination of the impact of actions on others. Thus, in addition to the capacity for moral judgment, choices involve considerations about the interests and welfare of others (Scriven, 1966). We suggest three approaches to assessing preservice students' level of moral responsibleness.

In his model of helping behavior, Schwartz (1967) proposed that two personality variables affect moral problem-solving. *Awareness of consequences* (AC) is defined as the tendency to recognize the impact of one's action for others. Persons with high AC are more likely to perceive situations in terms of the impact they have on others and are more likely to attend to personal moral values relevant to the consequences. *Ascription of responsibility* (AR) is the tendency to rationalize responsibility for action and/or consequences away from self. Persons with low AR deny personal responsibility while those with high AR tend to use personal moral values in decision-making. Persons with low AC and AR tend to be more defensive and do not recognize when they are faced with moral choice; they do not use moral values in decision-making and are less likely to exercise responsibleness.

The Awareness of Consequences Test (Schwartz, 1977) was designed to measure the extent to which an individual is aware of the consequences of their potential acts for the welfare of others. This type of assessment is a projective story completion questionnaire including six incidents in which the main character faces a decision that has consequences for the welfare of others. Respondents are asked to make inferences about the thoughts and feelings of the story main character as he/she decides what to do. It is assumed that thoughts and feelings attributed to the main character reflect personal considerations. A high score is assigned to descriptions of specific consequences, adoption of others' perspectives, and reflection about consequences from others' perspectives. The Ascription of Responsibility Test (Schwartz, 1977) also was designed to obtain an index of an individual's feelings of responsibility for personal actions and consequences. Respondents express agreement or disagreement on a 4-point scale with a series of 28 opinion and self-descriptive items. Each item refers to an action with interpersonal consequences together with implicit or explicit rationale for ascribing responsibility for this action away from the person performing it.

A second approach involves assessing the way people define crucial moral issues in a hypothetical conflict of rights situation. Rest's (1979) Defining Issues Test (DIT) reflects a cognitive–developmental approach similar to that used by Kohlberg. Respondents are asked to evaluate a set of 12 issues for each of six stories by rating the importance that each issue has in deciding what ought to be done in the situation posed by the story. Each item represents a different form of reasoning reflective of a particular stage of moral development. Items are rated and then the four most important items are ranked. The D index from this instrument reflects an individual's preference for principled reasoning stage items over lower stage reasoning. The D index has demonstrated consistent developmental trends in numerous longitudinal studies.

A third way of assessing moral responsibleness involves an informal judgment based on teacher educators' general observations of prospective teachers' performance during moral analysis. This approach would combine ongoing exposure to ethical dilemmas in the field with small group analysis of moral dilemmas. There is evidence that professionals can be encouraged to evaluate action with reference to ethical consequences. Shoemaker (1981), for example, has shown that participants in a 3-week course on decision-making about moral and social problems demonstrated significant gains in awareness of consequences. Similarly, developmentalists recognize that even though stage of development affects one's ability to do moral analysis, some skills in moral reasoning can be learned, for example, testing personal value principles (Coombs & Meux, 1971). Because studies have shown that conceptual, ego, and moral development are related (Sullivan, McCullough, & Stager, 1970), we envision screening for some minimum level of these characteristics early in the preparation program as well as systematic effort to plan for individual differences in development.

Integration of Self and Role

Another aspect of career preparation is the development of work identity rather than role confusion (Erickson, 1963). In addition to discovering one's vocational interests and areas of greater and lesser ability, such development requires an examination of the congruence between the choice of work tasks and one's identity. To do this prospective teachers need to go beyond an understanding of the physical and mental demands to grasp the social–psychological aspects of teaching: namely, teacher role. Examination of teacher roles includes ways in which attitudes and values are expressed through teaching; patterns of interaction with others; considerations of authority, responsibility, and status; and lifestyle preferences (Strom, 1980).

Much could be done through early assessment and contact with schools and young people to encourage evaluation of career choice and an examination of the degree of integration of self and role. As the discrepancy increases for some students, a self-screening and "out-placement" would be more likely.

In addition to feedback from assessments of the personal qualities and abilities just described, several other instruments may be of assistance in self-evaluation. Instrumentation used in a 5-year study which compared the vocational decision-making of students who left teacher preparation before completion to those who remained in the program (Thomas & Bruning, 1981, 1984) is suggestive of devices which might be used to check level of satisfaction with career choice, importance of career, general attitude toward career, certainty of career choice, and discrepancy of self-occupational perceptions. Thomas and Bruning used an adaption of Hoppock's Job Satisfaction Blank (Hoppock, 1970) to measure general satisfaction with career choice. The Career Salience Questionnaire (Greenhaus, 1971) was employed to assess perceptions of the importance of work and career in one's total life, and the Attitude Toward Teaching Scale (Merwin & DiVesta, 1959) was used as a measure of an individual's feeling of acceptance or rejection of teaching as a career. The certainty of career decision was measured by the Assessment of Career Decision-Making (Harren, 1976), and an extended Semantic Differential Scale was used to assess the degree of discrepancy between self-concept and occupational-concept.

Also, Kolb's Learning Style Inventory (LSI) (Kolb, 1971; Kolb, Rubin, & McIntyre, 1971), designed to measure an individual's relative emphasis of four learning abilities (Concrete Experience, Reflective-Observation, Abstract Conceptualization, Active Experimentation), has been used to examine the environmental demands of occupations as well (Kolb & Plovnick, 1977). Although the data are suggestive only of a general correspondence between learning style and careers, the LSI might provide students with another piece of information useful in examining the relationship of their own learning style and career choice.

Another type of experience designed to encourage development of work identity is the career dilemma (Strom & Tennyson, 1981; Sprinthall & Collins, 1984). It is a small group strategy designed to engage participants in critical examination of value dilemmas encountered in career decision-making and work. Prospective teachers would be asked to reflect on career and work-related issues (e.g., those involving conflicts over career involvement, career control, occupational colleagueship, job performance, and personal convictions) in order to identify, examine, and justify personal work values. Central to the career dilemma strategy is the invitation to share with others a personal conflict currently faced while pursuing one's career or work. When first initiating students to this strategy, the teacher educator would present specific examples of career dilemmas with which students can identify. After students have become familiar with a conflict resolution process and have developed mutual trust, personal dilemmas would form the core teaching/ learning material. For example:

A young teacher is worried — the teacher is in a highly authoritarian school atmosphere. That is, the teachers are to follow a set course of study; teachers have little voice in the operation of the school; emphasis is on being quiet and orderly, with punishment employed to remedy disruption. Formal classroom activity, teacher lecturing, and little student activity are the norms. Most rules are set by the administration, emphasis is on grades and achievement, and faculty and administration are proud of the social background of the students. The faculty will be discussing ways of improving the school and curriculum in a workshop before school starts. Should this teacher take a stand in the workshop and point out that what really needs to be changed first is the school atmosphere, and thereby risk offending the other teachers and the administration?

In trying to resolve this young teacher's dilemma, preservice students would identify the value issues which seem to be involved, such as: Should I become an active change agent (career control)? How should I deal with the teachers and administration — in a dependent, conforming way; as a competitor; with interdependence; (occupational colleagueship)? Whose interests should I seek to serve — my own, the school community, parents, students (occupational colleagueship)? Several basic values such as reasoned dissent, benevolence, and justice, as well as prudential concerns can be explored as the value bases for making a decision (Strom & Tennyson, 1981, pp. 31–32, reprinted by permission).

The discussion of career dilemmas when it is combined with early systematic observation in schools, interpretation of assessments of attitudes toward career and work, feedback about personal qualities and abilities could have a powerful effect on preservice student sense of purpose and style of work life.

SUMMARY

In this chapter we examined policy and practice regarding teacher selection. Limitations in current practice were identified. An illustrative framework was provided for explicating and applying additional criteria for selecting teachers consonant with a more fully defined conception of teaching. Thus, selected personal qualities and general cognitive abilities were identified and instrumentation and procedures which could be used to assess them discussed. In doing this we tried to highlight some of the central issues involved in teacher selection and point to possible new directions which would allow early identification of attitudes and behaviors which militate against the type of teacher and teaching the preservice program seeks to enable. It is our hope that this discussion will contribute to continuing reflection and dialogue on this important matter.

REFERENCES

American Association of Colleges for Teacher Education. (1984). *AACTE Briefs, 5*(5), 8.

Argyris, C., & Schon, D.A. (1977). *Theory in practice: Increasing professional effectiveness.* San Francisco: Jossey-Bass.

Aspy, D.N. (1965). *A study of three facilitative conditions and their relationships to the achievement of third grade students.* Unpublished doctoral dissertation, University of Kentucky.

Baker, L.W. (1970). *An analysis of some assumed predictors of success in teaching.* Unpublished doctoral dissertation, United States International University.

Barron, F. (1963). *Creativity and psychological health.* New York: Van Nostrand Rheinhold.

Bethune, S.B. (1984). *The impact of college selectivity on recruitment and retention in teacher education programs: Results from NLS.* Paper presented at the annual meeting of the American Educational Research Association, New Orleans, LA.

Brown, G.I. (1972). Growth of a felxible self through creativity and awareness. In B.R. Joyce & M. Weil (Eds.), *Perspectives for reform in teacher education* (pp. 89–115). Englewood Cliffs, NJ: Prentice-Hall.

Brown, M.M., & Strom, S.M. (1975–1976). *Curriculum materials in consumer education* (Vols. 1–4). St. Paul: Minnesota Department of Education.

Carkhuff, R.R. (1969). *Helping and human relations: Vol. 1. Selection and training.* New York: Holt, Rinehart, & Winston.

Carkhuff, R.R. (1971). *The development of human resources.* New York: Holt, Rinehart, & Winston.

Carpenter, J.A. (1972). *Survey of the criteria for the selection of undergraduate candidates for admission to teacher training* (Report No. Sp 006 037). Bowling Green, KY: Western Kentucky University. (ERIC Document Reproduction Service No. ED 070 758)

Coates, C.J., & Neva, E. (1970). *What is a quality school district?* (P.L. 89-10, Title III). Lakewood, CO: Jefferson County Public Schools, District, R-1.

College Entrance Examination Board. (1983). *National report on college-bound seniors*. New York: Author.

Cook, W.W., Leeds, C.H., & Callis, R. (1951). *The Minnesota Teacher Attitude*. New York: The Inventory Psychological Corporation.

Coombs, J.R., & Meux, M. (1971). Teaching strategies for value analysis. In L.E. Metcalf (Ed.), *Values education: Rationale, strategies, and procedures* (pp. 29-74). Washington, DC: National Council for the Social Studies.

Cronbach, L.J., & Snow, R.E. (1978). *Aptitudes and instructional method: A handbook of research on interactions*. Englewood Cliffs, NJ: Prentice-Hall.

deCharms, R. (1968). *Personal causation: The internal affective determinants of behavior*. New York: Academic Press.

deCharms, R., & Shea, D.J. (1976). *Enhancing motivation: Change in the classroom*. New York: Irvington.

Denton, J.J., & Smith, N.L. (1984). *Alternative teacher preparation programs: A cost-effective comparison*. Paper presented at the annual meeting of the American Educational Research Association, New Orleans, LA.

Dobson, R.L., & Dobson, J.E. (1983). Teacher beliefs-practice congruency. *Viewpoints in Teaching and Learning, 59*(1), 20-27.

Druva, C.A., & Anderson, R.D. (1983). Science teacher characteristics by teacher behavior and by student outcome: A meta-analysis of research. *Journal of Research on Science Teaching, 20*(5), 467-479.

Ducharme, R.J. (1970). *Selected preservice factors related to success of the beginning teacher*. Unpublished doctoral dissertation, Louisiana State and Agricultural and Mechanical College, LA.

Eash, M.J., & Rasher, S.P. (1977). *An evaluation of changed inputs on outcomes in teacher education curriculum*. Paper presented at the annual meeting of the American Educational Research Association, New York. (ERIC Document Reproduction Service No. ED 143 145)

Erickson, E.H. (1963). *Childhood and society*. New York: W.W. Norton.

Friere, P. (1981). The adult literacy process as cultural action for freedom. In J.R. Snarey, F. Epstein, C. Sienkiewicz, & P. Zodhiates (Eds.), *Conflict and continuity: A history of ideas on social equality and human development*. Boston: Harvard Educational Review. (Reprint Series No. 15)

Gauthier, D.P. (1963). *Practical reasoning: The structure and foundations of prudential and moral arguments and their exemplification in discourse*. London: Oxford University Press.

Goldenberg, I.I. (1978). *Oppression and social intervention*. Chicago: Nelson Hall.

Greenhaus, J. (1971). An investigation of the roles of career salience in vocational behavior. *Journal of Vocational Behavior, 1*, 209-216.

Griffin, G.A. (1983). The dilemma of determining essential planning and decision-making skills for beginning teachers. In D.C. Smith (Ed.), *Essential knowledge for beginning educators*. Washington, DC: AACTE/ERIC Clearinghouse on Teacher Education.

Guilford, J.P. (1967). *The nature of human intelligence*. New York: McGraw-Hill.

Haberman, M. (1984). Teacher education in 2000. *Education and Urban Society, 16*(4), 497-509.

Habermas, J. (1979). *Communication and the evolution of society*. (T. McCarthy, Trans.). Boston: Beacon Press. (Original work published 1976)

Habermas, J. (1984). *Theory of communicative action* (Vol. 1). (T. McCarthy, Trans.). Boston: Beacon Press. (Original work published 1981)

Harren, V. (1976). *Assessment of career decision-making*. Unpublished progress report. Carbondale, IL: Southern Illinois University.

Harvey, O.J. (1966). System structure, flexibility, and creativity. In O.J. Harvey (Ed.), *Experience, structure, and adaptability* (pp. 39–65). New York: Springer.

Harvey, O.J. (1967). Conceptual systems and attitude change. In C.W. Sherif & M. Sherif (Eds.), *Attitudes, ego-involvement, and change* (pp. 201–226). New York: Wiley.

Harvey, O.J., & Hoffmeister, J. (1975). *Conceptual systems test.* Boulder, CO: Test Analysis and Development Corporation.

Harvey, O.J., Hunt, D.E., & Schroder, H.M. (1961). *Conceptual systems and personality organization.* New York: Wiley.

Harvey, O.J., Prather, M.S., White, B.J., & Hoffmeister, J.K. (1968). Teacher beliefs, classroom atmosphere, and student behavior. *American Educational Research Journal, 5,* 151–166.

Heath, D. (1977). *Maturity and competence.* New York: Gardner.

Hoppock, R. (1970). *Manual for Job Satisfaction Blank No. 5.* New York: Author.

Hunt, D.E. (1970). Adaptability in interpersonal communication among training agents. *Merrill Palmer Quarterly, 16,* 325–344.

Hunt, D.E. (1971). *Matching models in education.* Toronto: Ontario Institute for Studies in Education.

Hunt, D.E. (1975). The B-P-E paradigm for theory, research, and practice. *Canadian Psychological Review, 16,* 185–197.

Hunt, D.E. (1976). Teachers' adaptation: 'Reading' and 'flexing' to students. *Journal of Teacher Education, 27*(3), 268–275.

Hunt, D.E., Butler, L.F., Noy, J.E., & Rosser, M.E. (1978). *Assessing conceptual level by the Paragraph Completion Method.* Toronto: Ontario Institute for Studies in Education.

Hunt, D.E., & Sullivan, E.V. (1974). *Between psychology and education.* Hinsdale, IL: Drydan.

Ishler, R.E. (1984). Requirements for admission to and graduation from teacher education. *Phi Delta Kappan, 66*(2), 121–122.

Joyce, B.R., Yarger, S.J., Howey, K.R., Harbeck, K.H., & Kluwin, T.N. (1977). *Preservice teacher education.* Palo Alto, CA: Lewin and Associates.

Kegan, R. (1982). *The evolving self.* Cambridge, MA: Harvard University Press.

Kohlberg, L. (1976). Moral stages and moralization. In T. Lickona (Ed.), *Moral development and behavior* (pp. 31–53). New York: Holt, Rinehart, & Winston.

Kolb, D.A. (1971). *Individual learning styles and the learning process.* (Sloan School of Management Working Paper, pp. 535–571). Cambridge: Massachusetts Institute of Technology.

Kolb, D.A., & Plovnick, M.S. (1977). The experiential learning theory of career development. In J. Van Maanen (Ed.), *Organizational careers: Some new perspectives* (pp. 65–87). New York: Wiley.

Kolb, D.A., Rubin, I., & McIntyre, J. (1971). *Organizational psychology: An experiential approach.* Englewood Cliffs, NJ: Prentice-Hall.

Laman, A.E., & Reeves, D.E. (1980). Admission to teacher education programs: Status and trends. *Journal of Teacher Education, 31*(1), 2–4.

Lewin, K. (1935). *A dynamic theory of personality.* York, PA: Maple Press.

Loevinger, J. (1976). *Ego development.* San Francisco, CA: Jossey-Bass Publishers.

Merwin, J., & DiVesta, F. (1959). A study of need theory and career change. *Journal of Counseling Psychology, 6,* 302–308.

Miller, A. (1981). Conceptual matching models and interactional research in education. *Review of Educational Research, 51*(1), 33–84.

Piaget, J. (1972). Intellectual evolution from adolescence to adulthood. *Human Development, 15,* 1–12.

Rathbone, C. (1970). *Teachers' information handling behavior when grouped with students by conceptual level.* Unpublished doctoral dissertation, Syracuse University, New York.

Raz, J. (Ed). (1978). *Practical reasoning.* New York: Oxford University Press.

Rest, J.R. (1979). *Development in juding moral issues*. Minneapolis: University of Minnesota Press.

Rogers, C. (1983). *Freedom to learn for the 80's*. Columbus, OH: Charles E. Merrill.

Rokeach, M. (1960). *The open and closed mind*. New York: Basic Books.

Rotter, J.B. (1966). Generalized expectancies for internal versus external control of reinforcement. *Psychological Monographs, 80* (1, Whole No. 609).

Sandefur, J.T. (1984, August 11). *Standards for admission to teacher education*. An issue paper prepared for the Minnesota Higher Education Board, St. Paul, Minnesota.

Schroder, H.M. (1977). *Developing adaptability to complexity*. Paper presented at a conference on Developing Cognitive Complexity, University of Augsburg, West Germany.

Schroder, H.M., Driver, M.J., & Streufert, S. (1967). *Human information processing*. New York: Holt, Rinehart, & Winston.

Schroder, H.M., Karlins, M., & Phares, J.O. (1973). *Education for freedom*. New York: Wiley.

Schroder, H.M., & Talbot, G.T. (1966). *The effectiveness of video feedback in sensitivity training*. Peace Corps Report, Princeton University.

Schwartz, S.H. (1967). *Moral orientation and interpersonal conduct in moral encounters*. Unpublished doctoral dissertation, University of Michigan.

Schwartz, S.H. (1977). Normative influences on altruism. In L. Berkowitz (Ed.), *Advances in Experimental Social Psychology, 10,* 221–279.

Scriven, M. (1966). *Primary philosophy*. New York: McGraw-Hill.

Selman, R. (1980). *The development of interpersonal understanding*. New York: Academic Press.

Shoemaker, S.F. (1981). *Training in awareness of consequences*. Unpublished doctoral dissertation, Fuller Theological Seminary.

Shulman, L. (1970). Reconstruction in educational research. *Review of Educational Research, 40,* 371–396.

Snow, R.E. (1974). Representative and quasi-representative designs for research on teaching. *Review of Educational Research, 44*(3), 265–291.

Sprinthall, N.A., & Collins, W.A. (1984). *Adolescent psychology* (The career dilemma approach and stages of work values, pp. 459–467). Reading, MA: Addison Wesley.

Sprinthall, N.A., & Thies-Sprinthall, L. (1983). The need for theoretical frameworks in educating teachers: A cognitive developmental perspective. In K.R. Howey & W.E. Gardner (Eds.), *The education of teachers: A look ahead* (pp. 74–97). New York: Longman.

Strom, S.M. (1980). Post high school career management tasks. In W.W. Tennyson, L.S. Hansen, M.K. Klaurens, & M.B. Antholz, (Eds.), *Career development education: A program approach for teachers and counselors* (pp. 121–132). St. Paul: National Vocational Guidance Association for the Minnesota Department of Education.

Strom, S.M., & Tennyson, W.W. (1981). *Influencing the development of work values*. Unpublished monograph, University of Minnesota, Minneapolis.

Sullivan, E.V., McCullough, G., & Stager, M. (1970). A developmental study of the relation between conceptual, ego, and moral development. *Child Development, 41,* 399–412.

Tabachnick, B.R., & Zeichner, K.M. (1984). The impact of student teaching experience on the development of teacher perspectives. *Journal of Teacher Education, 35*(6), 28–36.

Thomas, R.G., & Bruning, C.R. (1981). Validities and reliabilities of minor modifications of the Central Life Interests and Career Salience Questionnaires. *Measurement and Evaluation in Guidance, 14*(3), 128–135.

Thomas, R.G., & Bruning, C.R. (1984). Cognitive dissonance as a mechanism in vocational decision processes. *Journal of Vocational Behavior, 24,* 264–278.

Tom, A.R. (1984). *Teaching as a moral conflict*. New York: Longman.

Torrance, E.P. (1962). *Guiding creative talent*. Englewood Cliffs, NJ: Prentice-Hall.

Torrance, J.P., Torrance, E.P., & Crabbe, A.B. (1980–1981). *Handbook for training future problem solving teams.* Cedar Rapids, IA: Future Problem Solving.

Varga, K. (1984). Cultural pluralism and human liberty: A review of Cultural Pluralism in Education *Educational Theory, 34*(4), 389–396.

Victor, J.B. (1970). *A study of personality, attitudinal, and situational determinants of teacher behavior in regard to child misbehavior.* Unpublished doctoral dissertation, Syracuse University, New York.

Weinberg, C. (1972). Problems in the presentation of the "real" self. In B.R. Joyce & M. Weil (Eds.), *Perspectives for reform in teacher education* (pp. 69–87). Englewood Cliffs, NJ: Prentice-Hall.

Weinberg, C., McHugh, P., & Lamb, H. (1970). *Contexts of teacher alienation* (Report No. 5-10-170). Washington, DC: United States Office of Education.

Wehling, L.J., & Charters, W.W., Jr. (1969). Dimensions of teacher beliefs about the teaching process. *American Educational Research Journal, 6*(1), 7–29.

Wrightsman, L.S. (1974). *Assumptions about human nature: A social psychological approach.* Monterey, CA: Brooks/Cole.

Yarger, S.J., Howey, K.R., & Joyce, B.R. (1977). Reflection on preservice preparation: Impressions from the National Survey. *Journal of Teacher Education, 28*(6), 34–36.

Chapter 2

Preservice Teachers as Adult Learners: A New Framework for Teacher Education

Lois Thies-Sprinthall
Norman A. Sprinthall

North Carolina State University

One way to distinguish between general liberal arts education and almost any form of professional education is to view the problem from the learner's perspective. What are the goals of such experiences from the learner's view? Without belaboring the point, the liberal arts goals are heuristic and generic. The goal is to expand and open up the learner. From a developmental framework it is Erik Erikson's theory (1968) that is particularly helpful. College is a time for late adolescence to explore under conditions of a moratorium, that is to experience while deliberately postponing choice and commitment. A moratorium is like a rite of passage. The learner is encouraged by self and others to try new activities in both formal educational settings and in less formal. Studying unfamiliar subjects, such as art, anthropology, or the classics, represents a rather conventional response while doing the equivalent of Capetown to Cairo on a motorcycle represents a less conventional. In either case, however, the goal is to educate without commitment. Adolescence in this sense is a time to experiment, and to try out, as a necessary prior step to adulthood. The formation of one's own identity as a person, not as a professional, is the goal.

Contrast adolescent identity formation with early adulthood development. The goals are just opposite. The bench mark of transition from adolescence to adulthood is commitment. Professional education demands (or should demand) closure and choice as opposed to continued openness and tentativeness. Imagine being operated on by the equivalent of Benjamin Braddock from *The Graduate*. As he cuts, is he thinking about his next experience as a trial lawyer in order to "find himself"? As facetious as that seems it may help to remind us of some basic differences between heuristic, and hopefully, liberating experiences and professional development. Piaget and Inhelder (1958) in a rare commentary on adulthood have noted that the transition period is characterized by an increase in what they refer to as "decentered cognition." Instead of dwelling upon self exclusively the young adult becomes concerned with larger issues:

> The focal point of the decentering process is the entrance into the occupational world or the beginning of serious professional training. The adolescent becomes an adult when he (she) undertakes a real job. It is then that he/she is transformed from an idealistic reformer into an achiever. (p. 346)

In fact the concept of career entry is viewed as so important to Piaget that he has suggested a complete modification to the assessment of formal operations for young adults. Instead of measuring generic components of formal/abstract thought he suggests assessment within the field of study or discipline (Piaget, 1972). The main point, however, is to note the importance of the stage shift which marks the end of a developmental moratorium and the beginning of adulthood, or in the arcane language of Piaget, the beginning of decentered cognition at the level of formal operations. From a learner's perspective then, the process of professional training in education can be viewed as the onset of adulthood. With that established, we will now turn to the question of theory to guide professional education. A short-hand version of this larger question is, can we design teacher education to start where the young adult learner is? The answer is tentative yet affirmative if we use a developmental framework as a theory for choice.

TEACHER EDUCATION AND THEORY: SHIPS THAT HAVE PASSED IN THE NIGHT FOR TOO LONG

Teacher education as opposed to teaching itself has been a conspicuous example of practice without theory. In one sense this is very similar to much professional education in general. The selection of learning experiences, and even the content of professional curricula, are rarely based upon careful theoretically relevant criteria, let alone any basis in empirical validity. In an allied field such as counselor education Darley (1964) commented a number of years ago based on long years of experience as a department head, that the actual program content was decided in a manner more akin to a tribal ritual than objective or scientific direction:

First curricular planning and curricular revision represent the orgiastic, tribal ceremony of that strange primitive culture known as the faculty. Periodically, under malign or benign heavenly forces, we are gripped by the need to plan or replan a curriculum; we thrash through the arguments and compromises involved in establishing a training program, and fall back pleasantly exhausted and surfeited from the ceremonial task. (p. 69)

In a similar but less cynical vein Bok (1983, 1984) has recently reviewed professional education in both law and medicine. His conclusion was that both programs need a major overhaul with recommended changes (hopefully) to emerge from careful analysis as to professional goals as well as teaching strategies. In other words both need a more elaborated set of ideas to guide choice and process. For example, in medicine he was particularly critical of the folk-wisdom of medical school admission in prescribing so much science in the curriculum. Law, he suggested, needs a total reorientation toward a mediation model on one hand, and a careful reevaluation of admission away from its current practice of admitting unsure "boys" and "girls" on the other hand (e.g., law as an extended moratorium?).

We mention these examples as context to understand that criticism of current approaches to teacher education are not unique to professional education. Teacher education is simply another example of practice without theory. Thus commentary by critics such as Schalock, Ryan, Shutes, and Howey are contemporaneous examples to the same point. For example, Schalock (1979) underscored the almost total lack of valid research on current programs. Ryan (1979), with tongue only partly in cheek, echoes Darley's critique saying that teacher-education programs are camels — horses designed by a committee:

These creatures of committees are dumpy and lumpy, made by so many people with different views of human condition and of what are learning, teaching, and the characteristics of skillful teachers. In effect, a teacher-education program is a compromise of these many views and, sometimes, of many powerful factors. (p. 1)

Shutes (1975) points out that without theory any practice merely wanders. Teacher education itself, as a result, is subject to, and has been subject to, almost any fad or fanciful idea which pops up from time to time. Certainly there is no shortage of mindless fads whether we think back to the days of Admiral Rickover and basic education, more recently to George Leonard and education and ecstasy, or currently to a landscape strewn with "expert" ideas such as The Paedia Proposal, or even proposals to close schools of education themselves. These are and will be the fruits of professional education, atheroetically based. What this means, at a most serious level, is simply that

we have no basis to complain about the emergence of half-baked ideas and je-
june proposals for reform. We need to get our own house in order including
hard thinking and research to create the missing frameworks for program development. This may be harsh criticism directed at ourselves, but in our view
we will never be able to avoid present and future onslaughts of well-inten-
tioned but misinformed ideologues, unless we come up with more theoretically sound and empirically validated propositions to guide practice. Howey
(1977) has encapsulated the problem with his not-so-rhetorical question,
"Preservice teacher education: Lost in the shuffle?" (p. 26).

A COGNITIVE–DEVELOPMENTAL FRAMEWORK:
THE MISSING LINK?

In the past 20 years or so there has been a substantial body of research and
theory from a cognitive–developmental view which has important implications for the problems of teacher education. We will review some of the basic
assumptions of this view and then connect to program proposals. In general,
psychology as a discipline has avoided theory for normal adults. We've had
extremely complex and elaborated theory for normal and abnormal child development, as well as for abnormal adults. Even the field of adolescent development has progressed markedly as more than just a transition. A major la-
cunae, however, has been a framework for the process of adult development.
Recently there have been "pop" psychology case studies on adults, for example, sheehy's *Passages* (1977), yet nothing of real substance either theoretically or empirically as a basis for educative programming. In a somewhat
simplified sense psychology's preoccupation with normal children and abnormal adults has limited inquiry for too long, probably based on erroneous
assumption that adults, as such, don't grow anyway, only learn to adjust and
cope. Of course, the developmentalists themselves, have been slow to revise
their own earlier fixations on children and adolescents. Piaget, as noted
earlier, did not seriously comment on adult growth until the end of his long
career. Kohlberg (1969) similarly reflected this same preoccupation when he
commented in the early 1960s that adulthood could be conceptualized as a
time of change, but not developmental stage progression.

What caused the current revision and expansion of cognitive–developmental theory was a mistake in judgment by some of the researchers. The
mistake, ironically, was to conduct longitudinal studies. For example,
Kohlberg (1979) found that as some of his subjects matured their level of
value development continued to increase in the level of complexity. Similarly, under somewhat unique conditions, Heath (1977) found that adult
growth can continue along a variety of developmental domains such as conceptual development, altruism, and individualization. What such findings
mean is that we are in the process of creating a new and more complex theo-

retical paradigm to incorporate these new developmental facts. We can no longer assume that adulthood equals either stabilization or, worse, slow degeneration. If some adults demonstrate developmental stage growth as Kohlberg and Heath have shown then it is necessary to revise theory. If some can grow perhaps others can, so that developmental growth may not be an exception during adulthood but rather the rule?

What are these broad developmental assumptions? In the tradition of John Dewey, the cognitive–developmental view assumes the following:

1. All humans process experience through cognitive structures. Piaget uses the word schemata, for example, a cognitive system of thinking or symbolizing experience — an inner behavior of deep structure.
2. These cognitive structures are organized into a hierarchy of stages, a sequence from less complexity toward greater complexity.
3. Growth occurs first within a particular stage and then only to the next stage in the sequence. This latter change is a qualitative shift — a major quantum leap to a significantly more complex system of processing experience.
4. Growth is neither automatic nor unilateral, but occurs only with appropriate interaction between the human and the environment.
5. Behavior can be determined and predicted by an individual's particular stage of development. Predictions, however, are not exact.
6. The stages themselves are conceptualized as a series of partially independent domains. A domain is a major content–structure area of human activity, for example, how one understands an intellectual discipline, or value questions, or self and others, et al.

This last point deserves some elaboration because it represents a further revision from the earlier view of a developmental stage as a major global system. Instead we now know that humans can process experience ("be at" different stages) depending upon the quality and amount of interaction, in a growth sense, they may have experienced. Thus, as Heath has shown, an adult can process experience at an extremely high level in one domain such as mathematical/quantitative (Formal substage II on Piaget), yet process interpersonal and self-knowledge at an unintegrated/immature level.

There is a large body of research which is presented elsewhere in support of the developmental framework (Sprinthall & Thies-Sprinthall, 1983). Even more recently James Rest (1984) has commented that there is now in excess of 5000 studies just in the Kohlberg domain itself, as an example of the burgeoning interest in the cognitive–developmental field. The domain question is discussed later because that framework now makes it possible to view the preservice teacher from a variety of cognitive–developmental domains. A prior discussion is necessary. We need to ask an important question: What is the relation between the level of stage development of an individual and actual behavior? In other words, given that the six assumptions are logically coherent, as one test of theory, what is the empirical basis for significance? Does stage predict behavior?

In a recent article we reviewed much of the general research which indicates quite clearly that stage does predict behavior (Sprinthall & Thies-Sprinthall, 1983). What these studies show quite clearly is that persons at more complex levels of psychological development behave more humanely, based more on democratic principles, less in accord with social conformity, less other-directed, more empathically, and so on. If one reads across the brief descriptors of the higher stages on Piaget, Kohlberg, Loevinger, Hunt, et al., it will be perhaps obvious that persons who process experience with those characteristics "ought" to behave differently when compared to those who process at less complex levels. A wide variety of studies, with different subjects, and different measures, indicate they do. Rather than cover this ground in detail one more time, we will describe a few of the most recent investigations to further buttress the point. In each case the study examines the relation between stage and complex human behavior in a helping situation.

Walters and Stivers (1977) studied the process of student teaching with a large sample study ($N = 319$). Employing Erik Erikson's theory and an instrument designed to assess the developmental level of identity formation, they found that the developmental stage of the subjects was by far the most effective predictor of actual classroom preference. Following the Campbell and Stanley dictum of multiple measures of a dependent variable, the researchers used a combination of a Flanders index, a Bloom higher order questioning index, and a nine behavioral category observer index. The identity stage score explained the largest variance in student teaching, whereas traditional predictors (SAT & IQ) added nothing to the prediction equation. Probably the most interesting point in the study was the finding that it was a low score by males (Identity Diffusion) which accounted for the major differentiation. A male student teacher whose psychological identity is still diffuse, may be all right as a college student, but when required to perform in a complex role of managing instruction in a real classroom, that performance fails. In everyday language this suggests quite strongly that if a person does not know (in this case) who he is as a person, he is a poor risk for teaching.

A second recent study to the same general point was conducted with a sample of graduate students in counselor training (Strohmer, Biggs, Haase, & Purcell, 1983). The researchers, after assessing the developmental level with the Hunt Conceptional Level (CL) test, then presented the counselors with two sets of clients, "regular" and handicapped. With a sophisticated cross-over design to insure randomization, the results indicated that the counselors in training at more complex levels on the Hunt test were able to provide accurate empathy to both groups. Because one of the criticisms of cognitive–development research is that it often examines only verbal behavior, this study adds valuable new information. Counselor behavior was assessed exclusively at a nonverbal level, for example, eye contact, voice tone, interruptions in speech, and body posture. Experts in nonverbal communication such as Galloway (1968) have long maintained that such communication does speak more loudly than words. The SUNY Albany group provided a significant piece of detailing the nonverbal behavior and developmental level, in this case for counselors in a helping role. Those findings have also been cross-validated specifically with student teachers in a study by Mortenson (1983). She found, using the Galloway index, that student teachers with higher stage scores on the Hunt test were less restricting in nonverbal behavior compared to subjects with lower stage scores.

Finally, Eberhardy (1982) with a sample of nurses confronted with major decisions (to resuscitate or not); Libbey (1980) with a sample of junior high school teachers on approaches to discipline; and young mothers (Bielke, 1979) providing abundant and facilitating environments for their off-spring; all reached similar conclusions. The subjects assessed at higher stage levels perform more adequately in complex human interactions involved in helping situations.

A DEVELOPMENTAL FRAMEWORK: THREE FACES OF TEACHING

What these studies and theories suggest to us is the possibility of a synthesis for teacher education goals. It seems logical to view the teacher in a democratic society primarily through three developmental domains: (a) the teacher as a epistemologist and manager of instruction, (b) the teacher as a representer of democratic values, and (c) the teacher as a person or the teacher from a self-concept view. In a domain sense we can tentatively assign different theorists to these areas. In the first, how the teacher thinks about and acts out the instructional managerial role probably relates most closely to the Hunt (1974) area of intellecutal–conceptual development: What's the nature of teaching and learning? How do I conceptualize my role as transmitter/facilitator? These are the questions that are most often associated with this facet. Certainly the research evidence, given the huge number of studies in the Hunt area (see Miller's most comprehensive list in 1981), is indicative of a substantial empirical base for this aspect of teaching.

The second area, the teacher as a representative of democratic values and ethics, is based on the work of Kohlberg. If early public school advocates are correct such as Horace Mann (we can't teach for democracy through methods of slavery) or John Dewey (the role of schools is to nurture democratic participation), then it is obvious that a teacher's understanding of and ability to act upon democratic principles represents an important domain. The research does show that a person's ability to resist authoritarianism and to act autonomously on the basis of principle consistently lines up with the level of value judgment on the Kohlberg scheme (see Blasi's 1981 review of over 80 studies). These findings hold up cross-culturally, as well as for both sexes.

The third area, the self-concept of the teacher, relates to the work of a number of researcher theorists — primarily Loevinger, with Erikson as a precursor or contributor. The reason for the distinction is largely empirical. Erikson's evidence is mostly clinical, whereas Loevinger (1976) has done large sample empirical studies to cross-validate her stages especially through adulthood. Her levels of ego development suggest that it is the quality of the self that determines the person's ability to understand and reflect upon one's own self. Does one view one's ego as primarily an agent of social conformity, conscientious, self-directed, or integrated and mutually interdependent? Such are the different personality/ego milestones in her sequence. Her research studies indicate a consistent predictable relationship between these ego stages and performance. Some of our own studies indicate the quality or level of ego relates to performance in helping activities for samples of teenagers, and young adults (Sprinthall & Thies-Sprinthall, 1980). In an older sense this facet relates to the earlier socratic doctrine of levels of self-knowledge.

The synthesis can be conceptualized in at least two ways: as three separate strands or as three sides of a cube. It's problematic either way. Because the research intercorrelations across these domains is only moderate, it suggests that the domains are partly related and partly independent. This might be best represented by a cube, or perhaps a three-sided pyramid. Each side represents one of the three facets, allowing for simultaneous comparison of the three-way interaction. Figure 1 presents the synthesized cube.

At least at a theoretical level we could push the synthesis even further suggesting that the "ideal" teacher would reach high levels of development in all three domains. In fact if we review Douglas Heath's (1977) work in general that is exactly the case. He found in a cross-cultural study of males that the mark of psychological maturity was the ability to engage in a series of processes simultaneously, including (a) to symbolize experience abstractly, (b) to act allocentrically and with empathy, and (c) to act autonomously and with a commitment to democratic values. Such are the characteristics of an integrated, mature, stable personality. His work further shows that such individuals are more competent as adults in general, with success in life being measured by a broad multifaceted index.

In the specific case of teaching Greene's (1973) theory comes to mind. In her epic book, *The Teacher As Stranger,* she portrays the teacher as a philosopher who "does" philosophy in creating humane and facilitating growth experiences for the pupils. Clearly her description suggests a person who processes experience at a postconventional level on all three systems of our cube simultaneously. Greene's (1973) concept of the teacher as stranger is an ideal

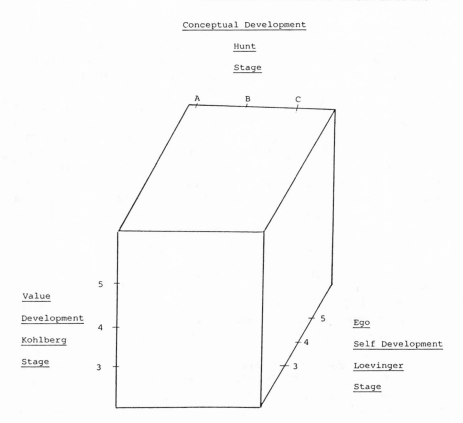

FIGURE 1. Three Faces of Teacher Development

and noble type. After quoting Rilke's poem, "Initiation," she says pointing to the phrase on raising a shadowy tree:

> The tree may represent the order, pattern, or perspective the individual creates when he learns. To grasp its meaning with one's will may signify the personal choice to integrate what has been disclosed, to put it to use in interpreting and ordering one's own life-world. The teacher, too, must raise his shadowy trees and let them ripen. Stranger and homecomer, questioner and goad to others, he can become visible to himself by doing philosophy. There are countless lives to be changed, worlds to be remade. (p. 298)

Thus a developmental synthesis seems adequate both theoretically and empirically as a framework for goals. One of the constant and long nagging problems in psychology as a science has been the difficulty to create a theory that is generically broad enough to be respectful of what we know about human complexity. Most prior theories have been conspicuous in what was left out. A broad-based developmental theory on the other hand seems to be a better approximation of human individuality and human similarity. Certainly the theory is less deterministic and reductionistic when compared to either humanistic or psychoanalytic psychology. We should also note that these cognitive–developmental domains themselves are not static. Work is continuing in related areas such as Selman's (1980) theory of interpersonal development, Dupont's (1978) work in levels of emotional development, and Fowler (1974) and Peatling (1981) who are investigating stages of faith/ spiritual development. Thus when we consider the specific cluster of developmental domains selected for focus vis á vis teacher education goals, these appear as a reasonable approximation of the level of complexity involved in teacher training on one hand, and the complexity of the person, on the other.

APPLYING THEORY TO PROGRAMS

Remembering the Kurt Lewin dictum of theory and practice as different sides of the same coin, we are now ready to sketch out the interactions between theory and practice for teacher education. The assumptions for applying developmental theory to educational programs designed for young adults in transition to professional careers are as follows:

1. Most young adults process experience in each of the three domains of Hunt, Loevinger, and Kohlberg with relative consistency and stability.
2. The mode of problem solving or processing experience itself is the current and preferred method of learning that the individual brings to a new educative task.
3. Developmental stage growth — a qualitative change to a higher and more complex level — generally requires a careful sequence of "matched" and "mis-matched" guided experiences.

These assumptions, in short, represent a shift from a theory which describes and explains human behavior to a theory which prescribes educational intervention. Years ago Bruner (1966) noted that a major difficulty in education was the lack of a theory for instruction. In other words there were multiple theories which described, but none that were capable of a second task, namely to detail educational prescriptions. One of the major advances of the developmental framework in the past 20 years has been a series of second generation studies to outline answers to the prescription question to be noted shortly. The reason for the second generation comment is simply that all these current attempts have their educational roots in the John Dewey turf. Programs designed to promote developmental growth and to enhance human potential, all are derivative of Dewey's philosophy. The recent research noted earlier now provides us with a much clearer picture of the nature and scope of stage learning characteristics. The careful basic research which began with Piaget and is now ongoing with developmental giants such as Hunt, Loevinger, & Kohlberg, indicate just how and where to start where the learner is and even (tentatively) what steps to take next. This research, for example, suggests that young adults potentially make meaning or process experience in the three domains outlined in Chart 1.

Longitudinal and cross-sectional studies indicate that college students and young adults generally function, for example, their preferred mode of problem solving, at either Stage A or B on the Hunt test, Stage 3 or 3/4 on Loevinger, and at Stage 3 or 4 on Kohlberg. To overgeneralize thus means that most candidates for the teaching profession are currently experiencing their world through one of two general modes:

Mode A — View learning from a concrete factual basis — there is one right way to teach.

- View self from a social conformity perspective — "other directed."
- View democratic values from the perspective of "the best way to get along is to go along." Follow orders and conventions without question.

Mode B — Views learning from an abstract perspective. Can distinguish theory from fact most of the time; not completely comfortable with successive approximations as a theory of knowing.

- More individuated as a self. Greater empathy for individual differences. Evidence of inner-direction and personal autonomy; some assertiveness, but not always consistent and still shows some evidence of social conformity.
- More understanding and action based on democratic principles. Distinguishes between social conventions and laws. Sometimes perceives differences between laws and principles.

These generalizations come from a synthesis of studies. In the specifications of students entering the teaching profession we have to be somewhat tentative as to the proportion "at" Mode A versus Mode B. We simply do not have a large number of nationally representative studies of the developmental characteristics of teachers in training. The specific research that does exist indicates that perhaps as many as one half of young adult teacher trainees are probably closer to Mode A than Mode B. For example Silverman and Creswell (1982) found over half of the preservice teachers in their study were functioning at the concrete level. This result was similar to an earlier study by Juraschek (1974). Both studies indicated that there was a greater tendency for elementary preservice to function at the concrete, whereas more secondary

CHART 1. Developmental Domains of Teacher Growth

Stage	Hunt Conceptual Educational	Stage	Loevinger Ego/Self	Stage	Kohlberg Value/Character
A	Knowledge seen as fixed and concrete. One way to teach and learn. High structure, detailed instructions, compliance as a learner. No differentiation between theories and facts. Needs advance organizers.	3	High on social conformity. Strong needs to fit in and please. Self as a follower. Banal and superficial emotions.	Three	Value orientation based on wishes of the "leading crowd". Other-directed values. High on ethnocentrism. Little ability to distinguish between social convention and laws and democratic principles.
B	Awareness of abstractions. Increased ability to separate fact, opinion and theory. Some unevenness in performance but increase in inductive and deductive reasoning. Greater enjoyment in open inquiry.	3/4	Beginnings of individuation. Growth toward an autonomous self. Some appreciation of abstract ideas and emotional complexity.	Four	Conscientious understanding of law. Some ability to understand principles. A "third" party perspective.
		4	Individuated as a self. Inner directed. Self-directed, competent achiever. Standards of excellence.		
C	Knowledge as successive approximations. Multiple solutions employed in problem solving. High on abstractions, symbolization. A balance between tentativeness and commitment.	4/5 & 5	Mutuality interdependence. Reciprocal interpersonal relations, rich and extensive "inner life," assertiveness balanced with compassion.	Five	Employs democratic principles in decision-making in a variety of circumstances. Ethical character understands difference between law and principle.

preservice could function at an abstract level. Similarly Hunt (1974) reports that in three samples of preservice, one group was primarily Stage A (concrete), whereas the other two were closer to Stage B (abstract). Unfortunately the level of the preservice groups was not noted. In any case the generalization holds that a substantial proportion of preservice teachers prefer to problem solve at a concrete level, whereas the other teachers (half or more) can process at an abstract level.

We may make similar inferences as to the approximate "base" rates for functioning in the other two domains of our modes. Kohlberg's (1979) longitudinal studies indicate that in the 20–22 and 26–28 age range about 40% of the subjects function primarily at Stage 3, with an equal percent at Stage 4. Similarly Loevinger's (1976) studies indicate a comparable split between these two stages as the major system employed by young adults. These base rates mean that almost all preservice teachers will share one of these two modes as their current preferred learning style. Before we proceed, however, it is important to underscore that last comment. Their current stage, or preferred learning mode, is not permanent, nor fixed. Hunt (1974) refers to the idea of a stage as representing the current "accessibility channel." It would be a major mistake to assume that such cognitive structures are similar to fixed personality traits or factors. Instead the developmental framework assumes just the opposite. Under particular learning environments it is clearly possible to promote growth to the next more complex level of functioning. Cronbach and Snow (1977) refer to this question as the "modifiability" of personality traits through trait–treatment interaction. Hunt (1974) denotes the question as the "malleability" of conceptual stage through appropriate environmental matching and mismatching. It is to that question which we now turn.

PROMOTING STAGE GROWTH: MATCHING AND MISMATCHING

Without getting bogged down in details, it is possible to assess preservice teachers in all these domains. Instruments are available and the scoring procedures are detailed in self-training manuals for both the Loevinger system (Loevinger & Wessler, 1970) and the Hunt system (Hunt et al., 1977). Rest (1979) has created an objective version for assessment of levels of value judgment on the Kohlberg scheme. Walters and Stivers (1977) employed an objective version of levels of ego identity formation in their study previously noted. Because no single measure of developmental stage functioning is adequate by itself, we recommend the use of multiple measures for increased cross-validation of the levels of functioning.

Given the entry-level characteristics of young adult learners in a professional training program such as teaching, the intervention question now becomes how do we start where the learner is from a developmental point of view? It seems almost obvious if we accept this cardinal principle of teaching that we ought to match the learning tasks to individuals' current preferred learning style or accessibility channel. Educators, in this regard, have long held that at least one aspect of instruction involved the differential use of structure, for example, how detailed, how concrete, how focused should be the instruction? Translating this idea into our framework can never be completely a literal adaption. However, we can set down some general guidelines for differentiation. Thus if we wish to match our instruction to current mode of Stage A learners we would arrange our educative experiences to match the characteristics of high structure as elaborated in Chart 2.

Following these general principles there have been some recent intervention studies designed to test out the effectiveness of such developmental matching and mismatching. Some of the earlier studies were only partially successful (Sprinthall & Bernier, 1978; Glassberg & Sprinthall, 1980; Oja & Sprinthall, 1978) largely because a careful differentiation was not followed. More recent studies have indicated that it is possible to differentiate instruction according to the developmental level of learners and promote stage growth as a consequence. These three studies are noteworthy because each was conducted independently and with subjects at different age and stage levels. Hedin (1979) devised differentiated strategies for a class of high school pupils, Widick and Simpson (1979) applied a similar method to a group of college students, and the first author conducted a study with inservice teachers (Thies-Sprinthall, 1984). In the latter case the researcher carefully differentiated the content and process of a graduate course in instructional supervision. To give the reader a sense of the extent of the differentiation we are including the following outline which represents an operational translation of the previous chart. Both the Hedin (1979) and the Widick and Simpson (1979) studies followed similar formats, although in the case of the college students, only the equivalent of the Stage A students improved.

CHART 2.   Differentiation of Structure (Thies-Sprinthall, 1984)

Factors	High Structure	Low Structure
Concepts	Concrete	Abstract
Time Span	Short	Long
Time on Task	Multiple practice	Single practice
Advance Organizers	Multiple use of organizers	Few (if any) advance organizers
Complexity of Learning Tasks	Divided into small steps and recycled	Learning tasks clustered into "wholes"
Theory	Concretely matched with experimental examples	Generalized including collaborative classroom research
Instructor Support	Consistent and frequent	Occasional

CHART 3.   Differentiated Curriculum Strategies (A Graduate Course in Instructional Supervision) (Thies-Sprinthall, 1982)

Stage	Examples of Strategies
Stage A	Simple, clear statements in class of theoretical considerations. Examples used were in the subject matter areas of the teachers.
	Opportunities to repeat practice during additional optional practice sessions.
	Careful sequencing of skills learned to assure graduate building on previous skill.
	Journal writing included specific questions to answer.
	All reflection discussions included concrete guidance by the instructor. A list of feeling words was given as a checklist.
	Support given by the instructor included extensive statements to journals, special conferences and reinforcement of contributions in class.
	Careful supervision to assure completion of assignments.
Stage B	Optional readings on theories presented in class.
	Optional research projects based on theoretical assumptions.
	Open-ended journal writing.
	Opportunities to present seminars on teaching models to colleagues.
	Less support needed from instructor.
	Option of doing cycle of differentiated supervision a second time with a colleague not in the class.

There are a number of important points to denote. First, the goals of such interventions are admittedly broad and complex. Attempting to promote developmental stage change is a tall order indeed. We are focusing on educational goals which are clearly greater than subject matter mastery or academic tasks in the traditional sense. The reason for this is simply because we are convinced that stage developmental growth does make a real difference in the person's ability to function as an effective professional in a helping relationship as the studies noted in the first section attest. In fact Hunt (1974) noted that we can consider education, psychotherapy, social case work, and child rearing as sharing a single common feature — to provide an interpersonal environment designed to nuture the developmental growth of the pupil, the patient, the client, or the child. Thus the developmental goals are ambitious.

Good (1980) has perhaps best summarized this point. After many years of seeking a high degree of teacher behavior specificity, he commented:

I suspect that the most important contribution of educational research has been the production of concepts for the classroom teacher that can be *examined, interpreted,* and applied in the context of his or her particular setting . . . Unfortunately too many educators ignore the indeterminate nature of their advice and argue for simple, unthinking application. (p. 65)

In our view this is precisely correct. The generic role of educational programs is to encourage the ability to examine, to interpret, and to act. If we want persons who can manage classrooms, attend to individual pupil differences, respond to the legitimate intellectual and emotional needs of pupils, and translate subjects into meaningful educative experiences for children, then we really must embrace developmental stage growth as our dependent variable.

A TWO-TRACK PROGRAM

Our final major point is that preservice teacher education programs should be organized in a manner which will deliberately accommodate the developmental differences of the students. This means reorganizing the entire program along developmental lines including all the components such as foundations, child/adolescent psychology, teaching methods, subject matter competence, and student teaching supervision. This also means reorganizing the faculty themselves into clusters or teams in order to insure consistency in application within each of the two modes. For those in Mode A, the structure, the amount of responsibility, and the concepts and skills would be oriented toward the concrete. Concepts and skills would be taught in a didactic manner, with substantial practice and recycling, immediate feedback, concrete rewards, and a heavy use of advance organizers. A less directive, more abstract and inductive method would form the context for those in Mode B. This does not mean, however, that each mode would remain exclusively in such a prescriptive environment. It does mean that each group would start in an environment matched to their current style. How quickly the environment for those in Mode A could be shifted to higher order, less structured, and more interactive instruction is clearly an empirical question. We do not know at this point how long an exposure is requisite for developmental readiness to shift to the next mode. Theoretically Piaget (1963) and Elkind (1967) have suggested that an individual cannot move upwards until the process of horizontal decalage has been completed. In everyday language this means the individual must grow "sideways" within a stage to fill out and generlize the ability to function successfully at that level before the individual can genuinely go through the period of disequilibrium associated with a stage shift upwards. For those at Mode A, a developmentally oriented teacher education program would need to build in careful and continuous assessment in a formative mode. Our own subjective experience concludes as one might guess, that it is the ability to generalize or transfer from one concept, skill, or situation to an analogous one that is most difficult for those at a concrete, social conformist level. Also, due to individual differences, not all persons whose current mode is "A" are at the same point within that stage; the concepts are dynamic, fluid. The faculty themselves, of course, need to be capable of functioning at the higher stages of development.

THE EDUCATION FACULTY: THE SINE QUA NON

Obviously for any of these propositions to work the single crucial element will be the faculty. Hunt and Joyce (1967), Murphy and Brown (1970), and others have shown that effective classroom teachers must be able to function at least at a Mode B level. Teachers in the moderate to high level of conceptual complexity are capable of "radiating" abundant and facilitating learning environments in the classroom; they can read and flex. This means that such teachers can adjust their methods and materials to meet the needs of pupils. Thus teachers at this level can impose high structure, employ concrete rewards, provide immediate feedback and/or use more open-ended, more abstract, more inductive, and more pupil-centered teaching depending on the learner characteristics. In other words the teacher changes and modifies instruction according to learner level. Such teachers are not committed to a single theory (ideology) of instruction. For example, such a flexible teacher selects from among Ausabel (advanced organizers), Skinner (reinforcement), Rogers (empathy), Bruner (induction), Flanders (a combination of direct and indirect strategies), and others. This means that the Mode B or C teachers are more effective because they can reach a greater variety of pupils. In a parallel sense we hold the same for a teacher education faculty. We do not suggest a simple-minded matching of Mode A faculty with Mode A student teachers or vice versa. Such a match would most likely result in no growth for many of the students. The study concluded by the first author on the negative effects of matched Mode A cooperating teachers and student teachers is to the point (Thies-Sprinthall, 1980). The faculty must be capable of and comfortable with the mode preferred by the students. In this regard we think that a team track approach would be the easiest way to facilitate a developmentally consistent learning environment. Following some ideas recently proposed by J. Lanier (personal communication, 1981) in reconstructing the Michigan State Program, we would organize groups of faculty from areas such as foundations, psychology, methods, and subject matter into teams.[1] Each team would select material activities and teaching methods

---

[1] In addition, the first author directed an analogous experiment at the University of Minnesota. "Project 60" grouped faculty and students into tracks (families). The project was modestly successful, but in retrospect could have had a greater impact if organized along developmental lines. As it turned out students at higher levels benefited from the largely inductive, abstract, student-centered mode that prevailed across all the tracks (families). Those at the concrete level never really "caught on" to the complexities involved in spite of faculty best effort (Thies, 1973).

consistent with either the Mode A or Mode B learners. Because there are sufficient assessment techniques to identify the developmental levels at entry, the student groups could be formed at the beginning points of the program. We have also found that it is extraordinarily difficult to modify instruction at the professional level within a single class. It can be done as the first author has shown (Thies-Sprinthall, 1984) but it requires immense energy and constant vigilence to make the necessary modifications on the spot with diverse subgroups within one classroom. A more realistic possibility is to separate the students as noted and fit the overall instruction to each group separately.

As each track proceeds, if our experience is accurate, then developmental growth will begin to be noticeable. The Mode A students will gradually show signs of a broader perspective. As comfort increases and anxiety decreases, then the instructional team can begin to employ higher order or more complex methods. This is the way the optimal mismatch begins, only after there is evidence of mastery at the concrete level. Then some constructive dissonance can be included as a first step toward more complex stage process. This would fit the educators dictum of turning the corner of the next page. There would be a gradual emersion, guided by the faculty, to help the students process more complexly.

A similar process could take place with the mode B group. Generally Mode B students will learn concepts more quickly and be ready for extended responsibility earlier than the Mode A group. There are, however, a number of important and challenging educative problems. Mode B students are usually comfortable and accepting of some theories and practices, but have trouble with others and hence resist. Thus some of the Mode B's may be competent with Ausabel or Skinner. They may fight tooth and nail, however, over some of the Rogerian, Synectic, or Gestalt theories and techniques. Others in the Mode B group may be just the reverse. Thus the atmosphere may be quite changed between clusters of competing theories and strategies. The challenge for the faculty in Mode B then will be to raise the level of consciousness and developmental complexity of such subgroups. They may then understand the connection between effective teaching and all our current theories as a synthesized comprehensive successive approximation to a "grand theory" for instruction. The same would hold for their understanding of the variety of theories concerning child/adolescent development and philosophical foundations. The goal is indeed ambitious, but from a developmental point of view no less ambitious than for those at Mode A. The shift from A to B requires just as much support and challenge by the faculty team as does the shift from B to C.

Such a track approach would continue through the student teaching experience. In this case the classroom teacher/supervisors need to be considered in the same way as the education faculty. Cooperating teachers have very significant influence upon student teachers. The first author has shown that such teachers can have positive or negative effect upon student teachers depending upon the developmental level of the classroom teacher (Thies-Sprinthall, 1980). A recent review by Veenam (1984) suggests that the impact of formal teacher education programs are generally "washed-out" by everyday experience in school. Similarly Zeichner and Tabachnick (1981) detail the multiple factors which reduce the impact of professional university training and maintain the influence of the work place through traditional occupational socialization. In any case it is clear that effective preservice must include careful attention to the culture of the work setting itself as well as the quality of the cooperating teacher as supervisor. On-site teacher educators need to practice the same differentiated approaches with student teachers as do the university faculty teams. There is obviously little point in creating a positive educative preservice university-based program and then see such effects washed out by the current traditions of the school as a work-place and by cooperating teachers who cannot practice differentiated supervision.

One final point on faculty teams: After a period of years, perhaps 3 to 5, we suggest that the teams switch tracks. This would help promote further growth by the faculty themselves because each group would, by necessity, have to realign its methods and goals.

SUMMARY

Basically we suggest that there is an urgent need to virtually reconstruct the entire approach to preservice teacher education if we accept, in Dewey's phrase, that such development is the aim of education. Joyce and Clift (1984) have provided an up-to-date and scathing indictment of preservice teacher education. There is no need to repeat the current problems of teacher education caught as it is between a whole series of conflicting demands, controlled more by political than educational issues, and responding inadequately through reactivity, defensiveness, and delay. Joyce and Clift (1984) give us a clear enough picture of what is wrong. Their proposals for change, however, do not give enough emphasis to the creation of a differentiated or optimally matched learning environment for the teachers in training. Although to be fair, they do suggest something analogous to our concepts when they suggest a "careful coordination" of training elements, a balance of theory and skill transfer, and careful on-site supervision (pp. 10–11). Our own research on the general cognitive developmental conditions designed to promote growth indicates that it is possible to synthesize such conditions with Joyce's long and extensive research on training. Through such a synthesis of a training model combined with a basis from cognitive–developmental theory and practice we can create a model for preservice teacher education.

At the outset we noted that a major difference between a liberal education and professional development was in terms of heuristic exploration versus choice and commitment. With the close of adolescence and the onset of early adulthood marked by entry into professional education, we need to create a framework for deliberate education to promote the requisite forms of developmental growth. From a realistic point of view and for the reasons so carefully innumerated by Schlecty and Vance (1982), students entering teacher training are most likely to present learner characteristics associated with either of our first two modes. At some point in the future, teaching as a career through a combination of status, salary, and working conditions may attract candidates further along the developmental scheme. In the near future that is highly unlikely. As a result we suggest programs which start where the learners currently are, developmentally.

In addition there is an intriguing educational and empirical question. Given an avowed developmental track approach, we would examine outcomes of such a program in a most rigorous research context. We really do not know how far young adults functioning at Mode A could develop in a typical 2-year preservice program followed by (say) 2 years of careful supervision in an emergent Beginning Teacher program. Our guess is over such a 4-year period with an adequate faculty and classroom mentors employing a sequenced developmental approach that most, if not all, the Mode A's could reach professional competence. Certainly it is most doubtful that our current pot pourri of politically organized teacher education programs and randomly supervised beginning teachers really demonstrate any developmental growth. There have been enough studies indicating the general negative effects of student teaching to prove our point. Also there is no current evidence that any of the new 2-year Beginning Teacher Programs do anything more than sort and cull rather than develop their charges (Griffin, 1984).

Our hope then is for a broader conception of our goals and a deliberate format to connect instructional strategies to those goals. Such a track system seems to us as the best approximation currently available. The directing concepts and the emerging empirical support combine to offer a framework. We hope for serious consideration and adoption of this view as teacher educations best answer to our current national hysteria over a nation at risk. Good and even great teachers are neither born nor made. They may be developed.

REFERENCES

Bielke, P. (1979). *The relationship of maternal ego development to parenting behavior and attitudes.* Unpublished doctoral dissertation, University of Minnesota.

Blasi, A. (1981). Bridging moral cognition and moral action: *Psychological Bulletin, 88*(1), 1–45.

Bok, D. (1983, May–June). A flawed system. *Harvard Magazine,* pp. 38–71.

Bok, D. (1984, May–June). Needed: A new way to train doctors. *Harvard Magazine,* pp. 32–71.

Bruner, J. (1966). *Toward a theory of instruction.* Cambridge, MA: Harvard University Press.

Cronbach, L., & Snow, R. (1977). *Aptitudes & instructional methods.* New York: Irvington.

Darley, J. (1964). The substantive basis for counceling psychology. In A.E. Thompson & D.E. Super (Eds.), *The professional preparation of counceling psychologists* (pp. 69–75). New York: Teacher's College.

Dupont, H. (1978). Meeting the emotional–social needs of students in a mainstreamed environment. *Counseling & Human Development, 10*(9), 1–12.

Eberhardy, J. (1982). *An analysis of moral decision making with nursing students facing professional problems.* Unpublished doctoral dissertation, University of Minnesota.

Elkind, D. (1967). Egocentrism in adolescence. *Child Development, 38,* 1025–1034.

Erikson, E. (1968). *Identity: Youth & Crises.* New York: Norton.

Fowler, J.W. (1974). Toward a developmental perspective on faith. *Religious Education, 69,* 207–219.

Galloway, C. (1968). Nonverbal communication. *Theory into Practice, 7,* 172–175.

Glassberg, S., & Sprinthall, N.A. (1980). Student teaching: A developmental approach. *Journal of Teacher Education, 31*(2) 31–38.

Good, T. (1980). Research on teaching. In G.E. Hall, S.M. Hord, & G. Brown (Eds.), *Exploring issues in teacher education* (pp. 51–73). Austin, TX: Research and Development Center for Teacher Education.

Greene, M. (1973). *Teacher as stranger.* Belmont, CA: Wadsworth.

Heath, D. (1977). *Maturity & competence.* New York: Gardner.

Hedin, D. (1979). *Teenage health educators: An action learning program to promote psychological development.* Unpublished doctoral dissertation, University of Minnesota.

Howey, K. (1977). Preservice teacher education: Lost in the shuffle? *Journal of Teacher Education, 38*(6), 26–28.

Hunt, D. (1974). *Matching models in education.* Toronto: Ontario Institute for Studies of Education.

Hunt, D., Butler, L., Noy, J., & Rosser, M. (1977). *Assessing conceptual level by the paragraph completion method.* Toronto: Ontario Institute for Studies of Education.

Hunt, D., & Joyce, B. (1967). Teacher trainee personality and initial teaching style. *American Educational Research Journal, 4,* 253–259.

Joyce, B., & Clift, R. (1984). The Phoenix agenda: Essential reform in teacher education. *Educational Research, 13*(4), 5–17.

Juraschek, W. (1974). *The performance of prospective teachers on certain Piagetian tasks.* Unpublished doctoral dissertation, University of Texas–Austin.

Kohlberg, L. (1969). *Stages in the development of moral thought and action.* New York: Holt, Rinehart, & Winston.

Kohlberg, L. (1979). *Meaning and measurement of moral development.* Worcester, MA: Clark University Press.

Libbey, P. (1980). *Teachers' conceptions of discipline: A cognitive developmental framework.* Unpublished doctoral dissertation, University of Minnesota.

Loevinger, J. (1976). *Ego development.* San Francisco: Jossey-Bass.

Loevinger, J., & Wessler, R. (1970). *Measuring ego development* (Vols. 1 & 2). San Francisco: Jossey-Bass.

Miller, A. (1981). Conceptual matching models and interactional research in education. *Review of Educational Research, 51*(1), 33–84.

Mortenson, J. (1983). *Predicting success in student teaching: A cognitive–developmental model.* Unpublished doctoral dissertation, University of Minnesota.

Murphy, P., & Brown, M. (1970). Conceptual systems and teaching styles. *American Educational Research Journal, 7,* 529–540.

Oja, S., & Sprinthall, N.A. (1980). Psychological & moral development for teachers. In N.A. Sprinthall & R.L. Mosher (Eds.), *Value development as the aim of education* (pp. 117–134). Schenectady, NY: Character Research Press.

Peatling, J. (1981). *Religious education in a psychological key.* Birmingham, AL: Religious Educator Press.

Piaget, J. (1963). *Psychology of intelligence.* Paterson, NJ: Littlefield Adams.

Piaget, J. (1972). Intellectual evolution from adolescence to adulthood. *Human Development, 15,* 1–12.

Piaget, J., & Inhelder, B. (1958). *The growth of logical thinking from childhood to adolescence.* New York: Basic Books.

Rest, J. (1979). *Development in judging moral issues.* Minneapolis: University of Minnesota Press.

Rest, J. (1984). Morality. In J. Flavell & E. Markman (Eds.), *Carmichael's manual of child psychology.* New York: Wiley.

Ryan, K. (1979). Mainstreaming and teacher education: The last straw. In M.C. Reynolds (Ed.), *A common body of practice for teachers.* Minneapolis: University of Minnesota National Support Systems Project—Draft Report.

Schalock, D. (1979). Research on teacher selection. In *Review of research in education* (chapter 9). Washington, DC: American Educational Research Association.

Schlecty, P., & Vance, V. (1982). The distribution of academic ability in the teaching force. *Phi Delta Kappan, 64*(1), 22–27.

Selman, R. (1980). *The growth of interpersonal understanding.* New York: Academic Press.

Sheehy, G. (1977). *Passages.* New York: Bantam.

Shutes, R. (1975). Needed: A theory of teacher education. *Texas Tech Journal of Education, 2,* 94–101.

Silverman, F., & Creswell, J. (1982). Preservice teachers: A profile of cognitive development. *Texas Tech Journal of Education, 9*(3), 175–186.

Sprinthall, N.A., & Bernier, J.E. (1978). Moral & cognitive development of teachers. *New Catholic World, 221,* 179–184.

Sprinthall, N.A., & Thies-Sprinthall, L. (1980). Educating for teacher growth: A cognitive developmental perspective. *Theory into Practice 19*(4), 278–288.

Sprinthall, N.A., & Thies-Sprinthall, L. (1983). The teacher as an adult learner: A cognitive developmental view. In G.A. Griffin (Ed.), *Staff development* (pp. 13–35). Chicago: University of Chicago Press.

Strohmer, D., Biggs, D., Haase, R., & Purcell, M. (1983). Training counselors to work with disabled clients: Cognitive and affective components. *Counselor Education and Supervision, 23*(2), 132–141.

Thies, L.M. (1973). *Project 60: An alternative teacher education project.* Unpublished Masters Degree Colloquium Paper, University of Minnesota.

Thies-Sprinthall, L. (1980). Supervision: An educative or miseducative process. *Journal of Teacher Education, 31*(2), 17–30.

Thies-Sprinthall, L. (1984). Promoting the developmental growth of supervising teachers: Theory, research programs, and implications. *Journal of Teacher Education, 35*(3), 53–60.

Veenam, S. (1984). Perceived problems of beginning teachers. *Review of Educational Research, 54*(2), 143–178.

Walters, S., & Stivers, E. (1977). The relation of student teachers classroom behavior and Eriksonian ego identity. *Journal of Teacher Education, 31*(6), 47–50.

Widick, C., & Simpson, D. (1979). Developmental concepts in college instruction. In C. Parker (Ed.), *Encouraging development in college students* (pp. 27–59). Minneapolis: University of Minnesota Press.

Zeichner, K., & Tabachnick, B. (1981). Are the effects of university teacher education "washed out" by school experience? *Journal of Teacher Education, 32*(3), 7–11.

Chapter 3

Implications from the Research on Teaching for Teacher Preparation*

Jane A. Stallings

University of Houston

Effective teaching was the focus of a great deal of research during the 1970s. This effort was reasonably rewarding. Many relationships between how teachers teach and what students learn were identified. The findings emerged from studies using a wide variety of methodologies. The question for this paper to consider is "What are the implications of those findings for teacher preparation?" In summarizing the papers prepared for the 1982 Conference on Research on Teaching held at Airlie House, Virginia, Gage (1983) says that findings from the research on teaching range along a continuum of strength:

> At the weakest extreme is what we might call a *shred* — a weak relationship based on a small sample or an ethnographer's glimmer of insight. Next is a *suggestion* that something mildly good will happen if teachers behave in a certain way. A *recommendation* follows from convincing evidence — a strong relationship or an educational connoisseur's ineluctable conviction. An *imperative* consists of a powerful recommendation — a moral cry for action. And finally, a *categorical imperative* is a moral law that is absolute and universally binding. (pp. 492–493)

* The original version of this chapter was published in Robert L. Egbert and Mary M. Kluender (Eds.), *Using Research to Improve Teacher Education: The Nebraska Consortium* (Teacher Education Monograph No. 1), Washington, DC: ERIC Clearinghouse on Teacher Education (1984).

Needless to say, there are few findings in the latter category. Gage (1983) goes on to say:

Implications for practice need to be considered carefully. Large effect sizes do not necessarily have important implications. Small effect sizes may amount to more than shreds or suggestions. Perhaps, if we think about them wisely, they can support recommendations or even imperatives. (p. 495)

In order to know whether research findings are useful in the classroom, the findings must be translated into workable teacher training programs. Using research-based curriculums, several training experiments have been conducted (Anderson, Evertson, & Brophy, 1979; Crawford et al., 1978; Good & Grouws, 1979; Stallings, Needels, & Stayrook, 1979). The training treatment received in these experiments ranged from a detailed list of recommendations to a series of seven 2½-hour training sessions with observation and feedback to guide and encourage continued teacher change. Notably, in all of the experiments, teachers changed their behavior and student achievement was significantly affected. The results of these several experiments are reported by Gage and Giaconia (1981).

Findings from the research on teaching have been used primarily to improve the instruction of inservice teachers. Comprehensive inservice training programs were financed by local, state, and national education agencies. An estimated $2000 per year per teacher was spent on inservice training during the 1970s. This included the cost of programs such as Teacher Corps, Follow Through, Head Start, the staff development components of migrant education, bilingual education, special education, and so on. Social changes required this massive effort to retrain teachers to help them work with mainstreamed handicapped students, multicultured student groups, recent immigrants, and low-achieving students. The avenue for educational improvement was considered by educators and funding agents to be through the schools rather than through colleges preparing new teachers. The primary reason for this was that very few new teachers were being hired; fewer children were in schools and tenured teachers were staying in their jobs longer.

However, time passes, children grow up and produce more children, and tenured teachers grow older. According to the National Center for Educational Statistics, by 1985 689,000 new teachers were needed, and we will need 983,000 by 1990. This need is created by the children of the baby boom children entering schools in the 1980s and the retirement of the many teachers who entered the work force in the 1950s to teach the baby boom children. The need to prepare new science and math teachers is particularly critical because business and industry have been luring these teachers away from the schools.

The spotlight for educational improvement in the 1980s is on preservice education. The task of preparing a whole new cadre of teachers is a wonderfully challenging opportunity. Old and well-worn curriculums must be examined in light of the knowledge and skills teachers need to provide effective instruction in schools today. The 1982 Conference on Research on Teaching, upon which this chapter is based, produced a synthesis of the most salient findings from schools and classrooms to that time.

As previously stated, the purpose of this chapter is to consider the implications of the research on teaching to the curriculum and instruction of preservice education. Because teaching occurs within a school, the effective school findings are considered first in this chapter. These are followed by the descriptive and statistical findings on classroom organization and management, instruction, and teacher expectations. A section on collaborative research describes a process rather than findings per se. Embedded in each section are suggestions of how these research findings might be incorporated into preservice programs. The final section considers some of the problems and challenges confronting those who are responsible for preparing new teachers.

THE SCHOOL COMMUNITY

Schools have been defined as "loosely coupled systems in which the work of the teacher is largely independent of the principal's immediate supervision" (Purkey & Smith, 1983, p. 441). Although it may be generally true that teachers are sovereign in their own classrooms, they do operate within schools and are subject to policies and practices that may limit or enhance what happens in the classroom. For example, if policies regarding cuts and tardiness are clear and well enforced, students are in class more often; if there are few interruptions from the intercom or from students leaving the class for special activities, there is more time to provide instruction; if the discipline policy is clear, students behave better in class (Stallings & Mohlman, 1981; Glenn & McClean, 1981).

In academically effective schools, Purkey and Smith (1983) report a greater degree of (a) collaborative planning and collegial relationships, (b) sense of community (parents, teachers, and students), (c) clear goals and high expectations commonly shared, and (d) order and discipline. The leadership of the principal is a primary factor in effective schools.

Given these criteria, if a new teacher is lucky enough to be hired into an effective school, he/she may be expected to participate in decision-making. Thus, some experience in collaborative planning and shared decision-making would be helpful. This could be accomplished during teacher preparation through simulated staff meetings at which program decisions are made. Discussions with local school principals regarding how school policies are formed could acquaint the preservice teacher with school issues and a range of administrative leadership styles.

How school policies are made ranges from collaboration among teachers, parents, students, and administrators to top–down orders issued by the principals. The principals' leadership style may be supportive, guiding and collaborative, or very directive depending upon the situation. It would be helpful for preservice teachers to be aware of and thus prepared for a variety of leadership styles. A very directive principal may not be all bad. Very clear rules for teachers, for example, checking in, attending meetings, being on time, being available 30 minutes after school, can be helpful to a new teacher. The point is that preservice education should prepare teachers for several eventualities. (See Gates, Blanchard, & Hersey, 1976.)

In fact, leadership may not always come from the principal. Leadership sometimes comes from a few influential teachers with energy and vision (Berman & McLaughlin, 1976). Such teachers may initiate policy and/or control policy. The preservice teacher needs to be able to recognize these power groups and consider how to function through them.

Teacher unions or associations are other sources of power that effect the school community (Purkey & Smith, 1983). The preservice curriculum should include how the unions or associations operate, how to influence them, and the options available. It would be informative to have a union or association representative discuss selected issues with preservice teachers.

Another influential sector of the school community is parents. Parental expectations and participation will differ by region, school size, grade level, and socioeconomic and ethnic background. It is of utmost importance that new teachers establish good rapport with parents and listen to their expectations. Without careful consideration, teachers may depend upon stereotypes of cultural groups and establish self-fulfilling prophesies for some groups of students (Hamilton, 1983).

Satisfied parents can be a great source of help and support (Purkey & Smith, 1983). Dissatisfied parents can hinder and hurt. The preservice curriculum should offer opportunities to observe a master teacher conducting parent conferences, meetings, and home visits. Parents can be helpful in increasing students' learning time. Duval County, Florida, has developed useful materials for parents to use with their children. The focus is toward helping children learn to learn at home. This county has been successful in raising student achievement through school and home cooperation. There is a unanimity of purpose and practice between home and school (Sang, 1982).

ATTRIBUTES OF EFFECTIVE CLASSROOMS

The preservice curriculum needs to be coordinated so that classrooms are considered total environments to be effected by teacher decisions. Physical things such as space, furniture, materials, curriculum, and time may be determined by others, but how they are used is determined by the teacher. The participants are also fixed, but the activities offered and the interactions that occur are determined by the teacher. Green and Smith (1983) make a convincing argument that teachers provide academic content and structure for student participation simultaneously; content and process are interactive. However, the total classroom environment is so complex that researchers have tended to study small pieces of that very large puzzle. The first piece in that puzzle to be considered here is space.

Space

Space and how it is used is important. In effective classrooms, Brophy (1983) reports that space is:

> . . . divided into distinct areas furnished and equipped for specific activities. Equipment that must be stored can be removed and replaced easily, and each item has its own place. Traffic patterns facilitate movement around the room, and minimize crowding or bumping. Transitions between activities are accomplished efficiently following a brief signal or a few directions from the teacher, and the students seem to know where they are supposed to be, what they are supposed to be doing, and what equipment they will need. (p. 266)

Nash (1981) reports that preplanning of classroom space can maximize student use of materials and participation in activities. Preservice curriculum should provide the opportunity for potential teachers to arrange doll-sized furniture in simulated classrooms of different sizes with 20 to 40 students. This would provide the experience of organizing a classroom and considering the issues Brophy mentions.

Use of Time

There is considerable research on the use of time in schools. Research in the 1970s indicates that more time is not necessarily better. A longer school day can simply mean longer lunch and recess periods (Harnischfeger & Wiley, 1978). Stallings' work in elementary and secondary schools did not indicate greater student achievement in longer school days or class periods. How the available time was used was the important factor (Stallings, 1975; Stallings, Needels, & Stayrook, 1979).

Fisher et al. (1978) report that on the average, children in California spend 6 hours in school a day. Of that time, only 2 to 4 hours were spent in instruction. Within that instructional time, students were engaged from 1.5 to 3.5 hours, and of the engaged time for the total school day, students were involved with appropriate materials only 36 minutes to 90 minutes. Preservice teachers should be made aware of these findings and consider how easy it is to waste those critical minutes.

Knowing that time should not be wasted does not provide much guidance for the beginning teacher. More specific information was needed regarding how effective teachers use their time. To this end Stallings and Mohlman (1981) assimilated four data sets from secondary schools and identified how effective teachers distributed their time across activities. They found that effective teachers spent 15% or less time in organizing or management tasks, 50% or more time in interactive instruction, and 35% or less time in monitoring seatwork (see Table 1). Effective teachers used some time to work with the total group, small groups, and individuals (Stallings & Mohlman, 1981). Although this distribution of time would not be appropriate for all grade levels or times of year, it is a framework that can help preservice teachers think about the use of available time. Bloom (1980) found in his Mastery Learning programs that 95% of the students in the classrooms could learn what is required if enough time was allowed and the instruction was at the appropriate level.

Lesson Plans

Decisions about the use of time should be made through a careful daily, weekly, and long-range plan. Yinger (1977) suggests the following:

1. Long range yearly — basic ideas for social studies, science — some for math and reading — basic structure of what will be done but not specific time.
2. Term — planning on a term basis for social studies, science, and for movies.

TABLE 1.   Time Allocations

Organizing/Management Activities (15% or less)

(E)	Take roll	
(E)	Make announcements	
(E)	Pass materials	
(E)	Make expectations clear for the period:	15% Non Academic
	Quality and quantity of work	
(S)	Organize groups	
(E)	Clarify and enforce behavioral expectations	

Interactive Instructional Activities (50% or more)

(E)	Review/Discuss previous work	
(E)	Inform/Instruct new concept	
	Demonstrate/Give examples	
	Link to prior knowledge	
(E)	Question/Check for understanding	85% Academic
(S)	Reteach small group (if necessary)	
(S)	Oral drill and practice	
(E)	Summarize	

Teacher Monitoring/Guiding Seatwork (35% or less)

(I)	Written work
(I)	Silent reading

Note. (E) = Total Class, (S) = Small Group; (L) = Large Group; (I) = Individual.

3. Monthly—deciding on basic units for social studies, science, and math. I decide on what I need the librarian to get or what movies I need.
4. Weekly—use teacher's plan book—specific units and time element added—more detailed.
5. Daily—put schedule on board, get actual materials out. (p. 172)

According to Madeline Hunter (1984), specific components should be included in preparing daily and weekly lesson plans. Hunter's widely used Instructional Skills Program offers a detailed 5-step lesson plan which includes establishing a set or focus, stating objectives, providing instruction, guided practice, and independent practice. Many school districts and state departments of education have adopted this program and are disseminating these strategies. Even though there is not solid evidence of the effectiveness of the program, a preservice curriculum should include exposure to the 5-step lesson plan. A study is in progress to evaluate the long-term relationship between teacher implementation of the Instructional Skills Program and student engaged rate and achievement (Stallings & Krasavage, 1986).

Long range plans are also important. According to Joyce (1978–1979):

> Most of the important preactive decisions by teachers are long-term in their influence as opposed to the influence of lesson by lesson planning. Relatively early in the year, most teachers set up a series of conditions which were to be powerfully influential on the possibilities of decision making thereafter. Lesson planning, to the extent that it goes on consciously, involves the selection and handling of materials and activities within the famework that has been set up by the long-term decisions. (p. 75)

In spite of best laid plans, the lesson may not go that way. Research by linguists indicates that although a teacher may plan a lesson, the lesson itself is modified as the teacher and students interact with the materials and activities (Green & Smith, 1983). In summarizing several studies on planning, Shavelson (1982) suggests that prolific planning may be counterproductive if the teachers become single minded and do not adapt their lessons to student needs. Thus the preservice curriculum should incorporate strategies for planning lessons and develop an awareness for when and how to alter plans.

Classroom Organization and Management

There is no doubt that students in classrooms that are well managed perform better on achievement tests (Brophy, 1979; Fisher et al., 1980; Good, 1979; Rosenshine & Berliner, 1978). "Because successful classroom managers maximize the time their students spend engaged in academic activities, their students have more opportunities to learn and this shows up in superior performance on achievement tests" (Brophy, 1983, p. 266). However, knowing this fact will not help the preservice teacher know how to do it. Observations by researchers Evertson, Anderson, and Emmer (1980a, 1980b) in both elementary and junior high schools were so specific that practice can be guided even for the first days of school. These researchers describe in detail how effective teachers established and carried out their management plans, and subsequently developed a set of checklists for teacher use. Preservice teachers should have the benefit of reviewing these materials.

Grouping is a part of classroom organization. Children are grouped within classrooms for several purposes. Traditionally, students were placed in ability groups (high, medium, and low) so that teachers could provide instruction that was appropriate to the approximate achievement levels of the children. This practice has raised serious controversy regarding children's self-images, motivations, and perceptions. Linguistic studies summarized by Green and Smith (1983) indicate that students in low groups have different input in terms of content, strategies for reading, and definitions of reading. Lessons for low groups consistently placed greater emphasis on pronunciation, grammer errors, and single word decoding. The high groups were encouraged to "go for the meaning"; their pronunciation and grammer errors were often ignored. Weinstein (1983) describes how children perceive the teachers' relationship to high- and low-achieving students. Students described as low achievers received more negative feedback and teacher direction, and more work and rule orientation than high achievers. High achievers were perceived as receiving higher expectations, more opportunity and choice than low achievers. No differences were documented in the perceived degree of supportive help. Unfortunately, we do not know the achievement effects upon the high- and low-achieving students who received differential treatment.

There is research from studies of reading and math that indicates ability grouping has a positive effect upon achievement. The Direct Instruction Follow Through Program (Becker, 1977) has consistently had a positive effect upon children within reading and math ability groups. This program does, however, allow for children to change from one group to another as their progress warrants. The National Follow Through Study also found a positive effect from ability grouping. Low-achieving students profited in math from a longer period of study more than did high-achieving students (Stallings, 1975).

When and how teachers work with each group is important. Work in progress indicates that it is more effective to work with the medium achievement reading group first, the low group second, and the high group last. In this manner, the lowest group, who are likely to have the shortest attention span, do not have as long a time at the beginning or end of the period to work independently (Stallings, Robbins, & Wolfe, 1984).

During group work, effective teachers make clear when students can ask questions and of whom they can ask questions. They do not allow students to interrupt during focused small group instruction (Evertson et al., 1981). However, Green and Smith (1983) report that this signaling of what is acceptable and what is not is a complex process. If teachers do not respond to students' requests for help as needed, the student has several alternatives: the student can (a) attempt to overcome the problem or make a decision on his/her own, (b) ask another student for help, (c) switch to an alternative activity, or (d) approach the teacher anyway. Each decision carries a different outcome for the student. Instruction for preservice teachers should help make them aware of these student options and have strategies to assist students to stay on task until help can be offered.

Groupings are also used for cooperative learning and to establish good interpersonal realtionships and group dynamics in the classroom. Several researchers have developed methods to bring about student cooperation (Aronson, 1978; Slavin, 1980). They have developed a variety of activities in which students of different achievement levels form groups that have a task to complete requiring the participation of all students. In one approach, each member of the group possesses at least one key item of unique information which is essential to the group's success. The problem encountered encourages everyone to participate. In some cooperative approaches, participants receive a group score rather than an individual score. The group score could be based upon the gain made by each participant. Such procedures motivate the high-, medium-, and low-achieving students to cooperate and achieve. There is clear evidence that students gain more academically (Slavin, 1980).

It is important to note that children are not likely to know how to work in groups productively unless some training is provided. Wilcox (1972) found that students who were trained to lead groups by encouraging all to participate and being certain that everyone had a turn were better at solving specific problems than were untrained or leaderless groups. The trained student leader groups were also better group problem solvers than were groups led by the classroom teachers. Teachers tended to do the problem solving themselves. It is important that preservice teachers be exposed to the cooperative group learning research because it offers an alternative to competitive and rote learning.

Disruptive Student Behavior

The findings on disruptive behavior are very clear in all of our studies. In classrooms where students evidence more misbehavior, less time is spent on task and less achievement gain is made by students (Stallings & Mohlman, 1981; Stallings et al., 1984). There are many techniques effective teachers use to manage student behavior. The first-days-of-school study by Evertson, Anderson, and Emmer (1980a, 1980b) yielded some specific recommendations: define rules and penalties before school starts (coordinate with school rules), teach rules and procedures to students during the first days of school, consistently monitor and reinforce rules, reward acceptable behavior and punish appropriate misbehavior.

There are some behavior management programs such as the Assertive Discipline Training Program (Lee Cantor, n.d.) and the Classroom Management Training Program (Fredric H. Jones, n.d.) that bring peer pressure to bear upon individuals. These programs offer rewards for good behavior (special games, activities, script, recognition) and withdraw privileges for bad behavior. These programs are effective in stopping the problem, but they do not necessarily solve the problem.

Problems of an interpersonal nature need to be solved. Glasser's *Schools Without Failure* (1969) offers group problem-solving methods and techniques to help students develop responsibility for their own behavior. Brophy (1983) summarizes the 10 steps of this process (p. 278). Although there is little systematic research on the Glasser (1977) program, survey data indicate fewer referrals to the office, fighting, or suspensions among students in classes implementing this program.

The preservice curriculum should include several approaches to controlling disruptive behavior. Of the several hundred teachers with whom I have worked and the student teachers interviewed in the last several months, there is solid agreement that most lacking in their preparation for teaching were techniques for managing classroom behavior.

Instruction

Now that the stage is set — furniture and materials placed, lessons planned, and strategies ready for dealing with disruptive behavior — instruction is about to begin. Instruction can and should follow several formats determined by the participants, subject matter, and objectives of the lesson. There are no panaceas for every situation.

There are several theories about how the mind works and the most effective instructional strategies. Three areas of research on learning have yielded useful implications for classroom teaching; these are: (1) memory, (2) understanding, and (3) reasoning or problem-solving. All three of these functions are necessary for students to process and use information. Memorizing facts increases students' ability to easily retrieve information from long term memory, thus allowing more space in the mind for understanding and problem-solving. For example, the more automatic a student's memory of the multiplication tables, the more mental energy can be devoted to solving word problems.

Memory. Memory skills are essential for lower elementary students to succeed in basic reading, writing, and computation. Ample research in the 1970s indicates that a very structured, carefully sequenced approach is effective in developing memory skills/basic skills. Rosenshine (1983) in summarizing this literature says:

In general, to the extent that students are younger, slower and/or have little prior background, teachers are most effective when they:

- Structure the learning [experience]
- Proceed in small steps but at a rapid pace
- . . . Give detailed and [more] redundant instructions and explanations
- Have a high frequency of questions and overt, active practice
- Provide feedback and corrections, particularly in the initial stages of learning new material
- Have a success rate of 80% or higher in initial learning
- Divide seatwork assignments into smaller [segments or devise ways to provide frequent monitoring]
- Provide for continued student practice [overlearning] so that they have a success rate of 90–100% . . . (pp. 336–337)

The interactions are started by the teacher presenting a small bit of information, asking a question, and calling for an individual or group response. Praise is offered if the answer is correct and correction is given if the response is incorrect (Anderson, Evertson, & Brophy, 1979).

In the 1970s ample research was done which shows most students can, through sufficient drill and practice, memorize most anything. The curriculum for preservice teachers should include instructional practice in using quick-paced interactions when children need to memorize material.

Understanding. In addition to facilitating students' memorization of facts, instruction should also develop students' understanding of the lesson content. Cognitive psychologists have studied linkages between new information and prior knowledge. Teachers need to help students make these linkages. Every student walks into the classroom with some experiences and knowledge. How the teacher structures the new information makes a difference in what students will be able to link to their existing information. Calfee and Shefelbine (1981) describe the mind as a filing system where there are hooks or pegs on which to hang information. This filing system is essentially the long-term memory from which the information can be retrieved and used in other situations.

For information to be filed, it must first be noticed. Broadbent (1975) wrote that only some of the information presented will receive attention, and if this selection is not decided deliberately, it will certainly be decided by chance factors. If something is not noticed at the time it happens, it has hardly any chance of affecting long-term memory (or the filing system as Calfee and Shefelbine describe it). It is the teacher's role to be certain that students have noticed the information and made a link with existing information, thus guaranteeing storage in long-term memory.

The importance of teachers' checking for understanding was shown in a study conducted by Webb (1980). In a group problem-solving task, those students who received an explanation after making an error solved the problem correctly on another trial. The explanation did not have to be directed toward the student, but could have been directed toward another student within the same group. Those students who never received explanations after an error were not able to solve the problem on the second trial.

Some educational programs, such as Madeline Hunter's (n.d.) Instructional Skills, include a step that requires teachers to check for student understanding before proceeding with instruction. If students do not understand, the teacher restructures the task and provides different examples and experiences to build the required background knowledge. The effects of this model are being tested (Stallings & Krasavage, 1986).

Although the theory on student understanding and the need for linkage is strong, the research findings are meager to date. The studies tend to have small samples, and experiments that teach teachers to use strategies that will increase understanding and lead to testable student outcomes are generally lacking. More studies such as Webb's (1980) are needed. Nevertheless, it is important to include this research in the preservice curriculum even if it is still a twinkle in the researcher's eye.

Problem-Solving/Reasoning.   The need to train students in problem-solving or reasoning skills has been receiving increasing attention, both from the educational system and from industry. In a recent survey of electronics firms in California's Silicon Valley, business leaders were asked to identify the skills most lacking in their recently hired employees, and which skills the educational system should help students to develop to become effective employees. The majority of the respondents reported that the schools should help students develop problem-solving skills, for such skills were needed by employees at all levels (Needels, 1982). The respondents reported that at the present, many of their recently hired employees, whether high school or college graduates, were deficient in that cognitive area.

G. H. Hanford (1983), President of the College Board notes that: "The decade-long decline in test scores appears largely due to the fact that reasoning ability in secondary schools is not what it used to be. In recent years, students in lower grades show marked improvement in reading, writing, and other basic skills, but students fall behind when problems get more complex" (p. 3). The College Board is currently funding a study to identify ways reasoning and problem-solving can be taught.

One of the difficulties in studying problem-solving has been the lack of group administered tests that can examine the thinking skills of young children. The tests usually require individual administration and this prohibits large scale studies. Another problem is in identifying and measuring the classroom teaching skills expected to be related to gain in thinking skills. One anomaly is a study of 52 Follow Through classrooms (Stallings, 1975) which reports the relationship between scores on a group-administered test of nonverbal problem-solving skills and teaching behaviors. These findings indicate that student scores were higher on that test in classrooms where the structure allowed students to take more initiative. In such classrooms, students asked more questions, worked more independently with manipulative materials, and worked more often on group tasks in cooperative activities. Teachers asked more thought-provoking questions and provided less overt praise and correction. The lessons were not quick paced such as those used to develop memory skills.

Inquiry methods are expected to develop problem-solving skills. Collins and Stevens (1982) identified instructional strategies used by expert teachers who use inquiry methods effectively. The authors identified five strategies: (1) systematic variation of examples, (2) counter examples, (3) entrapment strategies, (4) hypothesis identification strategies, and (5) hypothesis evaluation strategies. Even though the teachers observed by Collins and Stevens taught different content areas, the authors reported that these strategies were consistently used by all the teachers, thus the strategies most likely are not domain specific but can be applied to different content domains.

Preservice teachers need to be trained to think of the psychological processes and structures which the student must develop to produce the desired behavioral objectives. Any one lesson could require drill and practice, checks for understanding, and problem-solving. Certainly students should be aware of Bloom's Taxonomy and be able to ask questions at each of those six levels (Bloom, 1956). It is the instructional repertoire that teachers need, and the knowledge of which strategy is likely to develop memory, understanding, or reasoning. The important thing is that preservice teachers do not embrace extreme or singular points of view. Broadbent (1975), in speaking of extremes, says that:

> The lesson of cognitive psychology is that each of us acquires during life certain strategies of encoding the outside world, of organizing memory, and of proceeding from one step in an operation to the next, and that these may be highly general in their later use. The successful teacher, of course, has always known this, but in standing out for the middle ground between mechanical drill on the one hand and the abandonment of all positive teaching on the other, he/she can now claim the support of contemporary cognitive psychology. (p. 175)

TEACHER JUDGEMENT AND EXPECTATIONS

All teachers make judgements about students' abilities and develop a set of expectations which guide the curriculums they offer and the instructional strategies they use. Teacher judgements of student achievement are based upon student reputations and observations of classroom behavior, work habits, products, classroom participation, and test scores. Although these judgements are fairly accurate, they tend to impact upon expectations for low-achieving students in a self-fulfilling way.

In a summary of studies on teacher expectations, Brophy and Good (1974) indicate that students for whom teachers held low expectations were treated less well than other students. They tended to be seated farther away from the teacher. They received less eye contact and were smiled at less often. They received less instruction, had fewer opportunities to learn new materials, and were asked to do less work. Teachers called on these students less often and tended to ask them simple rote answer questions. They were given less time to respond and fewer guides or probing questions when their answers were wrong. Obviously, they remained low-achieving students.

In an effort to change teacher and student perceptions of low-achieving students, Morine-Dershimer (1983) trained a group of teachers to ask higher level questions of low-achieving students. The questions illicited ideas, hunches, and/or opinions. When students in the class were asked to check the names on a list of those who made good contributions to the class discussion, low-achieving students' names were checked. In classrooms where teachers asked low-achieving students simple questions, these students were not rated as making contributions. This point is important. If teachers do not expect that students can take part in a higher level discussion, these students are not even given a chance. In this case of high-achieving students, high achievement is reinforced, and similarly, low-achieving students' low achievement is reinforced.

When asked to list the outstanding qualities of the best teacher they ever had, a national sample of school administrators, teachers, and parents most often mentioned high expectations. Audience responses included, "He challenged me." "She made me think I could do it." "He thought I could, so I did." "She always made me stretch a little bit higher." "He never let me off the hook."

Based upon clinical and mildly good impirical evidence, there are implications that teacher judgements and expectations do impact upon student learning in terms of what is offered to students and how students perceive each other. According to Gage's (1983) continuum of importance, it seems "imperative" that the teacher preparation curriculum include exposure to the teacher judgement and expectation literature.

COLLABORATIVE RESEARCH

In order to continue to learn about effective instruction, the preservice teacher needs the opportunity to develop research skills. The teacher preparation courses should provide opportunities for students to develop questions which can be examined through naturalistic recordings, structured observations, criterion tests, surveys, or interviews.

The importance of research skills is exemplified by a project in San Diego conducted by Tikunoff, Ward, and Griffin (1979). The framework of this project required teachers at one school to select one pressing problem to study in depth. After several brainstorming sessions, the teachers decided to study classroom interruptions. With the assistance of the researchers, they developed methods to record the nature, purpose, and length of interruptions. The researchers helped the teachers process these data and write the results in a manner that could guide school practice. The beauty of this project is that teachers selected their most pressing problems and developed solutions.

During the project, the teachers were guided to read some of the research on teaching literature. Although classroom teachers expected it to be formidable, with a little help they did interpret and discuss the implications of the findings. Most classroom teachers do not have this opportunity and research studies remain formidable. It is the responsibility of preservice education to expose students to research terminology and possible flaws in research designs. If familiarity breeds contempt, they may be pressed to conduct their own studies on the issues that matter to them.

SUMMARY

Based upon the research on effective teaching, I highly recommend that several competences be taught during the teacher preparation years. These include the following domains:

Planning
    Long term and short term
    Lesson designs to include levels of thinking
Classroom Management
    Space
    Material Resources
    Time Management
    Grouping
    Behavior Management
Instructional Strategies
    Knowledge of Hunter's model
    Knowledge of Slavin's Cooperative Group model
    Knowledge of Bloom's Mastery Learning
    Knowledge of effective questioning strategies
    Knowledge of effective feedback strategies
    Knowledge of expectations and effects of self-fulfilling prophecies
Evaluation
    Knowledge of how to read research studies and conduct own research
        project

REFERENCES

Anderson, L., Evertson, C., & Brophy, J. (1979). An experimental study of effective teaching in first grade reading groups. *Elementary School Journal, 79,* 193–223.

Aronson, E. (1978). *The jigsaw classroom.* Beverly Hills, CA: Sage.

Becker, W.C. (1977). Teaching reading and language to the disadvantaged — what we have learned from field research. *Harvard Educational Review, 47,* 518–543.

Berman, P., & McLaughlin, M. (1976). Implementation of educational innovation. *Educational Forum, 40*(3), 347–370.

Bloom, B. (1956). *Taxonomy of educational objectives: I. Cognitive domain.* New York: David Mackay.

Bloom, B. (1980). *All our children learning.* New York: McGraw-Hill.

Broadbent, D. (1975). Cognitive psychology and education. *British Journal of Educational Psychology, 45,* 162–176.

Brophy, J. (1979). Teacher praise: A functional analysis. *Review of Educational Research, 51,* 5–32.

Brophy, J. (1983). Classroom organization and management. *Elementary School Journal, 83,* 265–285.

Brophy, J., & Good, T. (1974). *Teacher–student relationships: Causes and consequences.* New York: Holt, Rinehart, & Winston.

Calfee, R., & Shefelbine, J. (1981). A structured model of teaching. In A. Lewey & D. Denevo (Eds.), *Evaluation roles in education.* New York: Cordon & Breck.

Cantor, L. (n.d.). *Assertive discipline* (training program). 1553 Euclid St., Santa Monica, CA 90404: Lee Cantor and Associates.

Collins, A., & Stevens, A. (1982). Goals and strategies of inquiry teachers. In R. Glaser (Ed.), *Advances in instructional psychology* (Vol. II). Hillsdale, NJ: Erlbaum.

Crawford, J., Gage, N.L., Corno, L., Stayrook, N., Mitman, A., Schunk, D., Stallings, J. (1978). An experiment on teacher effectiveness and parent-assisted instruction in the third grade (Vols. 1–3). Stanford, CA: Center for Educational Research.

Evertson, C., Anderson, L., & Emmer, E. (1980a). Effective management at the beginning of the school year. *Elementary School Journal, 80,* 219–231.

Evertson, C., Anderson, L., & Emmer, E. (1980b). *Effective management at the beginning of the school year in junior high classes.* University of Texas at Austin: Research and Development Center for Teacher Education.

Evertson, C., Emmer, E., Clements, B., Sanford, J., Worsham, M., & Williams, E. (1981). *Organizing and managing the elementary school classroom.* University of Texas at Austin: Research and Development Center for Teacher Education.

Fisher, C., Berliner, D., Filby, N., Marliave, R., Cahen, L., & Dishaw, M. (1980). Teaching behaviors, academic learning time, and student achievement: An Overview. In C. Denham & A. Lieberman (Eds.), *Time to learn.* Washington, DC: National Institute of Education.

Fisher, C.W., Filby, N.N., Marliave, R.S., Cahern, L.S., Dishaw, M.M., Moore, J.E., & Berliner, D. (1978). *Teaching behaviors, academic learning time and student achievement: Final report of Phase III-B, Beginning Teacher Evaluation Study.* San Francisco, CA: Far West Regional Laboratory.

Gage, N. (1983). When does research on teaching yield implications for practice? *Elementary School Journal, 83*(4), 492–496.

Gage, N., & Giaconia, R. (1981). Teaching Practices and Student Achievement: Causal Connections. *New York University Education Quarterly, 13*(3), 2–9.

Gates, P., Blanchard, K., & Hersey, P. (1976). Diagnosing education leadership problems: A situational approach. *Educational Leadership, 33*(5), 348–354.

Glasser, W. (1969). *Schools without failure.* New York: Harper & Row.

Glasser, W. (1977). Ten steps to good discipline. *Today's Education, 66,* 61–63.

Glenn, B.C., & McClean, T. (1981). *What works? An examination of effective schools for poor children.* Cambridge, MA: Harvard University, Center for Law and Education.

Good, T. (1979). Teacher effectiveness in the elementary school: What we know about it now. *Journal of Teacher Education, 6,* 105–113.

Good, T.L., & Grouws, D.A. (1979). The Missouri mathematics effectiveness project: An experimental study in fourth grade classrooms. *Journal of Educational Psychology, 71,* 335–362.

Green, J., & Smith, D. (1983). Teaching and learning: A linguistic perspective. *Elementary School Journal, 83*(4), 353–391.

Hamilton, S.F. (1983). The social side of schooling: Ecological studies of classrooms and schools. *Elementary School Journal, 83*(4), 313–334.

Hanford, G. (1983, January 29). *San Francisco Chronicle,* p. 3.

Harnischfeger, A., & Wiley, D. (1978, March). *Conceptual and policy issues in elementary school teacher learning.* Paper presented at the annual meeting of the American Educational Research Association, Toronto, Canada.

Hunter, M. (1984). Knowing, teaching, and supervising. In P.L. Hosford (Ed.), *Using what we know about teaching.* Alexandria, VA: Association for Supervision and Curriculum Development.

Hunter, M. (n.d.). *Increasing teacher effectiveness* (training program). Los Angeles: University of California at Los Angeles.

Jones, F.H. (n.d.). *Classroom management training program.* 64 Alta Vista Dr., Santa Cruz, CA 95060: Author.

Joyce, B. (1978–1979). Toward a theory of information processing in teaching. *Educational Research Quarterly, 3,* 66–67.

Morine-Dershimer, G. (1983). Instructional strategy and the "creation" of classroom status. *American Educational Research Journal, 20,* 645–661.

Nash, B. (1981). The effects of classroom spatial organization on four-and-five-year-old children's learning. *British Journal of Educational Psychology, 51,* 144–155.

Needels, M. (1982). *Industry's willingness to collaborate with the education system: A survey of California's Silicon Valley.* Menlo Park, CA: SRI International.

Purkey, S., & Smith, M. (1983). Effective schools—A review. *Elementary School Journal, 83*(4), 427–452.

Rosenshine, B. (1983). Teaching functions in instructional programs. *Elementary School Journal, 83*(4), 335–351.

Rosenshine, B., & Berliner, D. (1978). Academic engaged time. *British Journal of Teacher Education, 4,* 3–16.

Sang, H. (1982, October). Education—A family affair. Jacksonville, FL: *The Newsletter.*

Shavelson, R. (1982). *Review of research on teachers' pedagogical judgments, plans and decisions.* Los Angeles, CA: The Rand Corporation and The University of California.

Slavin, R. (1980). Cooperative learning. *Review of Educational Research, 50,* 315–342.

Stallings, J. (1975). Implementations and child effects of teaching practices in Follow Through classrooms. *Monographs of the Society for Research in Child Development, 40,* 7–8.

Stallings, J., & Krasavage, E. (1986). Program implementation and student achievement in a four-year Madeline Hunter follow-through project. *Elementary School Journal, 87*(2).

Stallings, J., & Mohlman, G. (1981). *School policy, leadership style, teacher change and student behavior in eight schools.* Final Report for the National Institute of Education, Washington, DC: Grant No. NIE-G-80-0010.

Stallings, J., Needels, M., & Stayrook, N. (1979). *How to change the process of teaching basic reading skills in secondary schools.* Final report to the National Institute of Education. Menlo Park, CA: SRI International.

Stallings, J., Robbins, P., & Wolfe, P. (1984). *A follow-through staff development program to increase student learning time and achievement* (Phase II. Evaluation Report) Napa, CA: Grant No. NIE-R-81-0024.

Tikunoff, W., Ward, B., & Griffin, G. (1979). *Interactive research and development on teaching, final report.* San Francisco, CA: Far West Laboratory for Educational Research and Development.

Webb, N. (1980). A process outcome analysis of learning in group and individual settings. *Journal of Educational Psychology, 15,* 69–83.

Weinstein, R. (1983). Student perceptions of schooling. *Elementary School Journal, 83*(4), 287–312.

Wilcox, M. (1972). *Comparison of elementary school children's interactions in teacher-led and student-led small groups.* Unpublished doctoral dissertation, Stanford University, CA.

Yinger, R. (1977). *A study of teacher planning: Description and theory development using ethnographic and information processing models.* Unpublished doctoral dissertation, Michigan State University.

Chapter 4

Early Field Experiences: Three Viewpoints

Jane H. Applegate

Kent State University

Early field experiences emphasize active student involvement in the process of learning to teach. Unlike other instructional alternatives incorporated in teacher education programs, early field experiences provide prospective teachers with concrete, first-hand practice in actual school settings prior to student teaching. The belief that experiencing the classroom environment is necessary for a teacher's preparation is widely held by teacher educators, practicing teachers, and prospective teachers alike. Although practice under the guidance of an experienced teacher is the oldest form of teacher education, it is only within the last 25 years that practice in situ has infused the entire sequence of teacher preparation coursework. Surveys of teacher preparation programs nationally and internationally have revealed an increasing amount of first-hand experience either appended to or integrated into teacher education programs (see Shuff & Shuff, 1972; Ishler & Kay, 1981; Southall & Dumas, 1981; Twa & Dung, 1981; Pucket, 1981; Heath, 1984 for examples of such reports). These studies indicate that teacher educators have accepted and proliferated more and earlier field experiences, even though little is known about what these experiences actually contribute to a teacher's education.

The purpose of this chapter is to examine the character of early field experiences from three viewpoints: the college student, the cooperating teacher, and the university faculty member. These three roles provide diverse perspectives from which the relative value of field experiences can be assessed. Individual cases will provide frames of reference for the review of research following each case. Though what is known at this point about early field experiences is largely idiosyncratic, researchers are beginning to provide descriptions from which questions may be drawn for future inquiry. It is hoped that the cases which follow will prompt teacher educators, program administrators, researchers, and policy developers to examine the efficacy of early field experiences.

There are many reasons given for the inclusion of more field-based experience in teacher preparation. Historically, when teachers have been asked to critique their preparation for teaching they have cited their student teaching as the most practical and meaningful component of their preparation. Some program planners concluded then, if students found the culminating field experience to be so worthwhile, perhaps earlier field experiences would increase student satisfaction with the total preparation program. There has also been an increased demand among practicing teachers for more influence on teacher preparation. Requiring undergraduate students to spend more time in classrooms has given teachers the opportunity for this influence. Both undergraduate students and practicing teachers continue to call for relevant learning from schools, colleges, and departments of teacher education. Such relevance has taken the form of more field experiences. Some teacher educators, too, are committed to preparing teachers for the "real world" and see campus-based coursework as unable to meet that commitment. The questions which cannot be answered on-campus may be answered through experience.

Some commonly held assumptions are these: more experience in schools will make for more effective teaching; more experience in the teacher's role will make the transition from student to teacher less painful; more experience in schools will make campus-based theoretical knowledge more meaningful; more experience in schools will "weed out" those individuals who find they do not enjoy teaching as much as they thought they would; more experience in schools will enable prospective teachers to recognize the social, cultural, and political dimensions of the schools in which they will teach. But adding more experience in schools to an already crowded and controversial curriculum for teacher preparation has raised questions about these assumptions and has prompted researchers to begin examining the complexities of field experiences. (See Applegate, 1985, for a discussion of concerns about early field experiences.) What follows are three views of such experiences.

Viewpoint I: College Student

As early as the eighth grade, Tom Parry knew that he wanted to be a coach. His swimming coach in junior high had inspired him to go to college. Though his parents thought he should get a job and work for a while, Tom wanted nothing more than to go to State College and swim on the varsity team. Through the efforts of his high school coach he got a scholarship and prepared himself for college life.

In his first quarter a program counselor advised Tom to enroll in Freshman Field Experience during the winter. The course required that he spend three hours each morning in a school as a teacher's aide. The counselor told him he wouldn't have readings or tests with the course and that to pass, all he had to do was be there. Friends in his dorm told him the course was an easy "A," much better than calculus, for sure. He thought the course would fit in with his swimming practice in the afternoon and because it was required of education majors, he might as well take it. He thought the time in a school might help him decide if he wanted to teach and coach or if he should concentrate totally on coaching.

On the first morning of winter quarter the course convened in Union Auditorium. He was assigned to Mr. Stone at Hanson Middle School, and he met a "G.A." who was to be his advisor for the course. She would meet with Tom and 14 other freshmen for the course seminar. Tom thought all of this was confusing. He had no idea where the school was or what he was to do when he got there. The "G.A." was new, too, and didn't seem to know much more than he did, but she passed out maps and gave him a phone number in case problems arose. The major rules were to be at the school every day, on time, dressed like a teacher. Beyond that, the students were on their own. The "G.A." seemed to have great confidence in the teachers in the school. Suddenly Tom felt the class was going to take more time and gasoline than anticipated.

Mr. Stone, Tom's cooperating teacher, met Tom at the door the next morning when he arrived at the school. He told Tom that he was pleased to have him in his class, that he was the fifth field-experience student that he had worked with and that he had planned many things for Tom to do. When he introduced Tom to the eighth graders, Tom felt his confidence grow. He knew this would be a good course. Mr. Stone gave Tom a map of the building and a seating chart. He asked Tom to learn the students' names and to familiarize himself with the building. When Tom left the building that morning he felt great; Mr. Stone seemed to care about him and he was excited about working with the eighth graders. Three of the students had asked him after class if he would teach them to swim.

During the weeks to follow, Mr. Stone gave Tom many different kinds of responsibilities. One day he spent with the janitor; another day he had cafeteria duty (and was late getting back for swimming practice); another day he went with the home-school community agent to meet with parents. He also graded papers, constructed a bulletin board about the Olympics and tutored a group of students in spelling. He couldn't believe how complicated teaching was. He thought all teachers did was talk. He saw that he had a lot to learn if he wanted to be as good as Mr. Stone.

Tom discovered, though, that his experience was not like that of some of his peers. During the weekly seminars others in the course talked critically about the school and teachers with whom they worked. They talked about sitting for hours on end with nothing to do. They talked about the lack of concern teachers showed for their pupils. They compared the schools in which they worked with the schools they had attended. Some of them felt they would never teach; others were unsure. Some, like Tom, felt the experience was really helping them. The "G.A." seemed interested in all they said and though she came to class prepared to teach something, her lessons were never covered.

In the last week of the experience, Tom was asked to teach a lesson to the whole class. He was so nervous he thought he would never make it. Mr. Stone had really spent a lot of time with him in preparation and that helped. Though he felt he made many mistakes, the students were well behaved and the 40 minutes seemed to go so quickly. On the last day of class the students had a party for him. They asked Tom to come back again. Tom thought the experience had been terrific, that Mr. Stone was the best teacher he'd ever seen, and that teaching the eighth grade might be just what he should do. For the final seminar he had to write a paper about his experience. He passed the course.

What has this scenario revealed about the perceptions of college students engaged in early field experiences?

First, the decisions college students make about coursework and career may be arbitrary. There are many factors which influence course and career choices. General requirements as well as career-related coursework are frequently chosen for convenience, not because a clearly articulated curriculum design is being followed. Some courses are chosen because they have the reputation of being "easy." Tom enrolled in "Freshman Field Experience" because it fit with swimming practice, was required, had no books or tests, and he was advised to "take it now." Sometimes, though, students postpone taking "blocked" courses which require longer time commitments because of conflicting course schedules and thus such "early" field experiences may occur well into the second or third year of a student's preparation.

Many introductory education courses with early field experiences are intended to develop career commitment. Students enroll in these courses for self-assessment. They want to know if they have the aptitude, fortitude, and confidence it takes to teach (Book, Byers, & Freeman, 1983; Thompson, 1982; Applegate & Lasley, 1985; Gehrke, 1981). It is not clear at this point how early field experiences contribute to self-knowledge and concept of self-as-teacher. It is clear, however, that in students' eyes, learning about self is one of the principal outcomes of early field experiences.

Students believe that feeling confident about one's ability to teach is necessary for success as a teacher. They see field experiences as a vehicle for confidence building. Different hypotheses have been offered by researchers who have studied the relationship between confidence and field experiences. Scherer (1979) studied the relationship between participation in early field experiences and student teachers' self-concepts and performance. Her findings indicated that students who participated in early field experiences had more and earlier self-doubt at the beginning of student teaching, but at the conclusion of student teaching had significantly less self-doubt; also, the self-esteem of the early field experience group was significantly higher. Hardy and Mershon (1981) examined students' perceptions of learning style against preference for field-based coursework. They found that students who selected field-based courses were more confident in their learning abilities, more cooperative, and more interested in working with others.

When students begin a field experience they may experience a great deal of doubt and uncertainty, especially at the beginning of the experience. Not knowing where to go, whom to talk to, or what to do when arriving at the school contributes to such uncertainty. As noted by Kitchens (1983), adjustment to a field experience may depend upon the degree of structure provided by the college faculty member. Most other university coursework is highly structured; course requirements, books, and weekly assignments are all set forth in syllabi and all students are expected to learn material accordingly. In the experience described in the scenario, Tom entered the school with few specific rules to follow; the parameters of the experience were left largely to the cooperating teacher. Students with more need for structure may have a difficult time adjusting and, in fact, may never satisfactorily adjust, whereas others may thrive on the opportunity to test their own initiative.

The expectations and concerns of university students were studied by Applegate and Lasley (1984a, 1985). As students anticipate going into schools, they see the experience as an opportunity for learning about themselves as well as learning about teaching practices. Students expect the experience to give them practice; they expect to be active in the classroom; they expect the cooperating teacher to be a model of a successful professional. Students want to acquire practical and specific ideas for successful performance. Their expectations are frequently shaped by professional requirements. If, as part of a course, the professor requires students to practice particular teaching strategies, then that is what the students expect to do. Sometimes those expectations go unrealized and students find themselves caught between the demands of the university course and the realities of classroom practice. When students reported their concerns they focused upon problems that they did not anticipate while working with school-aged youth. Preservice teachers tend to assume that pupils will be attentive and interested in the lessons prepared; they are surprised when they are not. They also find that much of what a teacher does is managerial and many of the tasks assigned to the field-experience student are described as "menial, boring busywork." Students in field experiences are frustrated by the lack of the relationship they see between what is happening in the school and what they are learning in classes on campus. The amount of time allocated for conversation between the field-experience student and the cooperating teacher was also an expressed concern. Students seem to be wedging field experience in between other commitments as do teachers who deal with fixed schedules. Thus, there is little opportunity to question or reflect upon their observations and experiences with people in the school setting. Sometimes students end field experiences wondering what was to be learned; they have spent time watching teachers and students in classrooms, much the same as they did for 13 years previously as students themselves. Sometimes, they feel they have had a taste of teaching and that is enough. Sometimes the experience becomes a motivator for more coursework and more experience.

The important role the cooperating teacher played in shaping the early field experience is another point for consideration. In this particular situation the cooperating teacher was experienced in working with field-experience students and was prepared to introduce the student to the building and classroom. Unfortunately, not all cooperating teachers assume the responsibility "Mr. Stone" did. The effect that the cooperating teacher has, either positive or negative, will affect the student's satisfaction with the experience. The studies of Copeland (1978), Price (1961), and Seperson and Joyce (1973) have indicated that cooperating teachers have significant influence over the success of the student-teaching experience. Cooperating teachers have a similar impact on students participating in early field experiences (Kitchens, 1983).

Another point for consideration is the degree to which students' lives outside of their field experience may influence their performance during the field experience. Many university students hold outside jobs to support themselves while they study. Others have athletic scholarships or are in work-study programs. Although students know job considerations are separate from course requirements, frequently, for those who work, there is interference with field experience. Students also cite travel time to the school site as an interference with both performance in the field experience and performance in other coursework.

This scenario also illustrated that students in early field-experience programs, which are courses separate from regular university courses, need time to process their experiences with both peers and university faculty. A seminar such as the one Tom attended provided opportunity for him to listen to others and balance his judgments against those of his peers. He was able to consider his own immediate practical concerns. Frequently, however, university seminars are structured to meet the goals of the course rather than the needs of the field-experience students. When this occurs students perceive the seminar as unnecessary and not helpful.

Having a "successful" field experience depends upon a number of factors. Such elements as amount of time spent in early field experiences, previous coursework in education, previous experience working with children or youth, the sex and age of the college student, the level of the school placement, the number of times the cooperating teacher has worked with other field-experience students, the expectations the student holds for the field experience, the student's attitudes toward teaching as a career, the types of assignments required during the field experience, the student's interpersonal skills, the student's self-concept, the student's beliefs about learning, and frequency of supervisor feedback are all variables which have been identified and examined in relationship to perceived success in early field experiences (Applegate, 1985). When such variables are isolated and examined researchers have conflicting results, largely because measures of success have been perceptual. Most frequently success in field experiences has been related to personal relationships developed with the cooperating teacher, pupils in the classroom, other participants in early field experiences, and the university supervisor. The affective nature of the experience takes precedence over the cognitive. (See studies by Thompson, 1982; Harp, 1974; Poole, 1972; Gibson, 1976; Haddad, 1974; Buchanan, 1981; Palmer, 1980; and Ross, 1980 as examples of those designed for identifying and testing variables related to success in early field experiences.)

Most of the empirical work completed with regard to early field experiences has depended (perhaps unintentionally) upon students' perceptions of those experiences. Through "Tom's" experience we have noticed that what one learns through early field experience is somewhat arbitrary and idiosyncratic and dependent upon the decisions which prompt students to enroll in field-based courses. The commitment of the individual to teaching as a career, the degree of confidence an individual feels upon entering the classroom, the strength of personal relationships the student is able to establish with the cooperating teacher and pupils in the classroom, the structure given to the experience either by the cooperating teacher, the college faculty, or the individual himself all have some bearing on the success of the experience. Successful field experiences are in the eyes of the beholder. What might be deemed successful for one student might be ordinary for another. Researchers have sought to understand relationships among variables which may impact upon the success of the experience in students' eyes. That work is just beginning. No clear conclusions may yet be drawn.

Viewpoint II: Cooperating Teacher

Mr. Brill had been teaching general science for three years when the principal asked if he'd be willing to take two university students for a field experience. The principal thought that the students would be in the building 3 hours a week for a 10-week period. The principal also told Brill that the students would bring materials from the university to describe what they would be doing and that they would not interfere with his regular classroom activity. Mr. Brill remembered all too clearly what his own student teaching had been like . . . the day some students caught the chemistry lab on fire and told the regular classroom teacher that Brill had given them the wrong chemicals for the experiment . . . the time the cooperating teacher was ill for a week and he had to take over the whole schedule of classes after he had only been in the building a week . . . the last day of student teaching when a female student gave him a card that said "I'll Always Love You." Sure, he would take the students into his classroom. Perhaps he could give them advice that no one had given him; perhaps, too, they could help clean up the lab equipment and grade some papers. He knew he could give them a good experience.

The first day the students were to arrive during Mr. Brill's conference period. He waited and waited, but no students appeared. The principal assured him that the university professor had guaranteed their appearance. As his class began two young women rushed into the room and up to his desk. After apologizing for being late they explained they'd had a couple of quick errands to run and had gotten lost getting to the school. They assured him it wouldn't happen again. They took seats in the back of the room, said nothing more, and left at the end of the hour. Mr. Brill hoped this was not indicative of times to come.

The second week went much like the first. At the end of class, one of the field-experience students left a folder on the teacher's desk. In the folder was a letter from the university professor explaining the purpose of the experience, a weekly checklist describing the activities the students were expected to conduct, and two copies of a three-page evaluation form for the teacher to complete at the end of the experience. At the end of week two the students had done nothing on the list.

By the end of the fifth week the university students still had done nothing more than sit in the back of the room. Twice they had been late; once they had appeared in sweat clothes apologizing for having not had time to change after a physical education class. Mr. Brill realized they were not fulfilling their responsibilities and he wondered if he was fulfilling his. He decided to give the university professor a call. The professor seemed upset about the students' conduct. He assured Mr. Brill he would discuss the problems with the students and scheduled a visit to the building the next week.

The next week the university students came to the building early. They asked Mr. Brill what they could do. They told him their instructor threatened to fail them if they didn't do as he asked. Mr. Brill felt awkward. After all, didn't these students have responsibilities? Did they have no notion at all about what teaching is like? The teacher retrieved the materials from the professor, which were in a desk drawer. "According to your course requirements, this week you should have completed a bulletin board related to a lesson you are going to teach and should be reviewing with me your lesson plan for next week's experience." The students looked shocked. "What will we do? We've never taught before? We don't know how to plan a lesson."

At the end of the field experience Mr. Brill completed the checklists and mailed them back to the professor with this note: "Working with your students has not been a good experience for me. From the beginning neither they nor I knew what we were to do. We all felt uncomfortable. They were with me because they had to be, not because they wanted to be. The assignments they were given were beyond their level of preparation. I felt as if I were given two more students to teach."

The perceptions of cooperating teachers about early field experiences are quite different from those of the students involved in them. Although both students and university faculty members agree that the cooperating teacher is the single most important determinant of successful field experiences, the literature aimed at understanding the cooperating teacher's viewpoint is less substantial than that which has examined the viewpoints of students. There are a few studies suggesting issues for discussion about the place of cooperating teachers in early field experience. The scenario just mentioned illustrated several of them.

As with student teaching, the assignment of students to cooperating teachers is viewed as a critical factor in understanding early field experience. Kitchens (1983) noted that the placement of university students with cooperating teachers is done primarily by building-level administrators with some agreement from the teacher to whom students will be assigned. The criteria used for such selection and placement are typically arbitrary and as noted by Gregory (1971) usually depend upon observable, countable characteristics such as degrees held, numbers of years teaching, recommendations by administrators, certification, and willingness to serve as a cooperating teacher. (See Association for Student Teaching, 1966, for numerous other examples.) Cooperating teachers see their selection to work with university students as being either praise or punishment. Frequently cooperating teachers feel they are chosen because they are successful teachers and can provide a positive role model for a prospective teacher. They see working with university students as a service to the profession. Very few receive monetary rewards for such service (Black, 1979). In other cases, however, administrators place university students with weak teachers hoping that the presence of the students in the classroom will have a positive effect on the teacher.

There is a lack of knowledge, though, about what makes a cooperating teacher effective. It is widely known that effectiveness as a teacher does not mean that one will be an effective cooperating teacher. Stevens and Smith (1978) identified critical factors involved in evaluating cooperating teacher effects. Students identified four factors: personal relationship with the cooperating teacher, the cooperating teacher as a model teacher, the cooperating teacher as a guide to growth as a teacher, and the cooperating teacher and orientation to school personnel. Studies by Switzer (1976) and Funk, Long, Keithley, and Hoffman (1982) were also aimed at isolating the qualities of effective cooperating teachers. Both of these studies emphasized personal attributes such as support, enthusiasm, pleasant personality, and challenging teaching as being indicative of effectiveness in cooperating teachers from students' points of view.

Walker and Applegate (1985) studied the expressed concerns of cooperating teachers about working with field experience students. Nine areas of concern were noted. Of particular interest were: evaluation concerns (How am I to evaluate students in field experiences? How are my evaluations used? Am I responsible for the success or failure of the student in the course?); cooperating teacher preparation concerns (How much supervision is enough? When do I turn the student loose with the class alone? Am I expecting too much or too little?); college preparation concerns (What should I do if the student doesn't know course content? How do I deal with students who don't have standard English skills?); and university supervision concerns (What do I do if the university supervisor never appears? Whom do I contact at the university if I'm having trouble with the supervisor?).

A series of studies conducted by Applegate and Lasley (1982, 1984b) have attempted to unravel perceptions of cooperating teachers in two dimensions: the expectations they hold for working with field experiences and the problems that arise during the experiences. Cooperating teachers expect that, prior to coming into a field experience, students will have some knowledge and skills characteristic of effective teachers. They also expect students to show initiative in the classroom, to be enthusiastic about becoming teachers, to be flexible and adaptable in the school, and to behave professionally. They expect university faculty members to be on site and available to help. When cooperating teachers were asked about the problems they encounter when working with field experiences they report uncertainty about the purpose of the experience and their role in it. Cooperating teachers also expressed concerns about university students who are frequently tardy, those who have difficulty organizing and conducting lessons, and those who seem to see field experience as "just another class." Cooperating teachers, though identified as significant to the experience, know least about the intention of the experience and the ability of the teacher education student. Although teachers are generally willing to provide space and time for university students in classrooms, teachers are unsure about what to do. They act from the memories of their own teacher education experience; their knowledge base is personal. If they had no early field experiences as part of their own preparation, then they have difficulty distinguishing early field experiences from student teaching; expectations for students are like those they held for themselves in student teaching. However, personal experience in early field experiences or experience as a cooperating teacher working with early field-experience students helps cooperating teachers develop realistic expectations for what students should and can do (Martin & Wood, 1984).

To help cooperating teachers understand their role, especially with regard to expectations of the university for field experiences, many institutions are providing courses designed especially to prepare cooperating teachers for working with university students. (See Kapel, 1978; Applegate & Biedler, 1983; McIntyre & Killian, 1985.) Haberman and Harris (1982) conducted a status study to determine what states had legal requirements for cooperating teachers. Of the 50 states contacted, only two stated that they require teachers to be certified as cooperating teachers. A program or course related to the supervision of field-experience students is required of cooperating teachers in 9 states. The growing emphasis at both institutional and state policy levels is, perhaps, indicative of the recognition being given to the role of the cooperating teacher.

How students are assigned to cooperating teachers, how teachers adjust and adapt classroom routines for field-experience students, what personal qualities and professional skills are necessary for collegial, growth-producing relationships to develop between university students and practicing teachers, how expectations are established, and how problems are solved are a few of the issues affecting the quality of early field experience. A view of experiences from the cooperating teacher's angle has provided some insight into these issues. Research is just beginning to describe the relationship between university students and practicing teachers. An examination of "Mr. Brill's" experience has prompted further discussion.

Viewpoint III: College Faculty Member

Two years ago Denise Lawrence accepted a position as Assistant Professor of Elementary Education at State University. Jobs in higher education were scarce and even though the course load seemed heavy, she was pleased to have the position. During the interview the Department Chair described several changes the programs at State were undergoing to meet state standards for teacher education. Several times the Chair mentioned new field-based courses and stressed the importance of faculty supervision in these courses. Denise had supervised student teachers during her doctoral program and had enjoyed working with the undergraduate students. A field-based, teacher-education program sounded interesting.

As a new professor Denise was assigned two sections of "Teaching Social Studies in the Elementary School," one section of "Child Development," and a graduate level course, "Problems in Elementary School Curriculum." She was also assigned service on the college Undergraduate Curriculum Committee, the department Curriculum Committee, and was given a list of 30 advisees. Standard syllabi were provided for the undergraduate courses and Denise was told not to deviate from the content of those syllabi. She noticed that both courses had field components. In the social studies methods course students were to prepare units of instruction based upon some social studies topic and then were to teach those units to elementary children. In Child Development, students were to spend 30 hours during the course observing children from age 3 to age 12, both in and out of school. Both field assignments sounded interesting, but Denise could see from the beginning that managing these field experiences could be problematic.

At State University all contacts with schools for field placements were handled through a central administration office in the college of education. Denise found both logistics and paperwork for placements cumbersome. She also found that she had to take the sites and teachers the placement office provided. Choosing particular types of schools, classrooms, or teachers for her students' experiences was out of the question. According to the placement office some schools were unwilling to take the social studies minicourses; they had found some of the topics controversial and not in accord with standard elementary social studies curricula. Placements also were time consuming. All the university students had to complete placement forms, she had to complete a placement roster, and at the end of the experience students had to write about the school characteristics, the hours they spent in the school, the teacher's name, and a summary of what they did. That form had to be signed by the student, the teacher, and the course professor for a comprehensive field-experience file. Frequently her students were placed in as many as eight different schools in two or three different school districts. Adequate supervision of the minicourses was next to impossible. And evaluation of the students' performance was left to the cooperating teacher. Students always reported that the field work was the best part of the course, but Denise felt uncomfortable not knowing what the students were learning from such experiences. Denise could not understand the necessity for bureaucratic control. The whole process could be simplified and expedited if she could do the contacts herself. That way she could develop a working rapport with a group of schools and teachers who would always work with her students. But, the system just didn't work that way. When she brought her concerns before the department curriculum committee she was told that the faculty used to place its own students, but the schools preferred not to deal with so many different people calling with requests. Also, the paperwork was necessary for state audits. So much for academic freedom.

At the end of her first 2 years the Department Chairman reviewed with Denise her progress toward tenure at State University. He praised Denise for her teaching and for the seriousness with which she approached the field components of her courses. The Chair said school personnel were pleased to see Denise in the buildings and teachers had commented on the helpful suggestions she had given about the social studies curriculum. Some of the teachers had even enrolled in the graduate program at Denise's urging. The Chairman, however, was not pleased with Denise's publishing record, and for tenure and promotion, publication was expected. Denise talked with the Chair about the amount of time the field work took and about the value of that time in relationship to other priorities. She told the Chair that other colleagues had warned her that too much time in the schools would be detrimental to her career and unless her aim became research, writing, and grantsmanship, she would not be promoted. The Chair suggested that Denise develop written guidelines for the field components for the courses and only visit the schools if visits were requested by teachers. That should free her to write. Perhaps she could write about some of the experiences she'd had in the schools.

As Denise left the meeting she thought about the mixed messages she'd heard and the confusion she felt. She wondered what her role as a professor of education was. Although she felt successful as an instructor of preservice teachers and felt successful working in the schools to support the field components of her courses, that was not enough. She wondered why the assumptions and practices of the field component had not been questioned long ago. She wondered why it was necessary to have so much field experience when professors were unable to supervise and give students feedback. She wondered why each time she tried to question these practices, she was told that all her questions were dealt with years ago before she came to State University. It was clear she had decisions to make.

The least examined viewpoint in the consideration of early field experiences is that of the university faculty member. As McIntyre (1984) noted, research on the influence of university faculty members on any aspect of field experiences, except in the supervision of student teachers, is uncommon. Perhaps that is because faculty members studying the viewpoints of students and cooperating teachers assume their roles, decisions, and concerns are understood by their colleagues. Perhaps, also, the positions faculty members take with regard to field experiences and the impact made by university faculty on students, schools, and cooperating teachers is difficult to document. The points highlighted through the scenario of Denise Lawrence raise more questions than they answer.

How are faculty selected to teach field-based courses or supervise students in field experiences? Dyer (1976) cited seven possible selection criteria: (1) faculty members who are not yet ready or not capable of handling theory courses, (2) graduate assistants, (3) faculty members who seek a break from campus classroom routines, (4) faculty members who live close to cooperating schools, (5) faculty members whose regular courses don't fill, (6) new faculty members, and (7) faculty members who are perceived as out of touch with current school practices. These criteria are disparate and lack any mention of formal preparaton for working with early field experiences, or any interest among faculty for doing such work.

Why are faculty members involved in early field experiences? There appear to be two answers to this question: (1) Because they have to, and (2) because they want to. Those who answer "have to" look to the political forces of state standards and teacher pressure groups who acknowledge the gaps which have existed between theory and practice and have pushed for heavier field involvement in college curricular decision making. As a result many states have mandated more and earlier field experiences for preservice teachers. College faculty members who protest against the involvement of "outside factions" in academic matters view early field experiences as a concrete example of the dissolution of academic freedom. It is not field experiences, per se, that are in question; it is the traditional right of academicians to decide what the education of future teachers ought to be that is a concern.

The "want to" group who opt for the inclusion of early field experiences see early field experiences as the opportunity to practice and reinforce campus classroom content. Some are believers in the training model so well defined by Joyce and others and believe that transfer of theory to practice takes practice in context for the feedback and "coaching" to have effect on performance. (See Joyce, 1983, for a description of research related to the training model.) Others are believers in experiential learning and see field experiences as necessary for understanding concepts and theories taught in campus-based courses. It is the actions which result from these explanations, however, which affect the perceptions of both cooperating teachers and students in teacher preparation. Faculty members who see field experiences as external pressure frequently lack commitment to fulfill the expectations for the prescribed experience. Students may get no experience if a faculty member ignores the mandate or they may get experience without the benefit of supervised reflection if the faculty member does not visit schools to observe students in action. On the other hand, faculty members who value field experiences seem to communicate that value to their students. They visit school frequently, talk with teachers, observe, encourage, and provide support to all who are involved. Both postures may exist in a single department or college of teacher education. Both may contribute to unevenness in the effects of programs of teacher preparation.

How is supervision in early field experiences conducted? There is little evidence to suggest an answer to this question. So many variables seem to affect both the kind and quality of supervision which occurs. Applegate, Lasley, and Ellison (1985) and Lasley, Applegate, and Ellison (1985) in their studies of the expectations and problems of faculty members working in early field experiences cited the quality and quantity of supervision as both an expectation and a problem. Faculty members expect to supervise their students, but find that to do the supervision they feel students deserve, they could do nothing else. Variables such as commitment, interest, experience in field-based programs, course load, class size, placement distance, time restrictions, comfort with supervisory skills, and administrative red tape all may have some effect on a faculty member's supervision of early field experience. The multiple responsibilities of faculty members also interfere with supervisory duties, yet faculty are aware that both students and cooperating school personnel expect them to be on site and available to provide clinical support. As Koehler (1984) noted with regard to student teaching, most faculty assigned supervisory responsibilities emphasize orientation of students to course expectations and stress details like the importance of obeying school rules, but leave the bulk of site supervision to cooperating teachers. The research of both Heath (1984) and Thompson (1982) supports this conclusion in early field experiences. The lack of conceptual agreement about the place of supervision in early field experiences has left faculty members personally and professionally at odds with themselves and with one another.

What conflicts and concerns continue to exist for faculty who work in field experiences? Faculty who commit to field-based courses frequently feel that rewards for their work are minimal. The more time faculty members spend in schools, the less time they spend on campus, thereby creating feelings of isolation from campus-based colleagues. Faculty are also uncertain about the long-term effects of their actions. What overall impact will field-based courses have? Researchers who have addressed that question have examined such variables as preservice teachers' beliefs (Horak, 1981), achievement in coursework (Hedberg, 1979), concept learning (Ross, Hughes, and Hill, 1981), performance of inquiry skills (Sunal, 1980), performance in subsequent coursework (Denton, 1982), performance in student teaching

(Scherer, 1979), and subsequent employment (Baker, 1978). Results from these studies are unconvincing and leave the effects of early field experiences open for further study and debate. Faculty members are also concerned about the evaluation of field-based coursework: What role their judgments should play, what standards should be set, and how information should be gathered to provide documentation for successful experience. Faculty find themselves relying upon the "countables" (number of visits made to the school, number of hours spent in the classrooms, number of complaints registered by school personnel), rather than on the quality of performance as criteria for evaluating student performance.

The viewpoint of the faculty members needs further examination. Because others perceive the faculty member's decisions as critical to the success of early field experiences, a worthy investment of research time would be an examination of faculty decision making with respect to the questions raised in this review. Additional questions might be: What are the bases for faculty decision making? What influences faculty members to take classes into schools for instruction? What are attributes of more successful faculty in field-based courses? What feedback do faculty members receive about their performance in field-based courses? What forces and factors both support and mitigate against faculty who work in field-based programs?

SUMMARY AND CONCLUSIONS

This examination of early field experiences from three viewpoints has provided an opportunity for the reader to consider the complexities of early field experiences from different angles. Each angle was role governed and perceptual; each role had its own interests, agendas, and intentions. The college student approached field experience as a learning experience with nebulous goals. The cooperating teacher saw field experience as a teaching experience with crude lesson plans conceived by someone else. The college faculty member viewed field experience as a guided experience when the ideas and skills of students are tried and examined. But as with any role-governed activity, the person assuming the role makes the role meaningful and lively. Regardless of how clearly and carefully roles are defined, the actors' interpretations always must be watched and studied for the richness of the experience to be understood. Though the characters of "Tom Parry," "Mr. Brill," and "Denise Lawrence" were composites of several students, cooperating teachers, and college faculty members, their stories exemplified many of the issues studied by researchers.

Each of the cases also exemplified different forms for early field experiences. In the student's scenario the experience was the course. A large block of time for observation and limited participation was intended to give the student a feel for the classroom and teaching duties early in the student's college program. In the other two scenarios the experience was designed as an extension of campus-based coursework: One provided limited classroom exposure with sequenced activities leading toward whole class instruction; the other provided a short-term block of experience for instruction as a culminating experience in the campus-based course. These three forms are but three of many which are operational in teacher education programs. Whether the field experience is for observation, participation, tutoring, small group, or whole class instruction; whether the experience is one day, once a week, or semester long; whether the experience begins early in the student's preparation or begins when the student enters a professional semester of preparation; whether the experience is supervised, organized, or standardized does not appear to have certain substantial impact.

With early field experiences there are no guarantees. Studies reviewed in this chapter dealt with over 50 different variables associated with early field experiences. The interplay of relationships in the context of classrooms and teacher preparation programs mitigates against researchers who try to unravel problems as complex as those exemplified here. Research considered from these viewpoints has been heavily weighted by students' perceptions. Students have been viewed as dependent variables, affected most by the experiences in schools. This review has shown that the effects of early field experiences extend far beyond students' acquisition of teaching attitudes and skills.

All who participate in the experience are affected by it, but each to different ends. Although the viewpoints of the participants are each unique, there are some areas of common interest. Both the cooperating teacher and the student have expressed the need to know what is expected of them in the field experience and both view that as a responsibility of the college faculty member. All three participants share a sense of responsibility for what happens during the experience. All three see experience as a valuable aspect of teacher preparation. All three use past experience in schools and in teacher preparation to guide their decision making about the current experience. All three have multiple responsibilities which may affect the quality of the field experience. All three see the relationships they are able to establish with one another as critical to the success of the experience. All three know that communication and mutual respect are necessary for the experience to be beneficial. But parity does not yet exist across role groups. When problems arise resolution may be circular: The student can blame the cooperating teacher and the college professor for negative experiences; the teacher can blame the student and the college professor; the college professor can blame the teacher and the student.

Future examination of early field experiences calls for additional focus upon the roles of the cooperating teacher and the university faculty member and the ways they affect and are affected by early field experience. Additional work also needs to focus upon the context in which the experience occurs. Until a comprehensive description of this component of teacher preparation is provided, decisions affecting the nature and quality of field experience will remain arbitrary. As researchers continue to sort and sift through the problems in the area, program planners and policy makers must be cautioned not to assume too much about the place of experience in teacher preparation. These cautions are not intended as barriers to action. We must continue to challenge ourselves with hard questions by looking beyond our suppositions, and by talking with those directly and indirectly involved. Early field experiences can be satisfying and rewarding. What makes them so for each person involved still remains unknown.

REFERENCES

Applegate, J.H. (1985). Early field experiences: Recurring dilemmas. *Journal of Teacher Education, 36*(2), 60–64.

Applegate, J.H., & Biedler, F. (1983). Preparing cooperating teachers to work with teacher education students in urban field experiences: Instructor's guide. In *Providing positive urban field experiences for teacher education students*. Columbus, OH: Ohio Department of Education.

Applegate, J.H., & Lasley, T.J. (1982). Cooperating teachers' problems with preservice field experience students. *Journal of Teacher Education, 33*(2), 15–18.

Applegate, J.H., & Lasley, T.J. (1984a, April). *Perceived problems of students in early field experience*. Paper presented at the annual meeting of the American Education Research Association, Montreal, Quebec.

Applegate, J.H., & Lasley, T.J. (1984b, April). What cooperating teachers expect from preservice field experience students. *Teacher Education*, pp. 70–82.

Applegate, J.H., & Lasley, T.J. (1985). What undergraduate students expect from preservice field experiences. *Texas Tech Journal of Education, 12*(1), 27–36.

Applegate, J., Lasley, T., & Ellison, C. (1985, April). *Teacher education faculty member's expectations for early field experiences*. Paper presented at the annual meeting of the American Education Research Association, Chicago.

Association for Student Teaching (1966). *The supervising teacher: Standards for selection and function*. Washington, DC: Author.

Baker, H.H. (1978). *Effects of participation in a pre-student teaching field-based program on employment-related variables*. Unpublished doctoral dissertation, University of North Carolina at Chapel Hill.

Black, D. (1979). *Cooperating teacher remuneration: Where are we?* Reston, VA: Association of Teacher Educators.

Book, C., Byers, J., & Freeman, D. (1983). Student expectations and teacher education traditions with which we can and cannot live. *Journal of Teacher Education, 34*(1), 9–13.

Buchanan, L.L. (1981). *The effects of an early field experience upon the teaching concerns and pupil control orientations of beginning preservice teachers*. Unpublished doctoral dissertation, University of Florida.

Copeland, W.D. (1978). Processes mediating the relationship between cooperating-teacher behavior and student-teacher classroom performance. *Journal of Educational Psychology, 70*(1), 95–100.

Denton, J.J. (1982). Early field experience influence on performance in subsequent coursework. *Journal of Teacher Education, 33*(2), 19–23.

Dyer, C.J. (1976). *Humanistic competency training for supervisors and cooperating teachers.* Washington, DC: Association of Teacher Educators. (ERIC Document Reproduction Service No. ED 137 219)

Funk, F.F., Long, B., Keithley, A.M., & Hoffman, J.L. (1982). The cooperating teacher as most significant other: A competent humanist. *Action in Teacher Education, 4*(2), 57–63.

Gehrke, N. (1981). Rationale for field experiences in the professions. In C. Webb, N. Gehrke, P. Ishler, & A. Mendoza (Eds.), *Exploratory field experiences in teacher education.* Reston, VA: Association of Teacher Educators.

Gibson, R. (1976). The effect of school practice: The development of student perspectives. *British Journal of Teacher Education, 2*(3), 241–250.

Gregory, S.A. (1971). Criteria for selecting supervising teachers. *The Clearing House, 46*(3), 178–182.

Haberman, M., & Harris, P. (1982). State requirements for cooperating teachers. *Journal of Teacher Education, 33*(3), 45–47.

Haddad, F.A. (1974). *An assessment of the effects of early public school contact on preservice teachers.* Unpublished doctoral dissertation, Indiana University.

Hardy, C.A., & Mershon, B. (1981). Field-based vs. traditional teacher education: A study of learning style preference. *Teacher Educator, 16*(3), 23–26.

Harp, M.W. (1974). Early field experiences: A maturing force. *Elementary School Journal, 74*(6), 369–374.

Heath, P. (1984). *An examination of the curriculum of early field experiences in selected teacher education programs in Ohio.* Unpublished doctoral dissertation, Ohio State University, Columbus.

Hedberg, J.D. (1979). The effects of field experience in educational psychology. *Journal of Teacher Education, 30*(1), 75–76.

Horak, W.J. (1981). Field experiences: Their effects on beliefs of preservice elementary teachers. *Science Education, 65*(3), 277–284.

Ishler, P., & Kay, R.S. (1981). A survey of institutional practice. In C. Webb, N. Gehrke, P. Ishler, & A. Mendoza (Eds.), *Exploratory field experiences in teacher education.* Reston, VA: Association of Teacher Educators.

Joyce, B.R., Hersh, R.H., & McKibben, M. (1983). *The structure of school improvement.* New York: Longman.

Kapel, D.E. (1978). *Career education training and the role perceptions of cooperating teachers toward the field experience.* Paper presented at the meeting of Eastern Educational Research Association, Williamsburg, VA. (ERIC Document Reproduction Service No. ED 151 519)

Kitchens, R.H. (1983). *An early field experience program in teacher education: A grounded theory study.* Unpublished doctoral dissertation, Arizona State University.

Koehler, V. (1984, April). *University supervision of student teaching.* Paper presented at the National Conference of the American Educational Research Association, New Orleans, LA.

Lasley, T., Applegate, J., & Ellison, C. (1985, April). *Teacher education faculty members' problems with early field experiences.* Paper presented at the annual meeting of the American Educational Research Association, Chicago.

Martin, R.E., & Wood, G.H. (1984, April). *Early field experiences: Unification of cooperating teachers' and teacher education students' diverse perspectives.* Paper presented at the annual meeting of the American Educational Research Association, New Orleans, LA.

McIntyre, D.J. (1984). A response to the critics of field experience supervisors. *Journal of Teacher Education, 35*(3), 42–45.

McIntyre, D.J., & Killian, J.E. (1985, April). *The influence of cooperating teachers' supervisory training and experience on teacher development during early field experiences.* Paper presented at the meeting of the American Educational Research Association, Chicago, IL.

Palmer, M.J. (1980). *An analysis of pre-student teaching field work experiences at North Arizona University.* Unpublished doctoral dissertation, North Arizona University.

Poole, C. (1972). The influence of experiences in the schools on students' evaluations of teaching practice. *The Journal of Educational Research, 66*(4), 161-164.

Price, W. (1961). The influence of supervising teachers. *Journal of Teacher Education, 12*(1), 471-475.

Puckett, E.H. (1981). *A national survey of field experiences in elementary teaching preparation programs.* Unpublished manuscript. (ERIC Document Reproduction Service No. ED 217 044)

Ross, R.W. (1980). *The effects of an early field experience program on the pupil control ideology of teacher trainees.* Unpublished doctoral dissertation, North Arizona University.

Ross, R.W., Hughes, T.M., & Hill, R.E. (1981). Field experiences as meaningful contexts for learning about learning. *Journal of Educational Research, 75*(2), 103-107.

Scherer, C. (1979). Effects of early field experience on student teachers' self-concepts and performance. *Journal of Experimental Education, 47*(3), 208-214.

Seperson, M., & Joyce, B. (1973). Teaching styles of student teachers as related to those of their cooperating teachers. *Educational Leadership, 31,* 146-151.

Shuff, M., & Shuff, C. (1972). Designed for excellence: A program for laboratory experiences. *Journal of Teacher Education, 23*(2), 215-219.

Southhall, C.T., & Dumas, W. (1981). Early classroom field experiences in state universities of seven midwestern states. *Contemporary Education, 52*(4), 203-208.

Stevens, J.T., & Smith, C.L. (1978). Supervising teacher accountability: Evaluation by the student teacher. *Peabody Journal of Education, 56*(1), 64-74.

Sunal, D.W. (1980). Effect of field experience during elementary methods courses on preservice teacher behavior. *Journal of Research in Science Teaching, 17*(1), 17-23.

Switzer, R. (1976). Cooperating teachers: Strengths and weaknesses. *Colorado Journal of Educational Research, 15*(2), 37-45.

Thompson, L.L. (1982, March). *Faculty and student perceptions of early field experiences.* Paper presented at the annual meeting of the American Educational Research Association, New York.

Twa, R.J., & Dung, D.D. (1981, April). *Exploratory field experiences in Canadian teacher education: Phase 1.* Paper presented at the annual meeting of the American Educational Research Association, Los Angeles, CA.

Walker, L., & Applegate, J.H. (1985). *Expressed concerns of cooperating teachers.* Unpublished manuscript.

Chapter 5

The Ecology of Field Experience: Toward an Understanding of the Role of Field Experiences in Teacher Development

Kenneth M. Zeichner

University of Wisconsin–Madison

For many years researchers who have analyzed the empirical literature related to field experiences in teacher education have consistently characterized the knowledge base related to the socializing impact of these experiences as weak, ambiguous, and contradictory (Davies & Amershek, 1969; Peck & Tucker, 1973; Zeichner, 1980; Griffin et al., 1983; Feiman-Nemsor, 1983). Today despite the existence of numerous individual studies which have demonstrated specific effects of field experiences on the development of some individuals under particular conditions, there continues to be a great deal of debate in our field about the role that field experiences play in teacher development and about the relative contribution of various individual and institutional factors to the socialization process.

For example, several researchers have argued (often with the support of empirical data) that biography and the personal characteristics of education students are the key elements in teacher socialization and that field experiences play little part in altering the course of development that is set prior to these experiences (e.g., Lortie, 1975; Mardle & Walker, 1980; Zeichner & Grant, 1981). On the other hand, many other researchers have argued (also frequently with the support of empirical data) that field experiences by themselves or in combination with particular types of courses do indeed have a significant impact on teacher development. There is a great deal of disagreement, however, among those who view field experiences as potent socializing mechanisms as to the particular effects of these experiences, the particular socializing agents and mechanisms that play the most influential roles in affecting teacher development (e.g., see Tabachnick & Zeichner, 1983), and over the degree to which the dispositions, abilities, and personal characteristics of individual education students influence the role of field experiences in teacher development (Mardle & Walker, 1980).

Several analyses have recently been completed which provide us with very detailed and comprehensive summaries of the results of specific studies that have examined the influence of either early field experience or student teaching on various aspects of teacher development. Samson, Borger, Weinstein and Walberg's (1983) "Metaanalysis" of 38 studies on the effects of early field experiences on the attitudes of education students and McIntyre's (1983) analysis of studies of the relationships between all varieties of field experience and teacher development are two examples of recent attempts to synthesize this literature. Without exception, those who have attempted to summarize what research has to say about the role of field experiences in teacher development, whether they conclude that these experiences are impotent or not, have raised serious questions about the ways in which this research has been conceptualized and conducted and have offered many specific proposals aimed at a major restructuring of the dominant research paradigm in this area.

Rather than attempting to provide yet another compilation of the findings of specific studies, this paper will focus instead on bringing together in one place some of the conceptual and methodological limitations which have been identified in relation to this body of research and will offer a set of specific proposals based on these criticisms as to how research on field experiences can begin to move closer to providing us with the kinds of empirical data which will be useful for policy decisions. The general argument is that research to date has taken either too narrow or too broad a view of field experiences, too restrictive a view of teacher development (e.g., ignoring unanticipated outcomes), and that the failure of studies to attend to the complex, dynamic, and multidimensional nature of settings and people, individually and in interaction ("the ecology of field experiences") is a major reason for the current unsatisfactory state of our knowledge base related to the influence of field experience on teacher development.

THE ECOLOGY OF FIELD EXPERIENCES

Bronfenbrenner (1976) outlines what he considers to be the basic elements of the "ecology of education" and argues that educational research which seeks to understand how people learn in educational settings must attend to two sets of relations. First, research must be concerned with understanding the relations between the characteristics of learners and the surroundings in which they live and work (person–environment interactions). Second, research must investigate the relations and interconnections that exist between the various environments themselves (environment–environment interactions). This theme about the necessity for educational research to attend to the ecological characteristics of the learning process has frequently been reiterated by those who are concerned with the processes of teacher development (e.g., Doyle, 1977; Copeland, 1979; Zimpher, deVoss, & Nott, 1980). For example, Lortie (1973) concludes in his examination of "the riddle of teacher socialization" that "the socialization of teachers is undoubtedly a complex process not readily captured by a single-factor frame of reference" (p. 488). He calls for studies which assess the relative contribution of several agents or mechanisms under various conditions. Additionally, the work of Spencer-Hall (1982), Karmos and Jacko (1977), and Giroux (1980) underlines the importance of going beyond the immediate professional context in looking for sources of influence to investigate the contributions of various "nonprofessional" agents and factors to teacher development and the influence of the larger sociopolitical context in which both the personal and professional lives of teachers are embedded.

Others such as Popkewitz, Tabachnick, & Zeichner (1979) and Tabachnick (1981) have added to this concern about attending to a variety of simultaneous influences on teacher development at several levels, the concern that research must seek to investigate the processes of teacher development as they evolve over time. For example, Tabachnick (1981) characterizes experiences in teacher education as "dynamic social events" possessing the dual characteristics of "embeddedness" and "becoming" and feels that research on teacher development must seek to understand patterns of interaction between the intentions that participants bring to an event, the physical and social environments which exist during the unfolding of an event, and the ethical–psychological environments that develop as individual participants create and give meanings to the patterns of interactions that occur. Tabachnick (1981) argues that the processes of teacher development will inevitably entail unanticipated as well as anticipated "outcomes" and that in order to understand both the event and the development of participants one needs to be able to document the evolution of an event.

Finally, the works of Lacey (1977), Doyle (1977), and Zeichner and Tabachnick (1983) emphasize the importance of viewing patterns of interaction and influence between and among participants and social contexts as reciprocal in nature. The studies of Nerenz (1980) and Rosenfeld (1969), empirically document that influence during field experience does not always follow predicted directions and that those with the least formal power (i.e., the teacher education students) sometimes exert influence over those who are supposed to be influencing them and over the settings in which they work. In summary, an ecological approach to research in teacher education requires that studies: (a) seek to understand the simultaneous influence of a variety of people and factors under particular environmental conditions and at several levels, (b) document the evolution of an experience and patterns of influence over time, and (c) view influence in relation to teacher development as reciprocal in nature.

This ecological perspective toward research on teacher education has recently been set forth as a necessary ingredient in studies of field experiences. Consistent with Feiman-Nemser's (1983) general charge to researchers that they pay closer attention to the content and context of field experiences, Hersh, Hull, and Leighton (1982) have outlined the basic elements that need to be considered in research that attends to the complex ecology of field experiences. Hersh et al. (1982) in defining the ecology of field experiences as "the complex set of relationships among program features, settings and people" argue that research on field experiences needs to investigate:

1. *The structure and content of a field experience program* — This entails an examination of both the goals and substance of a program as viewed by program designers and an understanding of how a program is actually implemented (its "curriculum in use").
2. *The characteristics of placement sites* — This includes an examination of the classrooms, schools and communities in which field experiences are carried out.
3. *The relationships between education students and other people* — This presupposes an understanding of the characteristics, dispositions and behaviors of both the students and those with whom they interact. (p. 1812)

The extant literature on field experiences will now be examined in relation to these three ecological characteristics (see Table 1). The concern will be with how well researchers have attended to each of these areas and with what specific aspects of the ecology of field experiences need to be given more systematic attention in the future. Additionally, the construct of "teacher development" will be examined and suggestions will be offered as to how our notions of "development" need to be reformulated in studies of field experiences. Although the arguments to follow are directed at the literature on field experiences in general, most of the examples of studies to be cited have been drawn from a sample of 20 specific studies. These studies represent all of the reports of individual research efforts with a focus on field experience and teacher development which have appeared in the two major refereed U.S. journals devoted primarily to teacher education: (1) *Journal of Teacher Education,* 1976–1983; (2) *Action in Teacher Education,* 1978–1983. It is felt that these

TABLE 1. Conceptions of "Influence" in 20 Representative Studies

Study	Structure & Content of Field Experience Program	Field Experience or Not/Which of 2 Field Experiences	Supplementary Course or Seminar	Characteristics of Placement Sites			Characteristics/ Attitudes of Individual Education Ss	Characteristics/ Attitudes of "Significant Others"
				Classroom	School	Community		
Early Field Experience								
Denton (1982)	X	X						
Hedberg (1979)	X	X						
Henry (1983)	X	X						
Ross et al. (1980)	X	X					X (Maj-elem or sec)	
Student Teaching								
Boschee et al. (1978)							X (Maj-elem or sec)	X
Corcoran (1982)	X (Structure)			X			X	
Doyle (1977)				X				
Funk et al. (1982)			X					
Glassberg & Sprinthall (1982)			X					X
Hodges (1982)			X	X				
Holt & Peterson (1981)	X (Structure)				X			
Hoy & Rees (1977)					X*		X (gender)	X
Johnson et al. (1982)	X (Structure)							

Karmos & Jacko (1977)					X
Mahlios (1982)			X		X
McCaleb (1979)		X			
Silvernail & Costello (1983)	X		X	X	
Smith & Smith (1979)				X	
Walter & Stivers (1977)		X			X
Early Field Experience and Student Teaching					
Becher & Ade (1982)	X	X			X

*Hoy and Rees (1977) speculated as to the effects of school content on the developmental outcomes but did not directly investigate the schools in which the student teachers taught.

studies are representative of recently published studies and that they provide an accurate picture of the conceptual and methodological orientations of research in this area. Although a study by Zimpher et al. (1980) is within the time frame of this analysis and is published in one of the two journals that were reviewed, it was not included in the intensive sample because its primary emphasis is on the role of the university supervisor and the supervisor's functions in a student teaching program as a whole rather than on the development of student teachers. This study does, however, adopt an "ecological approach" to the study of student teaching and is an exception to many of the arguments to follow. These 20 studies, which were carefully reviewed in an attempt to validate the arguments made in the paper, will be referred to as the "intensive sample."

THE STRUCTURE AND CONTENT OF FIELD EXPERIENCE PROGRAMS

It is clear from any examination of the literature on field experiences that there is no agreed upon definition of the purpose and goals of either early field experience or student teaching and that there is a great deal of variety in the ways in which these experiences are conceptualized, organized, and actually implemented even within a single institution. Zeichner (1983) has outlined four paradigmatic orientations and two dimensions along which the substance of teacher education programs vary. This description of the "received–reflexive" and "problematic–certain" continuua are only examples of the wide range of theoretical orientations toward the organization and conduct of teacher education programs that have been discussed in the literature (see also Atkins & Raths, 1974).

With regard to field experiences Gehrke (1981) has reiterated Dewey's (1904) classic distinction between the "laboratory" and "apprenticeship" points of view regarding the purpose of field experience and has outlined two contemporary rationales for the conduct of early field experiences. Also, Zeichner and Teitelbaum (1982) have described two alternative orientations to the conduct of student teaching experiences ("personalized" and "inquiry-oriented") that are consistent with both Dewey's (1904) and Gehrke's (1981) analyses.

At the level of implementation numerous writers (e.g., McNaughton, Johns, & Rogus, 1978; Elliot & Mays, 1979; Ryan, 1982) have described various alternatives that exist in practice regarding the organization of field experiences, their relation to campus-based courses, patterns for involving supervisory personnel, and roles that are assumed by students (e.g., observer, tutor). Ishler and Kay's (1981) survey of current practices in early field experiences also emphasizes the great amount of diversity that exists in early field experience programs across the U.S. However, despite the overwhelming evidence of the wide variety of purposes, organizational patterns, and role configurations in field experience programs, studies that have investigated the relationships between field experiences and teacher development have not for the most part provided us with the kinds of information about programs which acknowledges this heterogeneity; nor have they provided us with information that reflects the complex interactions among the individual components within any given program.

Two different concerns have been raised in the literature regarding the treatment of field experience programs in individual studies. On the one hand, Gaskell (1975) and Ryan (1982) have criticized the common practice of examining changes in the attitudes and/or behaviors of education students as a result of participation in a "treatment" which is described simply as "field experience" or "student teaching." They argue that this lumping together of all of the constituent parts of a field experience masks the effects of the particular dimensions of a program or of a particular type of program. As a result, they argue, we frequently see reports of particular changes or of the lack of changes resulting from participation in a field experience, but we are very rarely given any insight into how and why education students were affected in particular ways.

A different criticism of the treatment of field experience programs in individual studies is concerned with the also common tendency to examine isolated bits of a field experience program in relation to developmental outcomes. Hersh et al. (1982) argue, for example, that these attempts to explain the influence of field experiences on the basis of a few isolated factors ignore the complex ecology of field experiences. As a result, they argue, we are also given little insight from such studies as to what particular components of programs influenced the developmental outcomes. The argument here is that we cannot understand the influence of any particular factor (e.g., cooperating teachers) without also understanding the influence of all of the other factors which are intimately linked to this factor.

When we examine the 20 studies in the intensive sample the information which is provided about the structure and content of the field experience programs varies according to whether the field experience is an early field experience or student teaching experience. Because Becher and Ade (1982) investigated the influence of early field experiences and student teaching their study is discussed under both categories. First, despite the fact that 3 of the 16 studies of student teaching provide relatively detailed information about the purposes and organization of courses or seminars which complement student teaching (McCaleb, 1979; Glassberg & Sprinthall, 1980; Hodges, 1982), only 3 of the 16 studies (Holt & Peterson, 1981; Corcoran, 1982; Johnson, Cox, & Wood, 1982) provide any information about the structure of the student teaching experience itself beyond descriptions of when it took place (e.g., senior year), its length, and the number of classroom placements. Silvernail and Costello (1983) differentiate between a student teaching experience and an internship, but they fail to provide any information about the differences and/or similarities in the structure, goals, or content of these two programs. None of the studies on student teaching offer any information about the content or curriculum of the student teaching program.

Thus, although all of these studies have examined various other influences on the attitudes and behaviors of student teachers (e.g., supplementary seminars, cooperating teachers, placement characteristics), the purpose, structure, and content of the student teaching program itself, for the most part, remains undefined. Consequently, we are presented with a lot of specific information about the influence (or lack of influence) of cooperating teachers and so forth, but we are given little if any insight into how the particular dimensions of the programs themselves contributed to the outcomes.

When we examine the five studies in the intensive sample which were concerned with the role of early field experiences in teacher development the picture is very different. Here, four of the five studies provide us with relatively detailed descriptions of the content and organization of both field experiences and related courses, even to the point of including in several cases lists of specific requirements and activities that students were expected to fulfill in the field. Consequently, when particular outcomes are reported in these studies (e.g., the field experience enhanced performance in a subsequent methods course, Denton, 1982), we have at least some idea of the nature of the field experience which is viewed as making a contribution to teacher development.

There is, however, an important issue which is not addressed by four of these five studies. Zeichner (1980) has argued that "the characteristics of field-based programs are not to be found in public statements of intention, but through an examination of the experiences themselves" (p. 53). Tabachnick and Zeichner (1983) elaborate on this theme when they argue that one cannot assume that all field experiences pose the same constraints and opportunities for all students and that the socialization of student teachers takes the same form and has the same meaning for all students even within a single program.

Fullan and Pomfret (1977) conclude with regard to curriculum and instruction generally that the process of implementation is not simply an extension of the planning process and that it is inappropriate to view the move from the drawing board to the school and classroom as unproblematic. Similarly, Parlett and Hamilton (1976) have noted that:

> An instructional system, when adopted, undergoes modifications that are rarely trivial. The instructional system may remain as a shared idea, abstract model, slogan or shorthand, but it assumes a different form in every situation. Its constituent elements are emphasized or de-emphasized, expanded or truncated, as teachers, administrators, technicians and students interpret and re-

interpret the instructional system for their particular setting. In practice objectives are commonly re-ordered, re-defined, abandoned, or forgotten. The original "ideal" formulation ceases to be accurate, or indeed, of much relevance. (p. 145)

There is some evidence from studies of both student teaching and early field experiences that supports these arguments and that underlines the inappropriateness of deriving an understanding of a field-based program solely from statements of goals and from instructional plans. For example, Zeichner and Tabachnick (1982) and Goodman (1983) have shown that even when the designers of a field-based program have articulated a specific emphasis, the actual implementation of a program reflects a diversity of orientations as the diverse perspectives of specific individuals are brought to bear on the coherent instructional plan in different contexts. In each of these studies there were differences in the degree to which various program goals and requirements were implemented in various classrooms.

Another example comes from one of the studies in the intensive sample. In the only study of early field experiences which examined the ways in which a program was in fact implemented, Ross, Raines, Cervetti, and Dellow (1980) found several discrepancies between the goals and requirements of the two programs under comparison and the actual implementation of the programs in classrooms. As a result of an analysis of students' reports of their activities during the semester (which were checked for validity by comparing them with reports from cooperating teachers), Ross et al. (1980) discovered that 16% of the students in the Tutoring Program did not have any involvement at all in tutoring, which was the main program requirement. They also discovered that as many as 25% of the students in the Teacher Apprentice Program reported involvement in only one activity other than observation. This was in conflict with the broad set of requirements for students in this program.

A final example can be found in probably the most comprehensive study of the student teaching experience to be undertaken to date. Griffin et al. (1983) concluded from a study of 93 student teachers from two universities that:

> Awareness of policies, expectations, purposes and desirable practices was not widespread across participants in the student teaching experience. It was rare that university and school-based teacher educators agreed upon, or could even articulate, the policies and practices which were supposed to guide student teaching. (p. 335)

As an example, Griffin et al. (1983) refer to a "pacing guide" that was supposed to influence the way in which student teachers assumed responsibility for instruction in their classrooms. They found little evidence that this guide was influential upon practice.

In summary, if one is to accept the 20 studies in the intensive sample as representative of contemporary studies on the relationship between field experience and teacher development, then we know very little from research about the nature of student teaching programs studied, something more about the instructional plans of early field experiences, and almost nothing about the ways in which either early field experiences or student teaching are implemented in the field in relation to program goals. Although there are some who hold the view that the goals, curricular plans, and substance of field experience programs have little influence on the manner in which programs are implemented in the field, it is premature for researchers to bypass systematic analysis of the influence of the explicit and implicit curricula of these programs and their organizational structures on the development of teacher education students. The influences of particular kinds of field-based programs and of particular components within programs on teacher development will remain unknown until we begin to include descriptions of individual programs and program components (as planned and as implemented) within the scope of our investigations.

THE CHARACTERISTICS OF PLACEMENT SITES

A second aspect of the ecology of field experiences to be considered is the nature of those classrooms, schools, and communities in which students work. Becher and Ade (1982) correctly point out "by their very nature no two placement sites are alike. All vary on a number of dimensions and it is likely that they may have potentially different effects and make potentially different contributions to a student's growth" (p. 25). McIntyre (1983) argues that "to understand the field experience, one must assay the elementary and secondary school settings and programs where students are placed and examine how that environment influences the triad's interaction" (p. 16).

When we examine the 20 studies in the intensive sample we find a variety of ways in which placement sites have been described. On the one hand, 13 of the 20 studies provide no information at all about the schools and classrooms beyond an occasional reference to the range of grade levels within a sample and the number of schools or school districts in which a program is carried out. On the other hand, 4 studies do provide some minimal information about the characteristics of placement sites:

1. In Hodges' (1982) study we are told that there was no cooperating teacher, at least two student teachers per semester in the classroom under study, and that the students were totally responsible for the instruction in the classroom. We are also given some information about the reading curriculum in the class and school based on the author's observations.

2. In Smith and Smith's (1979) study we are given information about the socioeconomic status of pupils in various schools.
3. In McCaleb's (1979) study we are told that all of the student teachers were placed in classrooms where the conditions for the teaching of language were in conflict with the approach that was emphasized in the students' courses.
4. Holt and Peterson (1981) speculate as to how the structure of their program influenced three school characteristics (isolation among staff, uncertainty as to teaching effectivenesss, and reward systems) and how in turn the school characteristics influenced student teacher–cooperating teacher relations and student teacher development. They provide very little information, however, related to the three school characteristics.

The most comprehensive approaches to the analysis of placement site characteristics are provided by Becher and Ade (1982), Doyle (1977), and Corcoran (1982). As part of a 3-year study of 58 student teachers who were observed for one full period per week during their 8–16 week student teaching experiences, Doyle maps out the ecological characteristics of the classrooms in which students taught and provides a description of the strategies student teachers used (both successfully and unsuccessfully) to attempt to reduce the complexity in their classrooms. Doyle argues that the ecological environment of a classroom together with the nature of specific activity structures are major determinants in influencing the actions of student teachers. Also, Becher and Ade utilizing the Placement Site Assessment Instrument analyze the relationships between three specific placement characteristics as judged by university supervisors (modeling of good teaching behavior, feedback to the student teacher, and opportunities for student teacher innovation), the students' potential field-performance abilities, and the quality of students' performance in several successive practica. Finally, Corcoran describes the instructional management system that was a part of the classroom in which an intern worked and discussed how the complexity of this system was related to the intern's problems in assuming instructional responsibilities.

Researchers have repeatedly emphasized the alleged importance of the schools (e.g., Horowitz, 1968; Sorenson & Hulpart, 1968) and classrooms (Copeland, 1979) in which students complete their field experiences in influencing student teacher attitudes and behaviors. If these 20 studies are accepted as representative of recent work in this area, then it appears that researchers have not paid much attention to the potential impact of particular types of classrooms, schools, and communities on the relationship between field experiences and teacher development. The approaches exemplified by the studies of Doyle (1977), Becher and Ade (1982), and Corcoran (1982) are exceptions and merit further attention by researchers in the future. Studies that seek to understand the role of field experiences in teacher development clearly need to place more emphasis on the specific constraints and opportunities which are present in specific school settings.

THE CHARACTERISTICS AND DISPOSITIONS OF INDIVIDUAL EDUCATION STUDENTS AND THEIR "SIGNIFICANT OTHERS"

The third and final aspect of the ecology of field experiences to be discussed is the characteristics and dispositions of individual education students and their "significant others," and how relationships among student characteristics and "significant others' characteristics" affect teacher development during field experiences. There are several rationales which have been presented in the literature for examining the influence of individual student characteristics on development during field experiences. First, Sprinthall and Thies-Sprinthall (1983) have presented a variety of empirical data in support of the view that the behavior of adults (including teacher education students) is affected by individual levels of cognitive development. Specifically, they conclude that there is empirical evidence now available that demonstrates:

> Persons at higher stages of development function more complexly, possess a wider repertoire of behavioral skills, perceive problems more broadly and respond more accurately and empathically to the needs of others. (p. 21)

If Sprinthall and Thies-Sprinthall (1983) are correct and there is abundant empirical evidence available that supports their general position, then it would seem that researchers who study field experiences would be obligated to examine how the particular developmental levels of individual students (e.g., ego development, conceptual levels) affect the influence of field experience on their development. Feiman-Nemser and Buchman (1983) suggest that students' dispositions toward inquiry (to learn and grow from experience) need to be given further attention in attempts to understand field experiences. Their suggestion is closely related to the "developmentalist" position of Sprinthall and Thies-Sprinthall (1983) and is especially interesting given the distinction between the "laboratory" and "apprenticeship" view of field experience which has permeated the literature since 1904. Similarly, McDonald (1980) in the recent Educational Testing Service review of the literature on beginning teachers has emphasized the importance of "coping skills" that beginning teachers bring to their jobs in helping or hindering their adaptation to the workplace:

> Many problems of teaching can be dealt with on the basis of skills that one uses in places and situations other than teaching. Maturity of point of view, inde-

pendence, self-reliance, confidence in seeking information and help are broadly useful characteristics in life and certainly must have some effect on how teachers make the transition into teaching. (p. 175)

McDonald's (1980) argument is analogous to the position of Sprinthall and Thies-Sprinthall (1983) and although he does not base his position on any particular stage theories of development there seems to be a close relationship between the messages conveyed by these authors. Additionally, although McDonald's remarks are directed at the adaptions made by beginning teachers, there is every reason to believe that his analysis is applicable to teacher education students as well.

Although the actions and the development of education students doing field experiences are clearly more than simple expressions of the ideas that they have in their heads and of who they are as people, the personality characteristics, dispositions and abilities that students bring to a field experience (including their unique biographical histories) are undoubtedly important factors in influencing the quality and strength of their socialization during the field experience. There is overwhelming support for the view from a variety of theoretical perspectives that teacher education students do not simply react to the people and forces around them. On the contrary, what teacher education students bring to a field experience and who they are as people interacts with contextual constraints and opportunities to affect the course of development during the experience (Tabachnick & Zeichner, 1983; Lacey, 1977).

When we examine the studies in the intensive sample we find that all of the 20 studies provide some minimal information about the general characteristics of students within a research sample. For example, we are frequently given information about the gender distribution within a sample, the distribution of student majors (e.g., elementary), the range of student ages, ethnicity characteristics, and so on. In most cases, however, this information is simply presented as background and does not enter into the analyses of how the field experiences affected particular developmental outcomes.

When we look at how the studies examined relationships between individual student characteristics and development during field experiences we find three general patterns. On the one hand, 13 of the 20 studies do not provide any analysis of how individual students' characteristics, dispositions, or abilities influenced the development. On the other hand, three of the studies give some, but still very minimal attention to how individual students' characteristics, and so forth, influenced their development. For example, Hoy and Rees (1977) sought to determine if there were differences in development related to gender, and Boschee, Prescott, and Hein (1978) and Ross et al. (1980) explored whether a student's subject major (e.g., elementary or secondary) influenced developmental outcomes. Together, these studies reflect an unfortunate lack of attention to the important role of individuals' characteristics in the process of teacher development.

Only four studies in the intensive sample gave any systematic attention to how individual students' characteristics, dispositions, or abilities were related to their development during field experiences. For example, Becher and Ade (1982) examined how students' potential field performance abilities (assessed prior to the experience) interacted with specific field placement characteristics in affecting the quality of a student's performance during successive field experiences. Another example is Walter and Stivers' (1977) analysis of how students' identity resolution/dissolution influenced their behavior and performance during a student teaching experience. Finally, Corcoran (1982), in speculating as to why a student's potential performance abilities were not actualized in her classroom, provides some insight into how individual student characteristics interact with the classroom context to affect development.

In summary, relatively few studies in the intensive sample have given systematic attention to how the individual characteristics, and so forth, of students interact with other influences to affect their development during field experiences. Furthermore, even where attention was given to the role of individual characteristics, only one of the studies provided any description of the structure of the student teaching program or field experience under study. None of the four studies described the content or curriculum of the program.

Another aspect of this ecological dimension is concerned with the influence of the characteristics, dispositions, and abilities of significant others and the relationships between individual student characteristics and significant other characteristics, and so forth, on development during field experiences. For many years studies have been demonstrating that cooperating teachers exert a great deal of influence on teacher education students (e.g., Yee, 1969). Recently, however, studies have begun to raise questions about this view and have identified the school and classroom in which both students and cooperating teachers work as a more potent source of influence (e.g., Copeland, 1979). There is almost no empirical support that the university supervisor exerts any substantial influence on development during field experiences (e.g., Bowman, 1979), but here again recent studies have emerged which document particular influences of supervisors on both students and cooperating teachers (e.g., Zimpher et al., 1980).

In the intensive sample only five studies gave any attention to the possible socializing role of the cooperating teacher and none investigated the role of the university supervisor. For example, Boschee et al. (1978) sought to determine if student teachers' educational philosophies were influenced by those of their cooperating teachers and found that there was no influence. Mahlios (1982) investigated whether the cooperating teachers' field independence/dependence in relation to that of their student teachers had any influence on student teacher performance and found that it did. Finally, although both Karmos and Jacko (1977) and Funk, Long, Keithley, and Hoffman (1982) discovered that student teachers viewed their cooperating teachers as the most significant source of influence on their development, the findings of Boschee et al. (1978), Corcoran (1982) and of a study conducted by Hodges (1982) raise questions about the view that locates a major source of influence in cooperating teachers. For example, Hodges placed groups of students in a classroom over two semesters without a cooperating teacher to see if the absence of the cooperating teacher facilitated the use of methods for the teaching of reading that had been taught in a campus course. Her discovery that the students did not employ the instructional methods taught in the course support Copeland's (1980) thesis about the significance of school and classroom characteristics.

In summary, the findings from this representative group of studies reflect the literature as a whole. There are conflicting results about how and to what degree cooperating teachers influence student development, and almost no inquiry into the possible influence exerted by university supervisors. Also, despite the evidence from several sources concerning the close connection between the personal and professional lives of teachers (e.g., Johnston & Ryan, 1983) only 2 of the 16 studies utilized a methodological approach that permitted the discovery of "non-professional" sources of influence.

Conceptions of Development

There were a variety of measures of "development" that were employed within the intensive sample (see Table 2). One interest was in assessing changes in student personality characteristics, developmental levels (according to a one or more stage theory), or attitudes from the beginning to the end of an experience either in isolation or in relation to other factors (e.g., attitudes of cooperating teachers). For example, we are given a lot of information in these studies about changes or the lack of changes in students' educational philosophies, attitudes toward pupil control, and language instruction and stages of cognitive development (e.g., ego development).

A second interest was in documenting the actual behaviors of teacher education students in classrooms or in interaction with cooperating teachers and supervisors. For example, Doyle (1977) describes the specific strategies used by student teachers in their attempts to reduce the complexity in their classrooms. Walter and Stivers (1977) document the degree to which student teachers employed specific teaching behaviors (e.g., accepted pupil ideas). Finally, Johnson et al. (1982) analyzed the substance and communicative structure of supervisory conferences between student teachers and supervisors.

A third interest was in assessing the quality of a student's performance in the field experience or in a campus course related to the field experience.

TABLE 2. Conceptions of "Development" in 20 Representative Studies

Study	Personality Characteristics/ Cognitive Development	Attitudes/ Perceptions	Behaviors (Self-Report)	Behaviors (Observed or Recorded)	Quality of Performance in F.E.	Quality of Performance in Campus Course
Early Field Experience						
Denton (1982)						X
Hedberg (1979)						X
Henry (1983)		X			X	
Ross et al. (1980)		X	X			
Student Teaching						
Boschee et al. (1978)		X				
Corcoran (1982)		X	X	X	X	
Doyle (1977)				X	X	
Funk et al. (1982)		X				
Glassberg & Sprinthall (1982)	X					
Hodges (1982)				X		
Holt & Peterson (1981)		X	X			
Hoy & Rees (1977)	X	X				
Johnson et al. (1982)			X	X		
Karmos & Jacko (1977)		X				
Mahlios (1982)					X	
McCaleb (1979)		X				
Silvernail & Costello (1983)	X	X				
Smith & Smith (1979)		X				
Walter & Stivers (1977)				X	X	
Early Field Experience and Student Teaching						
Becher & Ade (1982)					X	

Here some like Henry (1983) explored students' own perceptions of their success, whereas others relied upon grades (e.g., Denton, 1982) or on supervisors' ratings of teaching performance (Becher & Ade, 1982). Doyle (1977) and Corcoran (1982) both examined "success" in terms of mastery of the demands posed by the ecological environments of classrooms.

Two points merit discussion related to the conceptions of development that were employed in these studies. First, 11 of the studies determined the specific developmental outcomes that would be assessed and limited their analysis to only those few predetermined variables. Second, only 5 of the 20 studies included any observations (or recordings) of students' actions in classrooms or of their interactions with supervisors. Both of these trends: (a) to ignore unanticipated outcomes, and (b) to derive one's understanding of the influence of an experience without direct observation of that experience are problematic given the ecological reality of field experiences.

Gaskell (1975) correctly argues that investigations of only a particular set of predetermined "outcomes" in studies of field experiences ignore the numerous unintended outcomes and "side effects" that are inevitably associated with such experiences. Given all of the evidence regarding the inevitable discrepancies between program plans and implementation (some of which was discussed earlier), we have little reason to suspect that all of the significant developmental outcomes can be anticipated in advance. At most, according to Gaskell, these limited investigations of a few predefined variables can contribute to a particular theoretic viewpoint, but they will do little to further our understanding of the influence of field experiences on teacher education students.

Consequently, to assume that one can gain an understanding of the role of field experiences in teacher development without observing or in some way documenting the experience is a fallacy. There is much evidence that student attitudes expressed on questionnaires are inaccurate reflections of the teaching perspectives which guide their practice in classrooms (e.g., Shipman, 1967). There is also evidence concerning the discrepancies between teachers' self-reports of their behaviors and their actual behaviors in classrooms (e.g., Hook & Rosenshine, 1979). Griffin et al. (1983) succinctly summarize the importance of direct observation in studying field experiences:

> The use of multiple data sources is crucial to obtain as true a picture of classrooms and teachers as possible. In particular the use of multiple qualitative data sources in this study pointed out discrepancies in how student teaching activities were carried forward and how they were viewed by participants. This incongruity may not have surfaced had only a self-report method been used in place of collecting data about the actual event itself. (pp. 332–333)

In summary, without direct observation of field experiences or some other attempt to document the experience (e.g., through audio recordings), it becomes difficult to understand the nature and quality of the ecological elements of an experience and to discover developmental "outcomes" which may in some cases be more significant than those which were anticipated from a particular theoretical perspective. The failure of 13 of the 20 studies in the intensive sample to document either through observation or self-report actions and interactions during the experiences raises serious questions about their ecological validity and severely limits the usefulness of their findings for policy makers.

CONCLUSION

It has been argued in this chapter that field experiences in teacher education entail a complex set of interactions among program features, settings, and people (the ecology of field experiences) and that research that seeks to understand the role of these experiences in teacher development must reflect in its conceptualization and methodology the dynamic and multidimensional nature of the event being studied. If one accepts this ecological viewpoint, then it becomes necessary to understand the influence of a variety of interacting factors in order to understand the influence of any given factor. An understanding of three specific elements of this ecology was proposed as a necessary ingredient in studies of field experiences: (1) the structure and content of the field experience program, (2) the characteristics of placement sites, and (3) the characteristics, dispositions, and abilities of individual students and their significant others. It has also been argued that the conceptualization of development in these studies needs to be broadened to include the documentation of actual actions and interactions and the investigation of unanticipated outcomes. It should also be noted that the very process of studying field experiences may in fact alter the developmental outcomes under study. There is some evidence (e.g., Tabachnick & Zeichner, 1983) that studies of field experiences are *interventions* which influence development and which underscores the importance of studying how the research itself affects those being studied. It could even be argued that the research study itself is another dimension of the ecology of field experiences.

The 20 studies in the intensive sample have been utilized to provide a rough barometer of the conceptual and methodological orientations of contemporary studies in this area. When one examines these studies in terms of their exploration of the three dimensions of the ecology of field experiences, it is clear that each individual study emphasized a small part of one or two of the elements, but that none of the studies gave systematic attention to all three of the interacting factors. Corcoran's (1982) case study of one intern comes the closest to investigating all three elements. Also, this analysis of the studies in terms of their "coverage" of the three elements, does not consider the quality and scope of the investigations within each element. Most notable is the failure of all 16 studies of student teaching experience to describe the content of the programs studied and the almost total lack of attention to placement site characteristics in studies of early field experiences. Tables 1 and 2 summarize the degree to which each study has systematically investigated the various ecological elements and the conceptions of development which were employed in each study.

It should be pointed out that studies do exist that address the interactions among all three of the ecological elements of field experiences. The recently completed study of student teaching at the Texas R & D Center for Teacher Education (Griffin et al., 1983) is probably the best contemporary example of research that reflects the ecological reality of field experiences. However, these studies (see also Iannaccone & Button, 1964; Connor & Smith, 1967; Gaskell, 1975; Hultgren, 1982) are clearly in the minority. Most of the work that is curerntly being done in this area, particularly that which reaches professional journals, is not very different in its conceptualization from the studies described in this chapter.

Zeichner (1980) concluded that field experiences entail a complicated set of both positive and negative outcomes that are often subtle in nature and that research on field experiences does not provide much guidance for policy making in teacher education. The conclusions from two recent analyses of studies on field experiences confirm this assessment and underline the need for a major reorientation of research in this area. First, Samson et al. (1983) conclude in their analysis of 38 studies (both published and unpublished) related to the influence of early field experiences on the attitudes of education students:

> Insufficient information is available about aspects of the subjects and settings, the quality and character of the field experience, the field experience location and other important variables to recommend more specific policies than generally providing early teaching and related experiences in the first few years of college. (p. 11)

Griffin et al. (1983) conclude regarding the literature on student teaching (both published and unpublished):

> A survey of the literature related to teacher education reveals a paucity of information regarding student teaching from a research perspective. . . . Research-based propositions are conspicuous by their absence. . . . The current research derived knowledge base appears to be too limited to direct decisions and practices in clinical experiences for prospective teachers. (pp. 3–4)

The position which has been expressed in this analysis is that the usefulness of the findings of studies or field experiences is closely related to the degree to which individual studies respect the complex ecological reality of the event being studied. Consequently, we will only begin to move closer toward an understanding of the role of field experiences in teacher development when we begin to take more of the ecological reality of these experiences into account in our research. All of the ambiguity and contradiction that characterizes the findings from this body of research (examined as a whole) is not unrelated to the dominant tendency of investigating only isolated bits of this ecology.

At this point in our history there is little if any disagreement as to the importance of providing both early field experiences and student teaching in a teacher education program. The approximate question at this stage of our development as a field is not whether to offer such experiences or not. This is the major interest that is implied, however, in studies that do not describe the particular quality and substance of an experience. Given the undeniable evidence that field experience by itself is not necessarily beneficial in the development of a teacher (Feiman-Nemser, 1983), we must necessarily be concerned with developing conceptual and curricular frameworks for these experiences (e.g., Kindsvatter & Wilen, 1982) and with discovering which particular kinds of field experiences and which individual components within programs contribute to their educative functions. The particular quality of a field experience cannot be understood solely by its procedures (e.g., length), its organizational structure, or even by the curricular intentions and plans of its designers and its influence on teacher development cannot be discerned from the examination of only isolated fragments of its ecology. It is hoped that research on field experiences will give more attention in the future to the complex and multidimensional nature of these experiences and that this ecological approach to the study of field experiences will stimulate discussion and debate over which particular curricular and contextual dimensions of programs will help us more closely realize our goals for teacher development.

REFERENCES

Atkins, M., & Raths, J. (1974). *Changing patterns of teacher education in the U.S.* Paris: O.E.C.O.

Becher, R., & Ade, W. (1982). The relationship of field placement characteristics and students' potential field performance abilities to clinical experience performance ratings. *Journal of Teacher Education, 33*(2), 24–30.

Boschee, F., Prescott, D., & Hein, D. (1978). Do cooperating teachers influence the educational philosophies of student teachers? *Journal of Teacher Education, 24*(2), 57–61.

Bowman, N. (1979). College supervision of student teaching: A time to reconsider. *Journal of Teacher Education, 30*(3), 29–30.

Bronfenbrenner, U. (1976). The experimental ecology of education. *Educational Research, 5*(9), 5–15.

Connor, W., & Smith, L. (1967). *Analysis of patterns of student teaching* (Final Report 5-8204). Washington, DC: U.S. Office of Education, Bureau of Research.

Copeland, W. (1979). Student teachers and cooperating teachers: An ecological relationship. *Theory into Practice, 18*(7), 194–199.

Corcoran, E. (1982). Classroom contexts as settings for learning to teach. *Action in Teacher Education, 4*(1), 52–55.

Davies, D., & Amershek, K. (1969). Student teaching. In R. Ebel (Ed.), *The encyclopedia of educational research.* New York: Macmillan.

Denton, J. (1982). Early field experience influence on performance in subsequent coursework. *Journal of Teacher Education, 33*(2), 19–23.

Dewey, J. (1965). The relation of theory to practice in education. In M. Borrowman (Ed.), *Teacher education in America: A documentary history.* New York: Teachers College Press. (Original work published 1904)

Doyle, W. (1977). Learning to classroom environment: An ecological analysis. *Journal of Teacher Education, 28*(6), 51–55.

Elliott, P., & Mays, R. (1979). *Early field experiences in teacher education.* Bloomington, IN: Phi Delta Kappa (Fastback No. 125).

Feiman-Nemser, S. (1983). Learning to teach. In L. Shulman & G. Sykes (Eds.), *Handbook of teaching and policy.* New York: Longman.

Feiman-Nemser, S., & Buchman, M. (1983). *Pitfalls of experience in teacher preparation.* East Lansing, MI: Institute for Research on Teaching.

Fullan, M., & Pomfret, A. (1977). Research on curriculum and instruction implementation. *Review of Educational Research, 47*(2), 335–397.

Funk, F., Long, B., Keithley, A., & Hoffman, J. (1982). The cooperating teacher as most significant other: A competent humanist. *Action in Teacher Education, 4*(2), 57–64.

Gaskell, P. (1975). *Patterns and changes in the perspectives of student teachers: A participant observation study.* Unpublished doctoral dissertation, Harvard University.

Gehrke, N. (1981). Rationales for field experiences in the professions. In C. Webb, N. Gehrke, P. Ishler, & A. Mendoza (Eds.), *Exploratory field experiences in teacher education.* Reston, VA: Association of Teacher Educators.

Giroux, H. (1980). Teacher education and technology of social control. *Journal of Education, 162*(1), 5–27.

Glassberg, S., & Sprinthall, N. (1980). Student teaching: A developmental approach. *Journal of Teacher Education, 31*(2), 31–38.

Goodman, J. (1983). The seminar's role in the education of student teachers: A case study. *Journal of Teacher Education, 34,* 44–49.

Griffin, G., Barnes, S., Hughes, R. Jr., O'Neal, S., Defino, M., Edwards, S., & Hukill, H. (1983). *Clinical preservice teacher education: Final report of a descriptive study.* Austin, TX: University of Texas R & D Center for Teacher Education.

Henry, M. (1983). The effect of increased explanatory field experiences upon the perceptions and performance of student teachers. *Action in Teacher Education, 5*(1–2), 66–70.

Hersh, R., Hull, R., & Leighton, M. (1982). Student teaching. In H. Mitzel (Ed.), *Encyclopedia of educational research* (5th ed.). New York: The Free Press.

Hodges, C. (1982). Implementing methods: If you can't blame the cooperating teacher who can you blame? *Journal of Teacher Education, 33*(6), 25–29.

Holt, L., & Peterson, K. (1981). University and public school cooperation for professional growth. *Action in Teacher Education, 3*(1), 65–75.

Hook, C., & Rosenshine, B. (1979). Accuracy of teacher reports of their classroom behavior. *Review of Educational Research, 49,* 1–12.

Horowitz, M. (1968). Student teaching experiences and the attitudes of student teachers. *Journal of Teacher Education, 19*(3), 317–323.

Hoy, W., & Rees, R. (1977). The bureaucratic socialization of student teachers. *Journal of Teacher Education, 28*(1), 23–26.

Hultgren, F. (1982). *Reflecting on the meaning of curriculum through a hermeneutic interpretation of student teaching experiences in home economics.* Unpublished doctoral dissertation, Pennsylvania State University.

Iannacone, L., & Button, W. (1964). *Functions of student teaching: Attitude formation and initiation in elementary student teaching.* Washington, DC: U.S. OFfice of Education. (Cooperative Research Project No. 1026).

Ishler, P., & Kay, R. (1981). A survey of institutional practice. In C. Webb, N. Gehrke, P. Ishler, & A. Mendoza (Eds.), *Exploratory field experiences in teacher education.* Reston, VA: Association of Teacher Educators.

Johnson, W., Cox, C.B., & Wood, G. (1982). Communication patterns and topics of single and paired student teachers. *Action in Teacher Education, 4*(1), 56–60.

Johnston, J., & Ryan, K. (1983). Research on the beginning teacher: Implications for teacher education. In K. Howey & R. Dykstra (Eds.), *The education of teachers: A look ahead.* New York: Longman.

Karmos, A., & Jacko, C. (1977). The role of significant others during the student teaching experience. *Journal of Teacher Education, 28*(5), 51–55.

Kindsvatter, R., & Wilen, W. (1982). A clinical experience theory applied to clinical practice. *Action in Teacher Education, 4*(2), 17–26.

Lacey, C. (1977). *Socialization of teachers.* London: Methuen.

Lortie, D. (1973). Observations on teaching as work. In R. Travers (Ed.), *The second handbook of research on teaching.* Chicago: Rand McNally.

Lortie, D. (1975). *School teacher: A sociological study.* Chicago: University of Chicago Press.

Mahlios, M. (1982). Effects of pair formation on the performance of student teachers. *Action in Teacher Education, 4*(2), 65–69.

Mardle, G., & Walker, M. (1980). Strategies and structure: Critical notes on teacher socialization. In P. Woods (Ed.), *Teacher strategies: Explorations in the sociology of the school.* London: Croom Helm.

McCaleb, J. (1979). On reconciling dissonance between preparation and practice. *Journal of Teacher Education, 30*(4), 51–53.

McDonald, F. (1980). The problems of beginning teachers: A crisis in training (Vol. 1). *Study of induction programs for beginning teachers.* Princeton, NJ: Educational Testing Service.

McIntyre, D.J. (1983). *Field experiences in teacher education.* Washington, DC: Foundation for Excellence in Teacher Education and the ERIC Clearinghouse on Teacher Education.

McNaughton, R., Johns, F., & Rogus, J. (1978). Alternative models for revitalizing the school–university partnership. *Action in Teacher Education, 1*(1), 18–29.

Nerenz, A. (1980). *The influence of student teachers on their cooperating teachers' teaching strategies and beliefs about teaching and student teaching in foreign language instruction.* Unpublished doctoral dissertation, University of Wisconsin–Madison.

Parlett, M., & Hamilton, D. (1976). Evaluations as illumination: A new approach to the study of innovatory programs. In G. Glass (Ed.), *Evaluation studies: Review annual* (Vol. 1). Beverly Hills, CA: Sage.

Peck, R., & Tucker, J. (1973). Research on teacher education. In R. Travers (Ed.), *The second handbook of research on teaching.* Chicago: Rand McNally.

Popkewitz, T., Tabachnick, B.R., & Zeichner, K.M. (1979). Dulling the senses: Research in teacher education. *Journal of Teacher Education, 30*(5), 52–60.

Rosenfeld, V. (1969). Possible influences of student teachers on their cooperating teachers. *Journal of Teacher Education, 20*(1), 40–43.

Ross, S., Raines, F., Cervetti, M., & Dellow, D. (1980). Field experiences for teacher candidates: A comparison between tutorial and apprenticeship programs on student activities and attitudes. *Journal of Teacher Education, 31*(6), 57–61.

Ryan, T. (1982). Field experiences in teacher education. In H. Mitzel (Ed.), *Encyclopedia of educational research* (5th ed.). New York: The Free Press.

Samson, G., Borger, J., Weinstein, T., & Walberg, H. (1983, April). *Pre-teaching experiences and attitudes: A qualitative synthesis.* Paper presented at the annual meeting of American Educational Research Association, Montreal.

Shipman, M. (1967). Theory and practice in the education of teachers. *Educational Research, 9*(3), 208–212.

Silvernail, D., & Costello, M. (1983). The impact of student teaching and internship programs on preservice teachers/pupil control perspectives, anxiety levels and teaching concerns. *Journal of Teacher Education, 34*(4), 32–36.

Smith, D.S., & Smith, W. (1979). Teaching the poor: Its effect on student teacher self-concept. *Journal of Teacher Education, 30*(4), 45–49.

Sorenson, G., & Hulpert, R. (1968). Stress in student teaching. *California Journal of Educational Research, 19*(1), 28–33.

Spencer-Hall, D. (1982, March). *Teachers as persons: Case studies of home lives and the implications for staff development.* Paper presented at the annual meeting of American Educational Research Association.

Sprinthall, N., & Thies-Sprinthall, L. (1983). The teacher as an adult learner: A cognitive-developmental view. In G. Griffin (Ed.), *Staff development: The eighty-second yearbook of NSSE (Part II).* Chicago: University of Chicago Press.

Tabachnick, B.R. (1981). Teacher education as a set of dynamic social events. In B.R. Tabachnick, T. Popkewitz, & B. Bszekely (Eds.), *Studying teaching and learning: Trends in Soviet and American research.* New York: Praeger.

Tabachnick, B.R., Zeichner, K.M. (1983). *The impact of the student teaching experience on the development of teacher perspectives.* Madison, WI: Wisconsin Center for Education Research.

Walter, S., & Stivers, E. (1977). The relation of student teachers' classroom behavior and Eriksonian ego identity. *Journal of Teacher Education, 28*(6), 47–50.

Yee, A. (1969). Do cooperating teachers influence the attitudes of student teachers? *Journal of Educational Psychology, 60*(4), 327–332.

Zeichner, K. (1980). Myths and realities: Field-based experiences in preservice teacher education. *Journal of Teacher Education, 31*(6), 45–55.

Zeichner, K. (1983). Alternative paradigms of teacher education. *Journal of Teacher Education, 34*(3), 3–9.

Zeichner, K., & Grant, C. (1981). Biography and social structure in the socialization of student teachers. *Journal of Education for Teaching, 1*, 298–314.

Zeichner, K., & Tabachnick, B.R. (1982). The belief systems of university supervisions in an elementary student teaching program. *Journal of Education for Teaching, 8*(1), 34–54.

Zeichner, K., & Tabachnick, B.R. (1983). *The development of teacher perspectives: Social strategies and institutional control in the socialization of beginning teachers,* Madison, WI: Wisconsin Center for Education Research.

Zeichner, K., & Teitelbaum, K. (1982). Personalized and inquiry-oriented teacher education. *Journal of Education for Teaching, 8*(2), 95–117.

Zimpher, N., deVoss, G., & Nott, D. (1980). A closer look at university student teacher supervision. *Journal of Teacher Education, 31*(4), 11–15.

Chapter 6

Current Trends in Research on University Supervision of Student Teaching

Nancy L. Zimpher

Ohio State University

OVERVIEW

Literature on student teaching is almost excessive, to the point where much is produced annually, creating a case of exponential redundancy. The great books that guide our current understanding of student teaching stem from the works of Mead (1930), Curtis and Andrews (1954), Stratemeyer and Lindsey (1958), and Andrews (1964), to name but a few; all seminal works in outlining the nature of how we conduct the capstone experience for prospective teachers. Iterations of the last decade have added little to that base, except for a clearer understanding of the complex political and legal pitfalls (Hazard, 1976; Hazard, Freeman, Eisdorfer, & Tractenberg, 1977) of university–school collaboration (Lang, Quick, & Johnson, 1975). None of these citations would really be categorized as "research" on student teaching. Nonetheless, a recent Educational Resources Information Center (ERIC) search on the combined categories of "student teaching" and "field experiences" generated 1852 entries from 1966 to the present. The result of a subsequent search, combining field experience with "student teacher supervisors" (and also the descriptor "college faculty") reduced the number of specifically related entries to 412 references. Applying 16 category descriptors that refer to research, bibliographies, state-of-the-art reviews, and investigations (called by 12 more descriptors) reduced the entries to be considered to 73. If, to that search, the term "evaluation studies" is added, another 138 citations are produced. Further, a search of dissertation abstracts, using essentially the same descriptors, generated another 165 references. A decision was made to refer to dissertations only as they were referenced in journal articles, books, or other ERIC documents, leaving the 211 entries from the previous search to be reviewed. On final analysis, only about 35 of these entries dealt specifically with the role of the university supervisor in student teaching. The other entries, though often referring to the "supervsor," in reality dealt only with classroom or cooperating teacher supervision, or with the totality of the student teaching or field experience program, with little mention of the university supervisor. Most of the usual citations available through ERIC, through additional journal searches, and through random access to more fugitive and ephemeral documents (presentations, copied papers) constitute the substance of the review of research in the present study.

The text is organized first around extant research reviews on student teaching, field experiences, and teacher education, culling only those aspects relevant to the university supervisor's role. A second section is devoted to an in-depth analysis of three clusters of studies that shed light on the actual instructional supervision activities of the university supervisor. Finally, two conceptualizations consistently referred to in the existing literature base are posited to inform future inquiry into student teaching and university supervision. Although these conceptions have numerous referents in the literature, they have not systematically informed the nature of our activities and investigations. It is clearly the intent of the present study to summarize and then set aside much of the descriptive information available from our past efforts, in hopes that more intensive and extensive studies of a sound conceptual base will characterize our efforts in the future.

STATE-OF-THE-ART REVIEWS

Study and research related to student teaching can be characterized as meager, diverse, and trivial. Its meagerness is a function of the fact that the knowledgeable people who work with student teachers are essentially practitioners, not researchers. Its diversity is a function of the fact that there are few monies for research available in this area and thus the most common inquiry into student teaching has been one-time-only doctoral dissertations. These studies all conclude with a chapter advising others on ways to follow up on research but rarely if ever is this done. The often trivial nature of this research is a function of the fact that those who do an occasional study are unfamiliar with the basic nature of student teaching and regard it as teaching behavior rather than learning behavior. They also make the mistake of viewing it as largely individual behavior driven by knowledge and personality rather than as organizational behavior driven by the press of various conditions, norms, and events in the school setting. (Haberman, 1983, p. 98)

To further compound the work of the reviewer, rarely in the student teaching literature does the university supervisor become central to the discussion (Griffin & Edwards, 1981). Even in small sample studies, Griffin and Edwards (1981) found that "what attention *is* given is usually peripheral or a small part of one of the other participant's perceptions of the supervisor's role in such typical events as assignments, evaluation or reporting processess" (p. 121). Nevertheless, it is possible to extract for research syntheses bits and pieces of information that might ultimately contribute to some conception of who the university supervisor is, how supervisors think about their role, and how their beliefs and attitudes and their perception of role drive the nature of their interaction with student teachers (Koehler, 1984).

For purposes of this discussion, the reviewer has selected six significant research syntheses, some focused solely on student teaching, and some extending across all laboratory and clinical experiences, to organize the research information currently available regarding university supervision. These syntheses are as follows: Locke (1979), Griffin, Hughes, Defino, and Barnes (1981), McIntyre (1983), Haberman (1983), McIntyre (1984), and Zeichner (1984). Zeichner's chapter in this volume presents an extremely useful conceptualization for reviewing studies on field experience, and by implication draws references to overlooked areas of study regarding university supervision.

Being cautious not to oversimplify a rather disparate and unconnected literature base, an attempt is made to organize the themes presented in these syntheses to facilitate our discussion. The reviews referenced are displayed in chronological order in Table 1 against a set of constructs proposed in Griffin et al.'s (1981) review, which appear to be fairly compatable with issues addressed in the remaining reviews. This framework is as follows:

1. The characteristics of each of the individuals in the clinical experience.
2. The selection process applied to each.
3. The social/psychological interactions and mutual influences among the student teaching participants.
4. The planned and unplanned activities, as they relate to on-going functioning and goal-attainment of the student teaching experience.
5. The contextual influences which shape, frame, and to varying degrees determine the nature of the student teaching experience. (p. 4)

In this section of the chapter, a comparative analysis is drawn between and among findings cited in the contributing reviews. However, several comments need to be made first about the problems associated with such an analysis. First, the categories used by each of the reviewers are in no way precisely matched to the framework already proposed. Therefore, there is no intention to represent these categories as mutually exclusive. Further, certain areas of interest are in one review categorized one way and in other reviews differently. Perhaps the most salient example is teacher socialization, particularly in characterizing the role field experiences play in teacher development. Grif-

TABLE 1.   A Compilation of Recent Research Reviews According to the Griffin (1981) Framework

Concepts	Reviews					
	Locke (1979)	Griffin, et al. (1981)	McIntyre (1983)	Haberman (1983)	McIntyre (1984)	Zeichner (1984)
1. Characteristics of participants (ST, CT, US)		X				X
2. The selection process, characteristics of role		X				
3. Interactions and mutual influences of the participants	X	X	X	X	X	X
4. Planned and unplanned activities (supervising practice, evaluation, socialization)	X	X	X	X	X	X
5. Contextual features		X	X			X

Note. ST = Student teacher; CT = Cooperating teacher; US = University Supervisor.

fin et al. (1981) refers to socialization as a part of the planned and unplanned activities of student teaching. On the other hand, Zeichner (this volume) uses it as an ongoing concept for considering three major categories from the Griffin framework (i.e., structure and content of experiences, which is used synonymously with "planned and unplanned activities"; characteristics of placement sites, as "contextual influences"; and the relationships between education students and other people as "interactions and mutual influences" and "characteristics of participants").

Second, all six of these reviews go beyond the limited conception of the role of the university supervisor, reviewing in most cases a larger set of data regarding the totality of the student teaching experience, or the interaction of multiple participants in the experience. Because the focus of the present study is on the university supervisor, information extrapolated from the reviews attempt to focus primarily on aspects of university supervision and those factors or persons who interact with or influence that role.

Further, by virtue of my own review of research in this area, I found that across reviews, certain clusters of studies have been omitted from a particular reviewer's framework. So as topics are discussed, additional studies and clusters of studies will be inserted to attempt as comprehensive a picture as possible. And finally, this is not a synthesis that attempts to assess the particular nature of the six reviews or to claim their ownership of particular concepts or frameworks. Rather, the synthesis that follows is solely an attempt to categorize and characterize the nature of extant research on university supervision; a task made much more doable by the prior work of these reviewers.

The Characteristics of Participants

Both Griffin et al. (1981) and Zeichner (this volume) reflect on the characteristics of individuals involved in the student teaching triad: the student teacher (ST); the cooperating teacher (CT); and the university supervisor (US). Yarger, Howey, and Joyce (1977) present a demographic profile of the "typical" university education faculty member as a 43-year-old Anglo male, with working experience in public schools; a population from which the profession draws most of its USs (at least half of all teacher educators have supervisory duty). The issue of experience is addressed in a study by Lamb and Montague (1982), who found that STs perceived little difference in the effectiveness of supervisors who were graduate students and not faculty, and between those who had had significant teaching experiences and those who had not.

Griffin and Edwards (1981) confirms the wide variations in experience and expertise of persons assigned to the role, and Hanke (1967) confirms that supervisors have little training for their role. Johnson and Yates (1982) and McIntyre and Norris (1980) have identified measures of load, assignment, and use of time, but only descriptively, and not in relation to impact.

Studies of individual differences cover such concepts as self-concept, cognitive development, interpersonal characteristics, interest in other people, and measures of flexibility and creativity. University supervisor self-concept has generally been explored in regard to degree of comfort with role (Griffin, et al., 1983). Work in cognitive development stems from studies by Sprinthall and Thies-Sprinthall (1983) and McDonald (1980) and reflects the importance of theories of stage development, not just in relation to student teachers, but also of those with whom they work. Degree of empathy as characterized by the work of Carkhuff (1971) and in supervision models presented by Goldhammer (1969) and Cogan (1973) is attended to in several studies on supervision practice in student teaching, particularly in Jones (1980), Junell (1969), and Copeland and Atkinson (1978). The need for caring tendencies and an expressed interest in people is documented in studies by Yarger et al. (1977), Isam, Carter, and Stribling (1981), and Solliday (1982). Cirirelli (1969) verifies that the degree of creativity exhibited by USs helps them recognize creativity in their teachers.

Selection and Perception of Role

The literature on selection relates primarily to STs and CTs. Although many descriptive guides present preferred characteristics of effective supervisors, and by implication, criteria that could be used for selection, none of these references constitute actual research studies on selection of USs. Griffin et al. (1981) call for basic descriptive studies in this area. Instead, the literature is repleat with descriptive surveys of role characteristics and perception of role by both CTs and USs. In a study by Frenzel (1977) all respondents (STs, CTs, and principals) saw three aspects of US role as vital to student teaching: their visits and conferences, their insurance of a quality program, and their positive perception of the activities of the student teaching experience.

Other studies on US role describe the ideal characteristics of USs: in Stewig's (1970) survey of 1000 STs; five most frequent US activities, (in Solliday, 1982), including observation and evaluation of STs, leading seminars, teaching other methods courses, serving on university and school committees, and serving as a liaison between the university and field sites; English's (1971) study surveying practice of USs nationally, including three significant functions: of liaison, coordinator among all participants, and the administrator of the student teaching experience; and Nerenz's (1979) study which emphasizes the importance of US's "teachers" role, followed by the role of coordinator, counselor, curriculum specialist, and evaluator. The US role is reported by Waters (1974) to be below expected performance, even though the counseling function was rated as valuable, and Griffin and Edwards (1981) report lack of clarity of US role as to whether supervisors are to be teachers, mediators, guides, translators of policy, or role models. Koehler (1984) reports that USs perceive themselves to be, most importantly, liaisons and moral supporters.

Interactions and Mutual Influences

Probably no other category has received as much attention in the research literature as have studies that seek to determine the influence of the US and significant others (e.g., cooperating teacher) in the development of STs. The McIntyre (1984) review is devoted almost exclusively to this topic, and it is discussed in each of the other reviews as well.

The litany of results begins with a consideration of studies that attempt to determine the influence of the CT, and by implication, the lack of influence of the US. The direct influence of the CT, as reported by STs, is revealed in studies by Karmos and Jacko (1977) and Manning (1977); in regard to influence on ST attitude by Dunham (1958), Price (1961), Johnson (1969) Mahan and Lacefield (1976), Villeme and Hall (1975), Dutton (1982), Alper and Retish (1972), Dispoto (1980), Henry and Sa'ad (1977), Wilbur and Gooding (1977); in regard to influence through changes in personal characteristics by Coss (1959) and Scott and Brinkley (1960); in influencing aspects of classroom management by Hoy (1967, 1968, 1969), Fink (1976), Wilbur and Gooding (1977), Williamson and Campbell (1978), Iannacone (1963), and Iannacone and Button (1964); and finally, in general ST behavior by Seperson and Joyce (1973), Zevin (1974), and Price (1961).

The criticism that USs exercise little influence as instructional leaders espoused by Diamonti (1977) is dealt with directly and confirmed in studies by Sandgren and Schmidt (1956), Schueler, Gold, and Mitzel (1962), Morris (1974), Waters (1974), Barrows (1979), Evans (1976), Friebus (1977), and Yee (1969); wherein measures reflected no significant US influence on ST attitude or behavior. A study by Boschee, Prescott, and Hein (1978) suggests that neither CTs nor USs influence STs significantly. Such results reflecting either little or no nfluence of USs on STs have caused a host of educators to call for a shift in or the reduction or dissolution of the US role, and are cited here because of the ongoing debate on this particular issue, as follows: Patty (1973), Emans (1983), Bennie (1964), Spangler (1972), Andrews (1964), Spillane and Levenson (1976), Monson and Bebb (1970), Bowman (1979), Morris (1974), and Smith (1969). Those working in developing more effective supervision models (including Locke, 1979) ultimately call for a reduced role for the US, for instance, in Glassberg and Sprinthall's (1980) developmental approach to supervision and Siedentop's (1981) applied behavioral analysis model.

In an effort to counter arguments waged from one research study to another, McIntyre (1984) and Locke (1979) attempt to create a portrait that reflects negative CT influence on ST development. Locke's (1979) review is particularly pungent. He suggests that CTs encourage students to go with what works (Iannacone, 1963), to exercise order and authority in the classroom (Hoy & Rees, 1977), to adopt the CT's ideology (Salzillo & Van Fleet, 1977), to exhibit more hostility and authority as success indicators (Chabassol, 1968), to become more dogmatic (Johnson, 1969), more rigid and less liberal (Jacobs, 1968), less pupil centered (Walberg, 1968), more directed (Horowitz, 1968), and more bureaucratic (Pruitt & Lee, 1978).

In further opposition to the findings regarding US lack of influence, a cluster of studies have appeared that attempt to assess directly the influence of US, sources of influence on ST development, and the negative and positive dimensions of that influence. The Copenhaver, McIntyre, and Norris (1981) study and the Sacks and Harrington (1982) study counter the negative influence of CTs as forming custodial, authoritarian, and bureaucratic tendencies in STs, by documenting ST attitude at the end of student teaching to be more student centered and concerned for the emotional needs of pupils than control oriented. A study conducted by Zeichner (1978) suggest that ST socialization is less a function of the belief systems of CTs than the school sites.

Studies on role conflict further reflect the dilemma in sorting out lines of influence between CTs and USs. Differences of opinion among all three parties in the triad center on issues of evaluation and the resource consultant functions of the US (Kaplan, 1967); conflict about the ST assignment in the school site (Farley, 1973); and differing program expectations (Prokop, 1973; Simms, 1975; Clemons, 1973; Campbell & Williamson, 1973).

Almost all of the reviewers cited herein suggest that conclusions about CT influence, and the lack of US influence on ST development is in large part related to the design of studies used to establish lines of influence. Specifically, Locke (1979), McIntyre (1984), and Zeichner (1978) call for more naturalistic studies in regard to the complexities of influence, role, and ST development. One such study was conducted by Zimpher, deVoss, and Nott (1980) and revealed that without the influencing presence of the US little critical review of the ST's progress would have been conducted. Further, positive activities of the US include setting goals and expectations, serving as a personal confidante, intercepting problems with the principal, providing ST input into setting requirements, and encouraging self-analysis and improvement. Other studies, though not all of a qualitative mode, also support the positive influence of university supervisors, including studies reporting perceived US importance by STs (Smith & Alverman, 1983; Corrigan & Griswold, 1963; Seperson & Joyce, 1973; McIntyre, Buell, & Casey, 1979; Bennie, 1964). Even in studies where CT influence is primary, positive effects of US supervision were found (Friebus, 1977, as coaches; Karmos & Jacko, 1977, supervisors ranked second; and Becher and Ade, 1982, on reinforcement of goals and expectations of the experience).

Planned and Unplanned Activities

Structure and Content of the Field Experience Program. Zeichner contends in his chapter in this text, that references to structure and content (that is, the goals and substance of programs) are infrequently and inadequately examined in most studies of student teaching and field experience. Other studies suggest that the intended goals, when explicated, are often not, in fact, related to the activities that are actually implemented. Studies that support this contention include Zeicher and Tabachnick's (1982), Goodman's (1983), and Ross, Raines, Cervetti, and Dellow's (1980) conclusion that diverse orientations and perspectives impact on actual curriculum implementation. This finding is illustrated as Griffin (1983) reports little evidence of ST use of certain program guides during the course of student teaching. Surveys of other studies on student teaching, beyond the 20 reviewed by Zeichner and the others mentioned, do not reveal exemplary studies in regard to relating program structure to program outcomes. Rather there abound a considerable number of program description entries, but these descriptive data are not interwoven into any substained pattern of inquiry, with the exception of the Griffin et al. (1983) comprehensive study of student teaching.

From the perspective of considering the role of the US, another view of structure, purpose, and content would be that of the supervisory models used during student teaching. Locke (1979) carefully reiterates the categorical attempts reflected in recent student teaching research, using the three categories proposed by Metzler (1981) regarding systematic observation; that is, "eyeballing," the oral transmission to the ST from the supervisor's perceptions; anecdotal recording in which the supervisor writes down impressions; and rating scales, in which a permanent record of the ST's performance is categorized by some system or inventory of indicators or variables. Metzler cites research in physical education and general student teaching including critical incident research (Wright, 1965; Gibson, 1969), observation instrument studies (Weller, 1969; Kraft, 1974), interaction analysis studies (Keilty, 1975), and the applied behavioral analysis studies summarized by Siedentop (1981). Other supervision models recorded include peer supervision (Dodds, 1975) and self-supervision (Dessecher, 1975). Copeland's (1977) work on skill acquisition through supervision, and later studies on directive and nondirective supervision techniques (Copeland, 1980, 1982; Copeland & Atkinson, 1978) demonstrate the interaction of supervision models and styles with ST preferences in which STs generally preferred more directive supervision approaches.

It is difficult to distinguish studies that reflect supervisory approaches in many cases from those that assess approaches to ST evaluation. However, a cluster of studies on supervision practice related specifically to evaluation activity are not particularly complimentary to the university supervisor's ability to make evaluative judgments or to make judgments that are predictive of subsequent ST success on the job. McIntyre (1983) reports on a cluster of studies that reflect the personalized nature of US evaluation measures (Tom, 1974; Mahan & Hartse, 1977), the disagreement over the weight of agreed upon criteria (Morris, 1980), and the inability of USs to make distinctions between outstanding and ineffective teaching (Vittetoe, 1972), concurred with by Diamonti's (1977) perceptive observation that USs have difficulty making judgments about the STs that fall between the extremes. Barrows' (1979) contention is that USs exercise little authority in regard to the evaluation of STs readily accept the assessments offered by CTs (in conflict with the Zimpher et al., 1980 finding that CTs are rarely critical or evaluative), and give CTs much power in evaluation by default. Irvine (1983) found that high US ratings related to higher pupil learning achievement; however, this assumption is refuted in a study relating student teacher skill to learner cognitive attainment (Denton & Kazimi, 1982). Other studies using pupil performance to validate US ratings of ST performance are found in Capie, Eilett, and Johnson (1980) and Savage (1980).

Socialization.   Zeichner in this volume has reflected on the nature of teacher socialization and development, contrasting the views of scholars who judge the experiences of preservice teachers in elementary and secondary schools as inhibiting the development of innovative, reflective, and competent teachers (Friedenberg, 1973; Lortie, 1975; Salzillo & Van Fleet, 1977; Schoenrock, 1980) to those whose research refutes the "social-puppet" view

(McIntyre, 1983) of teacher socialization (Zeichner, 1980a; Egan, 1982; Roberts & Blankenship, 1970; Lacey, 1977; Lortie, 1975; Zeichner & Tabachnick, 1981). Determining the role of the US in enhancing positive teacher socialization is a complex effort, partly dependent on sorting out degrees of influence, on impact of program structures and supervisory purposes, and the ecological context in which the student teaching experience occurs. Initially socialization has been reflected in a series of stage studies (Iannacone, 1963; Caruso, 1977). There are more sophisticated studies representing the complexity of this process. Studies of discourse in supervisory conferences (Zeichner, this volume), personalized versus inquiry-oriented experiences (Zeichner, 1981; Tabachnick, Zeichner, Densmore, Adler, Egan, 1982) reflect these current trends and leave "the notion that preservice students passively absorb institutional doctrines" (McIntyre, 1983, p. 10) open to question.

Contextual Influences

Griffin and Edwards (1981) describes contextual influences as those that shape, frame, and to varying degrees determine the nature of the student teaching experiences. Influence of context are cited in the Becher and Ade (1982) study wherein STs were placed in three different classroom settings, the effects of which were mitigated, they speculate, by influences of the US discouraging modeling behavior of STs of their CT. In this case, contextual influences did not weigh as heavily as advice from the USs.

Properties of the school context are also influenced by the policies, procedures, and personnel provided by the university to guide the conduct of the student teaching experience. However, there is little evidence that these university contextual features are being addressed in the literature, beyond the supervisor's inclination to role assignment (cited in the discussion on role), time available to commit to the task (McIntyre & Norris, 1980), and status within the school site (Koehler, 1984). Studies of a more comprehensive nature, particularly Griffin et al. (1983), do document in more deliberate terms the activities of supervisors as does the Zimpher et al. (1980) study on university supervision. The schools as contexts are more heavily studied, and have been addressed in two previous sections of this report, particularly in reference to studies by Hoy and Rees (1977) and Pruitt and Lee (1978) on the bureaucratic net of the school site. Other contextual influences, such as home and personal interactions seem to arise in the influence studies where STs rank their peers as extremely influential sources of support during student teaching.

Summary

The present study has attempted a fairly technical and hopefully comprehensive reflection of the extant studies on student teaching and field experiences that bear even remotely on the role of the US. Employing a conceptual framework introduced by Griffin and Edwards (1981), the results of six recent research syntheses have been combined to reflect as comprehensive a portrait as possible of "what is out there." At every turn, the reviewer decried the sorry state of research on student teaching in general and on university supervision. Haberman (1983) has described the literature on student teaching and field experience as not research at all, but development, filled with "shoulds" and "oughts" to inform future practice. Zeichner (1980a) suggests that there is a great deal of confusion and contradiction surrounding the data that do exist. McIntyre (1984) refers to the literature base as superficial and misguided and in need of a more naturalistic, less statistical focus. Locke (1979) laments this psychometric focus, and calls for more in situ research. Griffin and Edwards (1981) say the research has been on isolated aspects of student teaching without consideration of the complexities of this phenomenon. His review of the literature uncovered a vast quantity of studies on student teaching and field experience, but few that were empirical, or large scaled in design.

EXEMPLARY STUDIES ON UNIVERSITY SUPERVISION OF STUDENT TEACHING

Reflecting on the collective criticisms of current research on university supervision of STs, occasional examples that ran counter to these criticisms did surface in this review of research. In particular, four studies will be reported that in method and substance represent more intensive and extensive explorations of university supervision than the norm of those reported so far. Although reference to these studies has been woven into the previous discussion, their expanded analysis here is to highlight their attempts to sort out the complex influences and interactions of USs. The results of these studies, viewed collectively, offer a provocative statement on the nature of the US's role in student teaching, in answer to the question, "What do university supervisors do?"

Further, there is little attention given in many of the studies reported to actual supervisory practice, with particular reference to the process of supervision (defined as critical attention to the ST in the classroom setting). Three clusters of studies are presented that are exemplary in this respect. After a rather exhaustive search, I have concluded that these efforts stand alone as longitudinal attempts to document supervisory practice and impact. This section is intended to answer the question, "What models exist of supervisory approach?"

The reviews of these two groups of studies are offered as models for further inquiry, both in respect to their methodologies and their substantive focus. In each instance neither method or focus is without fault, but together these efforts constitute sound direction for our continued inquiry.

What Do University Supervisors Do?

In probably the most comprehensive descriptive study of student teaching to date, the Research in Teacher Education (RITE) program of the Research and Development Center for Teacher Education and the University of Texas at Austin developed and implemented a multiside, multimethod, semester-long study during the 1981–82 school year (Griffin et al., 1983). The primary objective of the study was "to provide a rich description of the phenomenon such that it could be better understood and, it is hoped, made more effective" (p. xix). It was comprehensive in nature, using extensive data sets, with attention to a large number of variables, singly and in interaction, to focus on STs, CTs, and USs, and the contexts for their interactions. The data were collected at two univesity settings (a large urban area and a midsized less urban area), in 35 school sites, and involving 93 STs, 88 CTs, and 17 USs. Further, individual participants were described in personal, professional, and demographic terms, characterized through measures of empathy, locus of control, flexibility, educational preparation, teacher concerns, cognitive level and style, work-like perceptions, and vocabulary. In addition to descriptions and comparisons of these attributes, interactions between and among participants were described, as were the characteristics of each school site and the nature of the supervisory process.

For purposes of the present study, particular attention is given to exactly the nature of the supervisory process, with particular attention to the US's role and influence upon the totality of the student teaching process. As noted in the aforementioned comprehensive report, some overall findings are particularly worthy of attention here. There are, however, a series of published statements regarding particular dimensions of this study that should be reviewed concurrent with the overall summary, including the O'Neal (1983) study of supervision and feedback, and Defino (1983) investigation of evaluation practices, the Barnes (1983) study of STs' planning and decision-making related to pupil evaluation, and Griffin's (1983) focus on the commonplaces of schooling. Viewed in concert with the major study summary, the single most significant observation regarding student teaching is that supervision is viewed as the most important feature of the student teaching experience and that, in the second place, that process, the study finds, is dominated largely by the CT. The comprehensive summary appears to be not so much a summary of more or less influence by the US, but rather a characterization of the US's interaction being viewed in light of how USs interact with CTs, as well as STs. Further, the study profiles USs, in contrast to cooperating teachers, as more interpersonally tolerant, more secure in their role, more independent and more socially tolerant than either CTs or STs, more progressive in their educational philosophy, and exhibiting a higher level of self-esteem than CTs (p. 123).

As to a collective view of the supervisory practices exhibited in the triad, the following statements characterize the process revealed throughout the study:

1. Supervision is dominated by the CT, who assumed a major role in leading the ST through the total experience, and particularly the weekly conferences.
2. The context of supervisory comments and discussions were situation specific and temporally immediate, concerned with the day-to-day of classroom life.
3. The CT's influence was characterized by encouraging STs to "learn my way and find your way."
4. There was little attention in the triad to using or inventing a codified knowledge base to inform practice.
5. The supervisors (both CTs and USs) tended not to generalize the specific and temporal criticisms from the immediate situation to other possible settings and situations.
6. Most of the talk about the STs by their supervisors was more of a personal nature than professional or classroom-relevant.
7. The STs spoke of "liking" their CTs, and thought their university supervisors could have been more helpful.
8. The STs reported their experiences in personal rather than professional dimensions, liked their CTs if they were "warm," and thought of their USs as "someone the ST can come to for any reason whatever," in contrast to the strictly professional talk they shared with cooperating teachers.
9. The two dominant themes of the evaluative aspects of the supervision process focused on instruction and methods of lesson preparation. (Griffin, 1983, pp. 325–327)

To the extent reflected above, which is intended to capture the generally descriptive nature of this comprehensive study, we now have a well documented account of a number of student teaching experiences from which to generalize about common practice. This picture confirms in some ways the influential presence of the CT, but does not relegate the role of university supervision, contradicting other proposals to eliminate this role. The study does not, however, convey a profile of university supervision that is particularly rigorous, inquiry based, or clinical with respect to classroom observations. In fact, the report repeatedly reflects a social rather than professional orientation to student teaching that minimizes the presence of critical or analytical self-reflection on teaching by the ST, the CT, and the US. Through all of the description, the need to probe deeper into the antecedents and consequences of passive (i.e., lacking professional rigor) university supervision is apparent.

Fortunately, the Koehler (1984) study does just that. From the larger RITE population, Koehler draws a subsample "to explore the beliefs, intentions and knowledge bases of nine university supervisors; and their sense of efficacy in relation to their performance as supervisors" (p. 3). Also drawn from the data sources of the larger study are results of structured interviews, demographic information on supervisors, their notes on interactions with STs, and transcriptions of triad conferences. Again, as with the RITE study, two different university populations were used. This is a particularly rich analysis and provides some new and some corroborating information as to perceptions of role and activities, as well as sense of efficacy, particularly in relation to conditions of service on the two contrasting university–school sites. A new dimension, the exploration of US views on teaching, is correlated with their perceptions of ST success and problem analysis.

Specifically Koehler (1984) reports US role descriptions as follows: USs viewed their primary responsibility as serving a support function for STs, facilitating growth, and the reduction of conflict in the school sites. Other functions, in order as reported, include serving as a liaison between the university and the schools, providing STs and CTs with a set of expectations, providing clinical support for the personal and professional aspects of student teaching to the ST, securing good placements for the STs, orienting the ST to the school site, evaluating the ST (mostly in terms of growth, not in absolutes), providing observation feedback, and conducting seminars. Most supervisors reported major problems to be in the breakdown of communications, or in establishing group cohesiveness in the triad.

As a descriptive profile, effective supervisors were described by themselves and their CTs/STs as flexible, cooperative, hard working, humorous, and able to work with others. They also viewed themselves as pressed for time and overburdened with other responsibilities. They reported mostly weekly school/classroom visitations, felt they had received little in courses or instruction that actually prepared them for their role, relied heavily on their own experiences as teachers and STs as referents for their professional advice to their STs, viewed the seminar as critical and wished they had done a better job as seminar leaders, and reported, as did the STs, on the singular importance of the CT to the whole enterprise.

In terms of the USs' sense of efficacy, the value of their role, an assessment of their impact on the STs, both populations of USs agreed on several points: Collectively they felt they were actually able to teach the STs very little, particularly in regard to teaching skills (by implication the STs got these on their own or from their CTs). The impact the supervisors believed they did have fell in the personal dimension; that is, reinforcing the personal qualities of a sense of humor, a good attitude, and the fun of working with children. Upon reflection, this population of USs resented being put in a situation (presumably by the CTs and STs) where they "had to play the heavy," by being too critical of the STs. Efficacy was also determined largely by institutional affiliation, an issue addressed in much of the rhetorical literature on student teaching, but rarely reported, as in this study, in the bold relief of two very precise and different role orientations.

Specifically, supervisors from MU (a private, midsized institution in an urban area) were paid jointly by the university and the school district; supervisors from SU (a large state institution) were full-time university staff members. MU supervisors viewed themselves as school based, functioning in an extremely supportive atmosphere, enjoying considerable status in the school, whose primary purpose as a supervisor was to offer support to the STs, and not clinical supervision. These supervisors reported a strong sense of efficacy and role satisfaction. The SU supervisors were university based, did not feel that they "belonged" at the school, felt their job was almost impossible to accomplish, were more critical of the STs, felt one of their STs did not approve of their feedback, and suffered from a feeling of low status among their university colleagues. They enjoyed no strong sense of role efficacy.

This is an incredible statement of condition. In a situation where the assumed role of the US is to offer critical feedback, which is ignored by CTs and resented by STs, conditions of service that tie the supervisor more closely to the university (presumedly the base for an inquiry reference in student teaching) militate against supervisor sense of efficacy in that role. In contrast, supervisors who seem to enjoy more comfort in role and better interpersonal relations with the CTs and STs, deny their critical supervisory function in lieu of the social dimensions of student teaching, and consequently experience greater role efficacy. This portrait raises more questions than it answers, but undeniably confirms the findings of a more intensive, single-site study conducted by Zimpher, et al. (1980).

Zimpher et al. (1980) and Koehler (1984) report similar conceptions of the US role including the liaison and support function, the lack of supervisor impact in effecting critical feedback, and a professional, inquiry-based reflection on teaching on the part of STs. Both studies credit the US with establishment of role expectations, and Zimpher et al. further note that no goals would be set were it not for the presence of the US. The absence of CT critical feedback is confirmed by both studies, as is the role of all USs in the personal dimensions of student teaching, including personal support, serving as a confidante, and generally just being available to talk to both the CTs and the STs on any topic, but mostly in the personal dimension. In both studies the supervisors see themselves as trouble-shooters and problem solvers, who spend a great deal of their time resolving communication problems. Supervisors in both studies report being bothered by lack of time, failure to make adequate observations and to provide useful feedback, a sense of lost opportunity re-garding seminars, and a general sense of lack of efficacy. One can conclude from the results of the Koehler study that the characteristics that applied to the "SU" supervisors' conditions of service were precisely the same for the university supervisor in the Zimpher et al. study and may have been in large part the major contributing factor to lack of efficacy in the later case. The in-teraction of the results of these two studies draws a confounding portrait of USs, their belief system, and sense of efficacy.

In a fourth study, conducted by Zeichner and Tabachnick (1982) on a pop-ulation of USs, we are given yet another vantage point from which to con-sider what USs do. This study does not, in method, attempt the comprehen-sive analysis of all participants and contexts as do the other three studies cited, but rather focuses specifically on what supervisors believe about their roles and how those roles are executed. In a study of nine USs, the researchers conducted interviews of the supervisors, reviewed the specific criteria used by the USs to evaluate STs, and inquired as to the supervisors' sense of efficacy (perceived impact on the beliefs and practices of their STs), their perceptions of individual and institutional constraints which prevented goal attainment, and their view of themselves in relation to the cultures of the classrooms in which they offered supervision.

From this analysis, Zeichner and Tabachnick (1982) were able to draw three different profiles of the supervisors involved, each representing a dis-tinct belief system which influenced their actions as supervisors. Even though all nine supervisors saw their role as clinical supervisors, implementing prac-tices to support the program goal of critical reflection on the part of their STs, cared about students developing in directions the students valued, and were concerned about improving students' technical skills in teaching, they all went about their roles in distinctive ways, as follows:

1. *Technical–instrumental supervision* — a focus on the techniques of teach-ing in a specific classroom situation, or the "how" of teaching.
2. *Personal growth-centered supervision* — a focus on student identified goals, on the student's own development, on the "what" and "why" of spe-cific classroom teachings.
3. *Critical supervision* — a focus on the discovery of linkages between actors in specific classrooms, the character of schools, and how the student teachers might become a change agent in that context. (pp. 43–48)

Issues that distinguished these profiles involved the extent to which the super-visor saw teaching and learning as limited to the classroom or as a part of a larger social context; the kinds of questions supervisors raised to the STs about teaching, and whether supervisors focused only on teaching practices observed or tried to develop ST perspective in relation to larger social con-cerns and educational issues.

This study has to its credit an indepth analysis of some of the supervisory practices only intimated in Koehler (1984) and Zimpher et al. (1980). It may be possible to return to these studies and attempt a characterization of the MU/SU supervisors and the Zimpher et al. supervisor as one of these three types, although the data base may not be sufficient. On the other hand, Zeichner and Tabachnick (1982) caution that their analysis has limited utility because it deals more with intent than practice. They suggest that the supervisors may have been only partially conscious of the beliefs and assumptions that drove their actions, and that to determine the links with practice we must view beliefs and actions together, in the context not only of the conference role, or expanded expectations, but in terms of the totality of the student teaching phenomenon. What Koehler and Zimpher et al. sacrifice in depth, Zeichner and Tabachnick concede in limited context. But all three studies attempt an analysis that goes beyond overt practice to conceptions of belief, intention, action, and efficacy that provides a model conception for future studies.

What Models Exist of Supervisory Approach?

Models of supervisory practice abound, particularly in relation to the supervision of inservice teachers. The explications of clinical supervisions by Goldhammer (1969), Cogan (1973), and Acheson and Gall (1980); of counseling supervision by Mosher and Purpel (1972); and of developmental supervision by Glickman (1980) pose contrasting models of supervision from diverse conceptual referents. There exists little research on supervising practice in student teaching that strictly reflects any one of these approaches. In fact, little research in student teaching is devoted to a description of supervisory practice, regardless of the models just described. There are, however, at least three sets of studies that present contrasting approaches to supervisory practice in student teaching and reflect consistent attention to method and impact, assessed over time. These studies are as follows: Siedentop's (1981) use of an applied behavioral approach to supervision, Gitlin's (1981) development and impact, (Gitlin, Ogawa, & Rose's 1982, 1984) studies on horizontal supervision and Copeland and Atkinson (1978), Copeland (1980, 1982) analysis of directive and nondirective supervision. These studies do not by any means exhaust the available research on supervision practice, but have been selected because of their focus on STs, because they offer contrasting models, and because they beg the ultimate question of intent versus practice, raised again by Zeichner and Liston (1984) in a study on supervisory discourse.

In 1981, Siedentop reported on 8 years of study on the supervision of student teaching, using applied behavioral analysis to effect change in behavior of practicing STs. Driven by conclusions, pre 1972, that little evidence existed to suggest that supervision of teaching made any difference, a group of researchers launched an intensive effort to design a model of supervision that could impact on ST behavior. Their conceptual orientation was rooted in the belief that through behavior analysis, changes in behavior could be effected. The entire research program, reported in dissertations and a series of articles and conference proceedings is summarized in the Siedentop (1981) report. Specifically, the method relied on systematic observations and replications to insure both internal and external validity, and was consistently stable throughout the several studies. With each iteration of the observation systems, coding formats increased in complexity, certain behaviors were isolated or sampled over different periods of time, creating 80% reliability with scored internal rating techniques. Taped recording cues helped observers with internal consistency. Statistical tests, multiple baseline data, and visual analyses of graphic data served as rigorous tools for single-subject data analysis. The observation system (reported in Siedentop & Hughley, 1975) represented a small set of teacher behaviors, whose simplicity and reliability contributed to the ultimate refinement of more sophisticated observation systems as the project progressed.

Siedentop (1981) reports that changes in ST behavior did result from the observations of feedback, quickly and dramatically, as the interventions were applied. The designers added to this process packaged instructional materials, goals, instructions, and other information in a competency format. Ultimately, the structured materials became modules in classroom management and interpersonal relations, reduced the instructional responsibilities of the supervisor, and ultimately involved CTs in coding activities. Students, as well, were trained as peer observers. Supervisor visitations were reduced and still ST behavior continued to change and improve with each application of the observation and feedback model. In summary, Siedentop believes that the systematic attempt to impact on ST behavior, and the improvement of teaching behaviors was possible through a system of applied behavior analysis. The researchers were able to: (a) agree on a set of teacher behaviors (or competencies) which they wished to have STs demonstrate, (b) design a highly reliable and valid system for observing the frequency and degree of utilization of these behaviors, (c) observe significant behavior change as a result of the observation/feedback intervention, (d) utilize all three members of the student teaching triad in both the observation and feedback system, (e) package material to support or encourage use of the observed behaviors, and (f) insure maintenance of behavior change through continuous feedback and follow-up programming.

This system is highlighted in this review for several reasons. First, it represents a sustained effort to conduct supervisory interventions over time, in multiple settings and involving a number of replications. Second, the system of observation, its design and testing, and the associated materials development are clearly described and documented. Third, as a process, it was evaluated by the participants and judged to be the program's most successful model of supervision. Such a system, of course, presumes high agreement on the explicit goals of the program (in this case agreement on the initial set of teacher behaviors to be studied among program participants). Further, the process of behavioral analysis and the statistical analysis of the data had to be for the participants palitable methods of design and experimentation. Finally, this system focused on a limited set of variables related to the totality of the student teaching experience. While ignoring the interpersonal relations of the triad, the complexity of the school site, the process of teacher development or socialization as influenced by various aspects of the experience, this approach does focus on one aspect of student teaching that is regularly ignored in other studies; that is, reports of actual classroom observation.

In contrast to this applied behavioral approach to supervision, Gitlin (1981) has created an alternative approach to supervision, referred to as "horizontal evaluation," which includes a number of strategies supervisors can use with STs. Specifically, Gitlin takes issue with the competency-based approach to the assessment of STs, because of its "vertical" aim of laying out skills or competencies that are essential to good teaching in advance, determining a level of mastery, and observing the teacher to see if the competency is achieved (p. 47). The nature of these skills is technical, and does not allow for the reflective understanding of the linkage between theory and practice. Gitlin proposes a system of evaluation that has a horizontal aim, which is an adaptation of Simon's (1977) concept of educational platforms. "Espoused platforms are what students say govern their behavior. Platforms-in-use are inferred from actual behavior" (p. 581). Horizontal evaluation further expands this concept not only to examine the discrepancies or congruence between intent and practice, but also by introducing techniques that help STs question and revise beliefs (intents) that guide their practice (p. 48).

In a step-by-step procedure, supervisors and STs establish long- and short-term goals, define the goals, observe lessons focusing on these goals, and critique intent related to practice and also intent alone. Several strategies assist in analysis of intent to practice, including adopting historical perspectives on intent, generating alternative practices, and language analysis. Assessments of the justification of intent are pursued through a categorical review of intents, the appropriateness of intent within categories, and testing intents against hypothetical supervision-generated dilemmas. In this way Gitlin believes the supervisor assists the ST in acquisition of particular skills while also initially examining the political, moral, and ethical issues associated with teaching. Also the system assumes a collaborative agreement on the skills to be studied, unlike the underlying assumptions of the "vertical" system reflected in the competency-based Siedentop model.

Gitlin's agenda, in working with horizontal evaluation, included system development, the subsequent testing of the model in three field applications, and a comparative study of the model's effect. The initial test of the model (Gitlin, et al., 1982) involved three qualitative case studies in which teacher behavior, teacher intent, and teacher–supervisor interaction over time were investigated to determine the effects of the horizontal model. Researchers observed five supervising conferences, the first one allowing supervisors to use whatever method of evaluation they commonly practiced, and afterwards training the supervisor in horizontal evaluation, for use in the subsequent four conferences. Case study analysis was individual by researchers and then compared and discussed among the group.

An analysis of the case studies (Gitlin, 1981) uncovered five themes that characterize the application of the horizontal evaluation model, three in all cases, the remaining two in only two cases, as follows: (1) a focus of intent and practice did result in all cases, particularly noticeable in the amount and content of supervisor-initiated questions to STs in regard to intent and practice, and the focus of both participants beyond the strictly technical aspects of teaching; (2) both participants increased in critical reflection as opposed to more basic descriptions of instruction; (3) analysis reflected a holistic approach to teaching, not as a set of isolated concerns (such as curriculum, discipline, grading), but as connected activities to the total role of the ST; (4) STs had a view of educational practices as having valuative consequences; and (5) agenda setting, which got talked about in the conferences, represented a noticeable shift away from supervision dominated agendas to a greater balance between the supervisor and ST (p. 7). In summary, the most significant change in practice was in the observable relationship that the participants made between intents and practice. Student teachers were encouraged toward critical analysis, a holistic approach to the observation and assessment of teaching, and more mutually established the content of supervisory conferences.

A subsequent test of the horizontal evaluation model (reported in Gitlin et al., 1984) was a study of five supervisors trained in the technique compared to five supervisors who had not received such training. Five supervisory conferences were taped and analyzed for each of the cases involved, resulting in four related dimensions of the conferences: strategies, agenda setting, scope of issues, and type of analysis. These dimensions were found to be predictive, and tied one to another in the total supervisory process. The dimension descriptions resulted in the following conclusions: (a) horizontally trained supervisors allow ST role in setting agendas, and the use of a variety of approaches to analysis of teacher activity, whereas control group supervisors do not; (b) horizontal supervisors covered a wide scope of issues, the others did not; (c) control supervisors were more particularistic in their analysis of teaching, horizontal supervisors more relational and illuminating; and (d) with the contrast of control group supervisor domination of conferences versus horizontal supervisors openness and cultivation of an equal role with STs in agenda setting and discussion, ST behavior was effected. Control group student teachers tended to be more defensive, justifying behavior and attempting to correct it in accord with the supervisor's criticism. Horizontal ST defensiveness was minimized, and they were more reflective about their teaching. Gitlin (1981) concludes: Horizontal supervision creates more reflective and self-evaluative prospective teachers, who view teaching as a more holistic process than a collection of technical skills (pp. 48–51).

As with the Siedentop (1981) study, Gitlin et al. (1984) present a sustained effort to focus on analysis of the classroom instruction of STs, against an explicated model of classroom supervision. Again, the focus of the study is limited to that dimension of student teaching, but does cover in a comprehensive way many aspects of the supervising role as it relates to conferencing. In contrast to the prescriptive, competency approach described by Siedentop, similar to the control group in Gitlin, we see an emerging strategy that is reflective, holistic, relational and at least as much generated by the beliefs of the ST as the US.

If one could place these approaches on an imagined continuum, the referents could easily be between directive and nondirective supervision. This notion led the reviewer to a report of ST preference for supervisory approach, reported in another series of studies by Copeland et al. (1982, 1980) and Copeland (1978). At the University of California, Santa Barbara, Copeland et al. devised a system whereby STs could react to supervisory approach by viewing prerecorded actors depicting directive supervision (where the approach is to offer the teacher immediate and useful advice for overcoming instructional difficulties) and nondirective supervision (where the supervisor uses interrogative statements to solicit opinions and to encourage the teacher to make suggestions, reflecting the teacher's ideas and offering information as the teacher requests it).

Three studies report investigated preferences regarding these two approaches. In the first study, Copeland and Atkinson (1978) asked 66 elementary STs to rate supervisory approach against eight concepts: expertness, comprehension of problem, confidentiality, trustworthiness, ability to help, sincerity, knowledge of training, and utility. In all cases, contrary to predictions in the literature, the group means of these STs favored the directive over the nondirective supervisory approach. In the second study (Copeland, 1980), essentially the same approach was used, but for secondary STs, and the concepts were reduced from eight to three: trustworthiness, expertness, and utility. Again, STs preferred the directive over the nondirective supervisory approach. Because Copeland summarizes most current theoretical literature as favoring the more nondirective approach of clinical supervision, he speculates that STs may lack the experiential background necessary to analyze their teaching problems under nondirective supervision, but prefer instead the concrete solutions to their problems that are typical of directive supervision.

In a third study reported by Copeland (1982), he picks up on this speculation that beginning teachers (STs) prefer the more "supportive" or prescriptive model because of their initial insecurities, and studied the stability of this tendency over time. This factor, though ignored in the previous studies (when data were collected early in a new semester and a new placement for the students), became critical to the third study. Instead, in a mid-year assessment, half ($N = 35$) of the STs were tested for supervisory preference in October; the other group ($N = 25$) in May (at the beginning and end of the intern year). Again, the same three concepts used in the second study were used for analysis of the data. Several conclusions resulted from the analysis of results of this study (p. 35). First, individual preferences differed. Therefore supervisors cannot generalize that all STs prefer one supervisory approach to another. However, tendencies among participants were detectable. Significantly, in this third study, results suggest a progression from a mean preference for directive supervision early in the internship year to one for the nondirective approach toward the end of the student teaching placement. According to Copeland (1982), these findings also confirm reviews of other studies where experienced teachers preferred nondirective supervision and STs, more directive approaches. Therefore, the match of supervisory approach to ST preference might well require the supervisor to initiate conferencing and feedback more directly early in student teaching, with movement toward a more nondirective approach as the student gains more confidence and more self-analytic and reflective skills regarding teaching.

Of these three clusters, all propose a particular approach to supervision although the horizontal model is best explicated in terms of the conference process. We can conclude from the general descriptions of approach, that in the conduct of each of the two initial models (vertical and horizontal), STs responded favorably to the treatment. The Copeland studies offer at least one plausible explanation for why such conceptually different approaches might be attractive to students, given the elements of time and experience. Still, we have much to learn about the instructional supervision aspect of student teaching and the supervisor's role in that process. A recent study reported by Zeichner and Liston (1984) suggests yet another line of inquiry for unlocking the process and impact of the student teaching supervisory process; theirs on supervisory discourse. Briefly, this study analyzes verbal interaction from a population of STs and supervisors in order to ascertain the character of supervisory discourse, including the quality of thinking elicited and expressed with an explicit emphasis on promoting student reflection as a program goal. An elaborate category system was developed to distinguish types of discourse, and a score was computed to estimate the degree of reflective thinking exercised by the ST in the conference. Supervisory discourse was found to be predominantly factual or descriptive in nature; there was considerable lack of reflection on ST goals in the conferences; content consideration and autonomy in certain subjects did not lead to 'more reflective analysis; and measures of the conceptual levels of both the ST and US confirmed that high conceptual level of both participants led to more logical conference discourse. Such was not the case in instances where the US's conceptual level was higher than the ST's. Unlike revelations from other studies on this issue, results of Zeichner and Liston suggest that "it is the student teacher and not the supervisor who sets the tone for the level of complexity in supervising discourse" (p. 34).

Student teacher impact on supervising practices is alluded to in each of the studies just reported. It is not just that the US must contend with or compete for influence over the CT; the US must also exhibit considerable sensitivity in assessing the student's need for more or less structure in the supervisory process and also consider the student's cognitive development as a factor in fostering more logical and reflective discourse in the conferencing process.

Summary
This section of the present study offers extensive analysis of a small cluster of studies that represent one or all of the following characteristics:

1. In methodology, they offer an intensive and multidimensional perspective of role and process.
2. They reflect research conducted over time or are longitudinal in nature.
3. They attempt an assessment of impact.
4. They generally have an explicated conceptual base.

In a situation in which CTs play a dominant role, USs struggle for role clarification, acknowledge the limits of their impact on effecting ST practice, attempt clinical supervision in the fact of ST and CT tendencies to avoid critical analysis, experience more or less efficacy depending on the degree of influence they attempt to effect, and appear to be the sole model of reflection with regard to establishing a relationship between intent and practice in the habits of STs.

For those USs who execute classroom supervision, models of practice range from directive and nondirective approaches to observation and conferencing, which must be adjusted to the individual needs of each ST, initiating more directive approaches early in student teaching and more nondirective approaches as STs become more experienced.

From this new perspective on student teaching comes significant conceptual frameworks from which to organize new configurations of the practicum and more perceptive analyses of current practice. These concepts will be addressed in the remainder of the present study.

PROMISING DIRECTIONS FOR FUTURE RESEARCH

Along the way in this review of research on university supervision of student teaching, numerous references have been made to the current status of our research efforts, not only in regard to supervision of student teaching, but to the totality of the enterprise. Reference has been made to the largely atheoretical nature of our work (Shutes, 1975) and the need for new theory in studying the processes and outcomes of teacher education programs (Turner, 1975) in which the clinical aspect still plays an extremely important role. The research has also been fragmented, failing to recognize the antecedents and consequences of one member's behavior on all others in the experience (Zimpher et al., 1980), or to associate the contexts of student teaching to the actions of individuals within those contexts (Zeichner, this volume).

Two major conceptualizations of student teaching have surfaced repeatedly in this review of research. These conceptions apply equally to all aspects of the study of teacher education, not only to the didactic on-campus events, but to the field experiences in particular. One conception is an outgrowth of an interpretation of Dewey's (1904) distinction between the ways in which "the habits of a teacher as a teacher may be built up" (p. 15); a conception that differentiates between habits that help the teacher become thoughtful and alert as a student of teaching, as opposed to those that make the teacher immediately proficient, but not necessarily reflective about teaching. In references to field experiences, Dewey distinguishes outcomes as related either to an apprenticeship (having more of a utility character) or to a laboratory experience (fostering more personal inquiry and reflection). Much of the rhetorical literature reviewed for the present study and several of the research studies allude to this notion more or less directly. The reference to the habitual practice of what works (the instrumental perspective) in contrast to the specified educational purposes of reflective thinking epitomizes Dewey's distinctions.

Other scholars invoke Dewey to make a similar point. Haberman (1983) differentiates training and practice, perfected behaviors, command of knacks, tools of the trade, and the technicalities of teaching as "qualities of the apprenticeship," and monitoring one's own behavior, thoughtful and independent teaching, and becoming students of teaching through teacher education as the "laboratory" approach. Locke (1979, p. 13) calls for teacher education programs where "young interns must . . . receive intensive, supervisory assistance while they gradually learn how to function effectively as self-directed teachers," constituting his reference to Dewey's notion of the laboratory experience. In a program design offered by Emans (1983), conceptions of teacher education programs are presented in a continuum from more apprenticeship-oriented designs ("preparation approach," "imitation approach," and to some extent, "clinical approach") as differing from the more analytical "reflective" laboratory approach. Zeichner's (1983) alternative paradigms reflect the same range, from "behavioristic," "personalistic," and "traditional-craft" approaches to teacher education programs that are more apprenticeship in nature, to the "inquiry-oriented" laboratory paradigm.

Further delineations of programs are received or reflective, certain or problematic, draw a distinction consistent with Dewey's continuum. Zeichner and Teitelbaum (1982) differentiated the self and survival concerns of many STs (which they label "personalized") as an attempt to resolve early survival concerns by using what works (the apprenticeship approach), in contrast to a more "inquiry-oriented", reflective approach to the laboratory experience of student teaching. Other work by Zeichner (1980b) on teacher socialization investigates the tendencies of STs to follow established instructional patterns of the teachers and schools where they serve, versus their ability to maintain their own personal perspectives on teaching, which he describes as "functional" versus "dialectic" teacher socialization. In the differentiations of supervisory practice, Cohn (1981) refers to two models of supervision as a reflection of Dewey's apprenticeship (the "practical" model) and laboratory (the "situational" model) approaches.

The perspective presented in these various conceptions of the role and function of teacher education clearly portrays a concern with the reflective, critical, inquiry orientations that are a primary function of the practicum experience for prospective teachers.

> If we want field-based experience to contribute to the development of thoughtful and reflective teachers . . . then we must begin to focus our concerns on the quality of these experiences as they are actually implemented in the field. In this regard, we need more research that seeks to illuminate what is learned during these experiences as they are now constituted. (Zeichner, 1980a, p. 52)

The Deweyan distinction of prospective teacher experiences as either apprenticeship or laboratory in nature suggests not so much a methodology for studying student teaching and teacher education, as a conception for the dimensions of our inquiry. When we look at the activities of student teaching and the roles individuals play in those experiences, we need to consider the intentions and outcomes of the interactions that constitute the totality of student teaching, and measure those interactions against a continuum that ranges from utilitarian to critical. Our investigative measures must seek to distinguish the subtitles of interaction far beyond the descriptive data currently collected. We must probe intentionality and measure its effects on practice.

This further distinction of intent versus practice constitutes a second major conceptualization necessary for informing future inquiry in student teaching. Its referent (cited earlier) is associated with the notion of educational platforms (Simon, 1977): "Espoused platforms are what teachers say governs their behavior. Platforms-in-use are inferred from actual behavior" (p. 581). Simon created a 4-stage supervisory process employing this analysis. Gitlin (1981) proposed a supervision model that extended "platforms-espoused" and "platforms-in-use" by introducing techniques that help teachers question and revise the beliefs and intents that guide their practice (p. 47). In recognizing the need for a scientific theory for both the art and science of teaching, Diamonti (1977) suggests that even as irrefutable logic in teaching is derived, people (teacher educators and supervisors) will not necessarily adopt the theory in actual practice. Using Polyani's (1964) meaning for the "tacit dimensions" of knowing: "We can know more than we can tell and we can tell nothing without relying on our awareness of things we may not be able to tell" (p. x). Diamonti suggests that supervisors will not be able to help student teachers if they are not able themselves to bring their tacit knowledge to the conscious level. If teacher educators (and supervisors) are more effective at analyzing the intents (platforms-espoused) and practice (platforms-in-use) of their own teaching, they will be better able to support the reflective, critical-inquiry mode they seek in student teachers.

Again this conception tells us what to look for, not how to look. But together, seeking to reduce the functional, instrumental, and personalized approaches to learning to teach in lieu of more critical, analytical, and reflective discoveries of the relation of intent to practice will require elaborate qualitative, multi-data set, multi-source investigations into the events and interactions of the student teaching process. We must study the individuals, the programs, and the contexts of student teaching intensively and longitudinally to build an accurate portrayal of "which intervention by which interveners in what situations elicit what responses from which prospective teachers" (Fuller & Bown, 1972, p. 52). Therein lies the power to unlock the antecedents and consequences of university supervision needed to foster student teachers who can ultimately become lifetime students of teaching: "teachers who not only have the skills to do, but also the skills to analyze what they are doing and the habit of mind to do so" (Zeichner, 1981, p. 12).

REFERENCES

Acheson, K., & Gall, M. (1980). *Techniques in the clinical supervision of teachers: Preservice and inservice applications.* New York: Longman.

Alper, S., & Retish, P. (1972). A comparative study on the effects of student teaching on the attitudes of students in special education, elementary education, and secondary education. *The Training School Bulletin, 69*(2), 70–77.

Andrews, L. (1964). *Student teaching.* New York: Center for Applied Research in Education.

Barnes, S. (1983). *Student teachers' planning and decision making related to pupil evaluation.*

Austin: Research in Teacher Education Program, R&D Center for Teacher Education, The University of Texas at Austin.

Barrows, L. (1979). *Power relationships in the student teaching triad.* Paper presented at the Annual Meeting of the American Educational Research Association, San Francisco.

Becher, R., & Ade, W. (1982). The relationship of field placement characteristics and students' potential field performance abilities to clinical experience performance ratings. *Journal of Teacher Education, 33*(2), 24–30.

Bennie, W. (1964). Campus supervision of student teachers: A closer look. *Teachers College Journal, 36*(3), 131–133.

Boschee, F., Prescott, D., & Hein, D. (1978). Do cooperating teachers influence the educational philosophies of student teachers? *Journal of Teacher Education, 24,* 57–61.

Bowman, N. (1979). College supervision of student teaching: A time to reconsider. *Journal of Teacher Education, 30*(3), 29–30.

Campbell, L., & Williamson, J. (1973). Practical problems in the student teacher–cooperative teacher relationships. *Education, 94,* 168–169.

Capie, W., Eilett, C., & Johnson, C. (1980). *Relating pupil achievement gains to ratings of secondary student teachers' performance.* Paper presented at the Eastern Educational Research Association, Norfolk, CT.

Carkhuff, R. (1971). *The development of human resources.* New York: Holt, Rinehart, & Winston.

Caruso, J. (1977). Phases in student teaching. *Young Children, 33*(1), 57–63.

Chabassol, D. (1968). Possession of certain attitudes as predictors of success in practice teaching. *Journal of Educational Research, 61,* 304–306.

Cirirelli, V. (1969). University supervisors' creative ability and their appraisal of student teachers' classroom performance: An exploratory study. *Journal of Educational Research, 62*(8), 375–381.

Clemons, W. (1973). *Variations in role expectations and role realizations as perceived by teacher aide trainees, teachers of teacher aide trainees, teacher aides, and teachers utilizing teacher aides.* (Doctoral dissertation, Northern Illinois University). *Dissertation Abstracts International, 34,* 1160A.

Cogan, M. (1973). *Clinical supervision.* Boston: Houghton Mifflin.

Cohn, M. (1981). A new supervision model for linking theory to practice. *Journal of Teacher Education, 32*(3), 26–30.

Copeland, W. (1977). Some factors related to student teacher classroom performance following microteaching training. *American Educational Research Journal, 14*(2), 147–157.

Copeland, W. (1980). Affective dispositions of teachers in training toward examples of supervisory behavior. *Journal of Educational Research, 74*(1), 37–42.

Copeland, W. (1982). Student teachers' preference for supervisory approach. *Journal of Teacher Education, 33*(2), 32–36.

Copeland, W., & Atkinson, D. (1978). Student teachers' perceptions of directive and non-directive supervisory behavior. *Journal of Educational Research, 71*(3), 123–127.

Copenhaver, R., McIntyre, D., & Norris, W. (1981). Preservice teachers' reflections on the instructional process. *Peabody Journal of Education, 59*(1), 30–36.

Corrigan, D., & Griswold, K. (1963). Attitude change of student teachers. *Journal of Educational Research, 57*(2), 93–95.

Coss, A. (1959). *A comparative analysis of the expressed attitudes of elementary education student teachers, their university instructors, and their supervising teachers toward pupil-teacher relations as measured by the Minnesota teacher attitude inventory.* Unpublished doctoral dissertation, Indiana University.

Curtis, D., & Andrews, L. (1954). *Guiding your student teacher.* Englewood Cliffs, NJ: Prentice-Hall.

Defino, M. (1983). *The evaluation of student teachers*. Austin, TX: Research in Teacher Education Program, R&D Center for Teacher Education, The University of Texas at Austin.

Denton, J., & Kazimi, E. (1982). *Relationship among final supervisor skill ratings of student teachers and cognitive attainment values of learners taught by student teachers*. Paper presented at Southwest Educational Research Association, Austin, TX.

Dessecher, W. (1975). *The effects of audiotaped intervention on student teacher behaviors*. (Doctoral dissertation, The Ohio State University). *Dissertation Abstracts International*. (University Microfilms No. 76-9957)

Dewey, J. (1904). The relation of theory to practice in education. *The third yearbook of the National Society for the Scientific Study of Education*. Bloomington, IL: Public School Publishing.

Diamonti, M. (1977). Student teacher supervision. *Educational Forum, 41*(4), 477-486.

Dispoto, R. (1980). Affective changes associated with student teaching. *College Student Journal, 14*(2), 190-194.

Dodds, P. (1975). *A behavioral competency-based peer assessment model for student teacher and pupil behavior*. (Doctoral dissertation, The Ohio State University). *Dissertation Abstracts International*. (University Microfilms No. 75-26570)

Dunham, C. (1958). *Field attitudes of student teachers, college supervisors, and student teachers toward youth*. Unpublished doctoral dissertation, Indiana University.

Dutton, W. (1982). Attitude and anxiety change of elementary school student teachers. *Journal of Educational Research, 55*(6), 380-382.

Egan, K. (1982, March). *Carol, Laurie and Rita: Three persons in the act of becoming teachers*. Paper presented at the Annual Meeting of the American Educational Research Association, New York.

Emans, R. (1983). *Analysis of four different approaches to teacher education. College Student Journal, 15*(3), 209-216.

English, J. (1971). The university supervisor of student teachers. *Improving College and University Teaching, 19*(2), 157-188.

Evans, E. (1976). *Transition to teaching*. New York: Holt, Rinehart & Winston.

Farley, T. (1973). Comparisons of perceptions of elementary student teaching as perceived by cooperating teachers and student teachers. *Dissertation Abstracts International, 34*, 654B.

Fink, C. (1976, November). *Social studies student teachers— What do they really learn?* Paper presented at the Annual Meeting of the National Council for the Social Studies, Washington, DC.

Frenzel, N. (1977). Perceptions of university supervisors. *Teacher Educator, 12*(4), 14-17.

Friebus, R. (1977). Agents of socialization involved in student teaching. *Journal of Educational Research, 70*(5), 263-368.

Friedenberg, E. (1973). Critique of current practice. In D.J. McCartey (Ed.), *New perspectives on teacher education* (pp. 52-72). San Francisco: Jossey-Bass.

Fuller, F., & Bown, O. (1975). Becoming a teacher. In K. Ryan (Ed.), *The 74th yearbook of the National Society for the Study of Education, Part II*. Chicago: University of Chicago Press.

Gibson, J. (1969). *A study of effective and ineffective behaviors of college supervisors of student teachers in physical education*. (Doctoral dissertation, Teachers College, Columbus University). *Dissertation Abstracts International* (University Microfilms No. 71-7996).

Gitlin, A. (1981). Horizontal evaluation: An approach to student teacher supervision. *Journal of Teacher Education, 32*(5), 47-50.

Gitlin, A., Ogawa, R., & Rose, E. (1982). Horizontal evaluation: Its impact in three case studies. *CCBC Notebook, 3*(11), 1-13.

Gitlin, A., Ogawa, R., & Rose, E. (1984). Supervision, reflection and understanding: A case for horizontal evaluation. *Journal of Teacher Education, 35*(3), 46–52.

Glassberg, S., & Sprinthall, N. (1980). Student teaching: A developmental approach. *Journal of Teacher Education, 31*(2), 31–38.

Glickman, C. (1980). *Developmental supervision: Alternative practices for helping teachers improve instruction.* Alexandria, VA: Association for Supervision and Curriculum Development.

Goldhammer, R. (1969). *Clinical supervision.* New York: Holt, Rinehart, & Winston.

Goodman, J. (1983). The seminar's role in the education of student teachers: A case study. *Journal of Teacher Education, 34,* 44–49.

Griffin, G. (1983). *Student teaching and the commonplaces of schooling.* Austin: Research in Teacher Education Program, R&D Center for Teacher Education, The University of Texas at Austin.

Griffin, G., Barnes, S., Hughes, S., O'Neal, S., Defino, M., Edwards, S., & Hukill, H. (1983). *Clinical preservice teacher education: Final report of a descriptive study.* Austin: Research in Teacher Education Program, R&D Center for Teacher Education, The University of Texas at Austin.

Griffin, G., & Edwards, S. (1981). *Student teaching: Problems and promising practices.* Austin: Research in Teacher Education Program, R&D Center for Teacher Education, The University of Texas at Austin.

Griffin, G., Hughes, R., Defino, M., & Barnes, S. (1981). *Student teaching: A review.* Austin: Research in Teacher Education Program, R&D Center for Teacher Education, The University of Texas at Austin.

Haberman, M. (1983). Research on preservice laboratory and clinical experiences: Implications for teacher education. In K. Howey & W. Gardner (Eds.), *The education of teachers.* New York: Longman.

Hanke, D. (1967). The college supervisor: The unsung hero. *Teachers College Journal, 19,* 35–37.

Hazard, W. (1976). *Student teaching and the law.* Washington, DC: ERIC Clearinghouse on Teacher Education.

Hazard, W., Freeman, L., Eisdorfer, S., & Tractenberg, P. (1977). *Legal isseus in teacher preparation and certification.* Washington, DC: ERIC Clearinghouse on Teacher Education.

Henry, M., & Sa'ad, F. (1977). The impact of field experience on student teacher's perceptions of good and poor teaching. *Teacher Educator, 13*(2), 18–22.

Horowitz, M. (1968). Student-teaching experiences and the attitudes of student teachers. *Journal of Teacher Education, 19,* 317–324.

Hoy, W. (1967). Organizational socialization: The student teacher and pupil control ideology. *Journal of Educational Research, 61*(4), 153–155.

Hoy, W. (1968). The influence of experience on the beginning teacher. *School Review, 76*(4), 312–323.

Hoy, W. (1969). Pupil control ideology and organizational socialization: A further examination of the influence of experience on the beginning teacher. *School Review, 77*(3–4), 257–265.

Hoy, W., & Rees, R. (1977). The bureaucratic socialization of student teachers. *Journal of Teacher Education, 28*(1), 23–26.

Iannacone, L. (1963). Student teaching: A transitional stage in the making of a teacher. *Theory into Practice, 12*(2), 73–80.

Iannacone, L., & Button, W. (1964). *Functions of student teaching: Attitude formation and initiation in elementary student teaching.* Washington, DC: U.S. Office of Education.

Irvine, J. (1983). The accuracy of preservice teachers' assessments of their classroom behaviors. *Journal of Research and Development in Education, 17*(1), 25–31.

Isam, M., Carter, H., & Stribling, R. (1981). *A study of the entry mechanisms of university-based teacher educators.* Unpublished manuscript. University of Texas at Austin, Research and Development Center for Teacher Education.

Jacobs, E. (1968). Attitude change in teacher education: An inquiry into role of attitudes in changing teacher behavior. *Journal of Education, 19*(4), 410–416.

Johnson, J. (1969). Change in student teacher dogmatism. *Journal of Educational Research, 62*(5), 224–226.

Johnson, J., & Yates, J. (1982). *A national survey of student teaching programs.* DeKalb, IL: Northern Illinois University.

Jones, R. (1980). The supervisor and the teacher: An effective model of communication. *Clearinghouse, 53*(9), 433–437.

Junell, J. (1969). Abolish letter grades for student teaching activities. *Education, 89,* 255–256.

Kaplan, L. (1967). An investigation of the role expectations in college supervisors of student teaching as viewed by student teachers, supervising teachers, and college supervisors. Doctoral dissertation, The University of Rochester. *Dissertation Abstracts International, 28,* 517A.

Karmos, A., & Jacko, C. (1977). The role of significant others during the student teaching experience. *Journal of Teacher Education, 28,* 51–55.

Keilty, G. (1975). *The effect of instruction and supervision in interaction analysis on the preparation of student teachers.* Doctoral dissertation, Boston University. *Dissertation Abstracts International* (University Microfilms No. 75-20956).

Koehler, V. (1984, April). *University supervision of student teaching.* Paper presented at the National Conference of the American Educational Research Association, New Orleans.

Kraft, R. (1974). An analysis of supervisor/student teacher interaction. *Journal of Physical Education and Recreation, 45,* 37–38.

Lacey, C. (1977). *Socialization of teachers.* London: Methuen.

Lamb, C. & Montague, E. (1982). *Variables pertaining to the perceived effectiveness of university student teachers.* Papers presented at the Southwest Educational Research Association, Austin, TX.

Lang, D., Quick, A., & Johnson, J. (1975). *The supervision of student teachers.* Mt. Pleasant, MI: The Great Lakes Publishing Co.

Locke, L. (1979). *Supervision, schools and student teaching: Why things stay the same.* Reston, VA: American Academy of Physical Education.

Lortie, D. (1975). *School teacher: A sociological study.* Chicago: University of Chicago Press.

Mahan, G., & Harste, J. (1977). *Professional judgment as a criterion variable in preservice teacher education research.* Paper presented at the Annual Meeting of the American Educational Research Association, San Francisco.

Mahan, J., & Lacefield, W. (1976). *Changes in preservice teachers' value orientations toward education during year-long, cluster, student teaching placements.* Paper presented at the Annual Meeting of the American Educational Research Association.

Manning, D. (1977). The influence of key individuals on student teachers in urban and suburban settings. *Teacher Educator, 13*(2), 2–8.

McDonald, F. (1980). The problems of beginning teachers: A crisis in training (Vol. 1). *Study of induction programs for beginning teachers.* Princeton, NJ: Educational Testing Service, Washington, DC: National Institute of Education (ED).

McIntyre, D. (1983). *Field experience in teacher education.* Washington, DC: Foundation for Excellence in Teacher Education and the ERIC Clearinghouse on Teacher Education.

McIntyre, D. (1984). A response to the critics of field experience supervision. *Journal of Teacher Education, 35*(3), 42–45.

McIntyre, D., Buell, M., & Casey, J. (1979). Verbal behavior of student teachers and cooperating teachers. *College Student Journal, 13*(3), 240–244.

McIntyre, D., & Norris, W. (1980). The state of the art of preservice teacher education programs and supervision of field experiences. *Action in Teacher Education, 2*(3), 67–69.

Mead, A. (1930). *Supervised student teaching.* New York: Johnson Publishing.

Metzler, M. (1981). A multi-observational system for supervising student teachers in physical education. *Physical Educator, 38*(3), 152–159.

Monson, J., & Bebb, A. (1970). New roles for the supervisor of student teaching. *Educational Leadership, 28,* 44–47.

Morris, J. (1974). The effects of the university supervisor on the performance and adjustment of student teachers. *Journal of Educational Research, 67*(8), 358–362.

Morris, J. (1980). Evaluating the effectiveness of the university supervisor of student teachers: Role of the coordinator of field experiences. *Peabody Journal of Education, 57*(2), 148–151.

Mosher, R., & Purpel, D. (1972). *Supervision: The reluctant profession.* Boston: Houghton Mifflin.

Nerenz, A. (1979). The role of the university supervisor: Perceived importance and practical implications. *Foreign Language Annals, 12*(6), 471–475.

O'Neal, S. (1983). *Supervision of student teachers: Feedback and evaluation.* Austin: Research in Teacher Education Program, R&D Center for Teacher Education, The University of Texas at Austin.

Patty, A. (1973). Classroom teachers will replace college supervisors. *Contemporary Education, 54*(3), 179–183.

Polyani, M. (1964). *Personal knowledge.* New York: Harper Torchbook.

Price, R. (1961). The influence of supervising teachers. *Journal of Teacher Education, 12*(1), 471–475.

Prokop, M. (1973). *Role conflict in student teaching.* (ERIC Document Reproduction Service No. ED 080 498). Educational Resources Information Center.

Pruitt, W., & Lee, J. (1978). Hidden handcuffs in teacher education. *Journal of Teacher Education, 29*(5) 69–72.

Roberts, R., & Blankenship, J. (1970). The relationship between the change in pupil control ideology of student teachers and the student teacher's perception of the cooperating teacher's pupil control ideology. *Journal of Research in Science Teaching, 7*(4), 315–320.

Ross, S., Raines, F., Cervetti, M., & Dellow, D. (1980). Field experiences for teacher candidates: A comparison between tutorial and apprenticeship programs on student activities and attitudes. *Journal of Teacher Education, 31,* 57–61.

Sacks, S., & Harrington, G. (1982, April). *Student to teacher: The process of role transition.* Paper presented at the Annual Meeting of the American Educational Research Association, New York.

Salzillo, F. & Van Fleet, A. (1977). Student teaching and teacher education: A sociological model for change. *Journal of Teacher Education 28*(1), 27–31.

Sandgren, D., & Schmidt, L. (1956). Does practice teaching change attitudes toward teaching? *Journal of Educational Research, 50*(8), 673–680.

Savage, T. (1980). *Student teacher influence on learner cognitive attainment.* Paper presented at the Southwest Educational Research Association, San Antonio, TX, February.

Schoenrock, F. (1980). Student teaching—An entrenching "knowing that" and "knowing how." *Elements: Translating Theory into Practice, 11*(6), 3–4.

Schueler, R., Gold, B., & Mitzel, H. (1962). *Improvement of student teaching.* New York: City University of New York, Hunter College.

Scott, O., & Brinkley, S. (1960). Attitude changes in student teachers and validity of the MTAI. *Journal of Educational Psychology, 51*(4), 76–81.

Seperson, M., & Joyce, B. (1973). Teaching styles of student teachers as related to those of their cooperating teachers. *Educational Leadership, 31,* 146–151.

Shutes, R. (1975). Needed: A theory of teacher education. *Texas Tech Journal of Education, 2,* 94–101.

Siedentop, D. (1981). The Ohio State University supervision research program summary report. *Journal of Teaching in Physical Education.* Introductory Issue. Spring, 30–38.

Siedentop, D., & Hughley, C. (1975). The Ohio State teachers behavior scale. *Journal of Physical Education and Recreation, 46,* 45.

Simms, F. (1975). Role of the elementary and secondary student teachers as determined by current practices in student teaching. *Dissertation Abstracts International,* Kansas State University, *36,* 2755A.

Simon, A. (1977). Analyzing educational platforms: A supervisory strategy. *Educational Leadership, 34,* 580–584.

Smith, P. (1969). *Experimentation to determine the feasibility of remote supervision of student teachers.* (ERIC Document Reproduction Service No. 033 203). Educational Resources Information Center.

Smith, L., & Alverman, D. (1983). *Field-experience reading interns profile the effective/ineffective university supervisor.* Paper presented at the annual meeting of the College Reading Association, Atlanta.

Solliday, M. (1982). The university supervisor: A double image. *Teacher Educator, 18*(3), 11–15.

Spangler, R. (1972). *Teacher preparation: Supervision and performance.* Washington, DC: Association of Teacher Educators.

Spillane, R., & Levenson, D. (1976, March). Teacher training: A question of control, not content. *Phi Delta Kappan, 57*(7), 435–439.

Sprinthall, N., & Thies-Sprinthall, L. (1983). The teacher as an adult learner: A cognitive-developmental view. In G. Griffin (Ed.), *Staff development: The eighty-second yearbook of NSSE (Part II).* Chicago: University of Chicago Press.

Stewig, J. (1970). What should college supervisors do? *Journal of Teacher Education, 21*(2), 251–257.

Stratemeyer, F., & Lindsey, M. (1958). *Working with student teachers.* New York: Bureau of Publications, Teachers College, Columbia University.

Tabachnick, B., Zeichner, K., Densmore, K., Adler, S., & Egan, K. (1982, March). *The impact of the student teaching experience on the development of teacher perspectives.* Paper presented at the Annual Meeting of the American Educational Research Association, New York.

Tom, A. (1974). The case for pass/fail student teaching. *Teacher Educator, 10*(1), 2–8.

Turner, R. (1975). An overview of research in teacher education. In K. Ryan (Ed.), *The seventy-fourth yearbook of the National Society for the Study of Education (Part II).* Chicago: University of Chicago Press.

Villeme, M., & Hall, B. (1975). Professional education programs' effects of the attitudes of prospective teachers. *Humanist Educator, 14*(2), 64–70.

Vittetoe, J. (1972). Evaluation of product – An essential first step. *Journal of Teacher Education, 23*(2), 129–133.

Walberg, H. (1968). Personality-role conflict and self-conception in urban practice teachers. *The School Review, 76,* 41–48.

Waters, B. (1974). *Role expectations of the college supervisor of elementary student teachers in the state of Georgia.* Paper presented at the Annual Meeting of the American Educational Research Association, Chicago.

Weller, R. (1969). *An observation system for analyzing clinical supervision of teachers.* Doctoral dissertation, Harvard University. *Dissertation Abstracts International.* (University Microfilms No. 69–18245).

Wilbur, P., & Gooding, C. (1977). Attitude changes in student teachers. *College Student Journal, 11*(3), 227–231.

Williamson, J., & Campbell, L. (1978). The student teaching experience results in greater emphasis in pupil control. *Southern Journal of Educational Research, 12*(1), 1–6.

Wright, R. (1965). *An analysis of the techniques of guiding student teaching experiences.* Doctoral dissertation, University of Southern California. *Dissertation Abstracts Interna-*

tional. (University Microfilm Publications No. PE 1232).

Yarger, S., Howey, K., & Joyce, B. (1977). Reflections on preservice preparation: Impressions from the national survey. *Journal of Teacher Education, 28,* 34–37.

Yee, A. (1969). Do cooperating teachers influence the attitudes of student teachers? *Journal of Educational Psychology, 60*(4), 327–332.

Zeichner, K. (1978). *Student teaching experience: A methodological association of teacher educators.* Paper presented at the annual meeting of the Association of Teacher Educators, Las Vegas.

Zeichner, K. (1980a). Myths and realities: Field-based experiences in preservice teacher education. *Journal of Teacher Education, 31*(6), 45–55.

Zeichner, K. (1980b). *Key process in the socialization of student teacher: Limitations and conceptions of teacher socialization.* Paper presented at the meeting of the American Educational Research Association, Boston.

Zeichner, K. (1981). *Ethical problems in "personalizing" instruction during the student teaching experience.* Paper presented at the annual meeting of the Association of Teacher Educators, Dallas.

Zeichner, K. (1983). Alternative paradigms of teacher education. *Journal of Teacher Education, 34*(3), 3–9.

Zeichner, K., & Liston, D. (1984). *Varieties of discourse in supervisory conferences.* Paper presented at the Annual Meeting of the American Educational Research Association, New Orleans.

Zeichner, K., & Tabachnick, B. (1981). Are the effects of university teacher education "washed out" by school experience? *Journal of Teacher Education, 32*(3), 7–11.

Zeichner, K., & Tabachnick, B. (1982). The belief system of university supervisors in an elementary student teaching program. *Journal of Education for Teaching, 8*(2), 34–54.

Zeichner, K., & Teitelbaum, K. (1982). Personalized and inquiry-oriented teacher education. *Journal of Education for Teaching, 8*(2), 95–117.

Zevin, J. (1974). *In the cooperating teachers' image: Convergence of social studies student teachers' behavior patterns with cooperating teachers' behavior patterns.* (ERIC Document Reproduction Service No. ED 087 781). Paper presented at the Annual Meeting of the American Educational Research Association, Chicago.

Zimpher, N., deVoss, G., & Nott, D. (1980). A closer look at university student teacher supervision. *Journal of Teacher Education, 31*(4), 11–51.

Chapter 7

Student Teaching

Doyle Watts

Lamar University, Beaumont, TX

The support for requiring teacher trainees to student teach is almost universal. Practicing teachers usually identify their student teaching experience as the most valuable and helpful component of their total preparation program (Griffin et al., 1983). The National Education Association (NEA) considers field-based experiences essential to achieving excellence in teacher preparation (NEA, 1982). The American Association of Colleges for Teacher Education (AACTE) endorses experiences in student teaching as an important part of teacher preparation (AACTE, 1983). One accreditation standard established by the National Council for Accreditation of Teacher Education (NCATE) specifically stipulates that preparation programs are to provide teacher trainees with direct participation in teaching over an extended period of time (NCATE, 1982). The strong commitment to student teaching is also demonstrated by the fact that it is required in all 50 states for teacher certification (NEA, 1983).

Haberman (1982) correctly pointed out that student teaching is considered to be the heart and mind of teacher preparation. Does student teaching deserve its exalted position, or is it just another sacred cow which achieved its present status through tradition instead of merit? Does the call for excellence in education imply increased student teaching? Many schoolteachers, teacher educators, and legislators apparently believe that it does. There are, however, serious questions regarding the value of student teaching. These questions include the lack of research which supports student teaching, confusion over the legal status of student teachers, few etablished requirements for cooperating teachers or college supervisors, and some disturbing effects that the student teaching practicum has on teacher trainees.

PRESENT PRACTICES

A large proportion of teacher preparation programs is already committed to student teaching. The National Commission for Excellence in Teacher Education reported that approximately 10% of the entire teacher preparation program presently consists of field-based experiences (NCETE, 1984). This amount is, indeed, impressive in light of the fact that only about 6% of the secondary teacher trainee's program is comprised of coursework in curriculum and methods. The amount of time required for student teaching has increased substantially during the last few years (NCETE, 1984). Herald (1983) reported that the student teaching requirement now averages about 300 clock hours. In addition, a number of states are expanding even further the length and/or scope of teacher trainees' required activities in school settings (Beyer, 1984). As Beyer observed, "The general consensus seems to be that the greater the number of hours a student spends in the classroom — observing, assisting the teachers, teaching in formal and informal settings — the better prepared he/she will be" (p. 36).

The student teaching experience usually occurs during the final year of the teacher preparation program. A teacher trainee is placed in a school setting under the guidance and supervision of a practicing school teacher and a college supervisor. Tradition rather than empirical evidence seems to be the basis for this arrangement.

The purpose of the student teaching practicum remains poorly defined. According to NCATE standards, student teaching should provide "an opportunity for the student to assume major responsibility for the full range of teacher duties in a real school situation" (NCATE, 1982, p. 18). The professional skills that teacher trainees are expected to develop during the program, however, are not identified. Neither are any specific educational activities of the practicum experience described.

In view of student teaching's central position in teacher education, it is odd that the legal and professional position of student teachers while in the school setting has not been carefully defined. Should they be classified as junior school faculty or university students? Are they neophyte teachers who are expected to practice correct pedagogical behaviors or are they student teachers in the process of learning pedagogical principles and concepts (Haberman, 1982)? These questions are largely unanswered.

About three fourths of the states have no statutory definition of student teachers. Their legal status varies widely even among those states that have such definitions. Tennessee, for example, defines a student teacher as a student assigned to perform practice teaching, while in Nebraska a student teacher is a person assigned to student teach or intern under a regularly certified employee. Pennsylvania identifies a student teacher as a prospective teacher engaged in student teaching field experiences. In Wisconsin the student teacher is described as a university student assigned to practice through observation, participation, and actual teaching. New Mexico recognizes student teachers and interns as a part of the profession in the process of becoming professionals (Hoffman, 1979). It is apparent, therefore, that the legal status of student teachers remains largely unresolved, but as Hoffman noted, "A precise definition of student teaching is needed as teacher education programs become more extensive and sophisticated" (p. 8).

Many states have also failed to establish requirements for cooperating teachers. An article published in 1979 reported that at least two thirds of the states had no legal requirements or regulations for the appointment of a cooperating teacher (Hoffman, 1979). Three years later Haberman and Harris (1982) stated that 24 states reported no legal requirements for those serving as cooperating teachers. In states that have such requirements, standards usually consist of certificates held, degrees earned, teaching experience, and special courses in supervising student teachers (Haberman & Harris, 1982; Hoffman, 1979). Even these criteria seem to have been enacted without any empirical evidence to justify their selection.

The teaching profession has also failed to identify specific requirements for cooperating teachers. NCATE standards state only that the cooperating school personnel who are responsible for supervising practicums should be certificated, experienced, and that the school of education should establish and apply explicit criteria for their selection (NCATE, 1982). The NEA has stated that school-based teacher educators should model the attitudes and behaviors that they are attempting to develop in teacher trainees. In addition the NEA recommends that cooperating teachers have in-depth preparation, training, and experiences in their instructional fields (NEA, 1982). In addition to being vague and imprecise, these suggested requirements do not appear to be based on research information.

The standards and requirements for a college supervisor of student teachers are even less specific than those for the cooperating teacher. The determination of qualifications for, and the selection of, supervisors are largely left to the discretion of the university. NCATE standards state only that explicit criteria must be established and applied for the assignment of college personnel. The only qualification identified by NCATE for college supervisors is that they are experienced in, and have continuing experience with, elementary or secondary teaching (NCATE, 1982).

Universities and schools of education do not seem to take student teaching seriously or be willing to commit adequate resources to its operation. Judge (1982) observed, "Student teaching, or practice teaching, is required, but, for the most part, it appears to be held at arm's length by the university. Certainly there is none of the intimacy of involvement that characterizes medical education" (p. 34). The report by the National Commission for Excellence in Teacher Education noted that large universities have managed to keep the cost of their education programs low by staffing undergraduate courses and field experience supervision with graduate students (NCETE, 1984).

In addition to the problem of identifying appropriate criteria for the selection and assignment of cooperating teachers and college supervisors, the lack of agreement concerning a definition of effective teaching is a major stumbling block to designing high-quality student teaching programs. As Beyer (1984) noted, "There seem to be no clear, unassailable, fixed standards of what constitutes valuable teaching that may be employed to assess teaching excellence" (p. 40). Without any definition of or standards for effective teaching, it is impossible to design student teaching objectives, evaluate the effectiveness of the experience, or to conduct research to modify and improve practice.

RESEARCH

The lack of agreement about what constitutes valuable and effective teaching has resulted in a very limited body of research information concerning student teaching. Griffin et al. (1983) wrote, "there does not presently exist a solid knowledge base regarding student teaching. A survey of the literature related to teacher education reveals a paucity of information regarding student teaching from a research perspective. Research-based propositions are conspicuous by their absence" (p. 3).

The research studies that have been conducted are of questionable quality. Haberman (1982) described student teaching research as being meager, diverse, and trivial. McIntyre (1984) observed that the majority of studies used questionnaires to assess attitudes and behaviors and that student teaching performance was usually measured by grades received. McIntyre questioned the validity of these measurement techniques.

Consequently, the present body of research information is too meager to provide effective guidance for professional decisions and practices concerning student teaching programs (Griffin et al., 1983). Research has, therefore, had little impact on program design or modification. This lack of influence was pointed out by Haberman (1982), "There is no instance of any widespread practice in student teaching programs that is the result of research. Conversely, there are no common practices that have been dropped from student teaching programs on the basis of research evidence" (p. 74).

Most of the research that has been conducted on student teaching falls within one to five categories: (1) student teacher attitudes and personality characteristics, (2) the socialization of student teachers, (3) predictors of success in student teaching, (4) interpersonal relationships in student teaching, and (5) experimental attempts to modify student teacher behaviors (Zeichner, 1978). As noted earlier, most studies rely on data obtained from surveys, questionnaires, student teaching grades, and college supervisor or cooperating teacher evaluations. In addition, dependent variables usually consist of attitudes, self-concepts, or perceptions. Few carefully controlled, experimental studies have been reported to date.

In the paragraphs which follow, an effort has been made to collect and report the major findings from existing research on student teaching. A number of studies have found that the cooperating teacher has major influence on the student teacher, while the college supervisor has little or no effect. Research investigations indicate that the attitudes of student teachers incline more and more toward those of cooperating teachers as the student teaching practicum advances. When initial differences exist between the cooperating teacher and the student teacher, the student teacher adjusts his/her values toward those of the cooperating teacher (McIntyre, 1984).

It should come as no surprise that the cooperating teacher, who is in close contact with the student teacher on a one-to-one basis for 300 clock hours or more during the student teaching practicum, has a greater influence than the college supervisor who is unlikely to spend more than 10–12 hours with the teacher trainee. In fact, the cooperating teacher may well spend more time with the student teacher than the student teacher spent in all of his/her professional education courses combined. In addition, the student teaching experience occurs in the cooperating teacher's school and with the cooperating teacher's classes and students. In view of these circumstances, the student teacher is expected to be influenced by the cooperating teacher and to adopt many of his/her attitudes and teaching practices.

Some of the observed actions and activities of cooperating teachers, however, are not conducive to the professional development of student teachers. Zimpher, de Voss, and Nott (1980) reported that many cooperating teachers were not interested in observing student teachers and wanted to involve trainees fully within one week of placement. Cooperating teachers apparently perceived student teachers as aides who could lighten their duties. They did not consider them to be professional trainees to whom they had the responsibility of providing an approrpiate practicum to develop pedagogical knowledge, skills, and attitudes. This outlook may be a result of the lack of a role description which states the duties and responsibilities of cooperating teachers.

In addition, Zimpher et al. (1980) found that cooperating teachers tend to avoid critical remarks concerning student teachers assigned to them. Fink (1976) reported that cooperating teachers are inclined to write positive evaluations of student teachers without actually having observed them. In view of these disturbing findings, some educators have gone as far as suggesting that schools of education should take steps to offset the negative influence that cooperating teachers have on student teachers (McCaleb, 1979). Kilgore (1979) found, however, that when the cooperating teachers were trained in the techniques and strategies that the school of education was attempting to develop in the student teachers, the results were much more satisfactory.

Another consistent characteristic revealed by research studies is the negative shift in teacher trainees' attitudes toward pupils, discipline, teaching, and themselves during student teaching. Williamson and Campbell (1978) reported that as student teachers moved through their practicum, their attitudes became more custodial and they developed a pupil control frame of reference. Other researchers have found a decline in teacher trainees' attitudes toward children, teaching, and school following student teaching (Alper & Retish, 1972; Dispoto, 1980; Dutton, 1962). As the student teaching experience progressed, teacher trainees were found to associate poor teaching with teachers who were child-centered as opposed to subject-centered (Henry & Sa'ad, 1977). Wilbur and Gooding (1977) noted that teacher trainees became progressively more concealing and less willing to share professionally with their peers. Other studies indicate that student teachers become increasingly committed to finishing lessons on time rather than demonstrating a concern for individual differences and needs of pupils (Iannacone, 1963; Iannacone & Button, 1964). Tabachnick, Popkewitz, and Zeichner (1979–1980) found that cooperating teachers only involved teacher trainees in a narrow range of activities, and the trainees' pedagogical behaviors became routine and mechanical. Their chief objective seemed to become that of moving children through prescribed lessons in a given period of time, instead of attending to pupils' educational needs. Jones (1982) observed the negative shift to be greater for secondary than elementary student teachers.

A report by Moser (1982) revealed that prior to the student teaching experience, teacher trainees' general attitudes about the fairness and effectiveness of discipline were similar to those of sixth-grade pupils. Afterwards, they were significantly different. As their student teaching practicum proceeded, student teachers increasingly came to regard most methods of discipline to be fair and effective. They also became more willing to use harsher methods of discipline and to consider those harsh measures to be just. Student teachers reported that classroom control was more difficult than they had anticipated. Other research reports indicate that teacher trainees become more rigid, more authoritarian, less flexible, and less responsive to pupil needs during their student teaching practicum (Iannacone, 1963; Gerwinner, 1968; Zeichner, 1978).

The reasons for this change in student teachers are unknown. Beyer (1984) speculated, "Thrust into the existing culture of the school, and having less than the professional status of paid teachers and administrators, students may tend to accept existing conditions, patterns, and relationships as forming the boundaries beyond which one need not, or should not, trespass" (p. 36). Beyer goes on to state, "while exposure to classroom situations is increasingly mandated for students in education, this process — while apparently justified and appealing to common sense, almost at face value — can lead to a duplication of existing procedures and activities that are both noneducative and ideologically suspect" (p. 38). Finally, Beyer concludes that additional field experiences simply place teacher trainees in an accepted rut.

The previously cited studies generally place the responsibility for the negative shift of student teacher attitudes on the cooperating teacher and the school. However, some educators question whether teacher trainees begin student teaching with attitudes developed during professional training in schools of education. Zeichner and Tabachnick (1981) take the position that the effects of university teacher education are not "washed out" by student teaching because a substantial university effect never existed in the first place. Bartholomew (1976) stated that the belief that universities generate liberal views is false. Although institutions pay lip service to liberal philosophies and encourage teacher trainees to use liberal phrases and slogans, he contends that the facts of social interactions in the colleges are similar to those found in the public schools.

Lortie (1975) maintained that formal training in pedagogy plays little part in altering earlier and traditional attitudes which teacher trainees develop through the years as a function of close contact with, and observation of, many teachers. He argued that teacher socialization is completed before formal training begins, and the student teaching experience simply activates this latent culture. His conclusions were based, in part, on reports of teachers who referred to the continuing influence of their own teachers, not their formal pedagogical preparation, as affecting their current classroom practice.

It is also possible that professional practice as taught in schools of education is not achievable under present conditions. The organization and structure of schools, as well as the teaching profession's inferior status and unsatisfactory conditions of practice, may not permit a professional level of service. One study noted that teacher trainees stated that their perceptions of teaching, up to the time they began working with pupils, had been distorted (Felder, Hollis, & Houston, 1979). Perhaps the words of a preservice student, spoken to a teacher educator upon completion of the teacher preparation program, sums it up best: "Thanks. You've prepared me for the best of all non-existent worlds" (Haberman, 1981, p. 2).

The type of school and pupils also influence changes in student teachers' attitudes and self-concepts. Smith and Smith (1979) reported that a group of student teachers assigned to schools located in poorer neighborhoods had lower self-esteem, lower feelings of self-acceptance, described themselves in more negative terms, had greater reservations about things they did, and had doubts about their personal worth following their practicum experience. The negative shift was not observed in teacher trainees who completed their student teaching assignment in a middle class school.

As noted earlier, there is a general tendency to increase the amount of time teacher trainees are assigned to student teaching practicums. However, research studies do not support the notion that more time in school settings equates to better prepared teachers. Some investigations disclosed that student teachers who had longer assignments also had more pronounced negative attitude shifts. Covert and Clifton (1983) reported that students who had completed a 20-week practicum had significantly lower values (motivation toward teaching, attitudes toward a teaching career, lower self-concept) than those who had completed a 3-week practicum. Another investigation found no significant differences among self-ratings of performance, supervisor ratings of commitment to teaching, graduate ratings of the contribution of student teaching to skill development, and general satisfaction with student teaching as a function of the type of student teaching program (Freeman, Bradley, & Bornstein, 1979). These findings do not support the current trend to expand the student teaching experience.

Research information also fails to support the value of additional pre-student teaching field experiences. Henry (1983) reported that increased field experiences had little impact upon student teachers' perceptions of their ability to perform specific teaching tasks, the final evaluations of student teaching made by supervising teachers or the assessment of the major problems experienced during student teaching.

A number of research studies indicate that college supervisors have little or no impact on student teachers' attitudes and behaviors (McIntyre, 1984). Their apparently meager contributions to student teaching have lead some educators to question whether the present role of college supervisors should be continued (Bowman, 1978). Cohn (1981) pointed out that college supervisors serve largely in a public relations function. Their visits to the school usually have the three-fold purpose of monitering and assessing the progress of the student teacher's performance; identifying any specific areas of difficulty and offering assistance; and keeping in touch with cooperating teachers and principals. On a more positive note, Alvermann (1981) discovered that student teachers demonstrated a greater willingness to accept the university supervisor as an evaluator and a resource person when visitations were made more frequently.

UNANSWERED QUESTIONS

Because the research data are so meager, many questions concerning student teaching remain unanswered. Before confidence in our professional preparation system can be established, we simply must have a greater body of research information.

Student teachers are usually placed in a specific grade, age level, or subject matter area. Normally, placement decisions are made on the basis of the type of teaching certificate the trainee is seeking. But should clinical experiences be limited and restricted in that fashion? Would it be more beneficial to involve student teachers in practicum experiences with pupils in a variety of grades, ages, and subject matter? Would it also be better to provide each trainee with field-experiences in a mixture of school settings, taking into consideration such factors as size, location, student population characteristics and socio-economic conditions?

As already reported, the existing research does not indicate that student teaching facilitates the development of desirable professional attitudes in teacher trainees. In fact, many studies suggest just the opposite. Unfortunately, the contributions that student teaching experiences make to the acquisition and development of professional abilities is unclear. As a result of practicums in school settings, are teacher trainees better able to evaluate pupil needs, individualize instruction, construct instructional objectives and plans, design curriculum to achieve objectives, identify and effectively use appropriate pedagogical strategies and techniques, utilize support staff, make professional decisions, and function effectively as a member of a professional team? It seems that the merits of student teaching must ultimately be decided upon answers to these questions.

Information cited earlier revealed that most states do not establish any requirements for cooperating teachers. Where requirements are identified, they usually include certificates, degrees, and years of experience. These criteria are not, however, based on valid research evidence. Do the qualifications of the cooperating teacher affect the preparation of student teachers? Are practicing teachers with higher college grade point averages, higher scores on the Scholastic Aptitude Test, Graduate Record Exam, and intelligence tests more effective cooperating teachers? Is there a difference in supervisory effectiveness as a function of the number and/or type of degrees and certificates the cooperating teacher has earned? Does the philosophical preference (humanistic or behavioristic) of cooperating teachers determine their effectiveness? Are there personality variables that influence success? Do years of experience make any difference? Can school administrators and teachers accurately identify those teacher practitioners who will be the most successful cooperating teachers?

Many questions concerning variables that might contribute to the effectiveness of college supervisors also remain unanswered. Do the qualifications of college supervisors influence their effectiveness? Are professors more capable student teacher supervisors than graduate assistants? Are professors from the teaching field more successful supervisors than those from the school of education? Are instructors in methods more competent supervisors than those from foundations? Are there significant differences in college supervisors' effectiveness as a function of their previous school experiences, publication records, or their own teaching abilities?

Does the structure and organization of the student teaching activity influence its benefits? Does an approach that incorporates specifically stated objectives with preplanned student teacher activities result in a superior program as compared with traditional strategies? What would be the effect on program quality if all student teaching supervision were performed by college staff, teacher practitioners, or by school administrators? Would it be better to have professional teams? Is there a difference in the professional knowledge, skills, or attitudes of trainees who engage in student teaching and those who don't? Are alternative preparation activities more effective than student teaching in developing professional knowledge, skills, and attitudes in teacher trainees?

What is the optimum length of time for the student teaching experience? Some of the research cited earlier indicates that longer experiences are not necessarily more beneficial, at least in respect to the effects on trainee attitudes. Is it better for the trainee to be assigned to the school full-time? Or, is it more profitable for the trainee to divide his/her time between the university and the school? Is a continuous or an intermittent experience more effective? These are just some of the questions which the teaching profession and especially its preparation and service arm, schools of education, should be addressing. Answers to these questions are essential to the development of effective student teaching programs. Why then, does the research relating to student teaching remain meager, diverse, and trivial?

UNSOLVED PROBLEMS

Role confusion is undoubtedly a major cause for the anemic body of research relating to student teaching. Haberman (1982) observed that, "confusion between the role of practice and student teacher is a major cause for the low quality and quantity research on student teaching" (p. 72). Another major cause is the lack of agreement concerning the professional role of the schoolteacher. Is teaching simply a matter of presenting facts and information with the responsibility for learning those facts and information falling totally on the shoulders of students? Are teachers surrogate parents whose primary duties are to nurture and socialize children in an extended child care capacity? Are teachers providers of educational services with the obligation of utilizing their pedagogical abilities to facilitate the pupils' acquisition of knowledge and skills, and thus enhance the pupils' intellectual ability? Each of these roles requires different skills and preparation. Until teaching establishes its professional identity, it has no objectives to guide teacher preparation efforts and no standards with which to determine their success.

Another major reason for the low quality and quantity of research relating to student teaching is a general lack of commitment to educational research. Educational research efforts can best be described as poorly funded, disorganized, and largely the result of individual projects (Watts, 1982). Without a body of empirical knowledge, educators rely on experts' judgments, individual opinions, and group assumptions. This is an unwise strategy. As Coker, Medley, and Soar (1980) pointed out, "the history of science . . . has been a series of demonstrations that what is commonly believed about a phenomenon is untrue" (p. 132).

Inadequate research efforts are due, in part, to the teaching profession's lack of an effective research and development system. There is no appropriate structure to organize comprehensive research projects and disseminate findings throughout the profession. Until such a system is established, educational research will lack the quality and quantity needed to acquire the empirical foundation that the teaching profession desperately needs. Furthermore, too much of the research relating to student teaching is based on information obtained from questionnaires, opinion polls, and evaluations by students, cooperating teachers, or college supervisors. More experimental studies are needed and greater attention should also be given to long-term investigations. Dependent variables should consist of those professional abilities and skills that are directly related to effective teaching. Only when reliable information is available to guide professional teacher behavior can a preparation program be designed with confidence.

Organizational and structional problems also exist that contribute to complications in student teaching programs. Definite objectives for student teaching appear to be nonexistent. An American Association of Colleges for Teacher Education (AACTE) task force described the goal of student teaching as being "to enable teacher candidates to master pedagogical knowledge and skills to a level which allows them to enter the classroom with the confidence of knowing how to cope with planned and unexpected events" (AACTE, 1983, p. 14). This is indeed a worthy goal. But what are the specific objectives of student teaching that will lead to the achievement of that goal?

There is also a lack of coordination and continuity between the instructional program provided in the school of education and the field-based experiences in the schools. These two elements are not carefully designed and structured to complement one another in achieving the objectives of the preparation program. Thus, each functions independently and sometimes even in conflict with the other.

Without proper leadership from and involvement with the school of education, cooperating teachers may be forced to rely upon their own judgment concerning practicum objectives and activities. Consequently, cooperating teachers may simply instruct trainees in "this-is-how-I-do-it" methods and techniques. Thus, trainees learn only their cooperating teachers' pedagogical methods. This leads to an acceptance of and dependence upon the personal experiences of their cooperating teachers. As a result, teacher trainees fail to develop a body of professional knowledge, skills, and attitudes needed by and common to all teacher practitioners.

Also, there is confusion concerning the respective responsibilities of the cooperating teacher, college supervisor, and student teacher. Who is responsible for designing the trainees' program in the schools? Is it a team effort? Should the legal and professional status of the student teacher be that of a junior member of the teaching profession, of a student, or both? What professional duties and responsibilities should student teachers be assigned? Is the task of the college supervisor mainly that of sustaining good public relations? Should the college supervisor work primarily with the cooperating teacher in an advisory capacity and leave the actual contact and supervision of the trainee in the hands of the cooperating teacher? Is there even a need for college supervisors?

Furthermore, public schools are not designed to prepare student teachers. The basic function of schools is to provide educational services for pupils. Administrators and teachers may be reluctant to alter routines simply for the benefit of teacher trainees. This is especially so if they believe such alterations are not in the best interest of their pupils. Consequently, the student teacher may be perceived as a visitor from the university who must adjust to the procedures and practices of that school with few, if any, specific provisions for his/her own instructional needs.

Schools of education have no real authority over the content of the student teaching experience. Ordinarily, the cooperating teacher is paid by the school district and is administratively responsible to the building principal. Cooperating teachers are usually selected for essentially political or administrative reasons and not because they are uniquely qualified to serve as examples, advisors, and tutors. As Kaplan (1979) observed, "colleges of education must place their students with available teachers rather than appropriate ones" (p. 62). These cooperating teachers are paid little or nothing by the university for working with trainees and do so primarily as a professional courtesy. Schools of education, therefore, have limited influence on the content, organization, and structure of these field-based experiences. Thus, they cannot design these experiences as an integrated and compatible part of the entire teacher preparation program.

Within the present limited structure of teacher preparation programs, it may be impossible to make any modifications in student teaching that will have major impact. The length of the total teacher preparation program is far too short. Other professions have organized their practitioner preparation system into preprofessional (undergraduate) and professional (graduate) components, but teacher preparation is still confined to a brief, inadequate undergraduate program. Within this restricted "life space," it may be impossible to structure an effective student teaching practicum. We may discover that little can be done within the limits of a baccalaureate degree that will make a significant difference in our attempts to develop professional knowledge, skills, and attitudes in teacher trainees.

IMPLICATIONS FROM RESEARCH

Although the research on student teaching is sparse, it does suggest some tentative courses of action. The research data agree that the cooperating teacher is extremely influential in shaping the attitudes and behaviors of student teachers. Furthermore, several studies indicated that better identification and structure of a cooperating teacher's responsibilities and duties improve the quality of the student teaching experience.

It is clear, therefore, that cooperating teachers must become colleagues of teacher educators and be more intimately involved in the entire teacher preparation program. The objective of the student teaching experience and the practicum activities of the student teacher must be designed and agreed upon by college-based teacher educators and school-based cooperating teachers. The objectives and processes of the program should be clear to all involved. College- and school-based staff involved in teacher preparation should be striving for common objectives. Whether this can occur under present conditions and circumstances is certainly questionable.

A second finding that has occurred with considerable consistency is the student teachers' negative shift in attitudes during the student teaching experience. The research data do not reveal the cause for this undesirable effect. However, student teachers, cooperating teachers, and college supervisors should be aware of the tendency and pursue courses of action to instill and maintain in teacher trainees healthy, positive attitudes toward pupils, the profession, and themselves.

The present level of involvement and participation in the student teaching practicum by the college supervisor is of limited utility. In order to have an impact on the teacher trainee during the student teaching experience, the college supervisor must make frequent and lengthy visits to the schools. This has implications for the selection of cooperating schools. Schools serving as field-based training centers may have to be located near the school of education. Also, universities must be willing to commit the necessary college staff and resources to adequately perform this professional duty.

Research data also indicate that a structured approach with specific objectives and a carefully designed program would result in a more effective student teaching experience. Cooperating teachers should be involved in the design of the entire preservice program with special attention given to their specific duties and responsibilities. These are some of the courses of action that present research data indicate are needed. However, given the present organization, structure and financial status of schools of education, it is doubtful if even these modest measures can be instituted. Smith (1980) observed, "neither the local board of education nor the State has seriously committed itself to the task of providing the proper clinical conditions for pedagogical training. For another thing, colleges of pedagogy have never committed their resources or staffs to the task of pedagogical training nor provided the leadership to induce local school personnel to join in a study of the mutual problems of pedagogical education" (p. 21).

A PROPOSAL

Instead of continuing to make minor alterations in programs that are obsolete and ineffective, Smith (1980) advocates the redesign of the teacher preparation system. Smith described a model that would incorporate practicum experiences in clinical centers located in selected public schools with instructional activities in a school of pedagogy.

A formal, contractual relationship between the school of pedagogy and the public school systems that house the clinical training centers would resolve many present organizational problems. Schools of pedagogy would have a greater voice in the selection of cooperating teachers and the placement of trainees. Cooperating teachers would become administratively responsible to the school of pedagogy for their duties and assignments concerning teacher trainees. The school of pedagogy would also exert greater control over specific practicum objectives and activities.

In addition, it would require intimate involvement of teacher educators in field-based practicums; a condition that Judge (1982) noted is missing from present student teaching programs. Thus, instead of serving a political function, college supervisors would be actively involved with trainee programs in the clinical centers. In addition, cooperating teachers would also be more involved with that portion of the preparation program conducted in the university. Consequently, this should result in greater cooperation between college- and school-based staff.

This reorganization of teacher preparation would also create a unity between the field-based and university components of the preparation program. Trainees would have a continuous program of practicum experiences in conjunction with academic preparation in the school of pedagogy. This strategy appears superior to the divided and intermittent experiences that characterize present programs. The objectives and activities of the field-based and university-based components could be coordinated in a fashion so that each would be compatible with the other and make its unique contribution to the professional preparation of teachers.

The model designed by Smith (1980) would also provide a setting in which high quality research projects could be conducted. Consequently, many of the questions concerning student teaching could be empirically addressed.

FINAL OBSERVATIONS

Whether schools of education attempt to restructure teacher education completely as advised by Smith or simply continue their efforts to facelift present programs, the available information on student teaching leads us to two conclusions. First, existing research strongly indicates that present student teaching programs are generally unsatisfactory. They are not achieving the goals of teacher education and may, in fact, be regressive to the professional development of student teachers. In view of student teaching's meager contributions to the professional preparation of teachers, and with its present unsatisfactory structure and organization, it does not deserve its privileged status. The second conclusion is that current research efforts are inadequate. Present investigations cannot provide sufficient information to effectively guide professional actions and decisions in regard to student teaching. If excellence in education is to be achieved, then we must attack these issues with vigor and determination.

REFERENCES

Alper, S., & Retish, P. (1972). A comparative study on the effects of student teaching on the attitudes of students in special education, elementary education, and secondary education. *The Training School Bulletin, 69*(2), 70–77.

Alvermann, D. (1981). The possible values of dissonance in student teaching experiences. *Journal of Teacher Education, 32*(3), 24–25.

American Association of Colleges for Teacher Education. (1983). *Educating a profession: Profile of a beginning teacher.* Washington, DC: Author.

Bartholomew, J. (1976). Schooling teachers: The myth of the liberal college. In G. Whitty & M. Young (Eds.), *Explorations in the politics of school knowledge.* Drifferton, England: Nafferton.

Beyer, L. (1984). Field experience, ideology, and the development of critical reflectivity. *Journal of Teacher Education, 35*(3), 36–41.

Bowman, N. (1978). Student teacher supervision, practices and policies. *Action in Teacher Education, 1*(1), 62–65.

Cohn, M. (1981). A new supervision model for linking theory to practice. *Journal of Teacher Education, 32*(3), 26–30.

Coker, H., Medley, D., & Soar, R. (1980). How valid are expert opinions about effective teaching? *Phi Delta Kappan, 62*(2), 131–134; 149.

Covert, J., & Clifton, R. (1983). An examination of the effects of externalizing the practicum on the professional disposition of student teachers. *Alberta Journal of Educational Research, 29*(4), 297–307.

Dispoto, R. (1980). Affective changes associated with student teaching. *College Student Journal, 14*(2), 190–194.

Dutton, W. (1962). Attitude and anxiety change of elementary school student teachers. *Journal of Educational Research, 55*(6), 380–382.

Felder, B., Hollis, M., & Houston, W. (1979). *Problems and perceptions of beginning teachers: A follow-up study.* (ERIC Document Reproduction and Service No. ED 201 595). Washington, DC: US Government Printing Office.

Fink, C. (1976, November). *Social studies student teachers—What do they really learn?* Paper presented at the annual meeting of the National Council for the Social Studies, Washington, DC.

Freeman, D., Bradley, B., & Bornstein, T. (1979). *Survey of M.S.U. graduates of five student teaching programs: Trends and long-range outcomes of student teaching programs suggested by a survey of Michigan State University graduates and their supervisors.* (ERIC

Document Reproduction Service No. ED 166 163). Washington, DC: US Government Printing Office.

Gerwinner, M. (1968). *A study of the results of the interaction of student teachers and their supervising teachers.* Unpublished doctoral dissertation, Mississippi State University.

Griffin, G., Barnes, S., Hughes, R. Jr., O'Neal, S., Defino, M., Edwards, S., & Hukill, H. (1983). *Clinical preservice teacher education: Final report of a descriptive study.* Research and Development Center for Teacher Education. (Rep. No. 9025). Austin: University of Texas at Austin.

Haberman, M. (1981). Editorial. *Journal of Teacher Education, 32*(3), 2.

Haberman, M. (1982). Research needed on direct experience. In D. Corrigan, D. Palmer, & P. Alexander (Eds.), *The future of teacher education: Needed research and practice* (pp. 69–84). College Station: Texas A & M University.

Haberman, M., & Harris, P. (1982). State requirements for cooperating teachers. *Journal of Teacher Education, 33*(3), 45–57.

Henry, M. (1983). The effect of increased exploratory field experiences upon the perceptions and performance of student teachers. *Action in Teacher Education, 5*(1–2), 66–70.

Henry, M., & Sa'ad, F. (1977). The impact of field experience on student teachers' perceptions of good and poor teaching. *Teacher Educator, 13*(2), 18–22.

Herald, J. (1983). *Report to the profession.* Washington, DC: American Association of Colleges for Teacher Education.

Hoffman, E. (1979). Student teaching's legal status varies widely among states. *Journal of Teacher Education, 30*(4), 7–9.

Iannacone, L. (1963). Student teaching: A traditional stage in the making of teachers. *Theory into Practice, 12*(2), 73–80.

Iannacone, L., & Button, H. (1964). *Functions of student teaching: Attitude formation and initiation in elementary student teaching.* Washington, DC: United States Office of Education.

Jones, D. (1982). The influence of length and level of student teaching on pupil control ideology. *High School Journal, 65*(7), 220–225.

Judge, H. (1982). *American graduate schools of education.* New York: Ford Foundation Office Reports.

Kaplan, L. (1979). Does anyone want our student teachers? *Journal of Teacher Education, 30*(3), 62–63.

Kilgore, A. (1979). Pilot project shows definite link between pre-, in-service education. *Journal of Teacher Education, 30*(4), 10–12.

Lortie, D. (1975). *School teacher: A sociological study.* Chicago: University of Chicago Press.

McCaleb, J. (1979). On reconciling dissonance between preparation and practice. *Journal of Teacher Education, 30*(4), 50–53.

McIntyre, D. (1984). A response to the critics of field experience supervision. *Journal of Teacher Education, 35*(3), 42–45.

Moser, C. (1982). Changing attitudes of student teachers on classroom discipline. *Teacher Educator, 18*(1), 10–15.

National Commission for Excellence in Teacher Eduation. (1984). *The status of teacher education.* Washington, DC: American Association of Colleges for Teacher Education.

National Council for Accreditation of Teacher Education. (1982). *Standards for the accreditation of teacher education.* Washington, DC: Author.

National Education Association. (1982). *Excellence in our schools, teacher education: An action plan.* Washington, DC: Author.

National Education Association. (1983). *Standards and certification bodies in the teaching profession.* Washington DC: Author.

Smith, B. (1980). *A design for a school of pedagogy.* Washington, DC: U.S. Department of Education.

Smith, S., & Smith, W. (1979). Teaching the poor: Its effect on student teacher self-concept. *Journal of Teacher Education, 30*(4), 45–49.

Tabachnick, B., Popkewitz, T., & Zeichner, K. (1979–80). Teacher education and professional perspectives of student teachers. *Interchange on Educational Policy, 10*(4), 12–29.

Watts, D. (1982). Can campus-based pre-service teacher education survive? Part III. *Journal of Teacher Education, 33*(3), 48–52.

Wilbur, P., & Gooding, C. (1977). Attitude changes in student teachers. *College Student Journal, 11*(3), 227–231.

Williamson, J., & Campbell, L. (1978). The student teaching experience results in greater emphasis in pupil control. *Southern Journal of Educational Research, 12*(1), 1–6.

Zeichner, K. (1978). The student teaching experience. *Action in Teacher Education, 1,* 58–61.

Zeichner, K., & Tabachnick, B. (1981). Are the effects of university teacher education "washed out" by school experience? *Journal of Teacher Education, 32*(3), 7–11.

Zimpher, N., deVoss, G., & Nott, D. (1980). A closer look at university student teacher supervision. *Journal of Teacher Education 31*(4), 11–15.

Chapter 8
Fifth Year and Extended Programs

Dale P. Scannell

University of Maryland, College Park

In 1976 the Bicenntenial Commission appointed by the American Association of Colleges for Teacher Education presented its report, *Educating a Profession* (Howsam, Corrigan, Denemark, & Nash, 1976). Among the recommendations included was one calling on teacher education institutions to provide a comprehensive program, based on research and accepted best practice, for all prospective teachers. The report noted that such programs would require 150 semester hours or 5 years of study. Although not the first reference to the need for extended teacher education programs, *Educating a Profession* presented a major, compelling argument justifying 5-year programs as necessary for teaching to become a profession based on liberal education and a body of knowledge unique to education professionals.

Educating a Profession includes the recommendation: That teacher preparation for initial service be conducted in a 5-year sequence combining both bachelor's and master's degrees. Further the report noted:

> This plan will provide the "life space" urgently needed for adequate preparation in general education, academic specialization, preprofessional social and behavioral sciences, educational foundations, subculture study, and an appropriate blend of campus and field experiences emphasizing effective instructional strategies. The Commission is not recommending simply an expansion of existing liberal arts and professional components into an additional year of study. Instead, it is urging a bold new commitment of time, energy, and resources for an entirely original structure to prepare teachers. (p. 99-100)

Reactions to *Educating a Profession,* both within the Association which had commissioned the report and among member institutions, were lethargic. Several years elapsed before the Association took any action related to extended programs, and until the recent flurry of "reform" literature only a limited number of institutions had seriously considered extending their teacher education programs.

The major focus of this chapter will be on developments related to extended teacher education programs that have occurred since the publication of *Educating a Profession*. However, the present study will include a description of the four comprehensive extended programs now in existence, including two that preceded the Bicentennial Commission report.

During the early 1960s a substantial number of articles about extended programs appeared in professional journals (e.g., Cartwright, 1961; Fite, 1965; Finnegan, 1976; Heinemann, 1962). In general, the theme of the articles was a recommendation for higher education to consider extended programs as a possible solution to deficiencies in teacher education that were noted at that time. The calls for considering the extension of teacher education programs seems not to have generated widespread or consistent support. In retrospect it seems likely that two major reasons accounted for the lethargic reaction to the recommendations. First, at that time in the history of teacher education programs there was a tenuous knowledge base on which to justify the extension of teacher education programs. Second, and more importantly, the early 1960s were characterized by rapidly increasing K–12 enrollments with the attendant need for additional teachers to staff school classrooms. Thus, the persistent shortage of teachers prevented serious consideration by higher education of extending programs and thereby adding to the teacher shortage and, at the same time, there was an insufficient knowledge base to justify the expansion of the pedagogical aspect of teacher education.

The literature remained relatively silent on the topic of extended programs until the Bicentennial Commission report. Even then, however, higher education did not respond to the challenges of the report by seriously and formally considering the issues associated with extended teacher education programs. In fact, between 1976 and 1980, the most significant reference to more comprehensive teacher education programs was the Hunt Lecture at the 1978 annual meeting of the American Association of Colleges for Teacher Education, delivered by Lawrence Cremin, then President of Columbia Teacher's College.

In the fall of 1979 the Association of Colleges and Schools of Education in State Universities and Land Grant Colleges and Affiliated Private Universities established a task force on the Development of Specific Quality Standards for Teacher Preparation Programs. The task force was charged with developing a set of standards for Association members which included a high degree of specificity with regard to admission and graduation requirements, the nature of the program, and resources necessary for supporting high quality teacher education programs. The final report of the task force was adopted in October of 1982 along with eight recommendations for implementing the content of the task force proposal. The title of the report had evolved during the process of the task force activities and in its final form was "Proposed Standards for Extended Programs of Teacher Education". The report was consistent with the earlier *Educating a Profession* in that it also included a curriculum of approximately 150 semester hours.

In 1979 the membership of the American Association of Colleges for Teacher Education approved a resolution that related to extended teacher education programs, and in 1980 reaffirmed the resolution:

> AACTE encourages the development of major structural changes in college and university preparation programs for teachers. Such changes may address the development of programs of initial certification that go beyond the traditional four-year pattern. These changes may also include promising strategies that involve the redesign of general education, renovation of academic specialization, opportunity for greater depth of study in the professional culture, and more extensive cultivation of essential teacher competencies. (American Association of Colleges for Teacher Education, 1980)

In 1981 the AACTE Board of Directors established a task force on extended programs. The charge to the task force was to develop a paper that would stimulate study and discussion among member institutions and state units on the topic of extended models for initial teacher education programs. The paper also was to include a rationale for considering a major alteration of the prevailing model, a presentation of various models of extended programs, and a consideration of the issues related to adoption of extended programs. The work of the task force was to draw heavily on the product of a second task force which was charged to develop a position paper in cooperation with the National Education Association; *Profile of a Beginning Teacher* (AACTE, 1983b) was to be a statement of the guarantees that should be provided by graduation from an approved teacher education program. The recommendations of the task force on extended programs were to reflect the time required to accomplish the goals of the profile document. Because of a delay in the development of the Profiles, the task force could not accomplish that aspect of its charge. However, the task force reports did draw on the working Profile documents which included curricular recommendations more comprehensive than a 4-year program could accommodate.

The 1983 report of the task force on Extended Programs included a chapter on the reasons why institutions should consider the possibility of adopting an extended program model. The reasons cited included:

1. The rapid expansion of the knowledge base for teacher education during the 1970s. Research on effective schools and effective teachers identified

areas of professional training not included in most 4-year programs which impinged directly on the quality of learning in the K–12 schools. To include the related pedagogy in preservice teacher education programs would require institutions either to extend the length of study or to replace general education and teaching field subject matter with coursework in pedagogy. Because the options were deemed to be counterproductive, if even feasible, extending programs seemed to be the most logical course of action.

2. The evolution of teacher education programs had not followed the trend found in many professional fields. Examples of other fields were cited in which the comprehensiveness of the preservice program had been expanded periodically as the knowledge base for the field had evolved. In teacher education the high school diploma as a requirement was replaced by the normal school which in turn was repalced by the 4-year, baccalaureate model in the 1930s. The 4-year model had remained prevalent over a 50-year period of time, a longer period than found in other fields and the longest plateau in the evolution of teacher education.

3. The nature of the school and expectations of teachers had changed dramatically since the 1930s when the 4-year model had been adopted, and yet teacher education programs had not been changed to reflect those changes in society. In the 1930s the mission of K–12 schools was relatively simple and accepted by most people: the development of basic skills and knowledge of the basic academic disciplines. In addition, the retention rate in high school was relatively low, with non-college bound students leaving school after achieving the mandatory attendance age. In contrast, during the 1970s the holding power of high schools had increased dramatically, the enactment of Public Law 94–142 expanded the range of talent to be found in "regular" classrooms, desegregation and programs in multicultural and multilingual education had made an impact on the schools. Society in the 1970s and 80s was characterized by an increase in the incidence of single parent and two bread winner families, and schools were asked to give added attention to consumer economics, health and substance abuse, environmental education, and parent education. Teachers were no longer working with relatively homogenous groups of students in a monolithic setting on a narrow set of academic goals (AACTE, 1983a).

The report of the task force on extended programs also included a description of several models that could be considered. The models all included four generally accepted components of teacher education programs: general education, teaching field content, professional studies, and clinical application and practice. The models are described briefly in the following paragraphs.

The four plus one, BA: This model represents the typical 4-year program extended by an additional year of professional studies and practicum or internship. It culminates in the baccalaureate degree and generally splits the increased time available between professional studies and clinical experience.

Four plus one with internship: Again, the model includes 4 years as typically found in teacher education programs, and an extra year devoted to a year-long internship and the extensive professional practice which it includes. This program also results in the award of a baccalaureate degree.

Five year with BA plus Masters: The program described in this model includes close articulation between the work completed during the first 4 years and that completed during the fifth year. There are modest increases in subject matter and general education components, a more substantial increase in professional studies, and the possibility of additional clinical experiences. The model includes the award of a baccalaureate degree at the completion of year 4 and the master's degree at the completion of year 5.

A five plus one year, masters degree plus internship: This model is essentially the same as the previous model with the addition of a beginning year program or internship.

Four plus two years: In this model the first 4 years are almost entirely devoted to general education and teaching field requirements. The only exception is the inclusion of a pre-professional component derived from the behavioral sciences. A bachelor's degree is granted at the end of year 4. Year 5 is almost entirely comprised of professional studies with a small clinical component and the work in year 6 is largely a completion of professional studies with one third to one half of the year devoted to clinical experiences. This model can include the award of a master's degree and an Ed.S.

Four plus three with doctorate: The distribution of work in this model is very similar to the distribution found in the previous model. However, clinical work in year 5 and 6 is reduced somwhat and year 7 is an internship year.

Several observations are important to the interpretation of the various models just described. First, the different models vary in terms of the type of enrichment provided over a traditional program. The major components of teacher education programs are not uniformly strengthened in all types of extended programs. Second, some models represent a modest gain over a traditional program whereas others provide a more marked improvement. Figure 1, taken from the AACTE Task Force report, contrasts the various extended models with a traditional 4-year program.

In the early 1980s, B. Othanial Smith (1980), through several publications, called for the development of schools of pedagogy that would represent a marked departure from current curricula and organizations. The school of pedagogy would include, in the recommendations by Smith, a 4-year arts and science program culminating in a bachelor's degree and 2 years of post-baccalaureate study in pedagogy, including a substantial amount of clinical

FIGURE 1. **Contrast of Current Models with Alternative Models (from AACTE, 1983, p. 20)**

Model	Program Components					
	A	**B**	**C**	**D**	**E**	**F**
Typical 4 yr. Program	1	1	1	1	5	5
Four + 1 yr. (B.A.)	1	1	3	3	5	5
Four + 1 yr. (Internship)	1	1	1	1	5	4
Five year (B.A. + M.A.)	2	2	3	3	3	5
Five + 1 yr. (Master's & Internship)	2	2	3	3	3	4
Four + 2 yrs. (Ed. S.)	4	4	4	3	4	5
Four + 3 yrs. (Doc.)	4	4	4	3	4	4
Three + 3 yrs. (Doc.)	4	4	4	4	4	5

Degree of Change:
  1 = No change
  2 = Slight change
  3 = Moderate change
  4 = Substantial change
  5 = Not applicable

Program Components:
  A = General Education
  B = Teaching Field(s) Content
  C = Professional Studies
  D = Clinical Component
  E = Preprofessional Studies
  F = Internship

experience. The program recommended by Smith would be in many ways similar to the four-plus-two program included in the AACTE task force report.

In summarizing the recommendations for extending teacher education programs, there are several important characteristics that should be noted. All reports and recommendations note that a 4-year model cannot give adequate attention to all of the necessary components of teacher education: general education, study in the teaching field, clinical experiences, and the knowledge base of teaching. In other words, to accommodate preservice teacher education within a 4-year model, some or all components of the accepted teacher education program will have to receive less attention than is justified. The reports and recommendations stress the deficit nature of 4-year curricula.

In addition to calling for an increase in the amount of time given to preservice teacher education and the need to strengthen all components of the teacher education program, the reports and recommendations also call for major reorganization of teacher education programs. Most include a recommendation for integration of liberal arts, professional study, and clinical experiences. Some include a recommendation for a layered approach, with pedagogy and clinical experience building on a solid foundation in the arts and sciences. However, all reports stress the importance of cooperation between schools and colleges of education and the arts and science units of the college or university.

The reports also have in common a recommendation that cooperation between higher education and professionals in practice be increased. The importance of cooperating teachers as clinical instructors is stressed, and curriculum design and implementation decisions are noted as areas where improvement is needed.

Recently a study group established by the National Institute of Education (1984) submitted a report titled, *Involvement in Learning: Realizing the Potential of American Higher Education*. This report noted that in order to provide all students with 2 years of general education, some of the professional schools might find extended programs necessary. Among the fields cited was teacher education.

DESCRIPTIONS OF EXISTING 5-YEAR PROGRAMS

Four institutions have developed extended programs in teacher education. One institution is private with a liberal arts orientation. The other three are state supported universities. The programs at these four institutions differ in terms of content, organization and degrees awarded. They have in common a requirement that students complete 5 years of study to earn a recommendation for the initial teaching certificate.

Austin College, Sherman, Texas started a 5-year program in 1972. The University of New Hampshire program was initiated in 1974. The program at the University of Florida is the newest, started in 1984. The University of Kansas program was started in 1981. The first three will be described in broad terms, and the fourth will be described in more detail.

Austin College. The program at Austin College (Steinacher, 1979) is primarily a 4-year emphasis in liberal arts followed by a fifth year of professional study. Included in the undergraduate program are four laboratory experiences related to teaching and schools. The labs range from observation to actual teaching, providing an opportunity for the student to observe teacher behaviors and experience the role of the teacher; in addition the labs provide data for determining the type of assignment students will have during the fifth year.

During the fifth year students are assigned as interns or student teachers for one semester at full-time or two semesters half time. Interns are paid and receive a minimum of supervision. Student teachers are not paid and receive careful supervision. Field-based seminars are held for both interns and student teachers, primarily for a sharing of classroom experiences.

Students in this program can complete a masters degree by taking summer courses in addition to those required for certification.

New Hampshire. The program at the University of New Hampshire (Andrews, 1981) is somewhat more integrated than the Austin program. Although there are no undergraduate majors in education, students have a field experience in year 2 and take four professional courses during the upper division, each with a field component. Students receive a bachelors degree at the end of year 4.

During year 5 students are enrolled in coursework during the summers preceding and following the professional year. The summer enrollments include 12 semester hours in a field of specialization. The academic year is an internship with supervision provided by the regular classroom teacher and a university supervisor.

Florida. As noted earlier the extended program at the University of Florida (Smith, Carroll, & Fry, 1984) was implemented during the fall of 1984. Students aspiring to become secondary teachers will receive a bachelors degree after year 4 from the College of Liberal Arts and Sciences, with a major in a discipline. Elementary and special education students will receive a bachelors degree in education. For all three groups the program is integrated, with some professional course work in years 1–4 and with professional work in year 5 required for a recommendation for certification. Students also will receive a masters degree upon successful completion of the program.

The three programs just described have several important features in common. All three include a stronger general education component, more field experience, and more comprehensive professional training than are found in the prevailing traditional teacher education program model. All three programs were extended to provide more time for all aspects of the education needed by new teachers. All three represent attempts to ensure that beginning teachers have the academic background and professional skills required for success in schools with broad missions and high expectations.

University of Kansas. The 5-year teacher education program at the University of Kansas (Scannell, 1984) is an integrated program. During the first 4 years students complete approximately 132 hours and receive a bachelor's degree. The fifth year is a combination of assignments in the schools and graduate study.

As noted previously, the 5-year program was initiated in 1981. The then-existing 4-year program was scheduled to be phased out with the sophomore class of 1981 who would graduate in 1984. Planning for the extended program was officially started in the fall of 1979 and was intense through the 1980–1981 academic year.

In the fall of 1979 a representative faculty committee was charged with developing a concept paper for the teacher education program at the University of Kansas. The charge included an analysis of factors impinging on teachers, then and in the near future, an analysis of the knowledge base in teacher education, and a description of a program necessary for graduates to meet the challenges of schools and classrooms. The committee was told to ignore all time constraints and to concentrate on the goals needed to ensure graduates who were prepared for the immediate responsibilities of their job and capable of changing during their professional lifetime.

The concept paper included a rationale for a new teacher education program. The factors cited were:

- Educators need the ability to adapt to change. The constant expansion of knowledge and the changing perceptions held by society with regard to the role of education produce conditions requiring the ability of educators to initiate self-developed professional development programs.
- Teacher education should include a strong research utilization component. Research literacy is necessary for the critical analysis of published research and for the systematic study of an individual's classroom effectiveness.
- Prospective teachers need training and field experience to prepare them to individualize instruction for all students. Because of the increasing variability of talent, interests, and motivation in regular classrooms, instruction at an appropriate level for each student requires a high degree of individualization. This training includes skills in diagnosis and prescription, and includes familiarity with the curriculum materials available and the ability to create new materials as needed.
- Prospective teachers need a substantial period to study in the use of educational technology to improve instruction and to enhance student learning. Technology includes microcomputers, the more traditional media, instructional television, and interactive systems.

The concept paper included nine goals that the teacher education program should accomplish. Fifty-three objectives were identified for accomplishing the goals. The goals stated that the prospective teacher:

1. Possesses self-understanding.
2. Has knowledge of human growth, development, and learning and applies this knowledge to teaching children and adolescents.
3. Is skilled in human relations.
4. Understands curriculum planning and is skilled in choosing and adapting instructional strategies to implement varying curricula.
5. Manages a learning environment effectively.
6. Evaluates student learning and uses educational research methodologies to improve instruction and student learning.

7. Understands the scope of the teaching profession and the school as a social–political organization.
8. Is a liberally educated person.
9. Has thorough knowledge of the aspects of at least one subject matter area that is included in the public school curriculum.

The concept paper, and the goals and objectives included in it, served as the guiding structure for the development of a new teacher education program.

The coursework in the new teacher education program was designed to accomplish several major purposes, as follows:

1. To provide students an early opportunity in their college careers to make a well-informed decision about whether to major in teacher education or to seek a different collegiate major.
2. To provide a strong general education and teaching field areas of study.
3. To provide appropriate clinical experiences including frequent activities in K–12 classrooms.
4. To provide careful articulation between theory and practice.
5. To provide an opportunity for the study of theories of pedagogy and recent research.
6. To provide an opportunity for students to develop a teaching style best suited to their own preferences and personality.

These purposes are addressed through the requirements in general education, teaching field and professional education components of the program. The program includes 60 hours of general education. All teachers, regardless of subject or grade level taught, are role models for children and youth. General education is necessary so that teachers can relate content from one field to content in other fields. The 60 hours of general education are distributed among the major fields of English and other language arts, behavioral sciences, social sciences, arts and humanities, science and mathematics, and physical and mental health. The general education courses comprise the major part of the students' enrollments during the first 2 years of the program.

The second major component of a teacher education program, study in a teaching field, provides teachers with sufficient depth to understand how new knowledge in the field is created. Requirements in the teacher education program include a minimum of 40 semester hours in the fields to be taught. Students preparing for middle level and secondary endorsements are encouraged to take one major field and one minor. Elementary teachers are encouraged to take two minors, but they could elect to take one major.

The general education and teaching field requirements were designed by faculty in education and representatives of the arts and sciences disciplines. Although the courses are available to and taken by students from across the campus, the requirements were selected with the needs of K–12 teachers in mind.

The third major division of teacher education is professional education, including clinical experiences. Coursework in pedagogy occupies a very small part of the lower division curriculum, about half of the upper division, and for most students all of the fifth year.

Lower division coursework serves two primary functions, to provide an introduction for subsequent coursework and to provide a basis for a well-informed career decision by students. The first course is an introduction to teaching and is team-taught by a teacher educator and a faculty member from counseling with expertise in career planning. The other lower division courses are child study techniques and multicultural education. By the same time students complete the sophomore year they should have a solid basis for deciding on whether to remain in teacher education or to transfer to another program within the University.

Formal admission to teacher education occurs at the junior year. To be admitted students must have at least a 2.5 grade-point average and satisfactory scores on the writing and mathematics sections of the NTE Pre-Professional Skills Exam.

Professional education coursework is divided between those courses dealing with generic skills, those used by teachers of all levels and subjects, and those that are subject specific relating to a particular teaching field or level. The curriculum is tightly sequenced with subsequent courses building on those preceding. The courses in pedagogy are organized so that four major strands, or themes, spiral through the program. The themes include: child development and learning including attention to exceptionality; assessment, technology, and research literacy; interpersonal relationships; and induction into the role of a teacher, the clinical and experiential aspect of the program.

By the conclusion of the fourth year students will have spent approximately 200 clock hours in the K–12 schools. The field experiences are designed to provide articulation between theory and practice and evolve from observation through tutorial and aiding activities to the student teaching assignment.

Objectives in the program are assigned to specific courses at a specific level of accomplishment. The levels are introduction, acquisition, mastery and generalization. To illustrate, one of the program objectives is:

> Can differentiate normal from atypical pattern of behavior in children and adolescents.

This objective is introduced in a sophomore level course where exceptionalities are described in general terms. At the junior level the objective is covered again, with reading assignments from several well known educational psychology texts. In addition, students are presented video tapes showing atypical behavior for children classified as learning disabled, mentally retarded, and so on. Students in the course must not only differentiate atypical from normal behavior, they also discuss the teacher behavior appropriate for the behaviors observed.

In a senior level course students demonstrate mastery of the objective during field experiences or when viewing video tapes by identifying an atypical behavior and describing the impact on learning and adjustment. The demonstration of the ability to generalize this skill occurs during the final student teaching assignment; the student teacher must identify and deal with atypical behaviors.

Although each level of achievement for this objective is associated with a different course, some objectives have two levels associated with a given course. The most common arrangement is the introduction and acquisition levels occurring in the same course.

At the completion of 4 years students will have completed approximately 132 semester hours. A bachelor's degree is awarded but students at this level do not qualify for a recommendation for certification. To be admitted to the fifth year of the program students must be eligible for admission to the graduate school; an undergraduate G.P.A. of 3.0 is required for full admission, a 2.75 for admission on probation.

The fifth year of the program is divided into three parts. During the first 7 weeks students are assigned to a school for student teaching. During the last 10 weeks students are assigned to a different school, perhaps at a different grade level or in a second subject, for a second student teaching experience. Between these two assignments students will be enrolled in 15 hours of graduate study. Successful completion of year 5 earns the student an institutional recommendation for certification.

CONCLUSION

Educating a Profession (1976) was published 7 years before *A Nation at Risk* and the other recent reports referred to as the reform literature. The Bicentennial Commission was a group of professional educators imploring their colleagues to modify preservice teacher education programs to reflect current and foreseeable demands on teachers. *A Nation at Risk* and other reports were developed by groups of people most of whom were not associated with teacher education. These reports stated quite forcefully that "all is not well" in education and teacher education is part of the problem.

Because of the reports from groups outside of teacher education, the powerful message of *Educating a Profession* finally seems to be having an impact. Though only a few institutions have implemented extended programs, activity across the country suggests that the ranks will swell in the near future. To prepare teachers adequately, programs must have a solid general education foundation, depth in fields to be taught, and professional coursework and experiences drawing on an expanding knowledge base. Four years is not sufficient for accommodating the depth and breadth required to educate the people who educate the next generation of our society.

REFERENCES

American Association of Colleges for Teacher Education. (1980). *AACTE directory*. Washington, DC: Author.

American Association of Colleges for Teacher Education. (1983a). *Educating a profession: Extended programs for teacher education*. Washington, DC: Author.

American Association of Colleges for Teacher Education. (1983b). *Educating a profession: Profile of a beginning teacher*. Washington, DC: Author.

Andrews, M.D. (1981). Five year teaching program: Success and challenges. *Journal of Teacher Education, 32*(3), 40–43.

Cartwright, W.H. (1961). Fifth year programs in teacher education. *Journal of Higher Education, 32*(6), 297–311.

Finnegan, D. (1976, August). The way and how of organizing a five-year program of teacher education. *Bulletin of the National Catholic Education Association, 61,* 184–190.

Fite, E. (1965). Problems in developing a five-year program of teacher education. *Peabody Journal of Education, 42*(4), 206–209.

Heinemann, F.E. (1962, March). Five year teacher preparation. *Minnesota Journal of Education, 42,* 28–29.

Howsam, R.B., Corrigan, D.C., Denemark, G.W., & Nash, R.J. (1976). *Educating a profession* (Report of the AACTE Bicentennial Commission on Education for the Profession of Teaching). Washington, DC: American Association of Colleges for Teacher Education.

National Institute of Education. (1984). *Involvement in learning: Realizing the potential of American higher education*. Washington, DC: Author.

Scannell, D.P. (1984). The extended teacher education program at the University of Kansas. *Phi Delta Kappan, 66*(2), 130–133.

Smith, B.O. (1980). *A design for a school of pedagogy*. Washington, DC: U.S. Department of Education.

Smith, D. (Ed.). (1983). *Essential knowledge for beginning teachers*. Washington, DC: American Association of Colleges for Teacher Education.

Smith, D.C., Carroll, R.G., Fry, B. (1984). Proteach: Professional teacher preparation at the University of Florida. *Phi Delta Kappan, 66*(2), 134–135.

Steinacher, R.C. (1979). *The Austin teacher program and Buck Rogers, Jr.: Preparing teachers for the twenty first century*. Washington, DC: ERIC Clearinghouse on Teacher Education. (ERIC Document Reproduction Service No. ED 171 695)

Chapter 9

Follow-up Studies of Teacher Education Graduates

Ronald D. Adams

Western Kentucky University, Bowling Green

Prior to 1970, follow-up evaluation studies in teacher education were confined to mailed questionnaire findings from graduates which ascertained the respondents' perceptions of their teacher preparation experiences. Occasionally employers were surveyed in an attempt to determine if the institution's graduates were successful as first year teachers. These studies were infrequent and, for the most part, not reported in the professional literature.

Recent research studies on teacher education evaluation practice (Pegues, 1978; Adams & Craig, 1983) have shown that the practice of follow-up evaluation has become more wide-spread during the 1970s and early '80s. Additionally and more significantly, there has been experimentation with different approaches to evaluation of teacher education programs other than the mailed questionnaire to graduates and/or their employers. The purpose of this chapter is to review these recent practices and discuss how these developments and various other factors may impact current and future teacher education evaluation practice.

It may be naive to assume that teacher education evaluation was ever conducted out of an intrinsic value orientation of teacher educators to believe that evaluation is necessary to the improvement and development of teacher preparation. Yet, values toward and beliefs about the worth of evaluation are important if information obtained through evaluation systems is to contribute to the improvement in teacher preparation. The topic of utilization of evaluation studies will be discussed as a logical part of the evaluation process.

MODELS OF EVALUATION

Follow-up evaluation of graduates from teacher education programs has been a chief concern of teacher educators since the early 1970s. This concern was brought about undoubtedly by the rising demands for accountability at all levels of education, but it became a specific focus for teacher education through the accreditation process. In 1970 the National Council for Accreditation of Teacher Education (NCATE) adopted new standards for the accreditation of teacher education programs and contained the following statements:

> The ultimate criterion for judging a teacher education program is whether it produces competent graduates who enter the profession and perform effectively . . . . The institution systematically evaluates the teachers it educates when they complete their programs of study and after they enter the teaching profession, and uses the results of its evaluation in modification and improvement of its programs. (1970, p. 12)

These statements raised considerable concern on the part of those responsible for teacher education programs because the standards specifically called for systematic follow-up evaluation of graduates, an area which had been largely ignored by teacher education institutions (Sandefur, 1970).

A study of the 1970 version of the *Standards for the Accreditation of Teacher Education* was made over a 5-year period between 1975 and 1980. A revised edition was adopted by the NCATE Committee on Standards in 1982. Standard 6, Evaluation, Program Review, and Planning, included still more specificity on graduate evaluation, as related by the following statement:

> Maintenance of acceptable teacher education programs demands a continuous process of evaluation of the graduates of existing programs, modification of existing programs, and long-range planning. The faculty and administrators in teacher education evaluate the results of their programs not only through the assessment of graduates but also by seeking reactions from persons involved with the certification, employment, and supervision of its graduates. The findings of such evaluation are used in program modification. (NCATE, 1982, p. 26)

Christensen and Meade (1984) reported that in 1981 and 1982 all basic programs that were denied NCATE accreditation were cited for not meeting the evaluation standard. It has ranked number one among the standards as being most cited for noncompliance. Thus, the concern for follow-up evaluation of teacher education program graduates has continued as institutions prepare for NCATE accreditation.

There have been several responses to this concern for teacher education evaluation over the last decade and a half. One of the first and possibly best known was a publication by the American Association of Colleges for Teacher Education (AACTE). In response to the earlier NCATE Standard on Evaluation (1970 version), an AACTE Commission on Standards requested that J.T. Sandefur author a monograph specifically dealing with the evaluation of teacher education programs. It was to be the first of several monographs that addressed the new standards, but subsequently was the only such work actually received by the Commission.

In this monograph Sandefur (1970) suggested a model for the follow-up evaluation of graduates that was based on an analysis of the research literature on teaching and learning. He proceeded from two premises: (1) that a sufficient body of research existed from which inferences could be drawn about the characteristics of "good teaching and good teachers," and (2) that classroom observation systems and other evaluative tools were available for use in assessing these characteristics. Sandefur's model proposed a system of evaluation that was longitudinal and field-based. He suggested use of instrumentation that had been developed through research which would provide quantifiable data. Both high-inference and low-inference measures were included as part of the model. Finally, evaluation data would be obtained from multiple sources to include university-based observers trained in classroom observation techniques, peer teachers, supervisors, pupils, and participating graduates.

At least two institutions adopted Sandefur's model, Western Kentucky University in 1972 (Adams, 1978) and Tennessee Technological University in 1974 (Ayers, 1978). These evaluation efforts became widely known as exemplary evaluation programs in teacher education, and numerous reports and presentations were given describing these efforts (Huling & Hord, 1983). Procedurally these programs involved data collection during student teaching and subsequent follow-up for 5 years after graduation. Data were obtained through visitations to the graduate's classroom and maintained as a longitudinal record for continued analysis. A sample was chosen each year to begin a new 5-year cycle of follow-up data collection.

The evaluation efforts at Western Kentucky University and Tennessee Technological University have provided a tested alternative to the traditional mailed questionnaire follow-up evaluation of graduates. Although more costly than the mailed survey, these evaluation programs have demonstrated that rather complex large scale evaluation can occur over an extended period of time and provide quality evaluation information. Much has been learned about teacher education evaluation from these experiences.

The 10 years that Western Kentucky University operated their Teacher Preparation Evaluation Program (1972 through 1981) and the continuing effort by Tennessee Technological University to maintain their evaluation program have provided evidence that Sandefur's model could indeed be implemented and maintained over an extended period of time. These efforts have also provided an unprecedented means for evaluating the model itself. There appear to be three problems with this approach to evaluation. First, the longitudinal evaluation of graduates implies that the same data are obtained on the same teachers over a period of time (Sandefur recommended 5 years). To change instrumentation during this time would severely hamper the longitudinal study of graduates. Yet if an evaluation system is to continue over a number of years and provide meaningful feedback for program improvement, the emerging knowledge base resulting from current research would have to be ignored within the evaluation system. This was particularly true in 1970, as the reported research on teacher effectiveness was relatively prolific during the following decade. This suggests the need for some means of altering the evaluation system by making trade-off decisions between continuing the measurement of old variables and including new ones that have been found to be more relevant to the current knowledge base. It may be that changes can be made within cycles of follow-up rather than across-the-board changes.

A related problem is the rather recent realization of the complexity of the research surrounding teacher effectiveness. Medley's (1977) review of teacher effectiveness research clearly cites the numerous conditions and contexts under which research findings must be viewed before statements of teacher effectiveness may be made. Thus, the development of an evaluation system that would allow for the assessment of teacher education graduates utilizing instrumentation geared around generic, easily obtained measures of teaching effectiveness may not be feasible. This implies the need for increasingly complex evaluation systems that are developed for more specialized and targeted groups of teachers and students.

A final argument against this approach is the potential mismatch between program objectives and evaluation outcome measures. To expect an evaluation system developed externally to the teacher education program (even though the system is based on the most defensible and current research studies) to provide evaluative information that will be used for program modification or change is unrealistic. A system or procedure that encourages the simultaneous development of program objectives and evaluation design based on the knowledge/research base in teacher effectiveness and teacher education effectiveness would appear to be more desirable.

Several other models have been developed for follow-up evaluation since Sandefur's model appeared in 1970. Borich (1979) published a monograph describing three models for conducting follow-up studies of teacher education graduates. This monograph, commissioned by the Organization for Economic Cooperation and Development, suggested the following models: The Needs Assessment Model, The Relative Gain Model, and The Process-Product Model. The Needs Assessment Model utilizes follow-up questionnaires to teacher education graduates that asks the respondent to rate competency statements, derived from program objectives, as to the relevance to their job function and to their own level of attainment. Based on the difference between the perceived relevance and the attainment level reported, those areas of most importance to program change may be identified. The Relative Gain Model advocates the use of pupil achievement as the criterion against which the teacher (graduate) is measured. This model assumes that teacher competencies result in pupil performance and that confounding variables can be statistically controlled for to allow the effects of teacher training to be assessed. Utilizing multiple regression analysis, the prepost differences, together with covariables identified as potential confounding variables, are analyzed to determine if achievement scores of pupils fall above or below expected outcomes. The third model, Process-Product, was derived from research strategies that study the relationships between teacher behaviors and pupil outcome. A much more sophisticated model than either the Needs Assessment or Relative Gain Models, the Process-Product Model involves direct observation of teacher process variables and relates these to pupil outcome measures obtained similarly to those in the Relative Gain Model.

Each of these models has strengths and weaknesses. The Needs Assessment Model relies on teacher perceptions and suffers from the traditional weaknesses of survey research such as non-returns, item ambiguity, and response integrity. Its strengths lie in the relatively lower cost and ease of implementation. The Relative Gain Model is more expensive and has the added problem of lack of competency specificity. Decisions of program effectiveness can only be determined by comparing the pupil gain of teachers who have had a specific training to pupil gains of those teachers who have not. This system cannot specify areas of program weaknesses. The Process-Product, although the stronger of the models presented by Borich, has the distinct disadvantage of requiring a great amount of personnel and support costs, which would prove too expensive for most institutions given the current level of financing. Other considerations are the host of problems associated with process-product research presented by Soar and Soar (1983). Although Borich gives theoretical examples of various contexts in which the three models might be used, no examples of actual field testing were provided to suggest their feasibility of implementation.

Yeany (1980) has suggested a more complex process-product model that involves expanding the process to include teacher preparation as the process and the teacher education graduate as the product. This system would include a two-level process-product assessment with the teacher education program not only being evaluated in terms of their product (i.e., teachers who possess the desired knowledge, attitudes, and skills), but also the products of their graduates (e.g., pupil outcomes). Although this system has interesting possibilities for investigating the relative impact of teacher education on pupil outcome measures, it is doubtful if there are institutions that are able or willing to commit the kind of resources necessary to implement such a complex model. The model has more implications for research in teacher education than for evaluation, particularly if the teacher preparation process can be documented and systematically changed to test varying preparation theories.

Dillon and Starkman (1981) described a "model" approach to evaluation that, in their opinion, would meet the standards set by NCATE and provide reliable information about the effectiveness of teacher education program efforts. Their model calls for three or four programs to be selected for full evaluation each year, even though data are obtained from all entering and exiting students each term. During the fall, evaluation personnel meet with the program faculty and establish the particular evaluation design for that program. The winter is devoted primarily to interviewing graduates from the targeted programs and their supervisors as well as collecting written responses to various instruments. Data are analyzed during the late spring and summer. In the early fall, evaluators meet with program faculty to review findings, and the process begins again for other programs. Faculty are responsible for drawing conclusions from the evaluation findings and making appropriate program adjustments based on these conclusions. According to the authors, this decision making process has been successful. It is one of the few examples where user involvement, feedback, and decision making were included as part of the evaluation model, a desirable, even necessary, component if evaluation outcomes are to have impact on teacher preparation.

The Dillon and Starkman (1981) model has several advantages in addition to the built-in "program modification" element. It includes the analysis of data obtained from multiple sources, both field-based (graduates and supervisors) and campus-based (faculty and students). The system is longitudinal to permit, to some degree, the assessment of program impact on teachers both as students and as practicing teachers. Follow-up data are obtained from visits to the graduates' work places, permitting information to be gathered directly from the graduates and their supervisors as well as contextual data about pupils and the community.

There are also some disadvantages to this system. The authors state the data are "technically defensible" because they are longitudinal, collected from all students, interview-based rather than mailed questionnaires, computerized, and comprehensive. These are desirable characteristics methodologically, but they do not ensure the data are technically defensible from a measurement perspective, for example, validity and reliability considerations. For the most part, their instruments appear to be derived from perceptions of educators rather than from research, are ratings or rankings of those perceptions by educators, and do not have established relationships to pupil outcome measures. The use of such high inference measures are questionable according to Medley, Coker, and Soar (1984). The interview data are also questionable because they are obtained by evaluation staff for several programs and may involve professional judgements that require an in-depth knowledge of the specific program areas. The follow-up period for this model is for 1 or 2 years. There exists some evidence that this may not be long enough to allow the teacher to adjust to their new role. The induction of new teachers may take a period of at least 3 years before the desirable characteristics of teaching can emerge (Adams, 1982; Adams & Martray, 1980).

A recent book entitled *Measurement-Based Evaluation of Teacher Performance* by Medley, Coker, and Soar (1984) may provide a source of information that has implications for teacher education evaluation. The authors, well known for their research in teacher effectiveness, have explored means for evaluating teachers based on classroom performance. They argue quite convincingly that structured observational systems are the key to valid teacher evaluation systems that can lead to improvement of teaching and increased achievement of students. A sequence for developing the evaluation system included the selection of "Dimensions of Performance" to be evaluated. These dimensions must have specified behaviors that define them, but may come from educational theory, consensus of educators, or research on teaching.

The authors suggest that evaluators locate an existing structured observational system or systems that contain the dimensions chosen to be evaluated. They further suggest that a critical component in the evaluation process is the common understanding between the teacher and evaluator as to the nature of the tasks the teacher is to perform while her behavior is being observed. The resulting record of the teacher's classroom behavior is objectively obtained and scored. The final task in this developmental sequence is to decide how to use the information obtained from the evaluation process. The authors suggest developing individual profiles, group profiles, and norms that can be used for making judgements about a specific teacher's behavior.

One of the problems of using this system for developing evaluation studies of teachers would be (as the authors have admitted) the difficulty and complexity of design and implementation. This would become an even greater problem in adapting their system to follow-up studies of graduates from teacher education programs. In addition, the collection of low inference measures from structured classroom observational systems implies that the data obtained are mostly free from value judgements made by data collectors. That is, the Medley, Coker, & Soar (1984) approach would have the value judgements be made on the basis of an objective, highly descriptive set of data as opposed to more subjective approaches characterized by rating scales, checklists, or interviews. There are those who argue that the latter approach, although more subjective, has more meaning for evaluation purposes and takes advantage of the professional judgement dimension lacking in highly structured, low-inference observational systems. This argument is beyond resolution in this text but is one that is important when considering the development of observation systems.

CURRENT PRACTICE

The degree to which the models of teacher education evaluation are being or will be followed is unclear. However, it is clear that as late as 1981 the majority of institutions were reporting the conduct of follow-up evaluations of their teacher education graduates. Adams and Craig (1983) reported the results of a survey designed to describe the state-of-the-practice in teacher education practice. The population surveyed was 779 institutions on the AACTE membership list during the 1980–81 academic year. Surveys regarding institutional teacher education evaluation practices were mailed to deans or department heads of teacher education. A 57% return rate was obtained.

The results of this survey revealed that only 14.4% of the responding institutions reported conducting no evaluation, and 12.1% reported preservice evaluation only. The remaining 73.5% were involved in some form of follow-up evaluation. Yet, Katz, Raths, Mohanty, Kurachi, and Irving (1981) found only 26 studies of follow-up evaluation efforts in a literature search on the topic. Although there appear to be numerous institutions engaged in follow-up evaluation of graduates, these evaluation studies are not being included in the professional literature.

The Adams and Craig (1983) survey also found that by far the most often reported technique for collecting follow-up data on graduates was by questionnaires sent to first year graduates (53.8%) and supervisors of graduates (44.6%). Sustained contact with graduates was reported by roughly one fourth of the institutions, as follow-up questionnaires were sent to graduates as late as 4 to 11 or more years after graduation.

A survey on follow-up evaluation practice conducted by Pegues (1978) produced similar findings. Pegues found that approximately half of the respondents to her survey were engaged in follow-up evaluation and that by far the most prevalent schema was the "controversial one-shot questionnaire" sent to graduates the first year following graduation.

Between 9 and 10% of the respondents to the Adams and Craig (1983) survey reported first year follow-up visitations to gather interview or classroom observation data from graduates. In addition, several institutions reported interviews with employers. These approaches to evaluation support the notion that some experimentation with methods of evaluation beyond the one-shot questionnaire is occurring.

An interesting and important finding from the Adams and Craig (1983) survey was that evaluation of preservice students was occurring as regularly as was follow-up evaluation. Even though NCATE standards call primarily for follow-up evaluation, institutions reported gathering evaluative data on students at entry in teacher education, during their teacher education program, and at exit from their programs of study. The most often reported methods for gathering entry data were questionnaires (34.9%) and personal interviews (26.8%). Classroom observation was reported as the most frequent method of assessing students while they were matriculating through the teacher education programs (66.7%) followed by student questionnaires (48.3%) and supervisor questionnaires (42%). Exit data were collected through questionnaires given to students (64.7%) and supervisors (44.9%) and through direct classroom observation, probably during student teaching (39.9%).

These data suggest that evaluation of teacher education programs is occurring at various stages within the preparation process as well as through follow-up assessment of the graduate. It is not known the extent to which these evaluation efforts are conducted as part of a systematic approach to evaluation or if they represent longitudinal or cross-sectional studies of the student/graduate. There is some evidence that systematic and longitudinal studies are occurring, however.

Undoubtedly, many of the evaluation efforts conducted during preservice teacher education came about as part of the Competency Based Teacher Education movement in the early 1970s (Hall, 1981). For example, Weber and Cooper (1978) and Jones and Randall (1978) describe extensive development of student and curriculum evaluation strategies as part of the Competency Based Teacher Education (CBTE) program at the University of Houston. Other institutions strongly engaged in the early CBTE movement were the University of Nebraska, Oregon College of Education, and Weber State College. Only until recently, however, have institutions begun to plan and implement evaluation systems that bring together evaluative data on students as they enter teacher education, matriculate through the teacher education program, exit from teacher education and enter the teaching profession.

Galluzzo (1983) reported that Glassboro State College is conducting a longitudinal assessment of students enrolled in their teacher education programs. This system, based on Stufflebeam's (1971) CIPP (Context, Input, Process, Product) evaluation model, collects data repeatedly over four years of teacher preparation. These data include professional education knowledge, basic skills and attitudinal measures. Follow-up questionnaires based on program objectives are sent to first year graduates.

Current efforts in evaluation at The Ohio State University also indicate the marriage of data obtained during preservice and follow-up of graduates (Loadman, 1984). The Student Information System (SIS) is characterized by rather elaborate data collection procedures that document the students' experience within their preservice programs, diagnose student progress to assist in advisement and gather data on students and programs for evaluation and research purposes. Follow-up evaluation methods include a demographics survey, GRE scores, observation of graduates, a supervisor survey, and interviews with graduates and their supervisors. Loadman (1984) has suggested that the data will be triangulated where possible, providing a multifaceted overall picture of their teacher education programs.

Dravland and Green (1979) described teacher education evaluation activities at the University of Lethbridge in Alberta, Canada. The QUALTEP (Qualitative Analysis of the Lethbridge Teacher Education Program) was reported as an evaluation program designed to collect and analyze data obtained from five categories of variables: pre-education, selection, training, placement, and work success. The QUALTEP represents a signficant effort in teacher education evaluation that utilizes follow-up evaluation as the logical extension of an extensive preservice program evaluation system.

ACTIVITIES, ISSUES, AND TRENDS

Up to this point the intent of this chapter has been to describe and discuss evaluation models and current practice utilized for evaluating teacher education programs. However, it is important to realize that there have been significant activities other than NCATE and individual program efforts that have and will continue to influence the evaluation practices of institutions preparing teachers. There are issues and trends both within teacher education and from outside that will certainly contribute to a change in the conduct of evaluation practice.

One of the problematic issues in teacher education evaluation has been referred to repeatedly in the literature (Strathe, 1982; Katz et al., 1981; Adams, Craig, Hord, & Hall, 1981; Adams & Craig, 1983). This problem concerns communication among teacher educators who have the responsibility for or interest in evaluation of their programs. Although there is evidence that most institutions conduct evaluations of their teacher education programs, only a handful of reports have found their way into the professional literature. Thus, the literature has provided limited communication among those engaged in evaluation practice.

To address this problem the National Research and Development Center for Teacher Education has sponsored a number of activities that have resulted in more effective communication among individuals concerned with teacher education evaluation. In 1978 a colloquium on teacher education program follow-up studies was hosted by the R & D Center. Seven institutions identified as having experience with follow-up evaluation of graduates were invited to spend 3 days discussing common interests in follow-up evaluation. Two outcomes from this small conference emerged that are noteworthy. First, Hord and Hall (1978) edited a Research and Development Center for Teacher Education publication entitled *Teacher Education Program Evaluation and Follow-Up Studies: A Collection of Current Efforts*. This publication, which described the evaluation efforts of those institutions participating in the colloquium, was a first attempt to provide the profession with examples of "how to" in teacher education evaluation.

A second outcome of this meeting was the initiation of a network for individuals interested in teacher education evaluation. This network became known as TEPFU, Teacher Education Program Follow-Up studies group. Although no longer limited to individuals engaged in just follow-up studies, the TEPFU network has expanded its initial focus to include all aspects of teacher education program evaluation to include entry-level and preservice program evaluation. This somewhat loosely organized group has provided valuable services to members of the education profession concerned with teacher education evaluation including a TEPFU newsletter, supported by the R & D Center, with a mailing list of over 500. The R & D Center has also published a series of monographs that deal with current issues in teacher education evaluation. The TEPFU group meets on an annual basis often in conjunction with AACTE or AERA annual meetings, as well as special individual conferences, to address problems and issues of teacher education evaluation.

Another example of how communication is being facilitated is through the effort of Gary Galluzzo at Glassboro State University in New Jersey. Galluzzo is developing and maintaining a repository of teacher education program evaluation summaries. Currently more than 250 institutions have responded to the call for participation in the repository. Institutions join by providing a description of their evaluation procedures to include instrumentation and results of their evaluation efforts and in return have access to what other institutions have reported. Although not fully developed at this time, this activity has great potential for monitoring and promoting teacher education evaluation among institutions.

There is some evidence that professional associations are beginning to respond to the need for better communication. AACTE and Illinois State University co-sponsored an invitational conference on teacher education student assessment during the summer of 1984. This 3-day conference led to additional meetings planned during the 1985 annual conference of AACTE. AERA has recently formed a new Division K that is devoted primarily to teacher education research. This new division may lead to a forum for reporting follow-up evaluation studies.

The increase in conferencing and networking as evidenced by the TEPFU network and professional associations and groups may lead to a more effective means of communication among practitioners in teacher education evaluation. At present, this appears to be our best hope in providing solutions to the communication problem.

The national press for accountability in education and the call for educational reforms by virtually all segments of society must have an effect on teacher education programs and how they will be evaluated in the future. From the National Commission on Excellence in Education report, *A Nation at Risk* (1983) to recent articles and reports such as, "Why Teachers Fail" (*Newsweek,* 1984), and *The Making of a Teacher* (Feistretzer, 1984) lack of quality teacher education is being cited as one of the reasons public schools fail to meet public expectations for educating the nation's youth. That teacher education will become increasingly scrutinized for its contributions in preparing effective productive teachers is almost a certainty.

It stands to reason that institutions preparing teachers must respond to these demands of accountability through verifiable evidence of the quality of their programs. The logical means for providing such evidence is through defensible systems of program evaluation which contain a strong follow-up component. It may no longer be enough to produce findings from an occasional one-shot survey to graduates or employers of graduates indicating satisfaction with their teacher education program or with the products of those programs, respectively. Evidence of a quality teacher education program must begin to include the first hand successes and failures of graduates as they perform in their professional roles and build around these findings programs to prepare teachers for today's schools. Such an undertaking will not come easily and will not be inexpensive.

When certain social problems capture the public's attention to the degree that the quality of American education has, inevitably there is a political response. Recent publications citing the ills of American education have not escaped attention of state and national legislators. The almost phenomenal growth of mandated competency assessment for teacher certification has affected teacher education programs and their evaluation, and will undoubtedly continue to exert considerable influence.

Sandefur (1984) surveyed directors of teacher education and certification in each state to determine the status of mandatory competency assessment of teachers. In 1977 there were 3 states with such requirements. In 1983 30 states reported some type of teacher assessment program, and 12 others reported planning of such programs. Of these 30 states, 11 had legislative mandates and 22 had state board of education mandates (3 had both). Twenty-five of the 30 states had competency assessment for certification, with 10 of these states requiring on-the-job assessment — usually involving a visiting team.

A study by an AACTE (1983) Task Force on Shortage/Surplus/Quality Issues in Teacher Education provided evidence that changes in teacher certification standards affected teacher education program offerings, and these changes were perceived as positive. Yet, these same respondents saw teacher educators as the third most influential group in changing teacher certification standards, preceded by state departments of education and legislators, respectively. Other findings from this survey indicated that responses to questionnaire items differed when states with mandated competency assessment of teachers were compared to states without such requirements. Respondents from states with mandated competency assessment requirements placed more importance on entry tests of basic skills, increased hours for teacher preparation, and increased financial resources for teacher education than did respondents from states without mandates. Incidentally, evaluation of teacher education programs was ranked highly by both groups as an area that affected the quality of the teacher education graduate.

These findings indicate that state mandates for competency assessment of teachers for certification have impacted teacher education. It is equally clear that the movement is continuing toward determining entry criteria for the teaching profession through certification requirements by state departments of education, with some involvement from legislators and teacher educators. This holds tremendous implication for teacher education program development and evaluation, and, gives rise to questions such as the following: Will curricula in teacher education be determined by the state departments of education based on the evaluation of teachers for certification purposes? Will evaluation of teachers when they are certified become the yardstick by which programs of teacher education are measured and will those programs be given state approval if significant numbers of their graduates fail to become certified? Will the new certification assessment procedures permit individuals who are not graduates of teacher education programs to become teachers if they can successfully pass the required tests?

There is some evidence that these questions are already being posed in some states. For example, the AACTE (March, 1984) *Briefs* contains an article which describes the Georgia policy on linking program evaluation with student test performance. The following is the lead statement in that article, "Roughly 12 percent of all teacher education programs in public institutions in Georgia have been placed on probation under a new policy linking evaluation of teacher education programs to student's performance on a certification test . . . " (p. 14). Florida and Alabama have also considered a similar approach. New Jersey has approved a plan to permit the certification of individuals as teachers even though they are not graduates of a teacher education program and indeed may not have taken a single teacher education course.

The verdict is still out as to the degree of impact that mandated competency assessment of teachers for certification purposes will have on teacher education programs and their evaluation. However, it appears that there will be an impact. Whether it is positive or negative will in large measure be determined by the skill and persuasiveness of the leaders in teacher education and the amount of evaluative information at their disposal.

At a time when greater demands are being placed on institutions to produce evidence of quality teacher education, the funds available for higher education are becoming scarcer. This increased demand for quality has led to the screening of students at entry into teacher education through mandated assessment of basic skills, thus making it more difficult for students with marginal academic aptitude to become enrolled in teacher education programs. Add to this the low appeal of teaching as a career, noncompetitive salaries, and the expanded opportunities for women and minorities in other vocations, and the result is that fewer students are choosing to enter teacher education programs.

Because funding for higher education is dependent to a large extent on student enrollment, less dollars are being generated by teacher education than in the past. Also teacher education programs historically have been among the less expensive programs offered at most institutions as they require relatively little equipment, somewhat lower instructional costs, and maintain relatively higher student–teacher ratios than many programs in arts and sciences, the professional schools, business schools, or engineering. This translates into fewer dollars available to teacher education just to maintain quality instruction and supervision of teacher preparation.

To suggest substantial precious resources be devoted to evaluation of teacher education programs may be viewed by some institutions as heresy. Yet, the survival of these programs may depend upon such evaluations. Hearn (1981) addressed this issue and concluded that institutions must adequately fund these increasingly complex evaluation efforts if they expect to be accredited in the future, because little help can be expected from external funds.

Adams and Craig (1983) presented evidence that the general funding level for evaluation of teacher education was dismal. Of the institutions responding to their survey on teacher education evaluation practice, 23.1% were under $250, 27.5% were between $251 and $1,250, 30.6% were between $1,251 and $9,000, and only 18.8% reported budgets of more than $9,000. Given the costs associated with even the most unsophisticated survey, if properly conducted, there is little wonder that follow-up evaluation of teacher education graduates has not moved beyond the simple one-shot mailed questionnaire. Also, it was surprising to note the lack of association between the reported size of the evaluation budget and size of the teacher education program. Institutions with larger teacher education programs apparently do not financially support program evaluation any better than institutions with smaller programs.

Although the aforementioned data were subjected to error made by respondents' perceptions and estimations and a low response rate, they do indicate a serious problem in evaluating teacher education programs. Quality evaluation, like quality research, is expensive. Implementation of the models of evaluation discussed earlier or future models that may be developed will be impossible if there is not an increased commitment to finance the quality evaluation of teacher education. Basic costs associated with data collection, analyses, reporting, and maintenance do not appear to be reflected in at least 50% of the reported cases and are questionable in 30% of the others.

Teacher education evaluation results can help to justify program expenditures, thus, avoiding further budget reductions, and may even help reduce program costs due to unproductive practices in teacher education. For example, one institution has built an evaluation process around the idea of cost effectiveness. Savage, Denton, Colachio, and Salinas (1984) reported on an evaluation program at Texas A & M University in which two secondary certification programs of teacher education were compared. The first program, a major in the College of Education, involved a greater amount of professional education coursework (34 semester hours), while the alternative program, a major in another college, required the completion of 22 semester hours of professional education coursework. Building upon previous evaluation studies of student teacher effectiveness as measured by student cognitive gain, the cost effectiveness of both programs was compared. Results indicated that not only did the majors in teacher education produce greater student mean gains over their counterparts in other colleges, but also that their program costs averaged over $1,000 less. Studies of this type could serve teacher education well in demonstrating the cost efficiency of programs designed to prepare teachers as compared to other programs within the university. This would be particularly true if such studies could be expanded to include follow-up of graduates.

Another change is occurring outside of teacher education that will undoubtedly influence teacher education evaluation. Increasing numbers of states have demanded reform in public school education and are instituting master teacher and/or career ladder plans and merit pay incentives to bring about this reform. It is clear that these plans will require evaluation systems to assist in the determination of deserving recipients. How higher education institutions with teacher education programs will interface with these reforms is unclear at present, but they most certainly will be affected. It is predicted that the increased emphasis on evaluation brought about by these reforms will produce new ways and means of evaluating teacher education programs and graduates.

UTILIZATION

Any discussion of evaluation practice would be remiss without addressing the topic of utilization of evaluation results. Although teacher education accreditation standards dictate that evaluation results be used for program modification, there is little evidence that this is the case in most institutions. One reason may be that many institutions entering into evaluation studies simply do not give proper attention to feedback and utilization of evaluation results. Their initial concern is toward the mechanics of evaluation such as instrument selection, data collection and data analysis, with no planning for how the data will be used.

Adams and Craig (1983) reported findings that support this contention. The most often reported need among institutions not engaged in follow-up evaluation studies was "planning an evaluation system" (40.6%). For those institutions conducting evaluation studies, assistance in feedback and utilization of evaluation results were given as the most frequent needs (46.5%).

Part of this problem may also be attributed to the relative lack of information available to individuals on how to accomplish effective utilization of evaluation results. There are ways of approaching this problem that have come about rather indirectly but are applicable to utilization of teacher education evaluation results. Hall (1984) has suggested that evaluation results can be thought of as an innovation and that the research on "Levels of Use" (Hall, Loucks, Rutherford, & Newlove, 1975) is applicable to assessing the degree to which faculty are using evaluation results in affecting program change. He makes an interesting point that faculty will be spread along a continuum in which some will not be doing anything with the evaluation results, Level 0, while others will at least read the report and ask questions, Level I, and still others who have made the decision to do something, Level II, and so on. There are a number of levels through which faculty may progress with the use of evaluation results to include a routine use level and at later levels making suggestions for the improvement of the evaluation system. Hall's point is that it is unrealistic to expect all faculty to be at the same level of use, and that feedback and utilization strategies designed for faculty at the different levels can facilitate the utilization of evaluative information for program improvement.

Strathe (1984) makes a similar point about faculty being different, but bases her argument around faculty development. She suggests that faculty often do not understand program evaluation as a "mode for systematic inquiry," and there is usually no reward system for faculty to become involved in evaluation studies. She makes the point that faculty must understand the evaluation system and become involved in the process and this involvement must be rewarded. Further, faculty are at varying life stages and these stages reflect different concerns and needs—both professional and personal. The way one would approach one faculty to solicit involvement in evaluation may be quite different to the way one would approach another faculty at a different life stage. A reward for one may not be the same as for another. For example, release time, money, and recognition may have somewhat different values for faculty at different life stages.

Craig and Adams (1981) proposed a procedure for establishing an evaluation system intended to maximize the probable use of evaluation results in program decision making. This procedure is not method-bound and allows the flexibility to tailor the method of evaluation to the particular needs and preferences of individual teacher education program personnel. The following general points are summarized from their recommendations:

1. It is important that the chief administrative officer and his/her staff understand and value the evaluation process. It should be clear from the beginning that the major purpose of the evaluation system is not to meet external demands such as NCATE accreditation, but to provide useful and relevant information for program decision making. They should further emphasize that the administration has a long-term commitment to the evaluation of teacher education programs.

2. The organizational structure and staffing of the institution should be considered when planning and designing (or redesigning) the evaluation system. Both formal and informal faculty leaders should be identified for key roles and responsibilities in this process.

3. Formalized and effective systems of communication must be established and maintained to ensure all parties are kept informed of the progress made in developing the evaluation system, permitting suggestions, recommendations, concerns, and so on, of all parties to be considered in the planning of the evaluation system.

4. It is critical that the evaluation system be viewed by all parties as iterative where both the evaluation process and products evolve over time. The evaluation system itself should contain an evaluation component to allow the system to be continually improved to respond to the needs of program decision makers.

5. It should be understood that although the evaluation system can produce useful and relevant information, program decision making takes into account other information as well. Program decision making occurs in a socio-economic–political context in which decisions to change or modify programs are made in light of available resources, staff limitations or strengths, state mandates, and the like, as well as the information obtained from evaluation studies.

Those responsible for teacher education program evaluation must be concerned with more than methods and techniques of evaluation. They must also consider how the results will be disseminated and utilized for program improvements. This is not a simple reporting procedure where evaluation data are prepared and sent to faculty and administrators in hopes that somehow the information will result in desired program changes. If the results of program evaluation are to impact teacher education practice, they must impact the teacher educator and those who administer teacher education programs. Thus, if the desired result of informed program change is to occur, the evaluation system must include a planned systematic feedback and utilization procedure that takes into account the characteristics of the intended audience.

CONCLUDING REMARKS

To effect informed change in teacher education requires that evaluation systems be instituted that are designed to provide accurate and relevant information for program decision making. However, there is evidence that although leaders in teacher education view evaluation as a beneficial part of program improvement and necessary for accreditation, serious attention is not being given to development and implementation of effective evaluation systems. Inadequate funding, simplistic and outdated evaluation methods, and ineffective feedback and utilization mechanisms are the norm rather than the exception in institutions conducting teacher education evaluation. Even when advances are made or new ways of evaluating are tried, there are few avenues of communication available to share with others these successes or failures.

Public education is in the midst of reform brought about by recent criticism of schools in providing quality education for our nation's youth. Teacher education is not exempt from this criticism. On the contrary, teacher education is being cited as part of the problem and must become part of the reform as solutions are sought to the myriad of problems facing education in the next decade and beyond. Quality teacher education programs that assume responsibility for the products they prepare must be part of the reform movement. Teacher education institutions, together with other segments of the education community, must be accountable for the failures of our public education system and work toward its improvement.

Evaluation systems in teacher education must change to accommodate the changes in teacher education brought about by the reform of the total education system. As legislators and state departments of education become increasingly more active in setting educational policy and local education agencies and teacher organizations demand more voice in teacher education, both preservice and inservice, institutions preparing teachers must respond to these demands with more effective teacher education programs that are relevant and responsive to the needs of teachers. It may be that the emphasis on follow-up evaluation may shift to descriptions of program content and competencies of teacher educators who deliver that content. Follow-up evaluation of teacher education graduates may be accomplished through the state certification process and/or local school system evaluations for teachers' career development.

Whatever the direction taken, there will be opportunities to change both the means and the methods that have characterized teacher education evaluation in the past. Let us hope that the outcome will be a more dynamic and valued evaluation system based on the best available research and professional practice. Let us hope that the educational reform beginning in this country will foster evaluation systems that will unite the profession rather than promote further fragmentation.

REFERENCES

Adams, R.D. (1978). Western Kentucky University follow-up evaluation of teacher education graduates. In S.M. Hord & G.E. Hall (Eds.), *Teacher education program evaluation and follow-up studies: A collection of current efforts* (pp. 11–35). Austin, TX: Research and Development Center for Teacher Education.

Adams, R.D. (1982, March). *Teacher development: A look at changes in teacher perceptions across time.* Paper presented at the Annual Meeting of the American Educational Research Association, New York.

Adams, R.D., & Craig, J.R. (1983). A status report of teacher education program evaluation. *Journal of Teacher Education, 34*(2), 33–36.

Adams, R.D., Craig, J.R., Hord, S.M., & Hall, G.E. (1981). Program evaluation and program development in teacher education: A response to Katz, et al. *Journal of Teacher Education, 32*(5), 21–24.

Adams, R.D., & Martray, C.R. (1980, November). *Correlates of teacher perceived problems.* Paper presented at the 9th Annual Conference of the Mid-South Educational Research Association, New Orleans, LA.

American Association of Colleges for Teacher Education. (1983). *The impact of teacher shortage and surplus on quality issues in teacher education.* Washington, DC: Author.

American Association of Colleges for Teacher Education. (1984). Georgia policy: Program evaluation linked with student test performance. *AACTE Briefs, 5*(2), 14.

Ayers, J.B. (1978). Teacher education program study at Tennessee Technological University. In S.M. Hord & G.E. Hall (Eds.), *Teacher education program evaluation and follow-up studies: A collection of current efforts* (pp. 99–107). Austin, TX: Research and Development Center for Teacher Education.

Borich, G.D. (1979). *Three models for conducting follow-up studies of teacher education and training.* Unpublished manuscript, University of Texas at Austin.

Christenson, D.E., & Meade, M. (Speakers). (1984). *A tale of two standards* (Cassette Recording No. [TE74]). Presented at the Annual Meeting of the AACTE, San Antonio, TX.

Craig, J.R., & Adams, R.D. (1981). Use-oriented evaluation. In S.M. Hord & R.D. Adams (Eds.), *Teacher education program evaluation, 1981: Theory and practice* (pp. 38–48). Austin, TX: Research and Development Center for Teacher Education.

Dillon, J.T., & Starkman, S.S. (1981). A "model" approach to evaluation of teacher education programs. *Education, 101*(4), 366–371.

Dravland, V., & Greene, M. (1979, April). *Development of a model for the evaluation of teacher education programs.* Paper presented at the American Educational Research Association Annual Meeting, San Francisco, CA.

Feistritzer, C.E. (1984). *The making of a teacher: A report on teacher education and certification.* Washington, DC: The National Center for Education Information.

Galluzzo, G.R. (1983, April). *An evaluation of a teacher education program.* Paper presented at the Annual Meeting of the American Educational Research Association, Montreal, Canada.

Greene, M., & Dravland, V. (1979, April). *Relationship between success in an education program and success in the teaching profession.* Paper presented at the American Educational Research Association Annual Meeting, San Francisco, CA.

Hall, G.E. (1981). What is the future of teacher education program evaluation. In S.M. Hord & R.D. Adams (Eds.), *Teacher education program evaluation, 1981: Theory and practice* (pp. 65–75). Austin, TX: Research and Development Center for Teacher Education.

Hall, G.E. (1984). Implementation of evaluation results as an innovation. In S.M. Hord (Ed.), *Strategies for the implementation and utilization of teacher education program evaluations* (pp. 147–155). Austin, TX: Research and Development Center for Teacher

Education.

Hall, G.E., Loucks, S.F., Rutherford, W.E., & Newlove, B.W. (1975). Levels of use of the innovation: A framework for analyzing innovation adoption. *The Journal of Teacher Education, 29*(1), 52–56.

Hearn, Edell M. (1981). Finance and resource allocations relative to teacher education evaluation. In S.M. Hord & R.D. Adams (Eds.), *Teacher education program evaluation 1981: Theory and practice* (pp. 59–64). Austin, TX: Research and Development Center for Teacher Education.

Hord, S.M., & Hall, G. E. (Eds.). (1978). *Teacher education program evaluation and follow-up studies: A collection of current efforts.* Austin, TX: Research and Development Center for Teacher Education.

Huling, L., & Hord, S.M. (1983, August 29). Bibliography of literature on teacher education program evaluation and follow-up studies. *TEPFU Newsletter.*

Jones, H., & Randall, R. (1978). Professional teacher preparation program effectiveness studies: 1976–1977 affective testing. In S.M. Hord & G.E. Hall (Eds.), *Teacher education program evaluation and follow-up studies: A collection of current efforts* (pp. 155–165). Austin, TX: Research and Development Center for Teacher Education.

Katz, L., Raths, J., Mohanty, C., Kurachi, A., & Irving, J. (1981). Follow-up studies: Are they worth the trouble? *Journal of Teacher Education, 32*(2), 18–24.

Loadman, W.E. (1984). Overview of the student information system program evaluation at the Ohio State University College of Education. In S.M. Hord (Ed.), *Strategies for the implementation and utilization of teacher education program evaluations* (pp. 120–124). Austin, TX: Research and Development Center for Teacher Education.

Medley, D.M. (1977). *Teacher competence and teacher effectiveness: A review of process-product research.* Washington, DC: American Association of Colleges for Teacher Education.

Medley, D.M., Coker, H., & Soar, R.S. (1984). *Measurement-based evaluation of teacher performance.* New York: Longman.

National Commission on Excellence in Education. (1983). *A nation at risk: The imperative for educational reform.* Washington, DC: Author.

National Council for the Accreditation of Teacher Education. (1970). *Standards for the accreditation of teacher education.* Washington, DC: Author.

National Council for the Accreditation of Teacher Education. (1982). *Standards for the accreditation of teacher education.* Washington, DC: Author.

Pegues, W.W. (1978). *An assessment of teacher education follow-up evaluation in the United States: A descriptive analysis.* Unpublished doctoral dissertations, University of Tulsa.

Sandefur, J.T. (1970). *An illustrated model for the evaluation of teacher education graduates.* Washington, DC: American Association of Colleges of Teacher Education.

Sandefur, J.T. (1984). State assessment trends *AACTE Briefs, 5*(2), 17–19.

Savage, T.V., Denton, J.J., Colachico, D., & Salinas, L. (1984, February). *Cost effectiveness in program evaluation: A comparison of student costs in alternative preparation programs.* Paper presented at the Association of Teacher Educators Meeting, New Orleans, LA.

Soar, R.S., & Soar, R.M. (1983, February). *Context effects in the teaching–learning process.* Paper presented at the AACTE Meeting, Detroit.

Strathe, M.I. (1982). Program evaluation in teacher education: Future directions. In S.M. Hord, T.V. Savage, & L.J. Bethel (Eds.), *Toward usable strategies for teacher edcucation program evaluation* (pp. 169–178). Austin, TX: Research and Development Center for Teacher Education.

Strathe, M.I. (1984). Faculty development: Linking teacher education program evaluation and program change. In S.M. Hord (Ed.), *Strategies for the implementation and utilization of teacher education program evaluations* (pp. 143–146). Austin, TX: Research and Development Center for Teacher Education.

Stufflebaum, D.L. (1971). *Educational evaluation and decision making.* Itasca, IL: Peacock.

Weber, W.A., & Cooper, M.J. (1978). Evaluation of instructional system characteristics of the professional teacher preparation program at the University of Houston. In S.M. Hord & G.E. Hall (Eds.), *Teacher education program evaluation and follow-up studies: A collection of current efforts* (pp. 133–152). Austin, TX: Research and Development Center for Teacher Education.

Why teachers fail. (1984, September 24). *Newsweek,* pp. 64–70.

Yeany, R.H. (1980). Redefining process and product in teacher training: Alternative modes for evaluating teacher training programs. *Journal of Research in Science Teaching, 17*(5), 383–386.

Chapter 10

An Alternative View of the Evaluation of Teacher Education Programs

James D. Raths

University of Illinois, Urbana-Champaign

INTRODUCTION

The evaluation of teacher education programs is relevant to a number of interested audiences. Accrediting agencies want to recognize programs that are working well and to improve or to disestablish those that are weak. The organized professions would like to have a greater voice in raising the quality of teaching taking place in the public schools, and they are convinced that improving teacher education programs is a good place to start. Teacher educators themselves, having committed their time and energies to developing and implementing programs, are more than just curious about the impact they are having on candidates and ultimately upon schools. There can be little doubt that the evaluation of teacher education programs is a highly significant endeavor that merits our close attention.

Further, it would appear that evaluating teacher education programs should be a straightforward operation. What are some of the difficulties? Let's address this question by first asking what criteria evaluation efforts in teacher education programming should meet? Fox (1982) advocates three criteria that seem instructive.

Field Responsiveness

Fox suggests that this criterion implies engaging those who are to be evaluated in the intellectual demands of the process. Teacher educators need to tackle some of the substantive and methodological problems that are embedded in any evaluation. Evaluation should engage the interested parties and potential audiences in the planning of the process. Teachers, the organized professions, the public and many others should be invited to participate in both the planning of the evaluation and in the interpretation of the results.

Evaluation, according to Fox, is not an activity that is rightfully left to technicians to conduct, interpret, and report.

Policy Relevance

Evaluations, according to Fox, must analyze the information needs of those who make decisions about programs and plan to collect information that will, at least in part, accommodate those needs. If the faculty senate is to vote on program changes, then the information needs of senators must be taken into account. If cooperating teachers are to be influenced to implement changes in a program based on evaluation results, then the information needs of these participating groups must be considered in devising an evaluation plan. Fox warns that simply attributing information needs from the sidelines is no substitute for engaging in give-and-take with the persons who comprise the policy audience to whom the study is addressed. Efforts must be made to hypothesize the information needs of many audiences, to test out those hypotheses, and to modify evaluation proposals according to the fruits of this inquiry.

Professional Illumination

Fox asserts that evaluations should have relevance beyond the narrow scope of the program, which is the target of the evaluation. A professionally illuminating evaluation is one that sharpens discussion of the issues, provides information of interest to the field, and even perhaps increases uncertainties so as to advance the field beyond mere doctrine.

How well do standard evaluation practices stand up to these criteria? There are basically two patterns of teacher education program evaluation practiced in the U.S. today and another that is more advocated than practiced. Each of these approaches will be briefly described and evaluated against Fox's ideals.

STANDARD APPROACHES TO THE EVALUATION OF TEACHER EDUCATION

Follow-Up Studies

In this genre, recent graduates and/or their supervisors are sent a questionnaire or are engaged in a structured interview to identify general opinions about the program (or the performance of its graduates) and to solicit specific suggestions for making changes. The data resulting from such procedures are rarely seen as useful in making changes in programs. Two factors may account for this. First, there is the "feedforward" problem identified by Katz, Raths, Mohanty, Kurachi, and Irving (1981). The feedforward effect is evidenced in the testimony of the 18-year-old who argues that he "should have been made to study the piano at age 8." The problem, of course, is that at age 8 the child may not have been ready or willing to study the piano. The suggestion is logically valid, but psychologically naive. In a similar manner, the advice to increase clinical experience, for instance, emanating from the follow-up studies on the part of well-meaning experienced teachers, makes sense at a logical level, but perhaps less sense given the contexts of undergraduates faced with social and academic demands on campus that compete with their interests in working in schools. Second, the findings of follow-up studies are rarely course specific. That is, the advice that more work is needed in the area of classroom management and discipline is often accepted by faculty as sound, but with the implicit proviso that this important content ought to be covered in someone else's course. The information, then, is not relevant to the policymaker — in this case the course instructor. Besides being somewhat irrelevant to program improvement, the follow-up approach is almost never professionally illuminating. The private and personal theories that teachers have about teacher education, for example, that it should be an apprentice program, or that it should prepare teachers to cope with the anxieties of the first day or first week on the job, are generally found only implicitly in the responses; rarely are these theories and others explicated and analyzed. Questions such as, "If certain content is to be added to the program, what is to be removed" are hardly ever addressed.

The Accreditation Visit

Another standard approach to evaluation of teacher education programs is the accreditation visit. Voluntary association with NCATE on the national level and the mandated program approval process that is now in place in most states make use of this approach. The evaluation normally incorporates the following elements: A written report prepared by the program faculty or administration documenting the claim that it is effective; a team of experts visits the institution and substantiates the findings included in the report; and, the team review is sent ahead to a committee of experts which votes to accredit or not to accredit the program, based on the available evidence. This method of program evaluation rarely involves teacher educators or their students in the evaluation, except in the role of those being evaluated. In addition, the criteria that are applied in this process are almost always the result of a political process carried out in the state capital or in Washington, D.C. and are not fruits of an intellectual research-based inquiry. The results of an accreditation visit are transformed into policy, at one level, as an inherent part of the process. A program is accredited or not as an outcome, and that decision is in a sense "policy." It is rarely the case that the findings of an accreditation visit, if they are less dire than loss of accreditation, actually work to affect programs, practices, or policy at the program level (Wheeler, 1980). The crisis mentality that surrounds an accreditation visit ebbs once it is known that programs have been adjudged as meeting the criteria; administrators and faculty tend to relax and ignore subtle weaknesses that have been identified by the team or recommendations for change that have been shared as a result of the process. Further, it is extremely unlikely that an accreditation visit is professionally illuminating. To the contrary, the program faculty actually work to hide weaknesses and issues which may become a target for site visitors' inspection. And the process from the accreditors' side is cautious and veiled so that the likelihood of a lawsuit is reduced in the event of an adverse decision for the institution.

Examination of Teacher Effects

In response to an invitation to describe current practice in the U.S. for evaluating teacher educaion programs, Borich (1979) elected to describe a model which could be implemented — a model which evaluates a teacher education program in terms of the effects its graduates have on the learning of public school pupils. This approach appears to make use of the ultimate criterion — teacher efficacy as measured by pupil learning. The procedure for implementing Borich's plan is to ask all graduates in several elementary education programs, for instance, to teach an identical unit to pupils — after giving them a pretest. A posttest is administered at the close of the unit; comparisons are made between programs as to which is more effective, based on the learning rates of the pupils. The logistics required to carry out this plan are awesome. Graduates of the programs being compared have to be teaching in equivalent grade levels in sufficient numbers to adequately represent the programs. Further, they need to agree to teach an identical unit at an identical time. But assuming that all of these problems were solved in a satisfactory way, many still remain. There is the problem, first of all, of data reduction. Borich recommends some sort of covariance analysis, adjusting posttest scores for initial differences. This method makes a key assumption that seems questionable at best: namely, that regressions between pretests and posttests within each teacher's class are constant for all teachers. The more standard assumptions — that the adjustment procedure "equates" the pupils in the classrooms on variables such as interest, motivation, perseverance, and anxiety, all of which are likely to be imperfectly correlated with the prescores — makes the procedure problematic. Finally, what can one say if the difference on a 30-item test is significant at the .05 level. Although the findings may be statistically significant, what does it tell us about the teacher education programs? Not only is there a problem in comparing the achievement of pupils, because the classes may not have been equivalent to begin with, the differences in abilities among the teacher education candidates might vary from program to program. It would be difficult for an evaluator to attribute the significant differences that were observed to program differences. There are too many competing rival explanations for the hypothetical results.

Again, for these many reasons, this approach has not been implemented as far as I know, but its spirit is captured in a recent analysis of "effective teacher education programs" authored by Evertson, Hawley, and Zlotnik (1984). Aside from saying that one program scored better than another, there is little here that could be considered edifying. The results would not be useful for making program improvements because the results deal with the program in toto and not pieces of it. Unless the question which prompted the evaluation were whether to adopt one program or another, there is little here to offer policymakers.

Thus, in terms of how these approaches are implemented or could be implemented, it seems that they are unlikely to meet the criteria of field responsiveness, policy relevance, and professional illumination. Some of our conjectures of why this is the case are enumerated in the next section.

GENERALIZATION ABOUT PROGRAM EVALUATION

Given that the essays in this volume are written to communicate the knowledge base related to practice in preservice teacher education, we might ask: "What is known about the evaluation of teacher education programs?" What follows is a series of generalizations that represent some self-evident truths about evaluating teacher education programs. Actually, most of what is written here would apply to the evaluation of any educational program, not just teacher education programs. The generalizations may not be as applicable to training programs. The manifest truth value of the assertions is buttressed a bit by some argument in support of their validity.

1. A major task of any evaluation is to describe that which is being evaluated. This assignment represents a serious obstacle to the evaluation of teacher education programs.

As evaluators, we can obtain a number of descriptions of teacher education programs. We could, as observers, examine and describe the ways in which the program is implemented this semester, next semester, or the next. The descriptions of programs as perceived by candidates could be used as the basis of program evaluation. It is very unlikely that the descriptions of programs derived from these sources, and others, would be in complete agreement. Which one should serve as the basis for an evaluation? If the answer is "all of the above," and if the conclusions vary with the description that is used, then how helpful is the process?

2. There are no widely accepted criteria to apply to either the program components or to the graduates of the program to aid in making assessments of program quality.

Some evaluators assert that they know "quality" when they see it. However, they can't specify in advance what they are looking for in a high-quality program. Others work hard to generate criteria, to make them up, so as to give the evaluation process some substance. Accrediting agencies generate criteria by means of a series of compromises among the various stakeholders in teacher education; a similar process is found at the state level in the program approval process. Some research-based programs develop lists of competencies that serve as criteria. However, there is no set of criteria that represents a consensus within the profession. It is of little comfort to know that this state of affairs applies as well to other professions. Medical educators have no firm benchmarks against which to assess the competencies of first-year doctors; there is no wide acceptance of a vision of the well-trained lawyer. In these fields too, there are some "experts" who claim to know what the characteristics of an effective program are, but by and large their views do not represent a strong consensus in the respective professions.

3. The evaluation of teacher education programs by the imposition of pre-specified criteria can stifle diversity and creativity in teacher education.

In any evaluation effort, the use of standards in a telling way can bring about standardization. That is, the more precisely we specify the ways in which teachers ought to be prepared and the tests candidates should pass before they are graduated, the more likely it is that teacher education programs will become more and more similar. It is a matter here of choosing what error we want to make. If it is the case that only a few programs in teacher education are inferior, and most are satisfactory or better, it would probably be a mistake to implement evaluation procedures which standardize the field. On the other hand, if there are many teacher education programs that are patently weak and ineffective, the application of standards to all programs might be called for, accepting the likelihood that the effort will make the programs which are successful in the evaluation effort more alike.

4. The findings of an evaluation, if aversive, are likely to be challenged, discredited, and ignored.

Because evaluations are carried out making use of criteria that do not have wide acceptance, and because evaluations are usually flawed in their implementation from a methodological point of view, they can be rather easily criticized and discredited. For example, the sampling processes carried out in many evaluations are characterized by low return rates. In addition, surveys of graduates often make use of Likert scales with end points such as "often" or "rarely"—each of which has certain subjective meanings to the respondents. The instrumentation is problematic at best. These two areas alone, sampling and instrumentation, are almost always a source of justifiable criticism. As a result, the conclusions and recommendations that flow from evaluations are often attacked on procedural grounds.

5. A program is not evaluated solely by looking at the impact it has on candidates' careers or post-program attainments.

It is rather simplistic to argue that Harvard Law School has a good program because its graduates perform well on measures of achievement—such as attaining partnerships early in prestigious law firms, earning a great deal of money, or being appointed to judgeships. The program may have actually retarded or delayed the attainment of these accomplishments, and the attainments might well have occurred if these students had attended some other law school. Researchers into school effectiveness variables have cautioned us that only about 10% of the variance in outcome measures can be attributed to program variables (Cooley & Lohnes, 1975). The attributes of candidates entering a program are far more predictive of outputs than characteristics of faculty or curriculum. An implication of this thesis is that an important aspect of any program is the quality of the candidates it recruits or attracts.

6. *Traditional sources of standards for evaluating teacher education, seen as "necessary but not sufficient conditions for quality programs," are less compelling in these days of accountability ethics and public disquiet about teacher education.*

A number of standards were meant to define what was needed to implement an effective teacher education program. For example, it was important to have current curriculum guides in the library so that candidates could become familiar with what was taught in the public schools. In addition, it was long held that having a certain quantity and quality of library holdings was necessary for program quality. However, it was acknowledged that having the books in the library or the curriculum guides available to candidates did not ensure having a quality program, but almost surely not having these resources available would significantly reduce the chances that a quality program could be offered. There is apparently a problem with such standards today — especially as it is argued that there is something self-serving in their formulation. The librarians argue for the library standard; the AV people insist that minimums be set on the availability of overhead projectors; and the directors of student teaching call for more hours in clinical settings.

7. *Goals written at higher levels of abstraction, such as "to prepare effective teachers," are difficult to evaluate; goals which are written narrowly are more easily assessed, but are less valued.*

If an objective of a teacher education program were to prepare candidates to operate a video-tape recorder, the objective and others like it could be assessed with little difficulty, but critics would rightly ask: Is that objective sufficiently important to include in a teacher education program? On the other hand, objectives which point to "quality of teaching" or "effectiveness of teaching" as goals give little direction for program planning or evaluation. The middle ground is difficult to find.

8. *We know that the deepest irony of any evaluation effort is that if it is mandated or externally imposed on programs, its utility is diminished; we also know that self-evaluations tend to be self-congratulatory and benign.*

Seemingly, those who don't need evaluations for the sake of improvement seek them out, while those who are functioning poorly are usually the last to want to be involved in evaluation (Glass, 1975). In a sense, evaluations are seen as hostile processes, very unlikely to provide satisfying outcomes and more likely to provide data which are disquieting and troublesome.

As I noted earlier, the generalizations here apply perhaps with equal force not only to the evaluations of teacher education programs but to merit pay procedures, to the giving of grades, and to the judgments applied by referees to research papers submitted to professional journals. If all, or even most of what I have shared previously is true, why is the evaluation process seen as helpful? To many, evaluation is a process that makes the process of valuing and inquiry more rational. Often, the evaluation process, as we practice it, helps us understand what is happening in our own terms, from our own perspectives. Those with other epistemologies are less sanguine about evaluation, no matter how it is implemented. It is my belief that many of the pitfalls and limitations of the process just identified can be overcome at least in part by hard work and better thinking.

It is possible to become depressed by the litany of problems we are facing as evaluators of teacher education. At times, the position on program evaluation is akin to that of a high official in the central administration of a large research-oriented midwestern university. He was eager, in his role as principal budget officer of the university, to evaluate programs, professors, and anything else that came within his purview — and some things that did not. He saw himself as "hard-headed" and "data-based" in his orientation to evaluation. When he was confronted recently with a new policy statement approved by the university's Board of Trustees that he would have to undergo a periodic evaluation himself, his reaction was predictable. "No one can really understand my job sufficiently to carry out a valid evaluation of my performance," he asserted, "except for someone in exactly the same position in another university as distinguished as this one." It is likely we all feel this way about the particular assignment we hold. No one can evaluate us fairly unless, of course, they gush over our work. As teacher educators, many of us seem at times to claim "teacher education programs cannot be evaluated." Although attempts can be made at it, and reports can be written that purport to be evaluations, the task is so complex as to be nearly impossible to write an evaluation that meets the following "reasonable" criteria:

1. If the process is applied several times over a period of months or years, the outcomes will be quite similar.
2. There is widespread professional and public acceptance of the procedures and the criteria utilized in the process.
3. The evaluation process makes a difference in that weak programs are shut down or demonstrably improved and/or strong programs are recognized and acknowledged.

The problem with this line of thinking, of course, is that there is probably no evaluation of anything that meets these criteria. All of this brings to mind

that critics of the current U.S. defense policy have asserted that the continuum of preparedness in terms of the arms race is something like this: strong,
stronger, strongest, weak. The thesis is that once a nation becomes overly dependent on nuclear forces, it is unable to act in anything but Armageddon.
Many of us who engage in colleague watching at the university level see an
analogous continuum in the area of effective problem solving. It goes: smart,
smarter, smartest, dumb. We can know too much, be aware of too many pitfalls, anticipate too many problems so that our making solid contributions to
the solution of complex problems is inhibited. Perhaps that is the problem
with teacher education evaluation. We know too much, think too complexly,
engage in too many intellectual games to contribute to the solution of the
problem. What is needed, perhaps, is a more modest approach to the
conceptualization of the problem. What follows is an effort to get at just
such an approach.

First, it seems clear that there is a wide variety of approaches to program
evaluation. A number of authors have addressed the "methods" question
quite admirably (Fox, 1982; Fenstermacher & Berliner, 1983; Joint Committee, 1981). And yet, the generalizations already listed under the rubric "what
we know about evaluation" apply to all the methods that have been described
in the literature, albeit unequally. So all program evaluations, regardless of
method, have difficulty describing programs, making use of procedures that
match the extremely high standards of social science research and avoiding
the imposition of standards on programs or program directors. Understanding teacher education program evaluation is not likely to be advanced by
refining current evaluation methods or by inventing new ones.

Second, I should think most would agree, after Fox (1982), that findings
of any evaluation should be policy relevant, that persons who are the target
of an evaluation should be involved in the process, and that its findings
should be interesting to the professional at large.

The point here is that evaluation in teacher education shares with other
areas (a) program evaluation strategies, and (b) criteria to judge the evaluation itself. The key element of difference, it seems to me, in evaluating
teacher education is the set of criteria that is applied to the program. The critical issue in teacher education program evaluation is the substance of the
evaluation, and not the methodology. What are the critical elements of a
teacher education program that bear scrutiny? My general argument is that
evaluations would be most helpful if they were aimed at structural elements
that tap the extent to which programs are planned, maintained, and evaluated, and less helpful if they are focused on particular elements of the program such as: (a) Do candidates like the program? (b) Is mainstreaming covered in the curriculum?, or (c) Are candidates employed by the public schools
upon graduation? Although all of these considerations have merit, there is
really no end to the list of such "criteria" that could be used and very little ba-

sis to say that one set of criteria is more useful than another. The remaining sections of this chapter suggest particular program attributes that bear on this general proposition and focus on the implications of this position for teacher educators carrying out evaluations.

FOCI OF A TEACHER EDUCATION PROGRAM EVALUATION

Instead of trying to identify effective, outstanding programs in teacher education, in contrast to weak, ineffective ones, I suggest that we work to identify what elements or attributes of a required set of experiences constitute a teacher education program. The emphasis here is on the word "program." What is the distinction between a program and a sequence of courses? Between a program and a set of exit requirements? Between a program and a course of study? The answers to these questions are not likely to be based on empirical foundations, but perhaps in terms of ideology. The approach to defining programs instead of effective programs is akin to recognizing a home run in a baseball game. What is a home run? The definition is not simple, especially to those not familiar with the game, but it is an accomplishment that can be defined fairly concisely. The definition avoids the issue of what is a "good" home run. For someone to argue that some home runs are better than others, to make efforts to define home runs of high quality as distinguished from run-of-the-mill versions seems a fruitless task. The distinctions are more aesthetic than substantive. So, in teacher education evaluation, we should eschew the search for distinctions between effective and ineffective programs. Instead, we should seek to recognize and accredit programs that were duly determined to be programs and withhold accreditation, funds, or support from offerings that fail to meet the criteria.

In the next paragraphs, some criteria are set down that might be considered in such an evaluation. Of course, the criteria here need study, discussion, and revision. They are advanced as a starting point in the process of developing criteria dealing particularly with teacher education programs.

1. The admission to teacher education should be characterized by the application of rigorous academic and scholarly standards and by a concern for the personal attributes that candidates bring to the program.

For too long, teacher education has carried the burden of providing entry into the professions for persons from lower social classes and from minority groups. Although the goal of opening the profession to disadvantaged populations is still important, it must not be attained at the expense of scholarly ability. For reasons as crass as "image building" and as substantial as recruiting only the most able students into our programs, we need to be tougher at the entry level. It seems clear that in almost every profession, entry into the professional schools is tantamount to graduation. It is apparently very difficult to fail people out of programs. This finding certainly supports the need to be rigorous at the entry level. In addition, the quality of programs in many respects is set by the expectations and the performances of candidates within a program. As someone once said, "If the Harvard faculty were moved en masse to Podunk College, it would still be Podunk. But if the Harvard student body were moved to Podunk, Podunk would change dramatically and improve." Because most of the studies of program efficacy report that only about 10% of the variance in outcome measures can be attributed to program characteristics and almost 50% of the variance can be associated with the qualities that candidates bring to the program, the need to work with able candidates is paramount.

Also, the research of Sprinthall (1980), Heath (1980), and others has demonstrated that there are indicators of personal attributes that can be reliably used at age 19 or 20 to predict success in later life. They include allocentricity, articulateness, and autonomy. There are data to support the claim that professors working as juries can fairly reliably assess these qualities in interviews. Thus, the ideal program will harness the judgments of faculty in making entry decisions of candidates based in part on interviews.

2. The program in teacher education is characterized by its coherence. The teaching and learning experiences which comprise the program are unified through the adoption of "themes" that integrate the academic activities with the clinical experiences within the program.

Some programs are characterized by an ethic which supports each instructor's "doing his own thing." As a result, the task of making sense of the thrust of the program is left to the candidates who experience it. While this cannot be avoided altogether, nor should it be avoided entirely, it also makes some sense for faculty to share this burden. Thus, no matter how coherent a program might become, students still need help in making sense of what they are learning and experiencing. But, the task may be made easier, and the impact of the faculty and the program may be more promising if the goals of the program are stated explicitly and the expectations of students and faculty are generally shared. One approach is to adopt a competency model and list the 50 or so skills that the program intends to teach. There are a number of difficulties with this approach. It would be worthwhile to consider, in lieu of a statement of competencies, a description of the dispositions (habits) that are to be engendered in candidates. For example, Glaser (1984) has claimed that an important pedagogical principle is that "one must first understand an individual's current state of knowledge in a domain related to the subject matter to be learned, and within which thinking skills are to be exercised." This assertion suggests that a major role function of a teacher is to improve the understandings that pupils bring to learning tasks. Given that assumption, it would seem important to foster or strengthen the following dispositions of candidates: (a) to uncover the understandings of what is to be learned that the pupil currently holds, (b) to withhold intervening too early until the process of "uncovering" is complete, and (c) to use the occasion to "read" the pupil's current understandings. These habits on the part of a teacher come into play in a wide variety of teaching situations and suggest ways of working with candidates that are quite different from the "skill acquisition" procedures associated with teaching for competencies. The point here is not to quarrel with the vision that is imbued in a program designed to prepare teachers, but only to argue that a program should adopt a vision statement and share it widely with all who work with or within the program.

3. Candidates are assigned to cohort groups which experience the program together. The groups include some candidates just entering the program and some who are about to graduate.

Instead of teaching groups of students who are clustered into class groupings by a computer, students should be organized into cohort groups which develop some cohesion over time. These groups can promote dispositions of collaborating and sharing; they can work as support groups for individual candidates who run into difficulties; the members of the group can help one another interpret the teachings and experiences they undergo in the program. Such a practice might encourage potential teachers to see teaching and learning as a cooperative enterprise, and they might learn both the value of sharing and the skills associated with sharing effectively with others.

Further, working in groups, the candidates can have a say in the scheduling of their own learning; they can seek out experiences as helpful to their own group; and they can even provide each other with assessments of their work that might prove helpful. Finally, cohort groups could function as an advisory unit. A professor could be assigned to a group to counsel its members on program matters and to contribute through informal ways to their socialization to the profession. Professors working in this advisory role would be more advocates than evaluators or gatekeepers. Their role would include counseling and supporting students as they proceed through the program.

4. The teacher education program is characterized by an emphasis on the most recent research on teaching and learning and on encouraging candidates to see research as an important source of information about teaching.

Every program should include a research component that is a required part of the program. The purpose of this program would be less to establish a link between the specifics of research and professional practice than to provide students with an enduring frame of reference and way of thinking in support of more informed and reflective professional practice. The activities of the component would be designed to build a culture of reflective students who prize information and research as a source of knowledge about practice.

5. Candidates in a teacher education program should receive stringent and frequent evaluations of their progress in the program through a staffing procedure.

Often, evaluations and feedback are delivered to candidates on a one-to-one basis. These evaluations can be conflicting or so vague as to be not of much use. It is suggested that teams of faculty meet with a candidate periodically after reviewing portfolios which include the papers the student has written, logs of field experiences, and descriptions of teaching behavior. These staffings would bring together the views of faculty and enable candidates to hear about their progress in one consistent official voice.

6. *The evaluation function and the coaching function during the student teaching experience should be differentiated — with different staff members carrying out these distinct functions.*

The inherently conflicting roles of coach and evaluator, normally assigned to one person as supervisor, impede both functions. A cadre of evaluators needs to be developed who will take into account the preactive as well as the interactive functions of teachers in making evaluations. The coaching function should be separated and made distinct to permit supervisors as coaches to make sincere efforts to be supportive and helpful to the candidate. Of course, both the coaching functions and the evaluation functions should be disciplined by the goals of the program and the themes which link those goals.

7. *Courses meeting the general education component of a teacher education program should be elected from those that have been reviewed and approved by teacher educators as offering candidates opportunities to learn and to study that are consistent with the goals of the teacher education program. The courses approved as satisfying the general education requirements of the teacher education program should be open to any undergraduates in the university and should include work in philosophy, the arts, social science, literature, science, and mathematics. Professors who teach courses in the general education area, of course, would be free to decide not to share their course assignments and topics of study with teacher educators, but if their courses are not seen as contributing significantly to the goals of the teacher education program, candidates should be proscribed from electing them.*

In most institutions, the general education component is set down as a requirement to take so many credit hours in the social sciences, so many in the sciences, and so many in the humanities, and so on. The cafeteria approach has a number of virtues. It gives students the opportunity to make choices, to act on their own interests, and to give direction to their own preparation as scholars and as citizens. There is much here to be valued. On the other hand, the evidence suggests that the cafeteria approach is bewildering to some candidates and provides little basis for the kind of mental toughness and gentle appreciations that are normally expected from a general education program. To combine these values, it is recommended that the faculty of a teacher education program carefully review all general education courses before they are elected by candidates, and the courses that meet the expectations of faculty in preparing teachers should be specified as appropriate, and those that don't should not be open to teacher candidates to elect.

IMPLICATIONS

1. Would teachers who graduate from teacher education programs, as defined earlier, be better teachers than those already in the field, or those graduating from other programs, one of which does not meet the criteria? How could we know? I have suggested we now have no way of finding out.

2. Based on my experiences, very few programs extant in the U.S. would meet the criteria advanced earlier. Why is that the case? We can only surmise. One explanation has to do with the ambience of the university as a workplace. Most professors are striving to become recognized as scholars in their respective fields. Recognition is usually gained by "distancing" one's self from one's colleagues. It is not helpful to agree, to go along, to vote in the affirmative. Distinctions are associated with being separate, with advancing criticisms, with pointing out weaknesses. Socialized to this style of behavior, faculty make poor collaborators in teacher education. Second, there is a strong feeling in academia of academic freedom that carries over to classroom instruction. Professors want to have the freedom to teach whatever they want to teach — and they resist giving up this freedom to accommodate a faculty consensus with which they may have reservations. The concern for academic freedom has real and honest roots. It was not too long ago, for instance, when professors in Germany were directed to teach Nazi physics, Nazi literature, and Nazi history. On the other hand, the reaction to this threat, real or imagined in the U.S., leaves most programs in shambles in terms of developing themes or visions as described in goal statements. Finally, the need to evaluate students carefully and often as they progress through a program is time-consuming. It is hard for teachers to imagine the time press on university professors — when they learn that the normal teaching load at the university is close to 6 or 8 hours a week. And yet, professors are busy, even with that light teaching load, with committee work, with entrepreneurship, with professional activities, and coping with the publish or perish dicta. No question about it, evaluation of students is demanding, and to avoid contentious arguments with students, must be done carefully and precisely. Professors believe that time spent in such activities is not well rewarded at the university — and in fact may bring on problems as students complain of their evaluations, as they appeal from the professors' judgments to capricious grading committees, and the like. In sum, the criteria listed would be difficult to meet under the best of circumstances at most universities.

3. What are some of the benefits that might accrue in participating in a program meeting these criteria? Again, answers to these questions are only

surmises, and yet from what we know about group morale, it would seem salutary in general to participate in a process that had some rhyme and reason. Instead of teacher educators trying to make an impact with one methods course or one educational psychology course, if they perceived their efforts in the context of similar efforts being made by a large number of colleagues, then, at the very least, a sense of efficacy might be a by-product of such a program.

A second by-product would probably be manifest in the attitudes of students. Now, the candidates go from course to course, often learning contradictory precepts, becoming involved in activities they perceive to be irrelevant, and feeling that the entire program was a waste of time. A cohesive program might allay some of that feeling.

EPILOGUE

If not many teacher education programs can meet the standards suggested here, isn't it the case that advocating this approach is pie-in-the-sky thinking? Perhaps. However, it is the case that the standards described earlier are already included in most program standards. They are already a part of our expectations; the problem is that they are lost in the many, many others that are included and they are applied in ways that are generally judgmental and condescending. If the focus were placed solely on these criteria, then perhaps teacher education administrators would place their energies on seeing to it that they were met. The criteria might be unrealistic from another vantage point. It can be anticipated that a number of critics to this approach will argue that "faculty will never agree to a vision or a monitoring plan or an intensive effort to evaluate students." That may be true, but we can ask: How many of us have tried to harness the intellectual energies of faculty in this process? And for how long? My guess is that many of us have given up without trying. Let's get started.

REFERENCES

Borich, G.D. (1979). *Three models for conducting follow-up studies of teacher education and training*. (Report of the OECD on the Evaluation of Inserviced Education and Training). Paris: OECD.

Cooley, W.W., & Lohnes, P.R. (1976). *Evaluation research in education*. New York: Wiley.

Evertson, C., Hawley, W., & Zlotnik, M. (1984). *The characteristics of effective teacher preparation programs: A review of research*. Knoxville, TN: Vanderbilt University.

Fenstermacher, G.D., & Berliner, D.C. (1983). *A conceptual framework for the analysis of staff development*. Santa Monica, CA: Rand.

Fox, Jr., G.T. (1982). *Can a federal program evaluation be field responsive, policy relevant, and professionally illuminative?* Paper presented at the 1981 Annual Meeting of the American Educational Research Association, Los Angeles, CA.

Glaser, R. (1984). Education and thinking: The role of knowledge. *American Psychologist, 39*(2), 93–104.

Glass, G.V. (1975). A paradox about excellence of schools and the people in them. *Educational Researcher, 4,* 9–13.

Heath, D.H. (1980). Toward teaching as a self-renewing calling. In G.E. Hall, S.M. Hord, & G. Brown (Eds.), *Exploring issues in teacher education: Questions for future research.* Austin, TX: Research and Development Center for Teacher Education.

Joint Committee on Standards for Educational Evaluation. (1981). *Standards for evaluations of educational programs, projects and materials.* New York: McGraw-Hill.

Katz, L., Raths, J., Mohanty, C., Kurachi, A., & Irving, J. (1981). Follow-up studies: Are they worth the trouble? *Journal of Teacher Education, 32*(2), 18–24.

Sprinthall, N.A. (1980). Adults as learners: A developmental perspective. In G.E. Hall, S.M. Hord, & E. Brown (Eds.), *Exploring issues in teacher education: Question for future research.* Austin, TX: Research and Development Center for Teacher Education.

Wheeler, C.W. (1980). *NCATE: Does it matter?* (Research Series No. 92). East Lansing, MI: College of Education, Michigan State University.

Chapter 11

The Impact of Competency Tests on Teacher Education: Ethical and Legal Issues in Selecting and Certifying Teachers

G. Pritchy Smith

University of North Florida, Jacksonville

The society of the 21st century will inherit the fruits, both bitter and sweet, of sweeping changes in the professional preparation of teachers that are occurring during the last two decades of the 20th century. The present is perhaps an historic moment. The public is insisting on excellence in American education. This insistence has been underscored in no less than 100 regional and national reports. Never before has the public demanded reform in the public school system and simultaneously insisted on reform in the teacher training programs of American colleges and universities. Most state legislatures have enacted or are considering major reform legislation indicating that the destinies of teacher training programs and public school reform are clearly intertwined. Never before has there been such common agreement among professional educators, first, that there is a clearly identifiable knowledge base for teachers and, second, that the acquisition of the content of that knowledge base is measurable. It is an historic moment, too, because not since the years prior to the 1954 *Brown* decision have state legislatures and boards of education enacted regulations which directly bear upon the racial composition of the national teaching force. If not historic, the present is at least portentous, foreboding unfortunate consequences for minority teachers. No doubt, some legislated reforms and court determined precedents will leave a positive legacy for the future. However, two trends — the rise of competency tests and a supportive trend of conservative court decisions — constitute current seeds of reform which foretell a bitter harvest in the 21st century.

Responding to the increasing pressure of the public's mandate for excellence, state legislatures and state boards of education have been forced to respond with rapidly implemented, simplistic solutions to complex problems. Whereas little action has been directed toward curricular reform, increased teacher salaries, sufficient funding for education, the working conditions of teachers, or improved training models, great attention has been given to reforming the standards for selecting and certifying teachers. Hence, the single, most visible national response has been the adoption of state-mandated competency tests for the certification of teachers.

The consequences resulting from using competency tests as the primary determinant for certification, however, are tragic. In states where competency testing is occurring, disproportionate numbers of minority candidates are being excluded from the teaching profession. Philosophical and practical issues are being raised that threaten to splinter the profession with controversy at a time when solidarity is needed.

The use of competency tests to certify teachers has forced both educators and the public to challenge the most cherished premise underlying the philosophy of education in a democratic society: that persons regardless of socioeconomic status, race, or creed are guaranteed both excellence and equity in their pursuit of education. Furthermore, excellence has been reduced to a quality measurable by scores on standardized examinations; and, more specifically, excellence in teaching has been operationally defined in the narrowest sense, a high score on a pencil–paper test. Concomitantly, the issue of excellence has taken precedence over the issue of equity. In fact, with little protest from the public or the community of professional educators, definitions of excellence that are inclusive of equity have fallen by the wayside in preference for definitions of excellence that are dangerously akin to elitism. Signs of the time predict a brewing controversy and point to the need for an examination of the competency testing movement, related legal issues, and the impact of both on the American promise of equity.

PROFILE OF THE COMPETENCY TESTING MOVEMENT

Teacher competency testing is largely a pencil–paper test movement, although about 10 states have included in their assessment programs evaluation of teaching skills by teams of trained observers. Noting that state competency assessment programs have rapidly spread from 3 in 1977 to 30 in 1983, Sandefur (1984b) describes the movement:

Twelve states require testing for both admission and certification. Inclusively, however, 25 states require testing for certification and 17 require testing for admission to teacher education programs. In terms of skills tested, states are most concerned about basic skills (25), followed by professional or pedagogical skills (20) and academic skills (19). (p. 17)

Results of Sandefur's latest survey are shown in Table 1 and Table 2. Table 1 depicts states that have already mandated competency tests and Table 2 depicts states with reported discussion of adopting tests. Based on data in these charts, Sandefur (1984b) has made the following conclusions and predictions:

1. State competency-assessment programs . . . will continue to increase, especially since 12 states reported planning activity in 1983.
2. The pressing emphasis on basic skills testing for certification will continue.
3. Fewer states are using legislative action to mandate competency assessment; more are using state department-of-education regulations.
4. Most states are mandating an induction year prior to certification. The year is most frequently called an internship or beginning teacher year, and it usually includes assessment by a visiting team.
5. More states are choosing to use nationally standardized tests rather than develop their own. Apparently, this is a result of the prohibitive cost of test development and the additional advantages of national and state compatibility. (p. 17)

Based on an earlier survey, Sandefur (1984c) noted that the states were almost evenly divided in their use of nationally standardized versus customized tests. As Table 1 indicates, 18 states employ standardized tests; 16, customized. The National Teachers Examination (NTE), the American College Test (ACT), the Scholastic Aptitude Test (SAT), the California Achievement Test (CAT), and the more recently developed Pre-Professional Skills Test (P-PST) are the most commonly used standardized examinations. The NTE, published by Educational Testing Service (ETS), is either presently used in competency assessment programs or has been used on a trial basis in Arkansas, Louisiana, Mississippi, New Mexico, North Carolina, South Carolina, Tennessee, and Virginia. ETS was also involved in the development of the California Basic Education Skills Test (CBEST) and publishes the P-PST used in Delaware, Kansas, and Texas. The CAT has been adopted as a measure of basic skills in Colorado, Tennessee, and Wyoming. Scores on the SAT and/or ACT to determine admission to teacher education are used in Alabama, Florida, Missouri, and Mississippi. National Evaluations Systems, Inc. (NES) contracted for the development of customized examinations used in Alabama, Georgia, and Oklahoma.

TABLE 1. States Mandating Competency Assessment of Teachers – 1983

State	Mandate		Date Mandated/ Implemented	Level		Skills Tested				Type of Tests	
	Legislative	St. Bd. of Educ.		Admissions	Certification	Basic	Professional	Academic	On-the-Job	National Std.	Customized
Alabama		X	80/81	X	X	X	X	X		X	X
Arizona	X	X	80/81		X	X	X				X
Arkansas	X	X	79/83		X	X	X	X		X	
California		X	81/83	X	X	X		X			X
Colorado	X		81/83	X		X				X	
Connecticut		X	82/85	X	X	X	X	X			X
Delaware		X	82/85		X	X				X	
Florida	X		78/80	X	X	X	X		X		X
Georgia		X	75/78		X		X	X	X		X
Kentucky	X	X	82/83–85	X	X	X	X	X	X	X	
Louisiana	X		77/79		X	X	X	X		X	
Massachusetts		X	79/82		X	X	X	X			X
Mississippi		X	82/84	X	X	X	X			X	
Missouri		X	83/84	X	X	X				X	
Nevada	X		82/	X	X		X	X	X	X	
New Jersey		X	83/87		X	X	X	X		X	X
New Mexico	X	X	81/83	X	X	X	X	X			X
New York		X	83/84		X	X	X		X		
North Carolina		X	79/82	X	X	X	X			X	X

(Continued)

221

TABLE 1. (Continued)

| State | Mandate | | Date Mandated/ | Level | | Skills Tested | | | | Type of Tests | |
	Legislative	St. Bd. of Educ.	Implemented	Admissions	Certification	Basic	Professional	Academic	On-the-Job	National Std.	Customized
Oklahoma	X		80/82		X	X		X	X		X
Rhode Island		X	/81		X			X			X
South Carolina	X	X	79/83	X	X	X	X	X	X	X	X
Tennessee		X	79/79	X		X	X	X		X	
Texas	X		81/84–86	X	X	X		X		X	
Utah		X		X		X				X	
Vermont		X	/82		X		X	X	X		X
Virginia	X		80/84		X		X	X	X	X	X
Washington		X		X		X				X	
West Virginia		X	82/85	X	X	X	X	X	X		X
Wyoming		X		X		X				X	
Totals—30	*11*	*22*		*17*	*25*	*25*	*20*	*19*	*10*	*18*	*16*

Note. From "State Assessment Trends" by J. T. Sandefur, 1984, *ACCTE Briefs*, 18.

TABLE 2. States Reporting Planning or Discussion of Competency Assessment of Teachers – 1983

State	Level		Skills Tested				Type of Tests		Year First
	Admissions	Certification	Basic	Professional	Academic	On-the-Job	Standardized	Customized	Reported Planning
Illinois	X	X	X						1980
Indiana	X		X						1980
Kansas	X	X	X			X			1980
Maryland	X	X	X	X	X			X	1982
Montana									1982
Nebraska	X		X						1982
New Hampshire									1983
North Dakota		X	X						1983
Ohio		X	X	X	X			X	1982
Oregon	X	X	X				X		1983
Pennsylvania	X		X				X		1983
Wisconsin	X	X	X	X	X		X		1980
Totals – 12	*8*	*7*	*10*	*3*	*3*	*1*	*3*	*2*	

Note. From "State Assessment Trends" by J. T. Sandefur, 1984, *AACTE Briefs*, 19.

223

Although there is considerable diversity among the state testing programs, several significant patterns can be observed. One, the movement originated in a small band of southern states and spread rapidly to bordering states prior to adoption in most western, central, and northern states. It is significant that the impetus for the competency testing movement originated in roughly the same geographical region where massive displacement of black teachers occurred after the 1954 *Brown* decision. Using data gathered by a National Education Association (NEA) task force and the Southern Education Reporting Services, Ethridge (1979) reported that between 1954 and 1970 31,584 black teachers lost their positions in the 17 southern and border states. That a precedent for excluding minority teachers existed prior to the competency testing movement is well documented. Second, there is a geographical parallel between the early competency testing states and the 12 southern and border states under Federal mandate to desegregate their public colleges and universities (Blakely, 1983).

Third, it is significant that teachers and professional organizations have not presented a united, conclusive position on competency testing. The American Federation of Teachers (AFT) has strongly supported competency testing of teachers prior to their entry into the profession as well as the testing of practicing teachers. Noting the negative impact on minority teachers, NEA remained officially silent concerning the competency testing of new teachers during the early years of the competency testing movement. Recently, however, NEA has adopted a resolution that supports testing preservice teachers but has remained opposed to testing practicing teachers. A 1984 Louis Harris survey of 1,981 elementary and secondary teachers interviewed nationwide found that 57% would welcome periodic testing of teachers in their subject fields. NEA President Mary Hatwood Futrell refuted the Harris Poll findings on the basis of a survey of 2,000 randomly selected NEA members, which found overwhelming opposition to the competency testing of practicing teachers ("Poll Shows," 1984). The American Association of Colleges for Teacher Education (AACTE) (1983a) document, *Educating a Profession: Competency Assessment,* does not directly support the use of state-mandated competency tests. Defending institutional control of competency assessment, AACTE's position advocates flexibility:

> Teacher education institutions have an obligation to establish entry, retention, and exit criteria which measure the knowledge, skills, and attitudes of successful teachers . . . . Even though a comprehensive assessment system and rigorous standards are necessary for high quality teacher education programs, institutions have valid reasons for establishing flexible and special admission categories. These are particularly important and appropriate with experimental programs and with efforts to increase the representation of students who otherwise would be excluded because of limited pre-college educational programs.

Multiple assessments should be used on a regular basis from entry to exit
. . . . The use of multiple assessment procedures eliminates a reliance on paper-
and-pencil tests for establishing the competence of teacher education students.
(pp. 3–4)

AACTE's strongest position relative to the impact of competency tests on minority teachers is found in selected subparts of Resolution 7, "Affirmative
Action," passed by the membership at the 36th Annual Meeting on February
4, 1984:

Be it resolved that:

AACTE reaffirms the resolution that "no program shall be devised which
places sole reliance upon a single measure or upon a single assessment technique."

Further, no program of selection be devised by SCDEs and SEAs that eliminates disproportionate numbers of minority candidates from the teaching profession.

Further, AACTE work with state ACTE units and other appropriate agencies
to establish flexible, alternative admission requirements to state test scores to
increase the representation of minority candidates. *(AACTE Directory,* 1984,
p. 83)

Other observations can be made about the movement to test the competency of teachers. First, the initiative for the movement came from state legislatures and boards of education rather than from teacher organizations or
college and university schools and departments of education, thereby weak-
ening the position of educators to govern their profession. Second, in several
states the testing of teachers is paralleled by a movement to assess the basic
skills of public school students with the latter, more often than not, having
been mandated first. Third, competency testing of teachers has taken root
despite inadequate research to show a direct relationship between performance on pencil–paper tests and on-the-job competence. Fourth, recognizing
that predictive validity of the tests has been generally unsubstantiated, most
state departments of education and test developers have been cautious to establish content validity through textbook review and through test item review
by teachers and other groups of professional educators. Fifth, the tests are
more often norm-referenced rather than criterion-referenced, a fact that
makes designing successful college developmental and teacher preparation
programs extremely difficult. Finally, state determined cut scores have been
consistently set at a level high enough to eliminate disproportionate numbers
of minority students from the teaching profession.

MINORITY PERFORMANCE ON TEACHER COMPETENCY TESTS:
A STATE BY STATE ANALYSIS

Describing teaching as "the profession blacks may lose," Trammer (1980, p. 69) and others (Scott, 1979; Mohr, 1980; Wright, 1980; Kauchak, 1984; & Mercer, 1983, 1984) have noted the detrimental effects of competency testing on the professional pool of black teachers. Providing the most recent comprehensive analysis of historical and contemporary factors responsible for the diminishing number of black teachers, Witty (1982) identifies state-mandated competency testing as a threat to the very "survival of black teachers in America" (p. 1). In an analysis of unresolved issues posed by the newly adopted Texas teacher assessment program, Vargas (1984) forecasts a similar threat to Hispanic teachers. Questioning blind acceptance of competency tests as the major instrument for improving public schools and teacher training programs, Gallegos (1984) echoes concern for Native American teachers, particularly those being displaced by Anglos in Bureau of Indian Affairs schools in Arizona.

Enough evidence is now available from states that have had several years experience using testing in the certification process and from states that have completed initial validation studies to indicate that disproportionate numbers of minority students are being screened out of teaching. In fact, initial reports of minority performance have proved to be a source of embarrassment in many states, so much so that it is far easier to obtain data from newspaper sources than from state certification departments. Recognizing the growing use of standardized tests as one of several contributing factors, the American Association of Colleges for Teacher Education (AACTE, 1983b) reports that since 1978 the number of new teachers produced by 45 predominantly black AACTE member institutions has declined 47%. Table 3 shows pass rates on competency tests for 10 states.

Alabama

Since June, 1981, candidates who have completed an approved program and seek teacher certification in Alabama have been required to pass the Alabama Initial Teacher Competency Test (AITCT), an exit exam developed by NES that consists of the Basic Professional Studies test (basic literacy) and specialization tests. There are 36 specialization test areas, including elementary education, special education, language arts, and other academic disciplines. Admission requirements to an undergraduate teacher education program consist of a score of 16 on the ACT or 745 on the SAT and a passing score on the English Language Proficiency Test, also developed by NES.

Based on summary score reports from the Alabama Department of Education dated July 21, 1981; March 20, June 26, and December 11, 1982; and March 26, 1983, compiled data for five separate test administrations indicate

TABLE 3.   Teacher Competency Test Pass Rates By Ethnicity For Ten States

State	Anglos	Asians	Blacks	Hispanics	Native Americans	All	Test
	Pass Rates By Percent						
Alabama	86		43			81	AITCT (NES)
Arizona							
1/6/83	73	50	24	42	22	66	ATPE
7/9/83	70	25	41	36	19	59	
California	76	50	26	38	67	68	CBEST (ETS)
Florida							
6/82	92	67	37	57	90	85	FCTE Customized
2/83	90	63	35	51	100	84	
Georgia	87		34			78	CRTCT (NES)
Louisiana	78		15			77	NTE (ETS)
Mississippi*	97–100		54–70			NA	NTE (ETS)
Oklahoma	79	82	45	71	70	78	OCT (NES) Customized
Texas	62	47**	10	19	47**	54	P-PST (ETS)
Virginia* (Trial Testing)							NTE (ETS)
Communication Skills	97%		56%			NA	
General Knowledge	99%		69%			NA	
Professional Knowledge	99%		83%			NA	

*Pass rates at predominately white and black public institutions.
**Asian and Native American candidates are reported in a combined "Others" category in the Texas reporting system.

that approximately 10,028 tests, including both Professional Studies and specialization tests, were given. Table 4 indicates that black candidates passed 43% of the tests, compared to an Anglo pass rate of 86% and an overall pass rate of 81%.[1] Although the Alabama State Department of Education reports results by number of tests taken and passed rather than by number of persons, the data is still sufficient to estimate the impact of competency testing upon the racial composition of the Alabama teaching force. Assuming that the number of Professional Studies tests equals the number of candidates during these particular test administrations, 2,613 candidates passed sufficiently well to be certified. The 132 black candidates who passed the Profes-

[1] *Statewide summary score report by test of Alabama Initial Teacher Certification Program* (1981, July 21; 1982, March 20, June 20, December 11; 1983, March 26), unpublished, Office of Regulatory Services, Alabama Department of Education.

TABLE 4. Pass Rates By Ethnicity – Alabama Initial Teacher Certification Testing Program

	Black			Anglo			Overall Pass Rate		
Date/Exam	Number Tested	Number Passed	Percent Passed	Number Tested	Number Passed	Percent Passed	Number Tested	Number Passed	Percent Passed
July 21, 1981									
Professional									
Studies	40	18	45	555	455	82	597	475	80
Specialization	110	19	17	745	620	83	857	640	75
March 20, 1982									
Professional									
Studies	47	31	66	532	441	83	582	474	81
Specialization	133	58	44	988	856	87	1125	917	82
June 26, 1982									
Professional									
Studies	71	35	49	541	424	78	614	461	75
Specialization	272	120	44	1532	1356	89	1820	1489	82
December 11, 1982									
Professional									
Studies	48	24	50	553	441	82	606	478	79
Specialization	196	95	49	1044	923	84	1252	1027	82
March 26, 1983									
Professional									
Studies	55	24	44	813	693	85	875	725	82
Specialization	210	90	43	1479	1329	90	1700	1425	84
Total	1182	514	43	8782	7539	86	10028	8111	81

Source: Statewide Summary Report by Test of Alabama Initial Teacher Certification Testing Program (July 21, 1981; March 20, 1982; June 26, 1982; December 11, 1982; March 26, 1983), Office of Regulatory Services, Alabama Department of Education.

sional Studies test represent about half of the 261 black candidates who would have been certifiable had competency testing not been in force, a drop from 8% to 5% of the minority representation in the Alabama teacher candidacy pool. The actual impact in head count may even be more severe because students who passed the Professional Studies test may not be the same students who passed the specialization tests.

Two issues related to competency testing in Alabama are the pending litigation against the AITCT and the use of test scores to guage the quality of teacher education programs. In December, 1981, three black female students from Auburn University in Montgomery, the University of South Alabama, and Alabama A&M University filed suit in U.S. District Court to block the Alabama Board of Education from giving teacher certification tests. The suit asked the court to halt the tests until validated and until the state dismantled the dual system of higher education (C. Smith, 1981). In February, 1983, the Alabama Board of Education approved a resolution to begin using test scores as a measure of quality of teacher education programs in colleges and universities. A failure rate of 60% warrants a visit by a review team. Institutions have 4 years to make improvements based upon recommendations in the team's report ("Low Scores," 1983).

Arizona

Originally, the Arizona Teacher Proficiency Exam (ATPE) (1983) was a 150-item basic skills exit test designed to measure proficiency in reading, grammar, and mathematics. Presently, to obtain certification a prospective teacher education graduate must answer 80% of the items correctly. In July, 1981, the Arizona Board of Education added a second part to the test to measure professional knowledge, including classroom management, curriculum and instruction, assessment and evaluation, theories of growth and learning, educational foundations, and organization and administration. Although the professional knowledge test is being field-tested, candidates must get 50% correct responses to obtain a passing score. Table 5 shows test results for test administrations between January 1 and June 30, 1983.[2] Between July and September of 1983 an additional 1,366 candidates took the ATPE. Pass rates were 41% for blacks, 36% for Hispanics, 25% for Asians, 19% for native Americans, and 70% for Anglos (Knight, 1983).

---

[2]*Statewide ATPE results.* (1983, January 1–June 30). Office of Performance Based Certification. Arizona Department of Education. (The sum of the number of tests for each ethnic group do not equal the reported number for all tests administered. For example, the sum of tests by ethnic group equals 1,779 rather than 1,821, the total number of tests administered. Discrepancy may have been due to either test takers not reporting their ethnicity or a number of test takers whose ethnicity did not fit within the five categories used for reporting. Table 4 contains data as reported by the Arizona Department of Education with no adjustment for possible errors.)

TABLE 5. Arizona Teacher Proficiency Exam Results by Ethnicity, January 1–June 30, 1983

Ethnic Group	Basic Skills Test*			Professional Knowledge Test**		
	Number Tested	Number Passed	Percent Passed	Number Tested	Number Passed	Percent Passed
Blacks	54	13	24	27	24	89
Hispanics	123	51	42	58	56	97
Asians	12	6	50	8	8	100
Native Americans	100	22	22	39	33	85
Anglos	1490	1085	73	1008	1002	98
All	1821	1201	66	1162	1145	98

*Passing score of 80% correct responses
**Passing score of 50% correct responses
Source: "Statewide ATPE Results," (January 1–July 30), Office of Performance-Based Certification, Arizona Department of Education.

The Arizona Teacher Residency Program is a 2-year pilot program in which new teachers are evaluated by a committee including a master teacher, an administrator, and a member of a college of education faculty. The areas to be evaluated include assessing students, planning and implementing instructional strategies, developing positive relationships with students, monitoring and communicating student progress, evaluating the instructional program, and managing the classroom. Not yet mandated by the state, the program remains experimental. No data are available to determine the impact of the program on minority teachers.

California

Since February 1, 1983, new teachers, administrators, and some other school employees such as librarians, have been required to pass the CBEST, designed to measure proficiency in reading, writing, and mathematics. The reading and mathematics sections include only multiple-choice questions; the writing section requires written essay responses on two topics. To be certified, an examinee must obtain a total score (sum of reading, writing, and mathematics) of 123, with no section score lower than 37.

The California Commission of Teacher Credentialing (1984) has provided a detailed analysis of personal background factors and test performance scores in "CBEST Performance in Relation to Personal Background Factors," a study that includes data obtained at one field test and four regularly scheduled administrations (December, 1982; February, May, and July, 1983) during the first year of the testing program. Table 6 presents performance data for various ethnic groups and clearly shows the disproportionate impact on minority groups. The California Commission's (1984) study provides other significant findings that may be of interest to professional educators in other states that are considering competency testing:

1. Of those examinees who were attending college at the time of taking the CBEST, full-time students had a pass rate of 63% compared to a pass rate of 49% for part-time students (p. 3).
2. Recency of college attendance seems only slightly related to CBEST performance. Examinees who had graduated within the past two years had a 71% pass rate; those who had graduated within 3–9 years had a pass rate of 69%; those who had graduated 10 or more years ago had a 76% pass rate (p. 4).
3. There is considerable difference in the pass rates of those who attended a community college (53% for those still working on a baccalaureate and 60% for those who had completed a baccalaureate) and those who attended 4-year colleges and universities (65% for those still working toward a baccalaureate and 75% for those who had completed the baccalaureate) (pp. 4–5).
4. In general, those who did not have tutorial help had a higher passing rate than those who did require such help, but for both groups (examinees still attending college and examinees holding a baccalaureate) there is an exception if the tutorial work was limited to the combination of writing and mathematics (p. 6).
5. There is a low correlation between self-reported grade-point averages and pass–fail status on the CBEST. Correlations for both graduates and students working toward the baccalaureate range from .16 to .27 (p. 8).

Of the 33,586 examinees, a total of 5,183 or 15% had grade-point averages of 3.0 or above but failed the CBEST. That 21% of the college students and 18% of the graduates who reported senior grade-point averages of 3.5–4.0 and 39% of the college students and 28% of the graduates with self-reported

TABLE 6. Pass Rates By Ethnicity – California Basic Educational Skills Test, All First-Time Examinees December 1982

Ethnic Group	Number Responding	Number Passing	Percent Passing
American Indian, Eskimo or Aleut.	361	244	67
Black, Afro-American or Negro	2,040	539	26
Mexican American or Chicano	2,133	834	39
Oriental or Asian-American	1,259	637	50
Puerto Rican	110	45	40
Other Hispanic or Latin American	741	284	38
White	24,540	18,856	76
Other	855	533	62
Did not respond	1,547	965	62
TOTAL GROUP	33,586	22,937	68

Source: California Commission of Teacher Credentialing

grade-point averages of 3.0–3.49 failed raises serious questions. That all but 6,487 of the California examinees had completed 4-year programs magnifies the complexity of measuring competence not only of minority candidates but all candidates (California Commission of Teacher Credentialing, 1984).

Florida

The Florida legislature has enacted a number of testing laws which bear on the certification of teachers. A law passed in June, 1978 requires (1) a passing score on a nationally normed college entrance test (currently a score of 17 on the ACT or 835 on the SAT) for admission to a teacher education program, (2) demonstration of mastery of minimum essential generic and specialization competencies on a comprehensive written examination, and (3) completion of a fifth year internship. The current Florida Teacher Certification Examination (FTCE) is a 200-item test consisting of subtests in mathematics, reading, writing, and professional education. Although the FTCE was originally designed as an exit test, the Florida legislature made a change which permits the written examination to be taken by a prospective teacher prior to graduation (Sandefur, 1984a, 1984b). An added dimension to the competency testing program in Florida is a law passed in 1981 stating that 80% of the students must pass subject matter examinations for teacher education programs to maintain state approval. Enforcing the law for the first time in 1983, the State of Florida withdrew approval of 38 teacher education programs in 18 colleges and universities, primarily historically black institutions and other institutions with large minority enrollments ("In Brief," 1983).

Reports of minority performance on the FTCE are discouraging. In 1981 Florida certified approximately 200 black teachers out of a total of 5,500 teachers, a black representation of 3.6%. Table 7 shows results of the July, 1982 test report.

The July, 1982 data show a pass rate of 92% for white teacher candidates, 37% for black candidates, 57% for Hispanic candidates, 90% for native

TABLE 7.   Florida Teacher Certification Examination Test Results By Ethnicity, July 10, 1982

Group	Tests Taken	Tests Passed	Percent Passed
Black	369	138	37
Hispanic	156	89	57
Native American/Alaskan Native	10	9	90
Asian/Pacific	6	4	67
Anglo/White	3242	2973	92
Other	55	39	71
All	3838	3252	85

Source: Florida State Department of Education.

Americans or Alaskan natives, and 67% for Asian or Pacific Islanders (Florida Dept. of Education, 1982). Florida competency testing data released in February, 1983, show a first-time pass rate of 90% for white teacher candidates, 35% for black candidates, 51% for Hispanic candidates, 100% for four native American candidates, and 63% for Asian or Pacific Islanders (Andrews, 1983).

Georgia

In Georgia, one of the first states to develop and norm its own test, statistics on the performance of a total 22,261 students who took the 150-item Criterion Referenced Teacher Certification Test (CRTCT) were made public in 1983 by the State Department of Education for the first time since the program's inception 5 years ago. An article in the *Atlanta Journal and Constitution* (Hansen, 1983) indicated that on first attempt, 34% of the black candidates passed, compared to 87% of the white candidates.

Approximately 3,483 black students and 18,658 white students were tested between 1978 and 1983. The estimated first-time pass rate for all candidates for the 5-year period is 78%. The 3,483 black students in teacher training programs would have represented 15.6% of the newly certified teachers had competency tests not been required. The 1,184 black candidates who passed the Georgia CRTCT, however, constitute only 6.7% of the pool of 17,417 teachers qualifying for certification.

Students from the nine historically black institutions in Georgia had a first-time pass rate of 28% compared to the 34% pass rate for all black students. Forty-five percent of the students from historically black institutions eventually passed the CRTCT over the 5-year period, compared to a cumulative pass rate of 87% for all candidates. Despite the fact that black candidates failed the examination five times as often as their white counterparts, William Gorth, President of National Evaluations Systems, Inc., remarked, "There is no ethnic bias in the questions. The tests were reviewed by committees of people from all walks of life, black and white, in Georgia" ("Teacher Test," 1983, p. 30A). Noting that the CRTCT consists of 28 tests designed to measure minimum content knowledge in specified academic areas, Flippo and Foster (1984) have provided a comprehensive analysis of the procedures used to validate the test.

Since May 1, 1980, applicants have received nonrenewable, 3-year certificates. Beginning teachers must demonstrate competency on 14 generic teaching competencies as judged by evaluators on the Teachers Performance Assessment Instruments (TPAI). Although the precise impact of the TPAI on minority teachers is not known, 72% of all beginning teachers met their performance criteria in 1982–1983 during their first year (Sandefur, 1984a).

Louisiana

The superintendent of education selected the National Teacher Examination (NTE) to fulfill the Louisiana legislature's 1977 mandate that a teacher applying for initial certification must pass an examination of English proficiency, pedagogical knowledge, and specialization knowledge. Since 1978, 15% of the black teacher candidates compared to 78% of the white candidates have passed the NTE ("Teacher Test," 1983). Kauchak (1984) provides the most comprehensive analysis of the impact of competency testing on minority applicants in Louisiana:

> Since the beginning of competency testing in Louisiana in 1978, only 15% of the 1,394 black students from public institutions who took the NTE achieved a passing score. The figure represents a 10% passing rate for blacks at predominantly black public institutions and a 28% passing rate at predominantly white public institutions in the state.
>
> Since the inception of competency testing in Louisiana, only 211 black graduates of public institutions in the state have passed the NTE — just over 40 black students per year. This figure is well below the 580 black teachers that should have been hired each year if the racial composition of the teaching force was to be maintained at pre-1978 levels. (p. 627)

Noting a 49% decline in senior education majors from 768 in 1979–80 to 389 in 1982 at the two largest predominantly black institutions and a parallel decline of black graduates in predominantly white state institutions that produced an annual average of about 55 certified candidates over the last 4 years, Kauchak underscores the devastating impact of testing on minority teachers and challenges the myth that predominantly white institutions will rise to the occasion of providing substantial numbers of minority teachers. Using Kauchak's data, it is relatively easy to estimate that black teachers represent only about 5% of the total pool of new teachers certified between 1978 and 1982. The significance of this fact in determining the long-term effects of competency testing is magnified when viewed against Kauchak's findings that 37% of the school children are black and that 47% of the Louisiana teaching force with 15 or more years experience is black and rapidly approaching retirement.

Further reduction in the number of minority teachers is the likely result of implementation of a pending proposal by the Board of Regents to require an ACT composite score based on a sliding grade-point average for admission to a teacher program. The proposal recommends admission standards based on an ACT of 16 with a grade-point average of 2.2 and an ACT of 14 with a grade-point average of 3.2. Students with an ACT below 14 would be denied admission. Although the American College Testing Program is not prone to publish test results by ethnicity, inferred average ACT scores for black students enrolled in private and public historically black institutions range from 11 to 14.3 (Mercer, 1984).

Mississippi

The State of Mississippi originally required a score of 850 on the NTE for certification. Current certification requirements include a minimum score of 641 for the communications skill test, 636 for the general knowledge test, 639 for the professional knowledge test, and scores ranging from 445 to 512 for area examinations. The Board of Trustees of State Institutions of Higher Learning have approved an admission to teacher education policy that requires a satisfactory score on the College Outcomes Measures Project (COMP) Examination. A student is required to have a passing score only on the speaking or writing areas of the COMP if the student has a 3.2 cumulative grade-point average at the end of the first semester of the sophomore year or a composite ACT score of 18. The Education Reform Act of 1982 also requires competency assessment of a 1-year internship (Sandefur, 1984a).

The precise impact of competency assessment on minority teachers in Mississippi cannot be determined from the available evidence, particularly in relationship to admission requirements and internship assessment. Nor is the statewide impact of the NTE clear, particularly for graduates from private institutions. However, data in Table 8 does substantiate disproportionate impact on students enrolled in historically black state institutions as compared to students enrolled in predominantly white state institutions.

In 1982, pass rates for candidates at historically black state institutions ranged from 54% to 70% compared to pass rates for candidates at predominantly white state institutions that ranged from 97% to 100% (Warner, 1983).

TABLE 8.   National Teacher Examination Scores for Mississippi Universities

Institution	Composite Mean for 1982	Percent Scoring 850* or Above
Mississippi University for Women	1,156	100
Mississippi State University	1,140	98
University of Mississippi	1,123	97
Delta State University	1,132	97
University of Southern Mississippi	1,141	97
** Alcorn State University	895	70
** Jackson State University	874	60
** Mississippi Valley State University	851	54

*Required for certification in Mississippi.
**Historically and predominantly black institutions.
Source: Mississippi State College Board as reported in "Many Ed Majors Can't Pass Teacher's Exam" by Coleman Warner, January 30, 1983, *The Clarion Ledger,* p. 8B.

Oklahoma

In 1980, the Oklahoma legislature enacted House Bill 1706, which requires a teacher candidate to pass curriculum examinations in each subject that the candidate expects to teach. Any person completing a teacher education program after January 31, 1982, is required to pass the curriculum examination before being certified. The Oklahoma State Department of Education contracted with NES of Amherst, Massachusetts, for the development and administration of the Oklahoma Teacher Certification Testing (OTCT) program. The *Oklahoma Certification Testing Program: Registration Bulletin, 1984* provides the following description:

> The tests are criterion-referenced and competency based . . . designed to measure a candidate's knowledge and skills in relation to an established standard of competence rather than in relation to the performance of other candidates . . . . All competencies were reviewed by Oklahoma educators and committees of content experts for relevance to the teaching field. In addition, the tests were developed on the basis of textbooks, curriculum guides, and teacher education and certification standards. Further, a job analysis survey was conducted using some 4,000 randomly sampled Oklahoma educators to ensure that the com - etencies were accurate and reasonable. (p. 6)

Summary data from five selected test-result reports from January, 1982, to February, 1984, are shown in Table 9. Compared to an overall pass rate of 78%, black candidates passed 45% of the tests; Hispanic candidates, 71%; native American candidates, 70%; Oriental candidates, 82%; and Anglo candidates, 79% ("Sex and Race Results," 1982, 1983, 1984).

The Oklahoma Department of Education reports tests results by number of tests taken at a given test administration. Consequently, a true number of certifiable teachers cannot be extrapolated because candidates may seek certification in more than one area. However, by counting the number of individual major concentration tests, test figures for the total number of certifia-

TABLE 9. Oklahoma Certification Testing Program Test Results by Ethnicity, All Examinees/ All Tests (January, April, July, 1982; December, 1983; February, 1984)

Group	Tests Taken	Tests Passed	Percent Passed
Black	220	98	45
Hispanic	34	24	71
Native American	174	121	70
Oriental	11	9	82
White/Anglo	8284	6514	79
Other	36	33	92
All	8759	6799	78

Source: State Department of Education, Oklahoma. Compiled by the author

ble teachers and the number of certifiable teachers within each of the ethnic groups can be estimated; and, therefore, an estimate of the impact of competency testing upon the teaching force in Oklahoma can be computed. Compiled data from the July, 1982, December, 1983, and February, 1984 test administrations reveal that approximately 3,549 teachers were eligible for certification as a result of competency testing. Without competency testing, 4,357 teachers would have been eligible for certification. The overall effect of competency testing is a loss of 808 teachers, a 19% loss of prospective teachers. Approximately 118 black candidates took tests; 55 passed, a 53% loss in the pool of prospective black teachers. Approximately 86 native Americans took tests; the 55 native Americans who passed represent a 31% loss in the pool of prospective native American teachers. It is reasonably safe to conclude that competency testing will reduce certified black teachers to about 1.5% of the total pool of certified teachers. Likewise, native American teachers are likely not to represent more than 1.5% of the certified teachers. As a consequence of competency tests, minority teachers — Blacks, Hispanics, Native Americans, and Orientals — are likely not to represent more than 3.6% of the teachers certified in Oklahoma. Anglo teachers will constitute approximately 96.4% of the Oklahoma teaching force.

Texas

The Texas legislature enacted a law in 1981 requiring prospective teachers to pass both an entrance examination of basic skills and one or more exit examinations. Following a recommendation by the Commission on Standards for the Teaching Profession, the Texas State Board of Education adopted the Pre-Professional Skills Test (P-PST) as the entry examination. Like California's CBEST, the P-PST was developed by Educational Testing Service and consists of subtests in reading, writing, and mathematics. Permitted three attempts, candidates must pass all three subtests to be admitted to an approved teacher education program at a Texas college or university. Although an exit examination has not been adopted, the State Board of Education set cut scores for the entry level examination prior to March 3, 1984, the date of the first official administration of the P-PST. In the spring of 1983, a sample of 1,269 students from 61 Texas institutions participated in a data-gathering study conducted by IOX Assessment Associates to be used in establishing performance standards on P-PST. The Commission on Standards for the Teaching Profession has recommended to the State Board of Education cut scores for the reading, writing, and mathematics tests that will increase by 2 points every 2 years from 1984 through 1988. Based upon the 1983 performance data and the recommended cut scores for 1984, projections for the first administration indicate elimination of 84% of the black applicants and 61% of the Hispanic applicants on the math test, 87% of the black applicants and 65% of the Hispanic applicants on the reading test, and 80% of the black applicants and 56% of the Hispanic applicants on the writing test. By 1988, if minority scores do not show improvement and if the ruling that applicants must pass all three examinations is not amended, 96% of the black applicants and 84% of the Hispanic applicants may be denied admission to teacher education on the basis of the reading test alone (IOX, 1983). Recently released results from the March 3, 1984 test administration, the first official testing, indicate lower pass rates than originally projected with only 10% of the blacks, 19% of the Hispanics, and 62% of the whites passing the P-PST ("Performance," 1984).

Virginia

The Virginia General Assembly passed a 1981 law requiring that all new teachers hired after July 1, 1984, pass a battery of competency tests. During an 18-month study, portions of the NTE were administered to a total of 2,770 candidates for teaching certificates that included 1,654 graduates of predominantly white institutions and 89 graduates of predominantly black institutions. Compared to other states, relatively low cut scores of 644 for the communications skills test, 634 for the general knowledge test, and 633 for the professional knowledge test were used to establish pass rates. Findings of the study revealed a pass rate of 56% for candidates from black institutions compared to 97% for candidates from white institutions on the communications skills test; 69% compared to 99% on the general knowledge test; and 83% compared to 99% on the professional knowledge test. Only 50% of the candidates from black institutions passed all three portions of the NTE (Byrd & Keesler, 1984).

LEGAL TRENDS AND ISSUES IN TEACHER COMPETENCY TESTING

The decade of the 70s marked a reversal in the American legal system's view of the competency testing of teachers. Prior to the mid-70s, almost without question, competency tests for teachers were struck down by most courts. Courts seldom looked beyond discriminatory impact to rule tests and selection procedures unconstitutional. By the mid-70s competency tests, particularly outside teacher education, began to be struck down less frequently. The concept of discriminatory impact began to give way to the concept of discriminatory purpose and discriminatory intent. More lenient legal definitions of test validity began to emerge from the various court cases. Near the end of the decade, the U.S. Supreme Court upheld the use of the NTE for certifying teachers, a legal precedent which gave impetus to the rapid acceptance of competency testing. Clearly, increasingly more conservative court decisions throughout the decade charted the course, principle by principle, for how testing companies and state agencies could legally develop and use testing programs that would result in disproportionate failure rates for minority students. Thus, an examination of selected key cases serves as a primer for understanding the legal principles underlying testing and for understanding the relationship between the role of the courts and the phenomenal growth of the competency testing movement.

In the early 1970s most legal challenges to the testing of teachers focused on the use of the NTE for hiring rather than for certifying teachers. More often than not, the courts struck down testing requirements of school districts because the tests bore no rational relationship to an intended or legitimate purpose and/or because there were no studies of test validity or reliability. In *Baker v. Columbia Municipal Separate District* (1972) a hiring requirement of a minimum score of 1000 on the NTE was struck down on the basis that the school district had conducted no study of the validity and reliability of the test or the cut-off score. Similarly, a minimum score of 500 on the Common Examination, which was serving as an alternative to a required score on the Graduate Record Examination as prerequisite for hiring teachers was struck down on the basis of lacking rational relationship to a legitimate purpose in *Armistead v. Starkville Municipal Separate School District* (1972). In *U.S. v. Chesterfield County School District* (1973) the court struck down use of the NTE on the basis that the school district policy under which test scores were used was arbitrary and capricious. In *Walston v. County School Board of Nansemond County* (1974) where a minimum score of 500 on the Common Examination of the NTE was a prerequisite for hiring teachers, the court found no rational relationship to intended purpose.

By the mid-1970s, legal challenges to testing teachers began to focus upon the use of the NTE to certify teachers. Courts continued to strike down the use of competency tests but established a trend of clarifying legitimate uses of tests. In *U.S. v. North Carolina* (1975) a three judge court ruled that a state has a legitimate interest in determining whether candidates have the minimum knowledge necessary to teach but that the minimum score required by North Carolina violated the Fourteenth Amendment because it lacked any rational basis. Clarifying the absence of rational basis, the court said that although a cut-off "score somewhere on the scale would disclose the knowledge necessary as a prerequisite to effective teaching . . . that point — whether at 950 or some other score — is not established by the record" (p. 350). This ruling was a significant prelude to future cases because the court clearly established that the state has a legitimate interest in testing for the purpose of certification and implied that proper validation of a cut-off score would remove the only serious barrier.

As noted by Rebell (1977), in the case of *Georgia Association of Education v. Nix* (1976), the use of the NTE for certification was not upheld. The issue in this case centered upon a requirement that to obtain a 6-year certificate and higher pay, the teacher had to complete a specified post-graduate course of study and achieve a composite score of 1225 on the commons and the teaching field specialization portions of the NTE. The court found that the NTE was designed as a measure of knowledge gained at the undergraduate level rather than at the post-graduate level. The court further held that the NTE had not been shown to be related to the evaluation of a teacher's past performance for the purpose of determining "master teacher" status and therefore entitlement to higher salary. This case, however, did not throw any new light on the legality of using the NTE for certification of new teachers but did imply the possibility of validating the NTE against an undergraduate curriculum.

At the mid-point of the decade, two cases involving testing requirements for admission to training programs outside the field of education influenced the rationale underlying later court decisions directly concerned with teacher competency testing. In *Tyler v. Vickery* (1975) the Fifth Circuit rejected a challenge based on the Fourteenth Amendment to the Georgia Board of Bar Examiners' requirement of passing written tests as part of the criteria for admission to the bar. The court upheld the district court's use of a rational relationship test stating that "if a state has the right to insist on a minimum standard of legal competence as a condition of licensure, it would seem to follow a fortiori that it may require a demonstration of such competence in an examination designed to test fundamental ability to recognize and deal with legal principles" (p. 1101). Neither a validation study of the test nor validation against actual job performance was required to meet the rational relationship standard. *Washington v. Davis* (1976) clearly upheld the use of a verbal ability test as an eligibility requirement to enter a police training program. The U.S. Supreme Court stated that " . . . the test is neutral on its face and rationally may be said to serve a purpose the government is constitutionally empowered to pursue" (p. 4794) and " . . . that [the test] was directly related to the requirements of the police training program and that a positive relationship between the test and the training course performance was sufficient to validate the former, wholly aside from its possible relationship to actual performance to a police officer" (p. 4795). The court ruled that state laws or regulations cannot be invalidated under the Fourteenth Amendment solely on the basis of differential impact on persons of different racial groups but that state action must be proven to have *discriminatory purpose*. Thus, the test, in this instance, met the constitutional standard.

In 1978 the U.S. Supreme Court affirmed a district court decision in *U.S. v. State of South Carolina* that upheld the use of the NTE for certification. The decision was of such landmark significance that the legal particulars of the case bear careful examination. When plaintiffs in *U.S. v. South Carolina* (1977) stated that use of the NTE for certification and salary determination violated the equal protection clause of the Fourteenth Amendment and Title VII of the Civil Rights Act of 1964, the Educational Testing Service and the State of South Carolina presented an extensive validation study. In brief, the study consisted of validating items on the NTE Common Examinations and 13 of the 20 Area Examinations against the content of teacher training programs in South Carolina through jury judgment. Data presented to the district court indicated that 86% of the items on the Common Examinations and more than 90% of the items on the 13 Area Examinations were judged by 456 experienced educators from 25 teacher training institutions as appropriate for use in South Carolina. The validation study also proposed minimum cut-off scores for prospective teachers in South Carolina (Willens, 1976). The ruling of the district court, later upheld by the Supreme Court, has been summarized by Hyman (1984):

> A three-judge court held that the NTE met four legal standards: (a) They had a "fair and substantial relationship" to the governmental objectives for education (p. 1108); (b) They did not have a "discriminatory intent" in regard to race (p. 1104); rather they differentiated on a "rational basis" between persons who did and did not have some minimum verbal and communication skill. This created in turn some rational basis to the legitimate employment objectives of the State of South Carolina (p. 1112). In the words of the court, "the NTE creates classifications only on permissible bases (presence or absence of knowledge or skill and ability in applying knowledge), and they are not used pursuant to any intent to discriminate" (p. 1104); (c) They were "validated" in terms of job performance (p. 1114); the court accepted the NTE approach to validation, that is, they accepted the Educational Testing Services' procedure of validating against the academic training program rather than job performance (p. 1113); and (d) They met the "business necessity test under Title VII" of the Civil Rights Act of 1964 as amended (*U.S. v. South Carolina,* 434, U.S. 1026, 1978 as reported in Hyman [1984], pp. 15–16)

Whereas court acceptance of validation may appear weak in light of rigorous application of the American Psychological Association standards for establishing test validity and whereas the fine shades of difference between "discriminatory intent" and "discriminatory impact" may appear superficial to some critics, the court has spoken. A clear legal precedent for the use of competency tests to certify teachers has been established. However, not all the issues in teacher competency testing are resolved. Recent developments in the *Debra P. v. Turlington* (1979, 1981, 1983) case and future application of the revised *Uniform Guidelines on Employee Selection Procedures* (1978) to competency testing merit further discussion.

DEBRA P. AND COMPETENCY TESTING FOR TEACHERS

Despite the fact that this court decision is restricted to the use of a competency test to determine eligibility for receiving a high school diploma in Florida, *Debra P. v. Turlington* (1979, 1981, 1983) may have ramifications beyond its original parameters and influence the teacher competency movement. *Debra P.* was first filed in 1978 on behalf of several black high school students who challenged the constitutionality of a 1978 law that required high school students to pass a functional literacy test (later called the SSAT II) in communication and mathematics skills before receiving a high school diploma. Plaintiffs argued that the tests violated the Fourteenth Amendment Due Process and Equal Protection rights, Title VI of the Civil Rights Act, and the U.S.C. §1703, the Equal Opportunities Act. The results of three administrations of the test at the time of the case indicated a 36% overall failure rate with blacks constituting 78% and whites 25% of the failures. Although the *Debra P.* case has a lengthy legal history involving decisions in 1979, 1981, and 1983 at either the district court level or the U.S. Court of Appeals level, the decision rendered by the U.S. Court of Appeals for the eleventh Circuit in May, 1984, appears to have significant implications for the competency testing debate. In brief, a three-judge panel upheld the district judge's ruling that the Florida schools teach the skills on the test and that the disproportionate failure rate among black students was not due to the vestiges of past segregation.

In an analysis of the appeals panel's decision, Walton (1984) clarifies several important points. Plaintiffs claimed that because major changes in Florida curriculum had been enacted in 1976, a study conducted for the state that examined material taught during the 1981–82 school year did not reflect the entire time students had been in school. The appeals court, however, held that most of the skills were taught in the later grades and that extensive remedial studes conducted by Florida's schools after 1977 covered the necessary material. The appeals panel also cited a survey showing that a high percentage of high school students responded that they had been taught the skills on the test. In upholding that vestiges of past segregation are not responsible for the disproportionate impact upon black students, the panel cited several pieces of evidence. First, the expert witnesses of the state provided convincing evidence that factors other than schooling affected the success or failure of black students on the test. Second, the panel considered it significant that black students in districts that had black administrators as role models performed no better than those in districts with no black administrators. The panel cited the most compelling evidence to be the high percentage of black students who had passed the test over the past 6 years. For example, the pass rate for 1983 black seniors was 99.5% on the communication subtest and 91% on the mathematics subtest. Thus, the panel reasoned, the diploma sanction will effectively overcome effects of past discrimination.

There are several disturbing ramifications of the *Debra P.* decision for those who question the use of competency tests as the major determinant of eligibility for a high school diploma or a teaching certificate. First, high school minimum competency tests that have a disproportionate impact on minority students have been ruled as legal just as competency tests for the certification of teachers were ruled legal in *U.S. v. South Carolina.* Statistical evidence that minority students fail at a higher rate than white students has been judged not in and of itself evidence of discrimination. Second, student surveys asking students to indicate whether or not they have been taught skills measured on a test and other rather weak studies of curricular validity have been accepted by a court as sufficient means of test validation. Validation by opinion seems acceptable by the courts. Third, the concept of vestiges of past segregation in the form of dual school systems is no longer an acceptable explanation, at least in some courts, for the high failure rate of minority students on standardized tests. With the theory of educational deprivation laid to rest, can invidious claims of genetic inferiority and lack of motivation be far behind? Fourth, with the theory of educational deprivation laid to rest, testing companies, state legislatures, and state departments and boards of education across the nation are likely to interpret the court's decision as giving them a free hand to forge ahead with competency tests at all levels without regard to the impact on minorities.

Current Status of Legal Issues in Competency Testing

It appears that educators who are deeply concerned over the negative impact of competency testing on minorities may no longer look to the courts for protection against discriminatory testing. In fact, soon after the decision in *U.S. v. South Carolina,* the Supreme Court's ruling in *Personnel Administration of Massachusetts v. Feeney* (1979) could be interpreted as the proverbial "one more nail in the coffin." The Court stated: "[T]he Fourteenth Amendment guarantees equal laws, not equal results" (p. 273). Although this case involved a sex discrimination challenge to a veteran's preference law, its implication for competency testing litigation cannot be ignored. Certainly, the replacement of discriminatory impact by discriminatory intent to determine constitutionality of testing makes court challenges more difficult. Likewise, court acceptance of test validation by opinion makes a court challenge based on flaws of the test more difficult. Further, court challenges based upon vestiges of past discrimination have been weakened.

Despite the recent view of the courts, the distinction between discriminatory impact and discriminatory intent is likely to be perceived as superficial by minorities. After all, if a state conducts a validation study of a competency test whereby statistical evidence clearly forecasts disproportionate impact and then that state forges ahead with implementation of the testing program, such an action may be viewed by minority groups as a specific intent to discriminate. The subtleties of legal definitions offer little solace to minority parents who see their children denied high school diplomas or members of their group denied teaching certificates and, therefore, access to the social and economic advantages enjoyed by the majority population. To minority groups there is little difference between deliberate and unintended discrimination. The result is the same. When acts of unintentional discrimination are permitted to continue by the justice system and governmental agencies, unintentional discrimination becomes deliberate. A court may yet reopen this issue.

Not all the legal issues related to competency testing have been resolved at the national level. The parameters of the *Debra P.* rulings are restricted to the use of high school competency tests in Florida, and an appeal to a higher court is not likely. No court challenge to the use of competency tests for teacher certification has been initiated on the basis of the revised *Uniform Guidelines on Employee Selection Procedures* (1978), adopted by the Equal Employment Commission, Civil Service Commission, Department of Labor, and Department of Justice after the Supreme Court decision in *U.S. v. South Carolina* (1978). These standards appear to be directly related to the use of competency tests to certify teachers. First, a clear statement is made that the guidelines are applicable to *licensing and certifying* procedures, as well as to employment procedures. Secondly, a test for licensing and certification must be closely related to on-the-job performance and validated against a job analysis. A test must have content, construct, and/or criterion validity which is supported by empirical data. Third, selection processes should not have disproportionate impact and create a disadvantage for members of a race, sex, or ethnic group. As noted by Stedman (1984) and Hyman (1984), the Uniform Guidelines suggest further rulings on test validity because none of the current teacher competency tests have been validated against actual job performance.

PROJECTIONS

Prospects for the minority teaching force are indeed dim. The competency testing movement, fueled by recently supportive court decisions, will continue to grow. Actual and projected failure rates on teacher competency tests in Alabama, Arizona, California, Georgia, Florida, Louisiana, Mississippi, Oklahoma, Texas, and Virginia range from 30% to 90% for blacks, 29% to 81% for Hispanics; 18% to 75% for Asians; and 0% to 81% for native Americans. In 1980 minority teachers constituted approximately 12.5% of the national teaching force. Black teachers represented 8.6% of all teachers, K–12; Hispanics, 1.8%; and American Asians and American Indians, less than 1% (Andrews, 1983). However, if the currently observable impact of competency testing continues unabatedly along with normal rates of attrition through retirements and teacher burnout, minority representation in the national teaching force could be reduced to less than 5% by 1990 and, without question, by the beginning of the 21st century.

The competency testing movement will induce negative reverberations that will reach far beyond the single effect of excluding minority applicants from teaching. First, the presence of minority teachers contributes to the quality of education of all children in a pluralistic society. Whereas cross-cultural exposure for children of the majority population is an especially important factor in their development of healthy social attitudes, minority teachers as role models are essentail to the minority child's learning environment. The reduction of the number of minority teachers to less than 5% will be especially untimely as the minority elementary and secondary public school national enrollment reaches 30% by 1990. The National Center for Educational Statistics (as reported in Andrews, 1983) indicates that minority public school enrollment presently exceeds 50% in New Mexico and Mississippi. Minority public school enrollment is projected to approach 50% in California, Louisiana, South Carolina, and Texas by 1990. By the year 2000, Alabama, Arizona, Georgia, Florida, and North Carolina, which currently have minority public school enrollments ranging from 30% to 40%, are likely to approach the 50% mark. All of the above states are presently or will soon be engaged in competency testing for teachers. The impact of a reduced minority teaching force can be illustrated more graphically. If the minority teaching force is reduced to 5% and if schools become evenly integrated, the average school child, who has about 40 teachers during his/her K–12 school years, can expect only 2 of those 40 teachers to be from any minority group. Second, the options for higher education for minority youth who aspire to be teachers will become more and more restricted by 1990. As either more states follow the trend set in Alabama and Florida to tie approved program status to student test performance or as competency tests reduce enrollments, institutions that have historically been receptive to minority students will be forced to dismantle their teacher education programs. As these options become closed to minority students, other institutions that have exhibited little or no social conscience heretofore, many of which have been under considerable pressure for well over a decade to desegrate, are not likely to rush forward to recruit high-risk minority students whose test scores may either jeopardize accreditation or prove embarrassing in the media.

Additionally, with the exception of eliminating large numbers of minority teachers, the use of competency tests is not likely to alter significantly the general nature of the national teaching force that historically has been over 87% white. Almost without exception cut scores have been recommended or established, regardless of the examination, at the precise point that eliminates a majority of the black and Hispanic candidates but permits most white candidates to pass. For example, the pass rate for white students in Alabama has been 86%; in Arizona, 70–73%; in California, 76%; in Georgia, 87%; in Florida, 90–92%; in Louisiana, 78%; in Mississippi, 97–100%; in Oklahoma, 79%; in Texas, 62%; in Virginia, 97–99%. The teacher competency testing programs were designed to insure excellence in teaching. Yet they will have a negligible effect on changing the quality of the majority white teaching force of the past. In the next decade, testing will maintain the status quo rather than introduce an important innovation for achieving excellence. Testing appears only to guarantee the elimination of minority teachers in a decade when they will be sorely needed.

A CALL FOR A BALANCED SOLUTION

The one positive effect of the competency testing movement is that it has forced the nation to face its greatest failure in education — the failure to understand minority achievement and to develop instructional delivery systems that are successful with minority youth. Competency tesing that eliminates disproportionate numbers of minority candidates must be viewed within the context of this failure. Collaborative leadership from teachers, professional educators, and the public must rise to challenge new ways to perpetuate old inequities. In doing so, national leadership should consider these recommendations:

1. Establishment of a National Center for the Study of Minority Achievement. Needed is an effort of national magnitude that makes the understanding of minority achievement the nation's number one educational priority and that brings together the best minds the nation has to offer to review existing research, to conduct new research, and to develop a dissemination arm that directly impacts the public school classroom.
2. Negotiation with state departments of education to select alternatives to the use of standardized tests to identify, select, and certify minority teachers.
3. State and national funding for college and university developmental programs designed to prepare socioeconomically disadvantaged and minority youth to meet the challenge of stricter standards for teacher certification. This funding effort should have explicit provisions for those institutions that have demonstrated an historical commitment to equity.
4. State and national financial incentives to attract talented socioeconomically disadvantaged and minority youth to the teaching profession. Incentives should consist of both merit scholarships and loans with foregiveness provisions based on a designated term of service as a teacher.

Although the times call for a balanced solution and even if committed professional educators and grass roots organizations of minority parents formed coalitions to protest today, it may be too late to alter the direction of the competency testing movement. In recent years the critics of standardized testing have not been heard above the crusaders for testing. Mitchel Lazarus'

Goodbye to Excellence: A Critical Look at Minimum Competency Testing (1981), an insightful exposition of the intellectual, social, and legal problems of competency testing, passed largely unnoticed amidst the burgeoning crusade for testing teachers. Lazarus' treatise dealt exclusively with minimum competency testing in the public schools. Allen Nairn's (1980) *The Reign of ETS: The Corporation That Makes Up Minds,* the Nader report that charged Educational Testing Service with being the General Motors of testing, made a brief noise then seemingly receded into apathetic silence. Appearing on the *Phil Donahue Show,* Nader (1979) charged that "in 30 years, probably 90 million people have had their schooling, jobs, prospects for advancement, and beliefs in their own potential directly shaped by the quiet but pervasive power of ETS" (p. 1). Nairn and Nader's attacks were restricted almost entirely to testing for entrance into undergraduate, graduate, and professional schools. Sadly, no major book directly challenging the competency testing of teachers has appeared. For the time being, the balance of the matter seems to lean heavily in the direction of advocates of teacher testing. The state governmental agencies have spoken. With more to follow suit, 30 states have adopted teacher competency tests. The courts have spoken. The public has spoken. An overwhelming 95% of 1,243 respondents in a nationwide Associated Press–Media poll said teachers should have to pass exams periodically to keep their jobs ("Teacher Merit," 1984). Combined with the financial and political resources of the major testing companies, these separate constituencies collectively constitute a formidable voice amidst the current testing hysteria. Can so many be legally right but ethically wrong?

Initially considered a reasonable and acceptable solution for improving the quality of education, competency testing is now in danger of causing irreparable damage to the democratic character of education. Competency testing forces equity and excellence to be dichotomies and demands an elitist shift from equity to excellence in the nation's thinking. A pluralistic democratic society cannot have excellence in education without equity. Clearly, any professional practice that excludes disproportionate numbers of minorities represents neither excellence nor equity. If this nation is considered at risk now, a decade of willful elimination of minority teachers will result in a nation lost.

REFERENCES

American Association of Colleges for Teacher Education. (1983b). AACTE announces joint program to stem minority teacher shortage. *AACTE Briefs,* pp. 1, 8.

American Association of Colleges for Teacher Education. (1984). *AACTE Directory 1984.* Washington, DC: Author.

American Association of Colleges for Teacher Education. (1983a). *Educating a profession: Competency assessment.* Washington, DC: Author.

Andrews, T.E. (1983, May 26). *Teacher Education Reports,* pp. 2–4.

Armistead v. Starkville Municipal Separate School District, 461 F. 2d (5th Cir. 1972).

Baker v. Columbia Municipal Separate School District, 462 F. 2d 1112 (5th Cir. 1972).

Blakely, W.A. (1983). Black colleges and universities: Desegregation, disintegration or equity? *ISEP Monitor, 7* (1–2), 11–26.

Byrd, B., & Keesler, W. (1984, March 30). Black-college grads lag on tests: Failure rates high for prospective teachers. *The Virginia-Pilot,* pp. 1, 2A.

California Commission of Teacher Credentialing. (1984, January). *CBEST performance in relation to personal background factors.* Unpublished, Sacramento, CA.

Debra P. v. Turlington, 474 F. Supp. 244 (M. D. Fla. 1979).

Debra P. v. Turlington, 644 F. 2d 397 (1981).

Debra P. v. Turlington, No. 78-89 2- (M. D. Fla. 1983).

Ethridge, S.B. (1979). Impact of the 1954 Brown v. Topeka Board of Education decision on black educators. *The Negro Educational Review, 30*(4), 217–32. (ERIC No EJ 215 279)

Flippo, R.F., & Foster, C.R. (1984). Teacher competency testing and its impact on educators. *Journal of Teacher Education, 35*(2), 10–13.

Florida Department of Education. (1982, July 10). *Number and percent passing all subtests and each subtest by total candidates and by sex and ethnic designation: Florida teacher certification examination.* Unpublished report. Tallahassee, FL: Author.

Gallegos, A.M. (1984). The negative consequences of teacher competency testing. *Phi Delta Kappan, 65*(9), 631.

Georgia Association of Educators v. Nix, 407 F. Supp. 1102 (1976).

Hansen, J.O. (1983, October 9). 22% fail Georgia's teachers test. *Atlanta Journal and Constitution,* pp. 16, 17A.

Hyman, R.T. (1984). Testing for competence: The logic, the law, and the implications. *Journal of Teacher Education, 35*(2), 14–18.

In brief. (1983, July 29). *The Chronicle of Higher Education,* p. 2.

IOX Assessment Associates. (1983, June). *Standards advisor's booklet.* Austin: Texas Education Agency.

Kauchak, D. (1984). Testing teachers in Louisiana: A closer look. *Phi Delta Kappan, 65*(9), 626–628.

Knight, S.M. (1983, December 25). Proficiency testing: State's aspiring teachers sweat out last exam. *The Arizona Daily Star,* pp. 1, 2D.

Lazarus, M. (1981). *Goodbye to excellence: A critical look at minimum competency testing.* Boulder, CO: Westview.

Low scores to trigger reviews of colleges. (1983, February 11). *Alabama Journal,* p. 1.

Mercer, W. (1983, May). Standardized tests preserve a racial elite. *Instructor,* pp. 14, 89.

Mercer, W. (1984). Teacher education admission requirements: Alternatives for black prospective teachers and other minorities. *Journal of Teacher Education, 35*(1), 26–29.

Mohr, P. (1980, June). Research agenda for teacher education: Black perspective. In E.P. Witty (Ed.), *Proceedings of the National Invitational Conference on Problems, Issues, Plans, and Strategies Related to the Preparation and Survival of Black Public School Teachers* (pp. 99–109). Norfolk, VA: Norfolk State University.

Nader, R. (1979). The pervasive power of ETS. In *Additional resources.* Washington, DC: National Education Association. (Cited as excerpted and reprinted from an appearance by Ralph Nader on *The Phil Donahue Show,* May 2, 1979)

Nairn, A. (1980). *The reign of ETS: The corporation that makes up minds.* Washington, DC: Learning Research Project.

Oklahoma Teacher Certification Testing Program: Registration Bulletin, 1984. (1984). Amherst: National Evaluation Systems.

Performance by number of tests passed: P-PST data. (1984, March). Unpublished, Texas Education Agency.

Personnel Administration of Massachusetts v. Freeney, 442 U.S. 256(1979).

Poll shows teachers favor job tests. (1984, June 28). *Minneapolis Star and Tribune,* pp. 17, 18A.

Rebell, M.A. (1977, March). Recent developments in equal employment opportunity law and their effect on teacher credentialing practices. In *American Association of Colleges for Teacher Education yearbook: Professional relationships: Reality and action* (pp. 69–81). Washington, DC: AACTE.

Sandefur, J.T. (1984, March). *Addendum to state assessment trends.* Unpublished notes, Western Kentucky University, College of Education, Bowling Green.

Sandefur, J.T. (1984b, March). State assessment trends. *AACTE Briefs, 5*(2), 17–19.

Sandefur, J.T. (1984c). Teacher competency testing: The public's mandate. *Teacher Education and Practice, 1*(1), 11–16.

Scott, H.J. (1979). *Minimum competency-testing: The newest obstruction to the education of blacks and disadvantaged Americans.* Princeton, NJ: ERIC Clearinghouse on Tests, Measurement, and Evaluation and the Educational Testing Service. (ERIC Document Reproduction Service No. ED 178 618)

Sex and race results across all 7 test forms. (1982, January, April, July; 1983, December; 1984, February). Unpublished, Oklahoma Teacher Certification Testing Program, Oklahoma Department of Education.

Smith, C. (1981, December 23). Three file suit to block teacher test. *The Advertiser,* p. 11SF.

Stedman, C.H. (1984). Testing for competency: A pyrrhic victory. *Journal of Teacher Education, 35*(2), 2–5.

Teacher merit pay, competency tests favored. (1984, June 26). *Columbia Daily Tribune,* p. 2.

Teacher test raises questions (1983, October 30). *The Dallas Morning News,* p. 30A.

Trammer, M.D. (1980, February). Teaching: The profession blacks may lose. *Black Enterprise,* pp. 69–72.

Tyler v. Vickery, 517 F. 2nd 1089 (5th Cir. 1975).

Uniform Guidelines on Employee Selection Procedures. (1978, August 25). *Federal Register, Part VI, 43* (166).

U.S. v. Chesterfield County School District, 484 F. 2d 70 (4th Cir. 1973).

U.S. v. State of North Carolina, 400 F. Supp. 243 (E.D.N.C. 1975).

U.S. v. State of South Carolina, 445 F. Supp. 1094 (D. South Carolina, 1977), aff'd 434 U.S. 1026 (1978).

Vargas, Q., III. (1984). The screening of preservice teachers in Texas. *Texas Teacher Educator Forum, 11*(1), 1–11.

Washington v. Davis, 44 U.S.L.W. 4789 (June 7, 1976).

Walston v. County School Board of Nansemond County, 492 F. 2d 919 (4th Cir. 1974).

Walton, S. (1984, May 9). Federal appeals court upholds Florida high school graduation test. *Education Week, 3*(33), pp. 5–15.

Warner, C. (1983, January 30). Many ed majors can't pass teachers' exam. *The Clarion Ledger,* pp. 1, 8B.

Willens, H.P., Siemer, D.C., & Sims, T.S. (1976, July). *Brief Amicus Curiae For Educational Testing Service. United States of America, Plaintiff, and South Carolina Education Association, et al., Defendents. In the United States District Court for the District of South Carolina, Columbia Division.* (ED 157 905)

Witty, E.P. (1982). *Prospects for black teachers: Preparation, certification, employment.* Washington, DC: ERIC Clearinghouse on Teacher Education. (ERIC Document Reproduction Service No. ED 213 659)

Wright, M.D. (1980, June). The survival of black public school teachers: A challenge for black colleges and universities. In E.P. Witty (Ed.), *Proceedings of the National Invitational Conference on Problems, Issues, Plans, and Strategies Related to the Preparation and Survival of Black Public School Teachers* (pp. 63–70). Norfolk, VA: Norfolk State University. (ERIC Document Reproduction Service No. not yet assigned; Clearinghouse on Teacher Education No. SP 019 478)

Chapter 12

Liberal Education and Teacher Education: Two Forces in Search of Fusion

Edward R. Ducharme

University of Vermont, Burlington

A good liberal education—an education which liberates the mind from the shackles of prejudice and superstition and the confines of a single culture, that permits one to move freely and joyfully in the past and the present and to speculate objectively, with his fellowmen about the future—is a foremost aim of our schools. How far short we fall of ideal is probably directly related to how far the teachers in the classrooms of our schools have themselves fallen short in their liberal education . . . The reform needed in liberal education lies not in adding a few more hours of this or that. It is a matter of quality rather than quantity. (Bush, 1966, p. 4)

This quotation from Robert Bush, professor emeritus at Stanford University, remains as true in the 1980s as it was in 1960. To state this is not to say that things have gone nowhere. Rather, it is to say that the interrelationships between liberal and teacher education remain a continual source of unrest, a perennial concern, and a potentially rich resource.

The premises of this chapter are the following: Quality liberal education is desirable for teacher education students, but its definition remains elusive; liberal education is heavily value laden, often with values different from those of entering teacher education students; academicians who teach the liberal education courses for teacher education students are teacher educators, but they generally take little responsibility for this role; little of the impact of liberal education has been measured in any meaningful way; the cries for powerful liberal education in teacher education student curricula will continue to be made; if changes are to be made in the liberal education provided teacher education students, the changes will have to be forced by teacher educators within the faculties of schools, colleges, and departments of education (SCDEs); and, finally, it might be a better world if teacher education students had more potent liberal education.

DEFINITION AND DESIRABILITY

Despite much insistence that liberal education is valuable for educators, there is not always agreement on exactly what individuals mean when they use the phrase. I described some of the difficulty in an article I wrote several years ago.

> The definition of terms always presents a problem. There is rarely agreement on what is meant by "a liberal education." Surely, in time past, it meant much more attention to science than it now does. When students were expected to do some work in the sciences, even if their majors were philosophy, literature, or history, the intent was, of course, to "cover" the broad areas of human knowledge; but — perhaps more importantly — the intent also was to provide an introduction to what was naively called the scientific method. The expectation seemed to be that students majoring in the humanities would acquire some understanding of what scientists do, how they work, what methodologies they use.
>
> Quantum leaps in scientific and technological achievement over the last several decades have destroyed this unworkable premise, however laudable it may have been initially. Students majoring in the traditional humanities and social sciences often have not the slightest idea of what they are up to when they encounter scientific discourse later in life.
>
> Thus, when we discuss liberal education in the United States we are most likely speaking of a literary and historical education. We assume that some basic mathematical and scientific principles will be touched upon. We assume also that they will not be delved into very deeply. When editorialists, commentators, social critics, and others lament the lack of a liberal education in the citizenry, they are lamenting the lack of acquaintance with such things as the works of Shakespeare, the music of Mozart, the history of the Western civilizations.
>
> If I am right in this, the world has changed very little since Matthew Arnold visited the United States in the late 1890s and stated the case for education directed toward literary works. Science and mathematics people will, I am sure, resist this view, but I think they do so in spite of the evidence. It remains for them, on most campuses, to develop more dominant roles for science and mathematics. (Ducharme, 1980, p. 8)

Yet, whatever our definition of liberal arts education — and there are many — candidates for the teaching profession generally acquire their familiarity with the liberal arts through the general education component of their programs. Thus whereas the terms *liberal arts education* and *general educa-*

tion are not synonymous generally, they are, to a degree, interchangeable insofar as teacher education is concerned.

Part of the history of teacher education and liberal education has been a matter of avoidance of definition or the use of "definitions" of a loose manner. For example, in 1962, Woodring wrote that one of the four related but distinguishable parts of teacher education should be liberal education. No more was said. Similarly, Bush (1966) wrote: "The nature of this general and liberal education will need to be indicated as a part of the delineation of a program for teacher education" (p. 190). Beyond the listing of seven course areas, for example, mathematics, Bush did no further delineation. It is scarcely hyperbole to say that, except for some possible exceptions, delineation remains a task to be done. Hirst (1965) took the problem of definition a step further; namely, that definition is difficult and often writers attempt definition by stating what it is not.

> The phrase "liberal education" has today become something of a slogan which usually takes on different meanings according to its immediate context. It usually labels a form of education of which the author approves, but beyond that its meaning is often negatively defined. (p. 113)

Conant (1963) was conscious of the lack of precision in the term liberal education when he wrote his critique of teacher education in the 1960s:

> Let me caution the reader against the terms "liberal arts college" and "liberal education." Their meaning has become so varied as to render them almost useless in a study of this kind . . . it is absurd to assume that all holders of a bachelor's degree have received an education that can be described by any set of words. Those who proclaim "a teacher must be first of all a liberally educated person" are making a far from precise statement. (pp. 90–91)

Yet virtually no one questions the need for effective liberal education for teachers even though definition is rare. The "requirement" is written into state and regional guidelines and regulations, is part of national accreditations schema, and is integral to program descriptions at higher education institutions. Beyond a few vague, lofty statements, one looks in vain for much in the way of definitions of "effective" or reasoned rationales, or for evidence that the requirement works. The latter is true perhaps because almost no one well defines the purposes and subsequently measures if the purposes have been met. When stated at all, the purposes are generally vaguely but powerfully stated:

> The value of the liberal arts and sciences lies not only in the knowledge which they contain and produce, but in the spirit of inquiry which is their hallmark. (Sarason, Davidson, & Blatt, 1962, p. 32)

The value of inquiry is not contested; rather, its presence in individuals is difficult to demonstrate.

Do we want liberal education for educators because we believe there are particular things they should know in order to function well in American society or because we want them to be certain kinds of people? It seems that we have never been sure whether liberal education was intended as a fuel of the mind to promote change and growth in individuals, as a rites-of-passage for the socially and economically elite and those aspiring to such status, or as an entity in and for itself. Perhaps all three have existed simultaneously for many individuals and groups.

Much has been made in the past of liberal arts education as a means whereby one could understand the present and future by having well understood the past; that is, one might understand the complexities of a document describing political strife in the Middle East because of having taken high level history and political science courses. In others words, by having digested the "meaning" and mastered the skills of Political Science 147 or some such course, an individual could apply learnings to contemporary issues and emerge with understandings superior to that of citizens lacking such background. It is also assumed that individuals having a liberal arts education will have a vast catalogue in their minds filled with facts, examples, and data acquired through their studies ever at the ready for study, discussions, or thought. In brief, we have not concluded whether we want students to be wise and resourceful participants or culturally sophisticated conversationalists always prepared with the ready quip and the witty allusion. Perhaps we want both.

Certainly the goals cited for liberal education have been anything but modest. Reviewing the many statements made about the potential potency, one is struck by how all-encompassing some see the impacts of liberal studies, often indistinguishable in the literature from general education:

> To provide a program of education that will enable each man to put the parts of his culture together, to see the interdependence of its many social functions, and to have the patience and wisdom to remedy the dysfunctions that occur, is the task of those who are concerned with general education. An educational program that would lead to such results should be the basic education of a teacher. (Smith, 1962, p. 117)

Recently, Weber (1983) has argued that there is a relationship between creativity and the liberal arts. Certainly we want teachers to be creative:

> The key to the creativity of liberal arts students lies in their appreciation of seminal questions underlying human inquiry, consciousness of which liberates them from a slavish allegiance to any particular answers. Genuine creativity re-

quires not only mastery of a tradition, but the courage and breadth to free one-self from that tradition precisely to expand it. (p. 77)

Definition of a good program is equally broad and ill-defined. Smith (1962), writing of the deliberations at a national conference in the 1960s, set-tled for an extremely amorphous definition of a "good liberal education:"

> The members of the conference were unanimous in asserting that all teachers need a good liberal education without further definition and with a realization of the multitude of sins covered by the phrase "liberal education," it was consid-ered to be in general the mastery of the various programs of study normally rep-resented by the best of the four-year liberal arts college curriculums. (p. 16)

Sarason, writing in the same year, questioned the validity of the existent assumptions that the possession of a strong background in the liberal arts and sciences has any direct relationship to teaching effectiveness:

> What evidence warrants the conclusion that strengthening the background of teachers in the liberal arts and sciences will increase their effectiveness in communicating with children or in recognizing and adapting procedures to the range of individual differences found in any relationship between teaching ef-fectiveness and the degree of liberal arts and science background? (Sarason, et al., 1962, p. 32)

More than two decades later, teacher educators continue to deal with the same enigmatic questions: What is good liberal education? If we can define it, how can we provide it for prospective teachers? If we can both define and provide it, what implications are there for effective teaching? Nice conun-drums. But we still want "it."

VALUE-LADEN LIBERAL EDUCATION

Lortie (1975) and others have well documented that teachers in the public schools of America have come largely from lower middle and lower social and economic classes. A consequence of this fact is the general lack of a tradi-tion of education beyond secondary school and a near absence of any family or ethnic awareness and practice of the rites and customs of high culture as espoused by the private, 4-year, traditional liberal arts colleges, a custom em-ulated to higher and lower degrees across the spectrum of American higher education from 2-year community colleges to 4-year state universities. The tradition may find its greatest examples and models in the 4-year private colleges, but its presence is everywhere felt. Thus, regardless of where teachers took their undergraduate training, they were made aware, if not knowledgeable, of a tradition of knowledge and skills that they should aspire to and to which they should expose the young people they would in turn teach. That education was marked by:

- Survey courses in British literature.
- Survey courses in American literature.
- History of Western Civilization survey courses.
- Two or three years of foreign languages including an emphasis on the culture and literature of that country, usually a western European nation.
- An overview of a science or two.
- A mathematics course that, in retrospect, seemed designed to take students out of the "these are the problems for tomorrow" phase of high school mathematics to mathematics as another kind of language phase.
- Psychology or political science.
- Some physical education.

The purposes may have been many and varied, but two seem dominant: (a) to validate the cultural heritage of the Anglo-Americans in the institutions and enrich their understandings of it, and (b) to introduce and indoctrinate the ethnics in the classes to the major elements of the dominant referent group. So, for the one, it was a validating process, whereas for the others it was an annointing, a baptizing process.

I would argue, therefore, that valuable as the education was, it was inappropriate for the long view, but understandable in the short run. We were living, after all, in a world in which the "good guys" had not lost a war in decades despite near catastrophes, a world in which the enlightened nations went abroad to inform and convert the unknowing. Therefore the students learned the wisdom of Western poets, prophets, and philosophers. Knowledge of key figures and their work became the linguistic coin of the realm. As prospective educators we saw our future roles including these emphases as we would work with young people. The word would spread; the cultural tradition would be passed on. But there are no guarantees of the results of education in a splendid tradition. Real life provides the examples of the Nazi killers with refined tastes in art. The examples from literature are legion.

One must think occasionally of Kurtz, in Joseph Conrad's *The Heart of Darkness,* who brought his Western vision to a savage land and became both tyrant and victim, a tyrant who established a harsh and despotic rule and victim of the powers of darkness which he did not understand fully. The truths and strengths do not lie in a single tradition or way of life.

I do not intend these statements as latter-day accusations from the once-naive student. What occurred in liberal arts education at the time I described was the inevitable result of conditions that prevailed at the time. It is not surprising that, in Matthew Arnold's words, "the best that has been thought and said in the world" turned out to have been thought and said by English writers, that despite the scientific genius of a Leonardo, we learned about the scientific method by reading Thomas Huxley.

As I wrote the preceding words, a voice within me said, "Oh, how glib you are. Surely you remember the music course in which you listened to Italian and German music, the art course in which you looked at French, Italian, and Dutch painters." True, true. But why did I always see them as having composed and painted so that English speaking people could hear and view them?

This form, this content of liberal arts education, fell out of fashion in the late 1960s and 1970s as a host of curricula changes swept across American campuses. Electives proliferated; required courses disappeared; new areas of study emerged.

CURRENT EMPHASES AND DIRECTIONS

As educators, we always seem to be trying to figure out what we learned from something. What did we learn from the sixties that is applicable to liberal arts education?

- The very range and proliferation of mini-courses and other academic experiences taught us that, indeed, there is a world of things that are not widely known about people who are part of America.
- We need skills and knowledge to help understand these new learnings as the legitimate statements of different ethnic groups.
- We need to see the education of the '40s, '50s, and '60s as only one manifestation of the many cultures of the world.
- Institutions of higher education most likely cannot teach the content of everything, but they must teach the process for discovery and analysis of "new" materials.

These learnings must inform the reconceptualization of liberal arts education.

Now, after nearly a decade of social experimentation, of curricula innovation, and academic alternatives, American higher education seems to be hunkering down for a long period of its own version of Back-to-Basics. One finds everywhere the reemergence of the old Freshman composition courses, the skills-dominant mathematics classes, and the survey courses under new names.

For many, these developments are heartening. Students will have been exposed to directed writing experiences; students will have studied and perhaps even remember who the Romantic poets were; students will be at least modestly informed about specific events in the American past and general trends in the Western world. But they are inappropriate.

William Arrowsmith (1971) has written powerfully on our tendency to avoid the strange, to choose the familiar, or to make the strange into the familiar:

> What cannot be tolerated, what must be always shunned, is the direct experience of difference, the naked, unassimilated encounter with the "other." When school-children study foreign countries, it is not China or Pakistan or Chile they study, but Switzerland, Norway or France — that is, the always assimilable, the not-so-strange. The practice is defended on grounds of pedagogical necessity, but its real purpose is to evade encounter by domesticating the alien texture of reality. It is the same with the past as it is with the world.
>
> Programs in the humanities are anemic because humanists mindlessly view the past not as a great source of "otherness" — what we no longer have, the skills we have lost and need now, what we never knew we lacked — but as cultural reinforcement for the present. The past justifies the present; we teach students, not how we might become different or better, but merely how we became what we are. In the schools and universities the languages are being "phased out", apparently because their central educational purpose — the access they provide to alternate ways of being human, and hence to our undiscovered selves — is no longer understood. (pp. 6–7)

The simple reaffirmation of the past is inadequate. Professional educators have been at the forefront in advocating that professional students acquire a multicultural perspective, even though many of us have wondered from time to time exactly what that means. We have, however, agreed on some things it implies. Included are the ideas that students should see the world as multifaceted with respect to human experiences, that students should see American society as, perhaps, a tapestry woven of many different threads and fabrics, each contributing uniquely to the beauty and value of the whole. Such a vision need not, indeed ought not, lead to the wholesale abandonment or adoption of any one aspect of American culture. It implies an education preparation of students that would enable them to grasp both the dominant themes of American culture as well as the minor movements and recognize that without either there is no whole.

The future of liberal education for teachers must go beyond what I have described as often characterizing liberal education in the U.S.; namely, a preoccupation with Western traditions, knowledge and values or with "Westernizing" whatever appears unusual. If, for example, we reflect on only one of Dressel's (1979) six characteristics of the liberally educated person, we can gain a more appropriate perspective for teachers for the 21st century:

> They are aware of personal values that other persons and other cultures hold contrasting values which must be understood and respected in interaction with them. (p. 319)

The implications of this statement for the liberal education of teacher education students are enormous. First, there is the acknowledgement that personal values and value commitments are important; second, there must come
an awareness that other individuals and groups of individuals may have different values; third, there is the directive that these be not only understood
but respected as well. Dressel's characteristic relates not only broadly to liberal education sense but to the specific commitment of teacher education to
multiculturalism. Were such a characteristic to apply to emerging teachers
and were they so educated, we would truly be able to say that multiculturalism had been addressed. More significantly, it would be addressed
from the common liberal education component of all teacher preparation
students, not packaged in an SCDE module or special course for "covering
multiculturalism." Properly done, it would lead teacher education students,
indeed all students, to think in a multicultural dimension. We must demand
that educators graduating from a 4-year preparation program possess the following that relate to their liberal arts education:

- Effective use of English language, both written and spoken.
- Ability to read complex materials with understanding.
- Ability to use mathematical symbols and processes including computer
  applications.
- Ability to transcend their own ethnocentrism.
- Ability to honor cultural diversity.

These skills and learning go beyond the purpose of societal maintenance;
that is, providing educators to work with students in such manner as to introduce and indoctrinate them in the traditional values and texts of the West.
These force a shift in values and attitudes to accommodate new knowledge
and necessary skills.

Liberal education is intended to be liberating, but liberating to do something or liberating from something is a question that emerges. The liberation
of young people to a broader understanding of the values, forces, events and
beliefs that shaped the Western world in which they presently live is one thing
that goes on in quality general education programs; another is the separation
of young people from whatever values, forces, events, and beliefs that
shaped their own ethnic experience, if that experience is different from
Anglo-American tradition. This unplanned outcome for some students often
has unfortunate consequences. They work so hard to be the new that they
forget the old. A new emphasis must emerge that honors and respects diversity, that enables the minority to retain and value their experiences and past
while learning the majority.

ARTS AND SCIENCES PROFESSORS AS TEACHER EDUCATORS

There are those who continue to include academicians — those who teach the general education courses — as teacher educators. They are, of course, in that they provide courses that may or may not educate teachers. With rare exceptions, they are not teacher educators as is the language arts professor or the secondary methods professor. The latter individuals teach their material, generally speaking, with the specific audience in mind and are conscious that they have professional responsibilities for the students. The professors teaching the general education courses, on the other hand, are generally not concerned with career goals of their students, but rather with the content which they espouse and teach. One finds occasional exception to this general state of affairs in small, liberal arts colleges where the two or three persons responsible for professional education programs may have effective relationships with professors in other departments or programs and thus have occasional opportunity to talk about and share concerns. Clearly, such situations are the exceptions.

The result of all this is that teacher education students are dependent on the luck of the draw for a major portion of their undergraduate work, portions that many see as vital.

The unevenness of the situation is fostered by a number of conditions. Professional education is a late arrival, relatively speaking, to campus programs at liberal arts institutions and state universities, particularly with respect to those programs in elementary school preparation. Historically, higher education has not been greatly concerned with teacher preparation and there are few traditions to fall back on. Borrowman (1965) made the argument that teacher education was historically part of higher learning, but he clearly had in mind the period prior to the advent of professional training, the period when some liberal arts graduates went into teaching often because they had nothing better to do.

> There are no more authentic educational traditions than that teacher education is the central responsibility of institutions of higher learning and that the liberal arts and literature constitute the ideal curriculum for teacher preparation. (p. 1)

Teacher education may well have been the "central responsibility of higher learning" and liberal arts the "ideal" curriculum for teacher preparation, but between the early period in American educational history to which Borrowman alludes and the 1980s much occurred, including the normal school movement and the establishment of education as a field of study for those wishing to be teachers. Presently, the education of teachers is generally seen as anything but the central responsibility of higher education and the liberal arts form an often randomly chosen portion of teacher preparation rather than the total program.

> A second reseervation has to do with the meaning of the word "tradition," espe-
> cially as it applies to the liberal-arts college. There is a very definite sense in
> which the American liberal-arts college has no tradition of *teacher-education.*
> It is true enough that graduates of liberal-arts colleges taught in lower schools,
> but this was often the result of circumstances and not because the college had
> done anything in particular to prepare them for the occupation of teaching.
> (Anderson, 1962, p. 152)

Anderson inadvertently makes another point; namely, that graduates of liberal arts colleges have gone into the lower schools with minimal "profes-sional" preparation and often done quite well; at least, there have been few complaints recorded about the quality of their work relative to graduates of professional programs, thus producing some grist for the mill for those who advocate 4 years of liberal arts education as the only necessary preparation for teaching in the lower schools.

DIFFICULTIES OF MEASUREMENT

In *A New Case for the Liberal Arts,* the writers make the point that much of what students acquire in college may not be related to the mastery of intellec-tual skills and knowledge. They affirm that students learn such things as in-dependence from home, discovery of a mate, social poise, generalized work skills, organizational skills, rehearsal for management roles, and institu-tional motivation (Winter, McClelland, & Stewart, 1981, p. 11). Measure-ment of the learnings acquired through the liberal arts is less precise.

The case for effective liberal education has been made largely from rheto-ric, rarely from demonstration. Indeed, it may be that the providers of such education are totally inimicable to research on the effects of their work:

> The "guardians" of the liberal education tradition are not accustomed to think-
> ing this kind of support is necessary. From the classical tradition, they have ap-
> parently inherited both an emphasis on the power of rhetoric and form and a
> distrust of the empirical method . . . If the justification of liberal education
> were not self-evident, therefore, it could surely be established by personal testi-
> mony and eloquent rhetorical appeals stressing the emulation of classical mod-
> els, rather than by systematic collection and evaluation of empirical evidence
> . . . Thus . . . the tone and style of the celebrant override the proof of the scien-
> tist. (Winter, et al., 1981, p. 13)

This is but one of many statements over the years demonstrating how the effects of liberal education have not been systematically studied. It is doubly or trebly difficult to imagine studying the effects of liberal or general education on teachers in that nearly all the goals are idealistic statements rarely grounded in any systematic inquiry, their achievement dependent upon the application of knowledge and skills acquired in a process that merely assumes its value.

There are no studies demonstrating much of anything relative to the relationships between general education and teacher performance. There are, to be sure, the laments that if teachers had more or different general education they would be less likely to do things that some observers wish they would not do and more likely to do what the observers think they should do. None of these is grounded in anything much beyond individual preferences.

There may be very simple reasons why there has been so little effective research done on the impact of general education on the lives of students. It simply is very hard and very costly to do. A second, equally important reason, perhaps, is that many believe there is no necessity to do it because liberal education, like breathing and eating, is good for people; that is a given. It might well be that a multimillion dollar study, done over a period of several years would validate the efficacy of liberal education, would only demonstrate for many what they feel they already know. The response might well be: "Oh, really. Didn't we know that already?"

What Should Be

Lawler (1983) has perhaps forever confounded the prospects of those who seek finite distinctions:

> It is difficult to show the utility of a liberal education, especially its "classical" component, in our time. The problem is that utility is usually defined in a democratic, science-dependent context as a capacity for bringing forth a technological product. Technology, in turn, is understood to be a visible and tangible contribution to the comfortable self-preservation of the great mass of human beings. The utility of a "classical" education is usually defended in terms of its improvement of the "soul" or mind. A defense of this sort is questionable for a number of reasons, but the most important question concerns the thought that the "improved" recipient of a classical education may, in truth, have developed individual qualities destructive of his capacity for assuming his place as a productive member of our technological society. (p. 301)

Despite much conversation and writing about the topic, we remain unable to reach wide consensus on what graduates of teacher education programs should know and be able to do as a result of their experience in general education. Ernest Boyer (1981), writing on the role and function of general education, recently described six outcomes that he sees critical to society and integrally related to general education. Perhaps they are sufficiently broad and, conversely, adequately clear for widespread professional discussion:

1. All students should come to understand the shared use of symbols.
2. All students should understand their shared membership in groups and institutions.
3. Students should understand that everyone produces and consumes and that, through this process we are dependent on each other.
4. All life forms on the planet earth are inextricably interlocked, and no education is complete without an understanding of the ordered, interdependent nature of the universe.
5. All students should understand our shared sense of time.
6. All students should explore our shared values and beliefs. (pp. 11–16)

Of course, for many, Boyer's statements may well imply Western preoccupation with his continual use of *shared*.

Interestingly, Dressel (1979) also listed six characteristics of those who possess a liberal education:

1. They know how to acquire knowledge and how to use it.
2. They possess a high level of mastery at the skills of communication.
3. They are aware of personal values and value commitments and realize that other persons and other cultures hold contrasting values which must be understood and respected in interaction with them.
4. They cooperate and collaborate with others in studying, analyzing, and formulating solutions to problems and in taking actions on them.
5. They are aware of, concerned about, and accept some responsibility for contemporary events, and their implications.
6. They continually seek coherence and unity in accumulating knowledge and experience and use the insights thus achieved to further their development and to fulfill their obligations as responsible citizens in a democratic society. (p. 319)

Teacher educators could do worse than echo the sentiments expressed by Boyer and Dressel in any statements about the importance, content, and expectations about liberal education.

Still we might do well to remember that the possibility exists that some things in the universe may be undemonstrable, inexplicable. Herman Melville, in his short novel *Billy Budd,* a work often read by high school students, observes that William Claggart, the mendacious accuser of Billy Budd, is an example of innate moral depravity just as Budd is an example of pure, unalloyed innocence. Granted that Melville precedes Freud and the entire psychiatric structure that followed, nothing in Melville's narrative suggests that any new theories of man would change his opinion that Claggart's malevolence is inexplicable by any rational cause and effect analysis. Claggart is.

The connection between Claggart's moral depravity and the value of liberal education may be remote for many. The connection is that we perhaps cannot in our frenzied, data-driven searches find the precise cause of depravity in the Claggarts of the world, the goodness in the Budds of the world, nor the precise value of liberal education. However, because we cannot find the precise cause and effect does not mean that we deny the existence. Claggart, Budd, and the value of liberal education are.

We may never know precisely the relationship between liberal education and effective professional practice or, indeed, if there is one. The possibility that the search for predictable results may be futile is enough to unnerve the "hard" researchers among us who may say that if we do not know the effect of something, we surely should not do it. I suggest that we cannot follow that path, that we must continue to press for better liberal education for our students, that we continue to affirm the results.

It is axiomatic that teaching and learning are facilitated when connections and synthesis are experienced by learners, when they, more or less independent of teachers, are able to grasp the interactions among things which they are learning. It is axiomatic that among the variables that produce the synthesizing skills sits knowledge; the wider that knowledge is the higher the probability of student success.

We in the work of preparing educating professionals must demand that students in professional programs understand and know the critical persons, events, philosophical, social, and political movements, and the major texts that dramatically affected the world they live in. This, in itself, is a tall order; but we want more. We must demand more.

We also want persons entering professional education roles to be more world conscious, less chauvinistic than in the past. Such a position demands that students go beyond the present constraints of most undergraduate curricula.

CONTROL AND CHANGE

Some problems are thus never resolved. One of these in education is the relationship between teacher education and liberal or general education. Nearly every department or program in higher education is dependent on one or more of the departments in arts and sciences for portions of their students' programs. But virtually no one is as dependent both during the undergraduate phases of careers and at varied times with uneven emphases during their careers as teacher education students are. To illustrate: Elementary school teachers will generally have upward of 50% of their undergraduate course work at the hands of arts and sciences faculty; the same could be said for students in areas of studies such as engineering or computer sciences. But the elementary school teachers during their careers, are expected to model, demonstrate, and teach their charges in such manner so that somehow the evidence of their learning is present. It must be added, of course, that teachers who possess and demonstrate these vaguely defined characteristics are not cited; it is the absence of characteristics or readily available knowledge that gets cited whenever critics are sharpening their attacks. The other students, whether in engineering or nursing, never are required to give evidence of their general education as part of their careers.

Teacher education is thus dependent on the efforts of faculty over whom little control or direction can be exercised. For many professors in arts and sciences, teacher education students fill the required, introductory sections in sufficient numbers so that they can teach their majors and other advanced students in small seminars. Teacher educators can neither control the process by which their students are taught in more than half of their undergraduate education nor can they appeal subsequently when on-the-job deficiencies become visible.

Two decades ago, Combs (1965) described what he perceived to be one of the acute problems in the general education teachers acquire; the problem persists:

> Unhappily the level of teaching in general programs in many of our colleges leaves much to be desired. Overwhelmed with students and charged with the responsibility for "weeding them out," harassed instructors often cover the subjects as best they can and escape as quickly as possible to teaching the majors. As a consequence, general education programs are often badly taught and deadly dull. This is not good for any student. For education students it is disastrous. (p. 43)

Teacher education students, despite their large numbers on many campuses, remain low on the teaching priorities of many faculty:

> But our colleagues in the arts and sciences are rarely interested in these students, except as they may help to fill up enrollments in a summer course or figure into a grant. This dilemma leaves us and the students in a terrible position. We are aware of a problem of vast significance but seemingly unable to effect a solution. (Ducharme, 1980, p. 11)

Historically, teacher educators have been able to rely on their colleagues in arts and sciences in two kinds of situations: (1) When the SCDE unit obtains a grant enabling summer employment, curriculum development, or other paid activity for faculty from other units; and (2) when the NCATE team is on campus for a few days every 10 years, a few arts and sciences administrators and faculty will make tentative moves toward cooperation and collaboration because they realize that the consequences of not doing so might mean loss of accreditation with the accompanying demise of those education students who, although not particularly those which they would prefer to teach, do fill seats in the classrooms and keep enrollments up.

THE CRY FOR MORE OF THE ILL-DEFINED

The arguments on behalf of liberal education are endless and generally rhetorical. So much — both general and specific — is expected of an admittedly ill-defined curriculum.

> The use of the Socratic method does not require that we have a Socrates in every classroom, but the leader or questioner should understand the method and try to emulate Socrates in his approach. How much teachers should be prepared is a difficult question. Presumably they should have undergone the kind of liberal education that holds wisdom as its goal. (Woodring, p. 160)

The leaps of faith in this statement are enormous. And yet it is such leaps that sustain the practices in liberal education, both in institutions devoted exclusively to liberal arts preparation and in those, such as universities which prepare elementary school teachers, in which the liberal arts form the general education component.

Earlier, Borrowman (1956) placed weighty expectations on liberal education for teachers:

> The liberal function of education is to make certain that the individual sees every problem of living, *including the professional ones,* in the broadest scope possible. This includes a concern for what went before and what is to follow. (p. 4)

More recently, Kagan (1980) has been equally demanding:

> We have become such a technologically sophisticated community that we have grown overly dependent on those who not only understand the extant technology but also can easily learn or invent a new one. In short, we need adults who love the use of the mind and are good at it. This, it seems to me, is one of the defenses of a liberal arts education over a pragmatic one, for the former entices youth into seeing the excitement that follows analytic insight, synthesis of disparate ideas, and refutations of old claims. It creates a person who has faith in the power of thought. (p. 123)

We continue to have weighty expectations, powerful demands regarding the education of teachers. The 1980s and the following decades will require better prepared and better educated teachers than ever before. In summary, five observations seem in order:

1. Liberal arts education, as practiced through the 1940s, 1950s, and early 1960s vanished for a time and presently seems to be making a comeback.
2. This form of liberal arts education may have been adequate for the 1940s — and even that seems unlikely — but it is woefully inadequate for the 1980s.
3. The need exists to promote liberal arts education that (a) informs students about the dominant elements of the past of the Western world that helped shape the present; (b) promotes understanding and acceptance of the view that although it is necessary to learn the Western past in order to understand the Western present, these learnings and understandings do not explain the rest of the world; in fact, may lead to misconceptions; (c) develop scientific and mathematical literacy requisite for the 1980s and 1990s; and (d) foster curiosity and study of other cultural traditions.
4. This profession of teacher education must be proactive in forcing discussion and study of the attitudes, knowledge, and skills appropriate for a pluralistic society; this discussion and study must be carried on collaboratively with arts and sciences faculty.
5. The world grows dark and time grows short. There are national leaders who would counsel us to be more parochial, less outward-looking. This is fool's counsel. In the world of the 1980s changes in liberal arts education must go on in spite of disturbing national emphases and directions.

The issues are always critical in education. Teacher education and liberal education must, at last, become joined to effect the major results needed.

REFERENCES

Anderson, A.W. (1962). The teaching profession: An example of diversity in training and function. *Education for the professions.* Part II. Yearbook of the National Society for the Study of Education. Chicago: University of Chicago Press.

Arrowsmith, W. (1971). Teaching and the liberal arts: Notes toward an old frontier. In D. Bigelow (Ed.), *The liberal arts and teacher education.* Lincoln, NE: University of Nebraska Press.

Borrowman, M.L. (1956). *The liberal and technical in teacher education.* New York: Teachers College Press.

Borrowman, M.L. (1965). *Teacher education in America.* New York: Teachers College Press.

Boyer, E.L. (1981). The quest for common learning. In *Common learning.* Washington, DC: Carnegie Foundation for the Advancement of Teaching.

Bush, R. (1966). The formative years. In *The real world of the beginning teacher: Report of the 19th National TEPS Conference* (pp. 1–14). Washington, DC: National Education Association Press.

Combs, A.W. (1965). *The professional education of teachers.* Boston: Allyn & Bacon.

Conant, J.B. (1963). *The education of American teachers.* New York: McGraw-Hill.

Dressel, P. (1979). Liberal education: Developing the characteristics of a liberally educated person. *Liberal Education, 65*(3), 313–332.

Ducharme, D. (1980). Liberal arts in teacher education: The perennial challenge. *Journal of Teacher Education, 31*(3), 7–12.

Hirst, P. (1965). Liberal education and the nature of knowledge. In R. Archambault (Ed.), *Philosophical analysis and education*. New York: Humanities Press.

Kagan, T. (1980). Core competencies. In M. Kaplan (Ed.), *What is an educated person?* New York: Praeger Publishers.

Lawler, P.A. (1983). Tocqueville on the place of liberal education in a democracy. *Liberal Education, 69*(4), 301–306.

Lortie, D.C. (1975). *School-teacher: A sociological study*. Chicago: The University of Chicago.

Sarason, S., Davidson, K.S., & Blatt, B. (1962). *The preparation of teachers*. New York: Wiley.

Smith, E. (Ed.) (1962). *Teacher education: A reappraisal*. New York: Harper & Row.

Weber, S.L. (1983). Liberal learning: A learned ignorance. *Liberal Education, 69*(1), 75–80.

Winter, D.G., McClelland, D.G., & Stewart, A.J. (1981). *A new case for the liberal arts*. San Francisco: Jossey-Bass.

Woodring, P. (1962). The need for a unifying theory of teacher education: A reappraisal. In E. Smith (Ed.), *Teacher education: A reappraisal*. New York: Harper & Row.

Chapter 13

Epilogue: Open Letters to Those Most Responsible for the Quality of Teacher Education

Julie M. Backus

Director of Instruction, School District of Kewaskum, WI

The most pressing challenges to those responsible for the quality of teacher education derive from this volume's findings and recommendations. Each chapter provides new insights as well as updated reviews of issues which have been repeatedly examined in the journals and meetings of teacher educators. The letters which follow highlight a few of the major challenges to those most directly responsible.

TO: Deans of Education

The political and financial challenges to teacher education over the past few years have led to a number of knee-jerk solutions: raise admission standards, lengthen programs, or stop grade inflation. At the same time the resistance from department chairs and faculty anxious to continue in familiar and comfortable roles has also intensified. Tenured faculty are still not eager to exchange their comfortable on-campus roles for the daily grind of supervision at field sites. As a result, the proposals for additional on-campus credit requirements or extended years of preservice preparation may not reflect our acceptance of an expanded knowledge base as much as the faculty desire to generate additional student credit hours.

A common proposal for "excellence" has been the 5th year or extended program. Scannell describes the early history of such programs and provides a historical basis for examining their merits. The current pressure to provide extended programs may be difficult to resist in the face of the public clamor for increased competence. But in traditional 4-year institutions this presents a frightening spector of losing those students unable for pay for a 5th-year program or unwilling to commit the additional time.

Adams and Raths have recommended comprehensive rather than simple or one-shot methods of follow-up studies based on concurrent studies of program objectives. Adams has provided the rationale and overview — both pros and cons — for one such longitudinal assessment of program impact. He then challenges the schools of education to publish the results of their evaluation efforts for all to examine and critique. Evaluation of programs, as Raths points out, has not been a medium that has revealed quick, or even relevant, insights into program successes. He advocates that the teacher education institutions not spend as much time on the methodology or the choice of a particular evaluator as on the substance. What are the critical elements of the teacher education program that are effective and ineffective? Those responsible for programs must realize that money, time, and adequate resources for evaluation should be a high priority. Already overloaded faculty members in teacher education cannot be expected to add evaluation to other teaching and supervisory responsibilities.

Another pressure coming to bear on teacher education programs concerns field experiences — particularly student teaching. As Watts, Zeichner, and Zimpher all point out, the lack of well-conceived, systematic research on cooperating teachers, university supervisors, student teaching, and other field experiences may be the first place to begin serious study. Indeed, in spite of the popular misconceptions about the values of first-hand experience, many of the studies to date illustrate more negative than positive outcomes of early field experience and student teaching.

What might you, as Dean, do to utilize these trends and conditions to improve your programs? How might you begin to provide support to those directly involved in the program?

TO: Department Chairs and Directors of Teacher Education

Consider Smith's analysis of the moral issues involved in competency testing and its potential influence on the nature of our teaching staff for the 21st century. An increasingly multicultural and bilingual group of children may be taught by a more highly educated and over-tested, but monolingual, middle class white group of female teachers who, in a majority of cases, want to teach students of similar background (Howey and Strom). Howey and Strom are also concerned with the type of standards used for admission and the importance of further exploration into whether academic ability is the most critical variable leading to a good teacher. They, as well as Thies-Sprinthall and Sprinthall, cite research that indicates the opposite may be true: Scholastic aptitude may be inversely related to interpersonal competence and adult psychological maturity. Both of these chapters begin to high-light critical qualities and abilities (and methods for judging these attributes) which must be considered in designing the curricula of teacher education students.

Thies-Sprinthall and Sprinthall recommend a developmental track approach which differs greatly from the current pot pourri of arbitrarily programmed, placed, and supervised student trainees. Creating such a radical change will require the support of the deans, the faculty, and especially those responsible for placement of trainees into field experiences. Helping all these groups to perceive a need to change will be a critical first step.

As Ducharme points out, the debate over curriculum content and sequencing, particularly the role of liberal studies, has had a long history in teacher education. Ducharme's reaffirmation of the role of liberal education courses may be the source for a needed lively and productive interchange between the various departments on the university campus. But it cannot remain in a perpetual debate. The goal of a well-rounded education student is not just an academic ideal, but something to be achieved by priority setting and planning. Perhaps the elementary teacher should not take the same set of general or professional courses as the high school teacher. The focus of the debate should be on a better understanding of the actual content of specific courses, rather than on the traditional process of "horse trading" credits among departments.

In a critical review of supervision, Zimpher points out that although research is still sketchy, existing studies related to the role of the university supervisor can no longer be ignored. In some situations, the supervisor's sense of efficacy is very low, especially when the supervisor perceives a feeling of low status among university faculty and feels that student teachers are critical of the supervisory feedback they are getting. The various models of supervision which she describes, along with the review of research related to university supervisors, provides a basis for dialogue regarding the university supervisor's role and function.

What are the implications for your role? What are the implications for the roles of your colleagues of these findings related to the nature of education students, the content of the courses, and the effectiveness of direct experience and supervision?

TO: College and University Education Professors

There are obviously countless citations of research and avenues for action within the previous chapters. The following challenges are only a few which bear consideration.

The preservice student will need to be understood in terms of conceptual, value, and ego self-development dimensions. As Thies-Sprinthall and Sprinthall have proposed, we must take the students where they are conceptually and attempt, through well-designed instructional strategies, to move them to higher levels of thinking and perceiving. The consequences of failing to have teachers who can see multidimensional solutions to problems and who can keep an open attitude toward children and youth, particularly those of cultures different from the teacher, are serious. Their chapter not only describes the theories related to the area of developmental stage change, but instruments for assessing the students' levels. They also describe curricular strategies for matching and mismatching the students' instruction.

Stallings' description of many of the effective instructional strategies which have been isolated in the past 10 years might serve as the basis for preservice teacher curriculum as well as for cooperating teachers' inservice programs. Assisting the practitioners in the analysis of their own instruction and providing collegial and supervisory support to these teachers may be the first step in assisting the preservice students who will observe and often model their work after these experienced teachers. As Watts points out, the cooperating teacher may be far more effective in modeling the effective instruction techniques than attempting to have university faculty teach the strategies to preservice students through reading assignments or even microteaching examples.

What is the ultimate value to be preserved? Is your perception of yourself as a professor, a teacher educator, a researcher, or a school-oriented practitioner the top priority? How does your day-to-day work reflect our data?

TO: K–12 School-Based Administrators and Teacher Supervisors

Your help is needed to help create effective new teachers. The university must carefully select cooperating teachers (master teachers of teachers) and schools for the preservice student to complete observation and practice experiences (Applegate, Watts). The pressures from within and outside the university to increase the hours of early field experiences (Applegate) may mean that *any* live teacher and willing school will be picked to work with neophytes, regardless of practices which may be modeled. As Zeichner found from his comparison of field sites, the power of the instructional practices of the preservice student's own K–12 teachers and the expectations and setting of the school may be more powerful than the relatively few years within the school of education.

Administrators and experienced teachers may criticize the irrelevance of the university-based teacher education program, but until the university educators across the country develop ongoing partnerships with practitioners in K–12 settings (not just one-shot consultations or presentations), the practical knowledge base of the university-based educator may never be disseminated. Watts acknowledges this obstacle and recommends that students be placed in clinical centers — cooperative schools of pedagogy. This might be a collaboration effort between universities and K–12 schools. Such community-based clinical centers could bring together experienced teachers and principals seeking renewal and update with young preservice teachers seeking practical knowledge of teaching. The university resources and the K–12 inservice money might be more effectively utilized through this medium.

Another challenge is to change the environment of teaching from a semi-professional to a professional one in which teachers might leave the school between the hours of 8 a.m. and 4 p.m., design their own professional development experiences, or sit on teacher-chaired school governance committees. Thies-Sprinthall and Sprinthall have provided insights into the importance of cooperating teachers that are flexible and multidimensional and that can modify instruction to meet the needs of their own students, as well as the experience of the preservice students.

What does this evidence say to you regarding the conditions of professional practice and the role of school practitioners as models for preservice students?

TO: Cooperating Teachers

A number of the authors (Applegate, Watts, and Zeichner) reconfirm the critical role of cooperating teachers and your continuing influence on preservice students. The ability to provide support, be enthusiastic and pleasant, and be a master teacher makes one think that sainthood might be a prerequisite to being a cooperating teacher.

Some universities, and often the local school administration, have not taken your role seriously. A student teacher may provide new ideas and some assistance, but turning classes over to a struggling novice can often cause turmoil and personal and professional anguish. You should continue to request professional perks, for example, released time, university credit, and inservice, if these are not now provided to you. As Applegate and Watts note, the certification of cooperating teachers has been slow in coming, and an advocacy role at the local, university, and state levels may be one way to better represent your views and concerns.

What is your role in developing guidelines for assigning and working with student teachers? How can you influence the formation of standards for your work as supervisors and master teachers of preservice students?

TO: Preservice Teacher Education Students

Applegate provides some scenarios and challenges which cannot be ignored. Early field experiences are not just another course, but rather a time for you to sincerely evaluate whether or not teaching is a career to which you are suited. Although the challenges to change the environment of teaching are coming from many quarters, the change will be slow (Zeichner). The pressures on teachers to create optimal instructional environments with high achievement outcomes with pupils who may be unmotivated and often unruly will continue.

You will need to provide feedback to your university on the type of programs you have observed in schools and the nature of the experience. The opportunity to do multiple observations and the challenges to do preservice teaching in a number of schools and locations may be logistically inconvenient but are critical to your later experiences as a practitioner.

How do your abilities and predispositions match up with the roles of teachers you have observed? How do you approach the variety of required and volunteer teaching experiences available to you?

P.S.   To All Concerned with Teacher Education

We are hopeful that this volume will be helpful to school and university faculty in the process of revising or developing teacher education programs. The process of deciding admission requirements, the courses and experiences to be offered, and the evaluation of programs by simply having faculty vote their preferences and prejudices should finally be laid to rest. Before deciding anything about teacher education programs, we need to ask ourselves and each other: "How do you know that?" This volume will be successful to the degree that it helps answer that question.

Author Index

275

Subject Index